"David Limbaugh uniquely opens up the most beloved Book of all time, magnifying its greatest theme. Some may think the Bible is only a commentary on the struggle of good versus evil. But the two testaments are God's Word from eternity and testify about the Lord Jesus Christ. Anchored to the awe-striking account of Luke 24, David marks out the road map from Genesis to Revelation, reminding us of the two men who encountered the risen Christ as they walked along the road to Emmaus. The Lord opened their eyes to the truth that He was the One spoken of in Old Testament Scriptures, and they later exclaimed, 'How our hearts burned within us.'

David has written *The Emmaus Code* not only as an accomplished author, commentator, and attorney, but with vitality that conveys his love for the Lord and His inspired Word. Well-studied, he brings to light that Christ is not hidden in the early books of the Bible but is seen as the bearer of God's loving and redemptive plan of salvation from the beginning of time itself. You will see the unfolding of the promised Messiah before He came to earth in swaddling clothes as Savior and will come again as King, just as predicted, to be worshipped by all creation. Our hearts should burn within us as we anticipate that *someday* which is fast approaching. Don't miss following the road map found in *The Emmaus Code*."

> —FRANKLIN GRAHAM, president and CEO of Samaritan's Purse and of the Billy Graham Evangelistic Association

"Wow, what a book! My good friend David Limbaugh has outdone himself with *The Emmaus Code*. If you've ever been intimidated by the Old Testament, if you've ever wondered what ties the Old Testament and the New Testament together, then this is the book for you. It's the best Christian layman's guide to the Old Testament I've ever read. Fascinating—and highly recommended!"

> —SEAN HANNITY, host of *The Sean Hannity Show* and Fox News Channel's *Hannity*

"In his exciting new book *The Emmaus Code*, David Limbaugh takes the encounter with the risen Jesus on the road to Emmaus to show how the Old Testament affirms the truth claims of the New. It's a masterful performance, and, to coin a phrase, evidence that demands a verdict."
—JOSH D. McDOWELL, author and speaker

"David Limbaugh uses an ingenious approach to helping people understand God's Word in *The Emmaus Code*. The title refers to the resurrected Jesus appearing to two disciples on the road to Emmaus and explaining to them how the entire Old Testament focuses on Him and His redemptive ministry. Anyone wanting to better understand Holy Scripture will greatly benefit from reading *The Emmaus Code*, regardless of their previous level of understanding, beginning or advanced. This is truly a Christ-honoring book."
—DR. RICHARD LAND, president of Southern Evangelical Seminary

"If you've ever struggled to understand the unifying theme of the Old Testament and its relevance to your life today, *The Emmaus Code* will enlighten you. It's like seeing the box top to a jigsaw puzzle. David Limbaugh has written another gem filled with ah-ha moments that will leave you marveling at the Savior woven through every page of the Bible!"
—FRANK TUREK, founder and president of www.CrossExamined.org

THE EMMAUS CODE

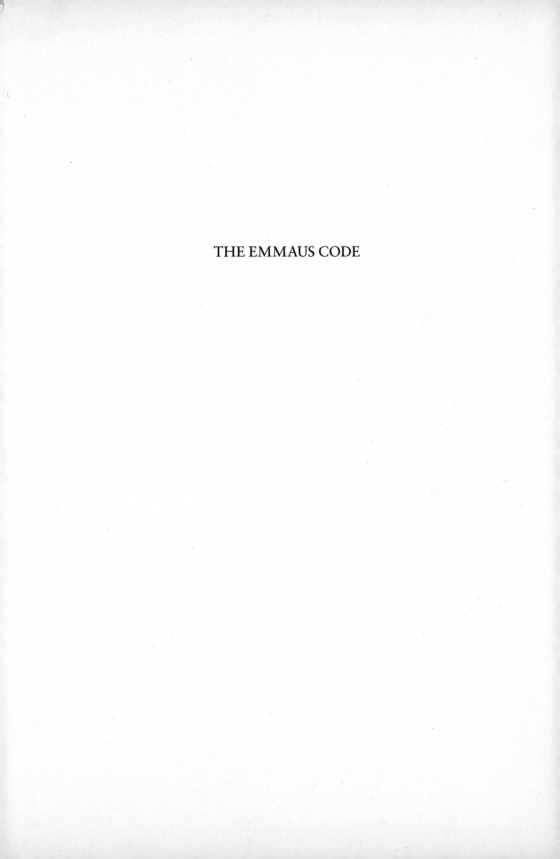

THE EMMAUS CODE

FINDING JESUS IN THE OLD TESTAMENT

DAVID LIMBAUGH

REGNERY
PUBLISHING
A Division of Salem Media Group

Regnery® is a registered trademark of Salem Communications Holding Corporation

Library of Congress Cataloging-in-Publication Data

Limbaugh, David, author.
  The Emmaus code : finding Jesus in the Old Testament / David Limbaugh.
     pages cm
  ISBN 978-1-62157-415-6 (hardback)
  1. Typology (Theology) 2. Bible. Old Testament--Criticism, interpretation, etc. 3. Jesus Christ--Biblical teaching. I. Title.
  BT225.L56 2015
  221.6'4--dc23
                         2015035812

Published in the United States by
Regnery Publishing
A Division of Salem Media Group
300 New Jersey Ave NW
Washington, DC 20001
www.Regnery.com

Manufactured in the United States of America

10 9 8 7 6 5 4 3 2 1

Books are available in quantity for promotional or premium use. For information on discounts and terms, please visit our website: www.Regnery.com.

Distributed to the trade by
Perseus Distribution
250 West 57th Street
New York, NY 10107

For our children—Christen, Courtney, Caitlyn, Scott, and Will—for whose faith we are grateful to God.

CONTENTS

INTRODUCTION

The Apostle Paul primarily ministered to Gentiles but also had an undying love for his fellow Jews. That is probably why, against the advice of his brethren, he traveled to Jerusalem at the end of his third missionary journey. When he is warned of the danger of going there, Paul replies, "What are you doing, weeping and breaking my heart? For I am ready not only to be imprisoned but even to die in Jerusalem for the name of the Lord Jesus" (Acts 21:13).

In Jerusalem Paul is accused of blasphemy and of defiling the Temple by bringing Gentiles into it, which is a capital offense. Paul is beaten in an ensuing riot and then arrested by Roman authorities. He ends up standing trial before Governor Felix in Caesarea on charges of inciting riots, being a leader of the Nazarene sect, and attempting to desecrate the Temple (Acts 24:5–8).

Paul denies the charges and pursues an unexpected line of defense. As one who never wastes an opportunity to evangelize—especially by exploiting acts of persecution against him—Paul gives a speech that is as much a celebration of Christ as it is a defense of his own actions. Mindful of his audience, he affirms his faith in Jesus Christ, paradoxically, by declaring common ground with Jewish believers. "But this I confess to you," he declares, "that according to the Way, which they call a sect, I worship the God of our fathers, believing everything laid down by the Law and written in the Prophets, having a hope in God, which these men themselves accept, that there will be a resurrection of both the just and the unjust.... It is with respect to the resurrection of the dead that I am on trial before you this day" (Acts 24:14–15, 21).

Don't miss the import of Paul's statement. He's saying he is not a rabble-rouser and he is not trying to upset his fellow Jews. Far from rejecting their religion, he affirms his belief in Old Testament Scripture, which he refers to as "the Law" and "the Prophets." As Judaism is protected under Roman law, preaching the truth of its Scripture surely can't be an illegal act.

Hoping to receive a bribe for Paul's release and seeking to placate his accusers, Felix leaves Paul in prison for two years despite knowing he is innocent. Felix is later succeeded in office by Festus, who summons Paul to the tribunal, asking him if he wants to stand trial in Jerusalem. Paul knows he won't get a fair trial there, so he demands to be tried in a Roman court. As a result King Agrippa, the ruler of territories northeast of Palestine, assists Felix in reviewing the charges against Paul so a written report can be prepared and forwarded to Rome.[1]

In explaining his position to Agrippa, Paul describes his background as a committed Pharisee who was an ardent enemy of Jesus Christ and brutal persecutor of Christians before encountering Jesus on the road to Damascus and undergoing a dramatic conversion. In stressing his innocence, Paul even more emphatically affirms the Jewish religion. "To this day I have had the help that comes from God," Paul contends, "and so I stand here testifying both to small and great, saying nothing but what the prophets and Moses said would come to pass: that the Christ must suffer and that by being the first to rise from the dead, he would proclaim light both to our people and to the Gentiles" (Acts 26:22).

Realizing Paul is innocent, Agrippa proclaims that he could have been set free had he not appealed to Caesar (Acts 26:31–32). Paul is then sent to Rome and placed in custody there, where he vigorously evangelizes to visitors and writes his Prison Epistles—Ephesians, Colossians, Philemon, and Philippians. The Bible is silent about the ultimate disposition of Paul's case and his later fate, but the oldest Christian traditions are that he died as a martyr in Rome.[2]

As we'll see later in this book, Paul's insistence that he remains faithful to Jewish Scripture echoes the arguments of Jesus, who had proclaimed that He came not to abolish the Scripture ("the Law") but to fulfill it. And indeed, Christianity doesn't abrogate the Old Testament; it completes it. True, the Jews don't interpret the Old Testament in the same light as converted Christians do—they don't see that it foretells the coming of Christ, Whom they reject as a false messiah. But as Paul emphasizes to Felix, he still worships the same God as the Jews do. He isn't embracing a new God, he's simply explaining that this same God—the God of the Jews—has now manifested Himself in the flesh. Christ is not mandating a new religion, Paul argues, but is completing the Jews' existing religion and expanding on God's original revelations to them. John Polhill notes that Paul's point is that "[h]e believed the same Scriptures, worshipped the same God, shared the same hope. But it was precisely at this point that 'the Way' parted ways with the rest of the Jews. The Christians believed that the resurrection already had begun in Christ."[3]

Undoubtedly, God's later revelations are not inconsistent with those of the Old Testament. Instead, the New Testament tells the rest of the story, offering a clearer picture of the eternal, never-changing God, Who can now be seen in His triune nature. Jesus Christ is God, the Holy Spirit is God, and the Father is God—three Persons of the Divine Godhead, all of Whom are featured in the Old Testament, if only in shadowy form. With the benefit of these later revelations, we can see truths in Scriptures that weren't evident to people in Old Testament times. Based on these revelations we understand those Scriptures in an entirely new light—we can see Christ on every page of the Old Testament as well as the New. It is my goal here to demonstrate that glorious truth.

This book has been a labor of love for me. In a sense, it completes a project I began many years ago. When I first studied the Bible in earnest some two decades ago, I was mildly frustrated, feeling I couldn't quite get a handle on the big picture, especially the Old Testament. As patience is not my strong suit, I tried various shortcuts to understand the major ideas, but nothing worked fast enough. I floundered until I approached it more deliberately and systematically. After a while I made some progress, but it took considerable effort.

Once I felt more comfortable with the material, I wanted to share what I'd learned, thinking that the process didn't have to be that difficult for others. I began writing a book on the Old Testament with the goal of publishing a primer from a layman's perspective. For various reasons, mainly because I just wasn't ready for the project yet, I finally abandoned it, but not without learning an enormous amount.

When my friend Harry Crocker at Regnery Publishing suggested last year that I write a book on Christian apologetics, I figured this was my chance to tackle the subject that had interested me many years before. Christian apologetics, of course, is different from a survey of the Old Testament, but I was gratified that I might finally write about Christianity as opposed to my usual commentaries on politics.

I found researching, writing, and promoting that book—*Jesus on Trial*—to be the most satisfying experience of my writing career. Afterward I was anxious to do another Christian book—specifically some sort of overview or introduction to the whole Bible. It was a daunting task, especially for a layman, but I thought I might be able to use my extensive studies over the past twenty years to resume the project I had begun long ago.

I quickly discovered I couldn't hope to do an adequate job on the entire Bible in one book, so I revisited the idea of covering just the Old Testament—which would still be plenty ambitious. I had titled my unfinished book *Roadmap to the Cross* because even then I understood that Jesus Christ is the key to understanding the Old Testament—and that is the central argument of *The Emmaus Code*.

The title refers to the road to Emmaus, which is where Jesus, in one of His resurrection appearances, opens the Old Testament to two men and explains how it all points to Him. None of us knows for sure, of course, exactly what Jesus said to these men, but with the hindsight perspective of the New Testament writers, we can get a pretty good idea. There are so many ways the Old Testament prefigures, anticipates, and predicts Christ and His redemptive plan, and I'm excited to share this material with you.

Many Bible readers seem intimidated by the Old Testament because they don't understand its grand sweep, they're overwhelmed by its difficult names and places, and they fail to see Jesus Christ on every page. They also cannot grasp the relevance of the Old Testament and its relationship to the New Testament. Decoding the Emmaus road, I believe, is the key to understanding the entirety of Scripture.

In this book I have set out to kill two birds with one stone in that I provide both an overview of the Old Testament and demonstrate how each of its books points to Christ. I first address the relevance of the Old Testament to the New, then outline Old Testament history, laying out the chronology of major events recorded in the Bible. My assumption is this: just as the Old Testament is foundational to the New, our basic understanding of the Old Testament is crucial to our comprehension of how Christ dominates its pages. This, I think, is what Paul is trying to explain as he is being falsely prosecuted for blasphemy.

Moreover, if you are confused about the historical events recorded in the Old Testament, you will likely find yourself distracted and frustrated as you struggle with its theological messages while failing to perceive Christ's pervasive presence. But once you grasp the flow of Old Testament history, you'll be better prepared to delve more deeply into the theological concepts. That was my experience, anyway.

After the historical summary, I discuss the various themes and threads in the Old Testament that point to Christ, from prophecy, to typology, to the biblical covenants, and more. I explain how each of these threads, in different and sometimes overlapping ways, points to Jesus Christ in the New Testament. Then I explore the Christ-centeredness of every book of the Bible while providing an overview of the books themselves.

This book features recurring themes that appear throughout the Bible. Many involve God's dealings with His chosen nation, Israel. Throughout Old Testament history the Israelites are repeatedly disobedient and sinful, and the prophets pronounce judgment upon them. But when they are obedient and faithful, they earn the prophets' blessings. The Bible's repetition of ideas and themes, however, is usually in different contexts and settings, showing God's consistency and faithfulness.

Christ is so essential to the Old Testament that one could fill tens of thousands of pages demonstrating it. My aim here is to introduce you to the most important categories, themes, and threads pointing to Christ, and to provide you as many examples of each as space permits. Though I hope you will find this book to be valuable, I must emphasize there is no substitute for reading the Bible for yourself.

Nevertheless, study aids and primers can enhance our biblical understanding, and I pray that this book helps you to comprehend the Old Testament and its sublime Christ-centeredness. And I hope that in these pages my enthusiasm for the Bible is apparent and even contagious. It is God speaking to us; how can anyone forego the privilege and opportunity He gives us, the portal He provides into His character, His purposes, His love, and His redemptive plan for our lives?

Jesus illuminates Scripture for the two men on the Emmaus road and does the same for His disciples. The New Testament is strikingly clear that He affirms the Old Testament is all about Him. Therefore, if we believe in Him and that all Scripture is God–breathed, as it professes to be, we too must accept that its singular focus is on our Savior. Once you acknowledge that, your understanding and reverence for the Bible will greatly increase.

I make no claim to being a Bible scholar, but I profoundly appreciate those who are. Accordingly, I tapped into them liberally in my research and have shared their invaluable insights. May the Holy Spirit enlighten you as you travel on your own Emmaus road to examine the Christ-centeredness of the Old Testament.

CHAPTER 1

IN DEFENSE OF THE OLD TESTAMENT

The Old Testament proclaims God's mighty acts of redemption. These acts reach a climax in the New Testament when God sends his Son. Redemptive history is the mighty river that runs from the old covenant to the new and holds the two together.

—SIDNEY GREIDANUS[1]

THE BIBLE'S OVERARCHING THEME

Many of the world's religions and secular philosophies seek to discover the existence and nature of God by either philosophical ruminations or experiential exercises. Christianity is different—it dispenses with the guesswork. It holds that God reveals Himself through general (e.g., nature) and special (e.g., Scripture) revelation, and that He revealed Himself in person in the incarnation of Jesus Christ. "For what can be known about God is plain to them, because God has shown it to them," writes the Apostle Paul. "For his invisible attributes, namely, his eternal power and divine nature, have been clearly perceived, ever since the creation of the world, in the things that have been made. So they are without excuse" (Romans 1:19–20). The writer of Hebrews says, "In the past God spoke to our forefathers through the prophets at many times and in various ways. But in these last days he has spoken to us by His Son, Whom He appointed heir of all things, and through Whom He made the universe" (1:1–2). Moreover, during His earthly ministry Jesus told us and showed us exactly Who He is, declaring, "I and the Father are one" (John 10:30). He asked, "Have I been with you so long, and you still do not know me, Philip? Whoever has seen me has seen the Father. How can you say, 'Show us the Father'? Do you not believe that I am in the Father and the Father is in me?" (John 14:9).

Thus, while many other religions involve the formulation of man's ideas about the existence and attributes of their gods, Christianity teaches that the God of the Bible has made Himself known to man through creation, by His direct communication and interactions with man through His chosen people, and by becoming man Himself during the incarnation, all as recorded in Scripture.

Let's not, then, be misled into believing the Bible is merely a written record of man's search for God. To the contrary, as some Christian sages have noted, it is a record of God's search for man: a chronicling of God's revelation of Himself to human beings. As Ambrose, Bishop of Milan in the fourth century, observed, "As in paradise, God walks in the Holy Scriptures seeking man."[2] Martin Luther personalized a similar sentiment: "The Bible is alive, it speaks to me; it has feet, it runs after me; it has hands, it lays hold on me."[3] Our omniscient God, of course, always knows where we are, but He wants a relationship with us and seeks us out, and through Scripture He opens the door for us to a relationship with Him.[4]

The Bible is more than just a collection of moral stories with colorful characters from whose experiences we can learn and grow. In *Jesus on Trial* I discussed the Bible's unity—its remarkable cohesiveness despite containing sixty-six books written by some forty authors over 1,500 years in three different languages, various literary styles, and diverse geographical settings. There is unity between the books of each Testament and between the books of the Old Testament and the New. There is unity in their structure, their history, their prophecies, their moral messages, the theological lessons they communicate, their revelation of God's unchanging character and divine attributes, and more.

Biblical theologians[5] acknowledge these different types of unity, but apparently no clear consensus has emerged as to what central idea unites the Old and New Testaments.[6] In my view, however, the overarching theme of the Bible is crystal clear: from first to last, it is Jesus Christ. Though the Bible comprises many diverse books with different stories, it is ultimately one story of God's redemptive plan for man, whom He created purposely in His image, for His glory, and for a personal relationship with Himself. The thirty-nine books of the Old Testament are united by a common thread centered on God's promise to redeem mankind, and this thread continues through the New Testament, where that promise is fulfilled and questions are answered. In fact, salvation is exactly what Paul says is the purpose of the Bible. In writing the last letter of his life before his execution, Paul reminds Timothy "how from childhood you have been acquainted with the sacred writings, which are able to make you wise for salvation through faith in Christ Jesus" (2 Tim. 3:15). Since Jesus accomplishes salvation, He's the theme of the entire Bible.

Understanding the Bible's unity couldn't be more important, yet some Christians regularly read portions of the Bible throughout their entire lifetimes without grasping the book as a whole. This is not to imply you must read the Bible from cover to cover to benefit from it—in fact, you can open the Bible to any page and profit by whatever portion you read. But your experience with God's Word will be greatly enhanced if you understand clearly how the Bible's individual books come together to form one dazzling, integrated work.

My primary goal with this book is to demonstrate how the entire Bible, not just the New Testament, centers on Jesus Christ, our Savior. Of course, few would doubt the Christ-centeredness of the New Testament. But it might strike some as counterintuitive to consider the Old Testament as being about Christ as well, albeit in a different sense. "Our Lord Jesus Christ is the key to the Bible, and it is impossible to understand the Old Testament apart from Him," explains Dr. Warren Wiersbe. "The experiences of the Jewish nation in the Old Testament are links in the chain that leads to His birth at Bethlehem." According to Wiersbe, there are numerous people, events, and symbols in the Old Testament that foreshadow Jesus Christ. "Look for Christ," he says, "and the Old Testament will become a new book to you."[7]

Counterintuitive or not, the notion that the Old Testament is centered on Jesus Christ is not something I made up or an idea that Christians and biblical scholars fashioned to support their belief system. In John 5:39 Jesus Himself exclaims, "You search the Scriptures because you think that in them you have eternal life; and it is they that bear witness about me, yet you refuse to come to me that you may have life." Don't pass over this lightly. Jesus is saying that His followers diligently studied the Old Testament (the New Testament hadn't been written yet) to find the key to eternal life, and the entire time they were missing what was right in front of their faces: *He* is the Key Who unlocks the treasures of the Old Testament, the Person to Whom the Old Testament points. He is Life and life eternal.

A few verses later, Jesus says, "For if you believed Moses, you would believe me; for he wrote of me. But if you do not believe his writings, how will you believe in me?" (John 5:46–47). Moreover, the New Testament Book of Hebrews attributes the words of Psalms 40:6–8 to Christ: "When Christ came into the world, he said … 'Behold, I have come to do your will, O God, as it is written of me in the scroll of the book'" (10:7). This passage validates that psalm as an Old Testament prophecy promising that Christ, in His incarnation, would come to accomplish what the Old Testament animal sacrifices could not—the full forgiveness of sin for believers in Him. Through the Book of Hebrews, then, Christ directly affirms that He is the core of salvation history.

But the most exciting quote of all is the one that inspired the title for this book. On the day Jesus rises from the dead He appears before two men headed to the village of Emmaus, some seven miles from Jerusalem. They are unaware of Jesus' identity and are talking about His crucifixion, death, and empty tomb while expressing disappointment that He had not redeemed Israel. Jesus quickly sets them straight, assuring them He is the promised Messiah Whose suffering and death is a necessary part of God's salvation plan. At that point, to their amazement, He illuminates the Scriptures for them, showing how they point to Him: "And beginning with Moses and all the Prophets, he interpreted to them in all the Scriptures the things concerning himself" (Luke 24:27).

Once this sinks in, their understanding is complete. Now, at last, they grasp the dominant theme of the Scriptures they had been reading for years: Jesus Christ. "They said to each other, 'Did not our hearts burn within us while he talked to us on the road, while he opened to us the Scriptures?'" (Luke 24:32). Shortly after that encounter, Jesus appears to His disciples and similarly enlightens them, declaring, "'These are my words that I spoke to you while I was still with you, that everything written about me in the Law of Moses and the Prophets and the Psalms must be fulfilled.' Then he opened their minds to understand the Scriptures, and said to them, 'Thus it is written, that the Christ should suffer and on the third day rise from the dead, and that repentance and forgiveness of sins should be proclaimed in his name to all nations, beginning from Jerusalem'" (Luke 24:44–47).

There are many different ways that Christ is revealed in the Old Testament, including by His titles; His work as creator; His role as the sustainer of God's creation; His appearances (known as "Christophanies"); the "types" and "portraits" of persons, institutions, events, and ceremonies pointing to Him; the Old Testament offices of prophet, priest, and king that prefigure His perfect work to come; God's promises, especially His major covenants that find their ultimate fulfillment in Him; and the many messianic prophecies.[8]

THE OLD TESTAMENT: A DELIBERATELY INCOMPLETE BOOK

Admittedly, the Old Testament overwhelms even some Christians, but I think that is partially because they don't see its big picture. Failing to understand how it can possibly be relevant to their lives or to the overall Christian story, they wonder, *Christ came to save us from our sins, didn't He, and isn't it enough that the New Testament fully lays out the Gospel and gives us all the instruction we need on how to be saved?*

By ignoring the Old Testament, however, Christians deprive themselves of deep and rich insights. A full understanding of the New Testament requires knowledge of the Old, which is, after all, the only Bible Jesus and the apostles had. Many Christians are familiar with Old Testament stories such as Noah and the ark, Moses and the Red Sea, and Jonah and the great fish, but have a vague impression of the Old Testament as being fragmented. The only remedy for this is to familiarize oneself with the Old Testament and learn how the two Testaments interrelate.

The New Testament does not begin from scratch—it builds on the Old. The Testaments are parts of a two-act play. "The New Testament presupposes the Old at every point, so much so that one can say that the New Testament is largely meaningless apart from its Old Testament orientation," writes Old Testament scholar Eugene Merrill. "The life, ministry, and teachings of Jesus as well as apostolic preaching and pronouncements betray on every hand their indebtedness to the Old Testament."[9]

The Old Testament prepares our hearts for the revelations of the New Testament. In fact, New Testament writers themselves believed that the Old Testament is foundational to the New, as evidenced by their voluminous quotes from and allusions to the Old Testament. Depending on how liberally you define "quotations," some say there are at least 295 New Testament quotations from the Old Testament, which occupy 352 verses.[10] If you add the New Testament's clear allusions to the Old Testament, the numbers grow substantially, with some maintaining that more than 10 percent of the New Testament text comprises citations or direct allusions to the Old Testament.[11] The Book of Revelation alone has some 331 allusions to the Old Testament.[12]

In his first letter to the Corinthians, Paul writes, "For I handed on to you as of first importance what I in turn had received: that Christ died for our sins in accordance with the Scriptures, and that he was buried, and that he was raised on the third day in accordance with the Scriptures" (15:3–4). When Paul refers to "Scriptures" he means the Old Testament. Paul knows that our understanding of the Gospel won't be complete if we believe Christianity came out of nowhere; it was a consummation of what had been promised in the Old Testament. Indeed, Paul says in the Book of Galatians, "The law was our guardian until Christ came" (3:24).

Pastor Ray Stedman confesses that he had read the New Testament's Book of Romans for years and had even taught it, but never fully appreciated it until he better understood the Old Testament background underlying Paul's arguments in that book. "I never grasped with real understanding the truth it contains," recounts Stedman. "I never let its mighty, liberating power come through to my own heart and experience until I had lived for a while out in the wilderness on the back side of the desert with the children of Israel, and had felt the burning desert heat— the barren, fruitless, defeated life they experienced. When I had been there too, and had seen how God delivered them, then I was able for the first time to understand what God is trying to tell us in Romans."[13]

Likewise Puritan Minister Stephen Charnock writes, "The Old Testament was writ to give credit to the New, when it should be manifested in the world. It must be read by us to give strength to our faith, and establish us in the doctrine of Christianity. How many view it as a bare story, an almanac out of date, and regard it as a dry bone, without sucking from it the evangelical marrow! Christ is, in Genesis, Abraham's seed; in David's Psalms and the prophets, the Messiah and Redeemer of the world."[14]

Nevertheless, many Christians are understandably intimidated by the Old Testament, with its bouts of extreme violence, its seemingly endless genealogies, and its arcane names and places. But we should not be discouraged because rich rewards await those who study it diligently, knowing it is every bit as divinely inspired as the New Testament. Theologian Vern Poythress admits that when he was a young Christian certain parts of the Old Testament were difficult for him. After reading through the entire Bible as a teenager, he was unable to respond to an older Christian woman who asked him how he made it through the Book of Leviticus, which many readers find painfully dry. He did not learn the answer until years later, when he grasped the significance of the Emmaus road story. It dawned on Poythress that when Jesus opened the Scriptures to two of His disciples that day, He not only walked them through the Old Testament witness to Himself, but also summarized its essence. "The whole Old Testament," explains Poythress, "finds its focus in Jesus Christ, His death, and His resurrection."[15]

Nor does the New Testament supersede the Old, though the Old Testament's ceremonial laws have been set aside and its sacrificial system, as the Book of Hebrews describes, has given way.[16] "The New Testament and the gospel never claim to have superseded the Old Testament in terms of its canonical status," Eugene Merrill explains, "Over and over again...it is cited as the Word of God.... It has lost nothing of its magisterial character for the Christian believer."[17] After all, Jesus told us in no uncertain terms that He came not to abolish the Law but to fulfill it (Matt. 5:17), and fulfilling the Law is a far cry from superseding it.

We must distinguish between the Old Testament and the New Testament on the one hand, and the Old Covenant and the New Covenant on the other. The Old Testament is a literary document that includes a written record of redemptive history. It provides a historical account of the legal contract God entered into with the Israelites at Mt. Sinai, which formed the basis of God's relationship to the nation of Israel. This contract is called the Old Covenant. The New Testament is also a literary document that includes the history of the early Christian Church. It records, among other things, the institution of a new contract between God and His people, which benefits all mankind. This contract is called the New Covenant and its mediator is Jesus Christ.[18] The New Covenant supersedes the Old Covenant, as we'll examine more closely in Chapter 5, but that doesn't mean the New Testament supersedes the Old Testament, and we should be mindful of this distinction.

The writer of Hebrews tells us, "In speaking of a new covenant, he makes the first one obsolete. And what is becoming obsolete and growing old is ready to vanish away" (8:13). This does not mean the major provisions of the Law God provided to Moses—the Ten Commandments—are less than perfectly holy. Nine of them (all except the command to keep the Sabbath) are restated in the New Testament, though sometimes with different promises attached and different penalties specified for disobedience.[19] But the fact that Jesus fulfilled the Law means, by definition, that He didn't negate it. To the contrary, Jesus affirmed the Law's moral teachings and rebuked the Pharisees for effectively nullifying those lessons and subordinating them to their traditions.[20]

And of course there's a simpler argument: if the Old Testament were no longer relevant to Christians, it would not be part of our Bible—but it most emphatically is.

Nevertheless, the New Testament forms "the last and most definitive word of God," as Hans K. LaRondelle and Jon Paulien maintain.[21] As such, we interpret the Old Testament in light of the revelations from the

New. This adage, attributed to St. Augustine, is instructive: "The New Testament is in the Old concealed; the Old is by the New revealed."[22] Elsewhere, he affirms, "What is concealed in [the books of the Old Testament] under the veil of earthly promises is clearly revealed in the preaching of the New Testament."[23]

The point is that we are introduced to "shadows" and "types" in the Old Testament, whose meaning becomes markedly clearer to us in the New Testament revelations. The writer of Hebrews, while explaining the insufficiency of sacrifices under the Old Covenant, argues, "For since the law has but a shadow of the good things to come instead of the true form of these realities, it can never, by the same sacrifices that are continually offered every year, make perfect those who draw near" (10:1). Referring to legal restrictions on food and drink in Old Testament times, Paul likewise notes, "These are a shadow of the things to come, but the substance belongs to Christ" (Col. 2:17).

We should read the Old Testament and the New as an indivisible unit with the same God present in both works.[24] Whereas students of the Hebrew Scriptures in Old Testament times read those Scriptures before Christ's incarnation and before the New Testament writers interpreted those Scriptures, we read them today with the benefit of hindsight and the illumination provided by the New Testament. So while Christians strive to read the Old Testament in its historical context—from the perspective of the Old Testament Jews who wrote it—we also benefit from the further revelations and perspective that Christ provides as the final Interpreter of Scripture, and as provided by the New Testament writers through the Holy Spirit.[25] Vern Poythress acknowledges we should try to understand the Old Testament within its own historical environment, explaining that "God intended it to be heard and understood by the Israelites who had recently been redeemed from Egypt."[26] But he notes that we also must read it from our own vantage point, understanding that the New Testament completes the story God began to communicate in the Old Testament.[27]

"The Old Testament is deliberately an incomplete book," writes Ray Stedman. "It never was intended by God to be His last word to the human race."[28] By itself it is a book of unexplained sacrifices, unfulfilled prophecies, and unsatisfied longings. But the second you open the New

Testament you read, "A record of the Genealogy of Jesus Christ." He is the one Who fulfills the prophecy, the one Who explains the sacrifice, the one Who satisfies the longings. Yet we cannot fully appreciate this until we have first been awakened by what the Old Testament has to say.[29] As Australian Anglican theologian Graeme Goldsworthy insists, "We can no more make sense of an Old Testament narrative isolated from the Christ who provides its meaning than we could make sense of one scene from a drama isolated from the climax and denouement."[30]

OUR UNCHANGING GOD

Another source of confusion is the mistaken idea that the God of the Old Testament is different in character from the God of the New. To believe that you would have to assume either that two different gods dominated the two periods, that God somehow evolved into a kinder and gentler Jesus Christ, or that the Old Testament is not God's inspired Word but just a book of allegories, beautiful poems, wisdom literature, and ancient stories unmoored from actual history.

Yet the Bible is clear throughout that God is unchanging and that He is one God, not two. The God Who speaks and reveals Himself to us in the Old Testament is the same God Who does so in the New. As God Himself assures us, "For I the Lord do not change" (Mal. 3:6), and as the prophet Balaam relates, "God is not man, that he should lie, or a son of man, that he should change his mind" (Num. 23:19).[31] Similarly James confirms, "Every good gift and every perfect gift is from above, coming down from the Father of lights with whom there is no variation or shadow due to change" (James 1:17).

Mark Dever argues that it would be easy to go through both Testaments piece by piece and show that God is the same throughout. But he maintains there is a more compelling way. All you need to do is consider Old Testament history, which demonstrates God's patience and loving forbearance toward mankind made in His image—and mankind in turn repeatedly rejecting Him. In fact, God's mercy is one reason Old Testament history extends over so many years. According to the Apostle Peter, "The Lord is not slow to fulfill his promise as some count slowness, but is patient toward you, not wishing that any should perish but that all should reach repentance" (2 Peter 3:9).

Dever explains that "God's forbearance can be seen in the fact that he did not end human history right at the Fall, when he would have been just to do so. Then throughout centuries and centuries of Israel's history, God patiently forbore with the wayward nation. Ultimately, the Old Testament presents God's grace, love, mercy, and patience on an epic scale."[32]

ALL SCRIPTURE IS GOD-BREATHED

Christians who deny that the Old Testament is the inspired Word of God face an unsolvable problem: the New Testament writers and Jesus Himself affirm that it is God's inspired Word. Indeed, "throughout its pages," writes Brian H. Edwards, "the Bible never expresses one sentence or word of doubt about either its divine origin or its absolute trustworthiness; on the contrary, it constantly asserts both."[33] Paul teaches that "all Scripture is breathed out by God and profitable for teaching, for reproof, for correction, and for training in righteousness, that the man of God may be complete, equipped for every good work" (2 Tim. 3:16–17). Along the same lines Peter asserts, "Knowing this first of all, that no prophecy of Scripture comes from someone's own interpretation. For no prophecy was ever produced by the will of man, but men spoke from God as they were carried along by the Holy Spirit" (2 Peter 1:20–21). And in the Book of Acts, Luke writes, "Brothers, the Scripture had to be fulfilled, which the Holy Spirit spoke beforehand by the mouth of David concerning Judas, who became a guide to those who arrested Jesus" (1:16).

Furthermore, consider the wording Jesus uses when declaring His intention to fulfill the Law: "Do not think that I have come to abolish the Law or the Prophets; I have not come to abolish them but to fulfill them. For truly, I say to you, until heaven and earth pass away, not an iota, not a dot, will pass from the Law until all is accomplished" (Matt. 5:17–18). Scholars agree that "the Law and the Prophets" refer to the entire Old Testament.[34] Jesus elsewhere affirms that "Scripture cannot be broken" (John 10:35), and He confirms the historical validity of specific claims of the Old Testament: God created Adam and Eve (Matt. 19:4); Cain killed Abel (Matt. 23:35); the flood destroyed the world during the time of Noah (Luke 17:27); God spoke to Moses from a burning bush (Luke 20:37); Elijah performed miracles (Luke 4:25); Jonah was inside the great fish for three days (Matt. 12:40); and Daniel prophesied truthfully and accurately (Matt. 24:15). Perhaps most interesting of all, Luke informs us that Jesus, in the synagogue of His hometown of Nazareth, establishes the program of His ministry by reading from the Book of Isaiah in chapter 61, verse 1 (Luke 4:18–19).[35]

And it wasn't just the New Testament writers asserting the inspiration of the Old Testament. The Old Testament Book of 2 Samuel relates that on his deathbed King David exclaimed, "The Spirit of the Lord speaks by me; his word is on my tongue" (23:2).

But in today's postmodern age, many people ridicule the very notion that the Bible—especially the Old Testament—is the Word of God. Dr. Ravi Zacharias, one of the most brilliant Christian thinkers of our time, explains that Americans used to implicitly accept that the Bible was divinely inspired. But in the mid-nineteenth century, assaults from within the Church did severe damage to scriptural authority. Betraying its own sacred trust as steward of the Word, the clergy allowed the Bible to be reduced to mere literature. "Now, into that frame of reference," recounts Ravi,

> the text of Scripture was brought under judgment. Suspect, and positioned as a piece of literature to be dissected and dismembered at the hands of scholars with unhidden pretexts, the Scriptures were well on their way to being dismissed as nothing more than ethnic utopianism punctuated with altruistic pronouncements. By stripping the Bible of divine authorship, liberal scholarship made it just another piece of literature, open to attack and critique.... It was no longer a God-authored book, but a man-concocted collection. This was no longer theology—from God to us—but anthropology—about us and our thoughts toward God. In short, the author of the Scriptures was renamed.[36]

We mustn't fall into that insidious trap. We shortchange ourselves and undermine a foundational aspect of our faith if we fail to fully appreciate that the Bible reveals the voice of God. As Christians we do not get to cherry-pick the Bible—it is all God's living, breathing Word. If we are to be obedient, let alone spiritually blessed, we should discipline ourselves to mine the abundant riches of the Old Testament.

The good news is that once you get over your anxiety and dig in, you will find that reading and studying the Old Testament is immensely profitable. God continues to speak to us through the Old Testament as well as the New. Indeed, the Old Testament addresses many subjects the New Testament doesn't discuss, and it provides practical guidelines on how we should conduct our lives.

But it's much more than that. The New Testament is anchored in the Old; without a firm grasp of the Old Testament one cannot fully comprehend its successor. Jesus Christ wasn't born in a vacuum. There is essential history preceding Christ's incarnation, which includes God's interactions with mankind.

As Dr. Wiersbe observes, "We would have no information concerning the origin of the universe, the origin of man, the beginnings of sin, the birth of the Hebrew nation, or the purposes of God for the world, were it not for the Old Testament record." He continues, "Every New Testament doctrine can be traced back to Old Testament history. An understanding of the Old Testament record is necessary if we are to interpret the New Testament correctly."[37]

Having established the enduring relevance of the Old Testament, the foundational importance of the Old Testament to the New, and the interconnectedness of both Testaments, we will next examine the nature and purpose of "salvation history" and present an overview of the Old Testament historical books.

CHAPTER 2

OLD TESTAMENT HISTORY
OVERVIEW

The Bible is the chart of history. It affords a panoramic view of the whole course of events.... It gives us, not events only, but their moral character, tracing the motives of the various actors in the drama, as well as the results of their actions. Events are shown in relation to their causes and effects, and the judgment of God as to their character is revealed. Without the Bible, history would be a spectacle of unknown rivers flowing from unknown sources to unknown seas; but under its guidance we can trace the complex currents to their springs, and see the end from the beginning.

—DR. H. GRATTAN GUINNESS[1]

SALVATION HISTORY

S ome assume the Bible is an inaccessible, impractical book. But the Bible couldn't be more practical, as it is grounded in actual history involving real human beings, their trials and tribulations, and their relationship with God. Yes, the Bible includes philosophy and instruction, but it is also a history book that reveals God's truths through the experiences of real-life people. It is, as D. Martyn Lloyd-Jones poignantly notes, "a textbook of the soul."[2]

Undeniably, the Bible contains extensive history, from the beginning of time through the entire span of mankind's existence. That includes the future, which is revealed in descriptions of the creation of the new heavens and the new earth (Isaiah 65:17, 66:22; 2 Peter 3:13; Rev. 21:1). Indeed, many of the future events predicted in the Bible are presented as history, as if they've already occurred. "It is clear that prophecy in the Old Testament and the eschatology [end times] of Jesus and the apostles is presented as a real projection of history in the future," contends Graeme Goldsworthy.[3] But biblical history is a specific type of history—referred to as "salvation history" or "redemptive history"—that only includes relevant slices of secular history. (In this book I use the term "salvation history" except when quoting authors who refer to "redemptive history.") The Bible's historical books were not written to give us history for its own sake, but to show how God works through history.[4]

Some critics emphasize the many gaps in the Bible's retelling of history. But those omissions simply mean that those periods are not relevant to salvation history. The Bible, for example, barely touches on the four-hundred-year period between the time of the patriarchs and the exodus, though many significant events in secular world history occurred during those times, such as the rise and fall of various Egyptian dynasties.[5] It's important to understand that salvation history is distinct from secular history, because salvation history relates God's sovereign workings in history, describing those events and people through which God reveals Himself and brings salvation to mankind.

Goldsworthy describes salvation history as the "framework within which God has worked, is now working, and will work in the future." It "implies a recognition that Yahweh, the God of Israel, and the God and Father of our Lord Jesus Christ, is the Lord of history. History happens because of his decrees."[6] B. K. Waltke says it "refers to the biblical texts propounding a glorious progressive history of redemption that runs through the entire biblical corpus, from the creation of the world to its fulfillment in the life, death, resurrection, and ascension of Jesus Christ and finally his second coming, which introduces the eschaton [the end of history]. The Israel of God establishes and advances the kingdom of God against the gates of hell itself."[7] In *Bible History: Old Testament*, Alfred Edersheim observes that "we notice large gaps in the history of Samuel, Saul, and David, long periods and important facts being omitted, with which the author *must* have been acquainted...while other periods and events are detailed in great length." These omissions are intentional, argues Edersheim, because "as in the case of other parts of Holy Scripture...we must not look for biographies...but *a history of the kingdom of God* during a new period in its development, and in a fresh stage of its onward movement towards that end."[8]

Despite its gaps, salvation history is a complete, coherent history for God's purposes, and it is a record of events that actually occurred, not a series of fictitious stories designed to teach various lessons. God's written revelation to us is tied to His purposeful interaction in history. As Ismael E. Amaya explains, "God's self-revelation to man did not consist primarily in the communication of certain ideas, propositions and doctrines about God to be believed by human beings, but rather consists in the confrontation of God with man in real historical events."[9] George Eldon Ladd affirms, "The Hebrew-Christian faith did not grow out of lofty philosophical speculations or profound mystical experiences. It arose out of historical experiences of Israel, old and new, in which God made Himself known."[10] As I noted in *Jesus on Trial*, this is true of the very establishment of Christianity, which was not based on theological ruminations into which the New Testament writers retrofitted certain historical events to suit their ideas. Instead, Christianity arose when men and women actually witnessed the bodily resurrected Jesus, and that experience radically transformed them from feckless skeptics to bold proclaimers of the Gospel.

Salvation history, then, traces the development of the nation of Israel and records God's dealings with His chosen people. The Israelites loom large in salvation history for numerous reasons. God chooses and forms the nation of Israel to bring salvation to all mankind, so His Word necessarily records the history of His dealings with that people. But the story of that love relationship, the history of Israel's obedience and disobedience, and God's corresponding blessings and judgment, is also instructive to us today. In His interactions with the Israelites, God reveals His nature and faithfulness and shows us, by their example, how we should conduct our lives and how to develop and sustain a relationship with Him. Through the pages of the Old Testament we can learn from Israel's mistakes and avoid making them ourselves, and we can also emulate its times of obedience.

Crucially, by seeing God's interaction with His people, we better understand His character. We discover that despite the Israelites' persistent disobedience, God refuses to give up on them and patiently brings them to spiritual maturity and ultimately back to a proper relationship with Himself—and He will do the same for us. As Jeremiah relates, "So I went down to the potter's house, and there he was working at his wheel. And the vessel he was making of clay was spoiled in the potter's hand, and he reworked it into another vessel, as it seemed good to the potter to do. Then the word of the LORD came to me: 'O house of Israel, can I not do with you as this potter has done?' declares the LORD. 'Behold, like the clay in the potter's hand, so are you in my hand, O house of Israel'" (Jer. 18:3–6).

BIBLE BASICS

To better understand the Bible and God's redemption plan we should comprehend how the books of the Bible are classified and arranged as well as the main events of Old Testament history.

There are thirty-nine books in the Old Testament and twenty-seven in the New, but these numbers don't reflect the respective lengths of these works—the Old Testament is actually about three times longer than the New. So if you're reading through the Bible, it's quite a relief to reach the beginning of the New Testament, knowing that you're three-fourths of the way done.

Old Testament books—which were written in Hebrew, except for several passages in Aramaic—are divided into three sections: there are seventeen historical books (Genesis through Esther); five poetical books (sometimes called Wisdom books, comprising Job through Song of Solomon); and seventeen prophetic books (Isaiah through Malachi). The New Testament books—which were written in Greek—are also in three sections: five historical books (The Gospels and Acts); twenty-one doctrinal books (Romans through Jude); and one prophetic book (Revelation).

The Old Testament historical books can be further broken down as follows: the first five books (Genesis through Deuteronomy) are the books of the Law (the Hebrew term is *torah*), or the Pentateuch. The next twelve books (Joshua through Esther) can be grouped into those

THE BOOKS OF THE BIBLE

39 OLD TESTAMENT BOOKS

■ **Historical**

■ **Poetical (Wisdom)**

☐ **Prophetic**

Job
Psalms
Proverbs
Ecclesiastes
Song of Solomon

BOOKS OF THE LAW (PENTATEUCH)
Genesis
Exodus
Leviticus
Numbers
Deuteronomy

PRE-BABYLONIAN CAPTIVITY
Joshua
Judges
Ruth
1 Samuel
2 Samuel
1 Kings
2 Kings
1 Chronicles
2 Chronicles

POST-BABYLONIAN CAPTIVITY
Ezra
Nehemiah
Esther

MAJOR PROPHETS
Isaiah
Jeremiah
Lamentations
Ezekiel
Daniel

MINOR PROPHETS
Hosea
Joel
Amos
Obadiah
Jonah
Micah
Nahum
Habakkuk
Zephaniah
Haggai
Zechariah
Malachi

27 NEW TESTAMENT BOOKS

■ **Historical**

■ **Doctrinal**

☐ **Prophetic**

Romans
1 Corinthians
2 Corinthians
Galatians
Ephesians
Philippians
Colossians
1 Thessalonians
2 Thessalonians
1 Timothy
2 Timothy
Titus
Philemon
Hebrews
James
1 Peter
2 Peter
1 John
2 John
3 John
Jude

Matthew
Mark
Luke
John
Acts

Revelation

describing events before the Babylonian captivity (the nine books spanning from Joshua through 2 Chronicles) and those relating events afterward (the Books of Ezra, Nehemiah, and Esther).[11]

Then come the poetical or wisdom books, which contain extensive verses of Hebrew poetry. Yet they are not the only Old Testament books that include poetry, and they also incorporate wisdom literature, such as the Book of Proverbs. Biblical wisdom, according to the ESV Study Bible, can be defined as "skill in the art of godly living, or more fully, that orientation which allows one to live in harmonious accord with God's ordering of the world."[12] Wisdom literature consists of biblical "writings that reflect on or inform that orientation."[13]

Finally, the seventeen prophetic books are divided into two categories. The Major Prophets (Major in the sense that their accounts are longer, not necessarily that they're more important) include Isaiah, Jeremiah (who is believed to have written both Jeremiah and Lamentations), Ezekiel, and Daniel. The twelve Minor Prophets are Hosea, Joel, Amos, Obadiah, Jonah, Micah, Nahum, Habakkuk, Zephaniah, Haggai, Zechariah, and Malachi.

The books of the Old Testament do not always appear in chronological order, especially the poetical and prophetic books. The historical books from Genesis through 2 Kings, however, are mostly arranged in chronological order, retelling events from creation to the Babylonian exile.[14]

OLD TESTAMENT HISTORY

The historical books of the Old Testament are a record of God's sovereign interaction with His chosen people. It is noteworthy that many of the biblical writers and figures, Old Testament and New, emphasize in their speeches and writings the importance of God's historical interaction with Israel by relating extensive summaries of that history. The repetition of these historical synopses throughout the Bible shows God's emphasis on salvation history. He wants us to see how He works in history and how He progressively unfolds His preordained plan for our redemption. These mini-histories also showcase

God's character—His loving-kindness, His patience, and His unfailing trustworthiness and grace, which in turn reinforce our faith. Though many people believe God acted harshly during Old Testament times, those acquainted with the full scope of this history understand that even when He brings judgment, there is almost always the promise of future redemption.

These historical summaries sprinkled throughout the Old Testament vary in scope, but they include many of the same central events. You will find such recapitulations in Deuteronomy 6:20–24 (covering from the exodus to the Israelites' occupation of Canaan); Deuteronomy 26:5–9 (from settlement in Egypt to the occupation); Joshua 24:2–13 (from Abraham to the occupation); Nehemiah (from creation to the return of the people from exile); Psalm 78 (from the exodus to the time of David); Psalm 105 (from Abraham to the occupation); Psalm 106 (from the exodus to the exile; also see 1 Chronicles 16:8–36); Psalms 135:8–12 (from the exodus to the occupation); and Psalm 136 (from creation through the exodus to the occupation).[15] New Testament writers followed suit, in that the recorded speeches of Stephen (Acts 7), Paul (Acts 13:17–41), and others in the Book of Acts include abridgments of Old Testament history. But because Christ had now come, these disciples told their histories from their New Testament perspective, demonstrating how Old Testament history paved the way for Christ and His Gospel.

As I've read the Bible through the years I have deeply appreciated these historical summaries because they refresh our memories of the seminal events in salvation history and remind us of their importance to understanding the Bible and God's will for us. These summaries were not designed just to inform and profit future readers of Scripture. They were also meant to remind the Israelites at the time what God had done for them and encourage them to turn back to Him. The biblical figures were telling their brethren, in essence, *Don't just take my word for it that God is great, that God is faithful. Remember what He has done for us unfailingly throughout history, a history with which you are all familiar, but which you must always keep at the forefront of your mind. God is great, God is faithful, and He has demonstrated that repeatedly since the time He called Abram out of Ur of the Chaldeans.*

So these historical summaries serve the dual purpose of reminding us of God's faithful dealings with His people and of informing us of the great importance the biblical figures and writers attached to these histories in calling people back to God through every phase of biblical history. "Scripture does not and could not summarize its story from a standpoint outside the story, which is unfinished," British theologian Richard Bauckham observes. "The summaries are themselves part of the story and even contribute to the story's own development."[16]

In my case, as I read and studied the Bible I wasn't interested in learning biblical history to win Bible trivia contests. At some point I came to realize the importance of understanding the grand sweep of Old Testament history because the message is inseparable from the history from which it emanates. Grasping the unity of the biblical narrative enhances our understanding of the Bible's overall message. As such, I now turn to Old Testament history with the goal of helping you get a handle on the main historical events in the Old Testament record. I will first provide a thumbnail sketch of each of the seventeen Old Testament historical books, then summarize the periods of Old Testament history and the major events covered in each.

SYNOPSIS OF THE OLD TESTAMENT HISTORICAL BOOKS

Genesis is a book of beginnings, the seed-plot of the whole Bible.[17] It opens with God's creation of the universe, its living creatures, and most important, man, whom He creates in His image. He places man in paradise and in peace, but man succumbs to the tempter's wiles and sins, leading to the fall and man's death. But as God pronounces punishment on mankind for his sin, He immediately provides a glimpse into His plan to redeem and reconcile man to Himself, restoring for him a pathway to life. Later, God sets apart the Hebrews as His chosen people and makes a nation out of them to bring His gift of salvation to all the people and nations of the world. The book closes with the Israelites in bondage to the Egyptians.

Exodus is about redemption. It teaches that God saves. It records God's people beginning as a nation and incubating for centuries in Egypt. God frees the Israelites through a series of plagues He imposes on Egypt and cements His special relationship with them by giving them His Law and establishing the priesthood. Despite God's graciousness and blessings, however, Israel continually disobeys and rebels, mostly through idolatrous practices.

Leviticus is a book of atonement and worship. It includes the detailed laws God gives to the people for their benefit in the wilderness, which form an instruction manual for holiness—a condition they must acquire and maintain to be in the presence of the Holy God and to serve as a nation of priests.

Numbers traces the Israelites' journey to the Promised Land, which is interrupted by their sin and leads to their wanderings in the wilderness. This period serves as a transition from the old generations that left Egypt to the new generation that is poised to enter Canaan.

Deuteronomy is a record of God's restatement of the Law to His people, led by Moses, and of the renewal of His covenant with them. It signifies a new beginning for the Israelites as they prepare to conquer Canaan.

Joshua chronicles the Israelites' conquest of Canaan under Joshua, Moses' chosen successor, and the division of the land among the twelve tribes. God doesn't free Israel from Egypt simply to wander forever without a home. He promised them the land, and this book records His initial fulfillment of that vow and the onset of a new historical era for the Israelites in that land.

Judges tells the story of the Israelites' habitual degeneration into sin, the punishment that God enforces against them—usually through attacks by foreign nations—and the important leaders (called "judges") whom God raises up to deliver the people from these invaders and to restore order in the land. In a sense the book is a microcosm of the entire span of Israel's history in that it involves a recurring cycle whereby the people sin and turn away from God, later repent, and are finally restored. Aside from the intervening, remedial actions of God's judges, this period is marked by apostasy, chaos, and lawlessness during which "there was no king in Israel. Everyone did what was right in his own eyes" (Judges 21:25).

Ruth is a short book about a Moabite widow, living in the time of the judges, who leaves her own culture out of love for her Israelite mother-in-law Naomi. "Your people shall be my people, and your God my God," she declares (Ruth 1:16). Ruth falls in love with Boaz, a prosperous Hebrew farmer, who takes care of her. This book is included in the biblical canon primarily because it shows God's intention to accept Gentiles who seek Him and because Ruth, who would become the great-grandmother of David, was an ancestor of Christ.

1 Samuel describes Israel's transition from theocracy to monarchy and Samuel's leadership of the nation as a prophet, priest, and as the last of the judges. Samuel anoints Israel's first king, Saul, whose trials and tribulations are recounted, including his conflict with David. The book also relates the loving friendship between David and Saul's son Jonathan. The book ends with Saul's death in battle.

2 Samuel covers David's reign and God's promise to him of an everlasting dynasty, David's triumphs as a man after God's heart, and the consequences of his terrible sins of adultery and murder.

1 Kings opens with King David's death and Solomon's succession to the throne. Solomon becomes the wisest and richest king on earth and has an auspicious beginning with the dedication of the Temple in Jerusalem, where God will dwell with His people. But Solomon's story is ultimately tragic because he squanders all his God-given blessings and falls into unfaithfulness and sin, which leads to apostasy among the people and the division of the nation into northern and southern kingdoms. The book also recounts the ministry of the great prophet Elijah, who warns the people against idolatry.

2 Kings records the final part of Elijah's ministry and the beginning of the ministry of his successor Elisha. It describes the ongoing idolatry of the people of the Northern Kingdom of Israel and their resulting conquest by the Assyrians, who take them into captivity. The Southern Kingdom of Judah lasts more than a century longer, but in the end its sins are no less severe, leading to its fall and the Babylonian captivity.

1 Chronicles deals with the history of Judah after the fall of Israel.

2 Chronicles continues with the history of Judah and its fall into apostasy, leading to the people's exile in Babylon.

Ezra tells of the release of the Jewish people from their Babylonian captivity by Persian king Cyrus, who had conquered Babylon, and the people's return to Jerusalem to rebuild the Temple despite strong opposition arising mostly from Judea's non-Jewish inhabitants—those who had been living in the area since the fall of the Northern Kingdom.

Nehemiah follows up with the restoration of the Jewish people to Jerusalem, telling of their rebuilding of the city's walls under the authority of Persian king Artaxerxes, again in the face of fierce opposition.

Esther, the last of the historical books, describes God's preservation and deliverance of the Jewish people from the threat of extinction at the hands of the evil Persian official Haman. God thwarts Haman's diabolical scheme through Esther, whom He has prepared "for such a time as this" (4:14) to save His people.[18]

I found that it was easier to understand the individual Old Testament books once I grasped the broad flow of the history they cover. Accordingly, in the next chapter we'll take a closer look at the various periods of Old Testament history to illuminate the continuous unfolding of God's redemptive plan.

CHAPTER 3

OLD TESTAMENT HISTORY
CREATION THROUGH THE UNITED KINGDOM

*For the Bible should be viewed, not only in its single books,
but in their connection, and in the unity of the whole. The
Old Testament could not be broken off from the New, and
each considered as independent of the other. Nor yet could
any part of the Old Testament be disjoined from the rest.
The full meaning and beauty of each appears only in the
harmony and unity of the whole. Thus they all form links
of one unbroken chain, reaching from the beginning to the
time when the Lord Jesus Christ came, for whom all previous history had prepared, to whom all the types pointed,
and in whom all the promises are "Yea and Amen."*

—ALFRED EDERSHEIM[1]

OUTLINE OF OLD TESTAMENT
HISTORICAL PERIODS

I fondly remember my law professor Grant Nelson excitedly telling
us second-year students that having the first year under our belts,
we were about to discover the interconnectedness of the entire field

of law. He assured us that a light would soon turn on, and our subsequent studies would become richer and more meaningful as the big picture came into focus. He couldn't have been more right. Professor Nelson's enthusiasm for imparting the law to us was infectious, and I hope my enthusiasm for the Bible is contagious as well.

When I first began to study the Bible I felt lost and overwhelmed, having no idea how the pieces fit together to form a comprehensive story. But the more I studied, the clearer the picture became. As I described in *Jesus on Trial*, my understanding increased as I began to notice recurring themes and other evidence of the Bible's unity. Another key step was learning the flow of Old Testament history, after which, as in law school, the Bible's broad sweep came into clearer view and the details started falling into place.

Scholars outline Old Testament history in various ways. Professor Paul Benware frames it in two main sections, the first involving God's dealings with mankind generally from creation to the Tower of Babel (Genesis 1–11) and the second focusing on God's dealings with Israel specifically (Genesis 12 to the end of the Old Testament).[2] Why did God devote so little space to the beginning period? Because the Bible's purpose is to relate salvation history, not secular history. God gives us a brief albeit vitally important account of the creation and man's fall, then proceeds in short order to unveil His sovereign plan for the salvation of mankind through His chosen nation of Israel.

Most scholars break the span of Old Testament history into smaller periods, but I've found the divisions to be somewhat arbitrary. I've seen various writers create five periods,[3] six periods,[4] seven periods,[5] eleven periods,[6] and even twelve periods.[7]

The most helpful outline I've found divides Old Testament history into ten periods, though scholars do not agree on all the precise dates:

1. Primeval Period: from Creation to the Patriarchs (Creation–2166 BC)
2. Patriarchal Period (2166 BC–1446 BC)
3. Exodus Period (1446 BC–1406 BC)
4. Conquest of Canaan (1406 BC–1390 BC)
5. Time of Judges (1390 BC–1050 BC)
6. United Kingdom (1050 BC–931 BC)

7. Divided Kingdom (931 BC–722 BC)
8. Surviving Kingdom: Judah (722 BC–586 BC)
9. Babylonian Captivity (586 BC–538 BC or 516 BC)
10. Restoration (538 BC–400 BC)[8]

In this chapter and the next we'll summarize many, but by no means all, of the major events of Old Testament history in these periods. I discuss these periods not only because learning them helps us to understand Scripture overall, but also to create a backdrop for our examination of the centrality of Christ to all of Scripture—for at every turn in these historical periods we will see God's redemptive plan at work.

PRIMEVAL PERIOD: FROM CREATION TO THE PATRIARCHS

The first eleven chapters of Genesis deal with beginnings: God speaks the universe into existence, creates the world, makes mankind in His image, and establishes work, family, nations, and languages. Beyond creation, numerous other major events are recorded in these chapters: man's temptation and fall, which bring God's judgment; fratricide, with Cain murdering Abel; the flood and Noah's ark; and the division of man and the dispersion of his language at Babel. Though man's fall occurs early in the Bible, God unveils His promise of redemption as He administers His judgment for man's sin. He curses the serpent, which represents Satan, and tells him that the Redeemer will triumph over him (and thus over sin and death): "I will put enmity between you and the woman, and between your offspring and her offspring; he shall bruise your head, and you shall bruise his heel" (Gen. 3:15).

This passage is considered the first messianic prophecy (a prophecy concerning the Messiah). It is also regarded as the *protevangelium*, meaning the first announcement of the Gospel or a foreshadowing of the Gospel and of the Redeemer—who will come from the offspring of a woman and will be "bruised," but will crush the head of the tempter (Satan).[9] As the New Testament explains, the offspring or seed of the woman referred to here is Jesus Christ—He is to be born of woman, not man, because He is to be sired not by Joseph but by the Holy Spirit. Though He will suffer (His heel will be struck), He will crush Satan's head, which indicates He will triumph over Satan and redeem believers through His sacrificial death on the cross.

In chapter 4 of Genesis we have the beginnings of civilization with Adam and Eve begetting Cain and Abel. After Cain murders Abel in a jealous rage because God approves Abel's sacrifice and not his own, God sends Cain to be a wandering fugitive. The rebellious Cain, however, settles down and builds a city, glorifying himself while excluding God. But God does not allow this to go unanswered. He intervenes to preserve the godly line in furtherance of His redemptive plan. Adam and Eve then produce another son, the virtuous Seth, to take Abel's place. Significantly, the chapter ends with this uplifting passage: "At that time people began to call upon the name of the Lord" (Gen. 4:26).

Despite God's preservation of the godly line, the cumulative effects of sin ravage mankind and "the Lord saw that the wickedness of man was great in the earth, and that every intention of the thoughts of his heart was only evil continually" (Gen. 6:5). Humanity degenerates to the point that God decides to purify mankind by bringing on the flood and eradicating the evil line of humanity while preserving, through Noah, the godly line.

The Tower of Babel tells the story of man's ongoing rebellion, idolatry, and his attempt to glorify himself apart from God, even though God has preserved His promise of redemption by sparing Noah (and his descendants) in the flood. In building the tower man brazenly defies God's mandate to "fill the earth." In response, God disperses humanity and confuses its language (Gen. 1:28).

These first eleven chapters, then, are foundational to the entire Bible. The identity and role of human beings in God's creation are established here, and the reality and destructiveness of sin are plainly demonstrated. God displays His superintending providence over sin and His proactive intervention to redeem man each time he succumbs to its devastation. Long before He gives Moses the Law, God moves in judgment against sinful and prideful man with His first rendering of punishment at the fall in chapter 3. Then Cain rebels, and just as sin appears to be carrying the day, God steps in remedially, preserving His godly line through Seth. Despite man's subsequent descent into further corruption, God refuses to destroy mankind in the flood and spares it through the righteous Noah. When incorrigible mankind rebels at Babel, God refrains again from destroying the human race but thwarts the people's independence and confuses their language. This is in preparation for calling Abram (chapter 12) and setting in motion His plan for mankind's redemption.[10]

Richard P. Belcher Jr. observes that our worldview will be distorted if we don't grasp the essential truths set forth in these first eleven chapters.[11] If we don't understand that God created the material world to be good, we'll either believe the falsehood that the material world is evil, or we might, at the other extreme, deify the material world (as do some religions and belief systems), unaware of the boundaries God established for His creation. Unless we comprehend the reality and nature of sin, and God's attitude and response to it, we won't understand our fellow man or how to govern ourselves in light of our nature. If we don't have a clear picture of God's character as revealed in these pages, we'll fail to see God's justice or His grace in dealing with our sin. That's why chapters 1–11 are crucial to our formation of a proper biblical worldview and our understanding of God, the world, and ourselves.

To avoid sliding into cynicism, let's keep in mind that no revealed truth in Genesis is more important than God's creation of human beings in His image. Singling man out from His other created beings on earth, God proclaims, "Let the earth bring forth living creatures according to their kinds" (Gen. 1:24) and "Let us make man in our image, after our likeness" (Gen. 1:26). As Kenneth Mathews writes, "The crown of God's handiwork is human life."[12] Man is the apex of God's creation, he is superior to other creatures and is to have dominion over them (Gen. 1:26–28). The revelations about sin and redemption would be superfluous and meaningless outside this context. Only man is capable of sinning, and only man is in God's redemptive plan.

PATRIARCHAL PERIOD: ABRAHAM TO MOSES

Pastor Roy Gingrich breaks the Bible into a three-part outline: "generation," when paradise is established, as recorded in Genesis 1–2;

"degeneration," when paradise is lost through man's sin, according to Genesis 3; and "regeneration," when paradise is regained, which is related in the rest of the Bible. As "God's great redemptive plan of the ages" unfolds, explains Gingrich, "a new creation is gradually coming out of the old ruined creation."[13] Interestingly, British Bible scholar G. Campbell Morgan, writing in the early twentieth century—some one hundred years before Gingrich—used the same three themes to describe Genesis as a microcosm of the entire Bible: chapters 1 and 2 involve "generation," i.e. the creation; chapters 3–11 involve "degeneration," or man's fall into sin; and chapters 12–50 involve the beginnings of "regeneration" that "culminated in the person of the Messiah [in the New Testament]."[14]

One of the most important events of the Old Testament occurs early in Genesis, when God makes an everlasting covenant with Abraham known as the "Abrahamic Covenant." This is perhaps the most significant of all the Old Testament covenants. God calls Abram (later renamed Abraham) out of his land, telling him to go to the land that God would show him. God promises Abram, "And I will make of you a great nation, and I will bless you and make your name great, so that you will be a blessing. I will bless those who bless you, and him who dishonors you I will curse, and in you all the families of the earth shall be blessed" (Gen. 12:1–3). In this passage and later ones (e.g., Gen. 15:18–21), God promises Abram that He will make a nation out of him and that He will give his people the land of Canaan as an everlasting possession (thus the designation "the Promised Land").

It's important to distinguish God's promise to make Abram's name great from the Babel event in which people try to make their own names great. Consistent with God's command that we focus on Him and put no other gods before Him, we cannot navigate our existence on our own power, intentionally apart from God.[15] God does not promise to make Abram's name great for Abram's glory but for His own and in accordance with His sovereign plan to bless all mankind.

So at the beginning of this second section of Genesis, God unveils His plan to set apart the Hebrew people as a nation for the ultimate purpose of blessing (redeeming) all peoples and nations of the earth. As subsequent books of the Old Testament reveal, God will accomplish this redemption through the Messiah, Who will come from the Hebrew nation as a descendant of King David. God sets apart and establishes a chosen nation of people to whom He would entrust the Holy Scriptures, be His witness to the other nations, and through whom He would bring the Messiah and salvation to mankind.

In several places, the New Testament confirms God's plan to bless all people through Abram and the Hebrew nation. Peter invokes Genesis 12:3 when he tells his people, "You are the sons of the prophets and of the covenant that God made with your fathers, saying to Abraham, 'And in your offspring shall all the families of the earth be blessed'" (Acts 3:25). Paul, in his letter to the Galatians, cites the same Scripture passage, describing it as "the gospel" that was preached beforehand to Abraham. He exclaims, "And the Scripture, foreseeing that God would justify the Gentiles by faith, preached the gospel beforehand to Abraham, saying, 'In you shall all the nations be blessed'" (Gal. 3:8). Abraham, as both Genesis (15:6) and the New Testament Book of Hebrews affirm (11:8, 9; 17–18), distinguishes himself as a man of faith, especially because he is willing to sacrifice his son and trust that God will bring him back to life (Heb. 11:19; James 2:21).

Abraham's son Isaac does not occupy much of the Genesis narrative, but he is important as the son that Abraham is commanded by God to sacrifice (chapter 22). As such, Isaac becomes a type of Christ.[16] Also significant is his "miraculous birth," his obedience unto death, his stead-fast love for his father despite his father's agreeing to sacrifice him, and his victory over death, which foreshadows Christ's resurrection.[17] More important, God passes on His covenant promises to Isaac and through him to his son Jacob, who will become father of the nation of Israel. Isaac is also recognized in Hebrews as a man of faith who invokes blessings on his sons Jacob and Esau (11:20).

Jacob is a colorful figure who steals his brother Esau's blessing, wrestles with God, and sires twelve sons who will be the leaders of the tribes of Israel. The fascinating story of Jacob's favorite son Joseph is told in Genesis, chapters 37–50. Joseph too is a type of Christ, as we'll examine in Chapter 9, and through Joseph, God gloriously demon-strates the outworking of His sovereign plan to preserve His chosen nation despite the recalcitrance and evil of man. He even uses man's evil to advance His will, as Scripture repeatedly avers that God is ever active in His creation and in history, using the wrongs of man for His own glory. (See, for example, these passages from Isaiah alone: 10:5–19, 13:1–27:13, 36:1–39:8, 40:12–26, 44:24–45:13.)

I want to mention one other seemingly minor story in Genesis—in chapter 38, which briefly diverges from the life of Joseph to tell the story of Judah, founder of Israel's Tribe of Judah, and his daughter-in-law Tamar. In brief, God strikes down Tamar's husband due to his wicked ways and also kills Tamar's second husband, who was the sinful brother of her first. Later, disguised as a prostitute, she sleeps with an unsuspecting Judah and eventually bears twin sons, one of whom becomes an ancestor to King David. This short story provides a crucial link in the genealogical line to the Messiah, Jesus having descended from the tribe of Judah (Heb. 7:14; Rev. 5:5). Furthermore, the astonishing way in which Tamar becomes impregnated—and thereby protects the line of David—is further resounding proof of God's sovereignty and His unwavering commitment to fulfill His covenant promises.

In sum, Genesis tells of God's creation of man in His image, man's disappointing fall into sin and death, and ultimately, God's promise to redeem man. As scholars point out, Genesis ends in death, with Joseph being placed in a coffin in Egypt. Although the book includes God's promise of future redemption, that promise is not yet fulfilled as Genesis closes. Rather, man's utter hopelessness apart from God and his bondage to physical death punctuate God's first book of divine revelation. As stated in 1 Corinthians, "For as in Adam all die" (15:22).

EXODUS PERIOD

In Exodus, God begins to actualize His promises of redemption. As the story unfolds, God takes affirmative steps to realize His promise to make Abraham the father of a nation. In this second book of the Bible, which is a continuation of the first, God formalizes His election of this special nation as He delivers Israel from the oppressive bondage of Egyptian rule.

But remember: God's election of Israel is not primarily for the sake of Israel, but to enable the salvation of all mankind. "It is important that we should understand the meaning of the creation of this nation," argues G. Campbell Morgan. "It cannot be too often emphasized that it was not the election of a nation from among others in order that upon that nation God might lavish His love while He abandoned the others. The purpose of God was far wider than that of the creation of this nation; it was that of the creation of a testimony through this nation, for the sake of the others."[18] Along the same lines, Roy Zuck writes, "Israel itself and its covenant relationship to [God] cannot be the focal point of biblical theology. Israel's role is not an ultimate objective but merely a means of facilitating that objective—that God and the peoples of the earth might have unbroken communion. Israel's importance, then, is functional.... Israel was made a priestly nation to achieve communion between man and God."[19]

So Exodus is important because it records God's initial redemptive activities on behalf of mankind by liberating this wayward people from their Egyptian slave masters and molding them into a nation. But God's redemptive activities merely begin in Exodus—the remainder of the Old Testament and the entire New Testament progressively reveal the rest of the story.

Moses is the central character of this period and is widely considered to have authored the books covering it in addition to having written Genesis. He is adopted by pharaoh's daughter and trained in the finest Egyptian culture and education, but flees for his life to Midian after slaying an Egyptian who beat a Hebrew slave. In Midian he marries Jethro's daughter Zipporah, stays there forty years, and returns to Egypt. At that point God, in the guise of the burning bush, calls Moses to lead the people to Canaan in fulfillment of His promise to deliver the people after four hundred years of Egyptian bondage (Gen. 15:13–16). God is not deterred by Moses' reluctance and doesn't demur when Moses asks Him how to respond when people ask, "What is his name?" (Exodus 3:13). In a profoundly significant theological revelation denoting God's self-existence, His infinity, and His intention to reveal Himself to Moses, He answers, "I AM WHO I AM" or "I AM THAT I AM" (Exodus 3:14), which is as power-packed an expression as human language permits.

Christ would later apply this name to Himself (John 8:58), which prompts the Pharisees' attempt to stone Him for blasphemy (John 8:59).

Other major events in Exodus include God's plagues on the hard-hearted pharaoh (chapters 5–10); the institution of the Passover (chapters 11–12) to commemorate God's deliverance of His people; Israel's exodus from Egypt with the miraculous parting of the Red Sea (chapters 13–14); God's miraculous provision of manna to sustain His people (chapter 16); His miraculous provision of water (chapter 17); the giving of the Law (chapters 19–24), including the Ten Commandments (chapter 20); and the design and construction of the Tabernacle (chapters 25–40).

In giving the Law to the Israelites, and the Israelites accepting it, God enters into another covenant with His people—the "Mosaic Covenant," which we will discuss in Chapter 5. In return for His deliverance of the people from Egypt, they need to obey Him, foremost by following His commandments, which is essential to their relationship with Him. The Israelites are to be a holy people, set apart and distinguished from other nations[20] and serving as an example to them—and ultimately to all people through the ages. Indeed, two months after the exodus (Exodus 19:1), before God presents the Law to Moses, He instructs Moses to tell the people of Israel, "Now therefore, if you will indeed obey my voice and keep my covenant, you shall be my treasured possession among all peoples, for all the earth is mine; and you shall be to me a kingdom of priests and a holy nation" (Exodus 19:5–6).

By giving the people of Israel the Law, God provides the standards by which they should live, become holy, and distinguish themselves from other people. As the first two of the Ten Commandments emphasize, above all, they must worship Him and Him alone, and scrupulously avoid idol worship. As part of these duties, He forbids them from inter-marrying with other peoples, primarily because foreign wives would woo them to worship false gods (Exodus 34:16). He has them build the Tabernacle—a portable structure for Israel to use for worshipping Him while in the wilderness—because He will dwell with them. He gives specific instructions on its design and orders that it be placed in the center of their camp (Num. 2). Notably, Israel is to have only one sanctuary, in contrast to the numerous temples in Egypt.[21]

In Leviticus, sometimes called a "handbook on holiness," God gives explicit instructions to the Israelites for establishing a priesthood, instituting a system of sacrifices and feasts that would be mediated by the priests, and learning how to worship and obey Him. (As a point of interest and to further illustrate the interconnectedness of the Old and New Testaments, it's noteworthy that some have called chapter 9 of the Book of Hebrews a divine commentary on Leviticus, especially Leviticus 16,[22] and a "divine commentary on the prophetic meaning of the ceremonial law.")[23] God's provision for man's holiness is meant to make him fit for the presence of His own holiness. Accordingly, Leviticus provides the requirements and means by which finite man may approach an infinite God—namely, man must have an offering provided to God by the priests.[24] These requirements carry through to the New Testament, where they are perfectly and finally fulfilled in Jesus Christ.

Significantly, as soon as God gives His people the Law they begin to break it freely, making an idolatrous golden calf and building an altar to place before it (Exodus 32:1–6). This incurs God's wrath, and He only refrains from destroying the nation due to Moses' pleas. God then directs Moses to continue to lead the people to Canaan (Exodus 33:1–6) and renews His covenant with the people (Exodus 34:1–9).

Some Bible scholars believe the narrative of these sections is structured to showcase Israel's sin and to illustrate its consequences. For example, the instructions for building the Tabernacle given in Exodus 25–31 are interrupted by the story of Israel's idolatry. Thereafter the instructions are repeated and the Tabernacle is constructed. This literary framework demonstrates the people's desperate need for the Tabernacle and the notion that they will be denied God's presence and blessing when they degenerate into sin.[25]

In the Book of Numbers the people head toward the Promised Land but display marked discontent along the way, grumbling to Moses about God's provisions for them (Num. 11). This pattern continues as they near the border of Canaan and send twelve spies to scout it. Only two of the spies, Joshua and Caleb (Num. 14:6), recommend proceeding, while the other ten, representing the people's collective lack of faith in God's promises, fear entering (Num. 13–14). This is the final straw, as God responds by denying this generation, except for Joshua and Caleb, entry into the land and relegating it to wandering and dying in the wilderness (Num. 14.30; Psalms 106:24–27).[26] At the close of this period Moses relinquishes his power, and God commissions Joshua to take his place (Deut. 31:23). As always, no setback will interfere with God's sovereign plan to march forward toward His redemptive ends.

CONQUEST OF CANAAN

The Israelites are now ready to enter and conquer Canaan, the land God promised Abraham and his descendants some four hundred years before (Gen. 15:18–21). They already have a king—God Himself—and a governing constitution through the Law that God has given them. But to fulfill their corporate duty of serving as priestly mediator to the world ("a kingdom of priests and a holy nation," according to Exodus 19:6), they must occupy their own land (Deut. 8:1–10).[27] The land, for numerous reasons, will be pivotal to God's unfolding plan of redemption.

Dwelling across the Jordan River from the Israelites' encampment, the Canaanites reside in city-states, many of which are protected by walls and by their high elevations. (The term Canaanite, as used here, describes all those who lived in Canaan prior to its conquest by the Hebrew people, including the actual Canaanites as well as the Hittites, Amorites, Jebusites, Perizzites, Hivites, and others.)[28] They were pagans through and through, polytheistic, with sexual beings as their gods. The Canaanite gods El and Baal, for example, had female deities such as Asherah and Anat as their consorts.[29]

Bible readers sometimes shudder at the Israelites' wartime brutality against the Canaanites, and even more so at the thought that God directed some of it. But such practices are not random or sadistic and must be understood in the context of the Canaanite culture and God's overall redemptive plans for mankind. Anything or any people who interfere with the outworking of God's salvation purposes must be removed as God's enemy.[30]

By every account, and confirmed by archaeological discoveries, the Canaanites were unrivaled in their immorality and barbarity, as shown in their religious rituals of child sacrifice, prostitution, and snake worship.[31] Knowing these practices, Moses tells the Israelites they have no choice but to wholly destroy these people, lest they fall prey to their vile practices, thereby corrupting themselves and their worship of the one true God, whose message they are entrusted to preserve through the ages for humanity (Lev. 18:24–28, 20–23; Deut. 12:31, 20:17, 18).[32] Also keep in mind that God's judgment on these wicked people was rendered only after patiently enduring them and allowing their sinful condition to pass the point of redemption. For example, when Abram was in that land centuries earlier, God told him that he and his people would be sojourners in another land (Egypt) for four hundred years, but "they shall come back here in the fourth generation, for the iniquity of the Amorites is not yet complete" (Gen. 15:16).

As they stand poised to begin their conquest, the Israelites know they have blown their first opportunity due to their lack of faith, which cost them thirty-eight long years in the wilderness. To acquire the Promised Land they have to accept that these events aren't about them, but ultimately about God's sovereign plan to reconcile human beings to Himself,[33] and that they must surrender their will to Him to inherit this gift.[34] Though God is absolutely sovereign, He makes human beings accountable for their conduct. Moreover, their conquest of the land would not end their duties to God. God deliberately places them among pagan nations (Ezek. 5:5) so they can show the consequences of serving the real God and honoring His laws (Isaiah 43:10).

Informing the Israelites' new leader that He is about to fulfill His land promise, God instructs Joshua, "Do not be frightened, and do not be dismayed, for the Lord your God is with you wherever you go" (Joshua 1:11). He tells Joshua that the people must steep themselves in the Book of the Law and "meditate on it day and night, so that you may be careful to do according to all that is written in it" (Joshua 1:8).

Joshua's first order of business is to dispatch two spies, who are ordered to "go view the land, especially Jericho" (Joshua 2:1). The spies get help from an unlikely source—Rahab, a Canaanite prostitute who shelters them, hides them from the King of Jericho, and helps them to escape. Rahab, though not an Israelite, expresses her faith in the true God and not the false gods of the Canaanites. The writer of Hebrews includes Rahab in his list of the faithful: "By faith Rahab the prostitute did not perish with those who were disobedient, because she had given a friendly welcome to the spies" (11:31).

God meticulously superintends the people's crossing of the Jordan River, telling Joshua, "Today I will begin to exalt you in the sight of all Israel, that they may know that, as I was with Moses, so I will be with you" (Joshua 3:7). Joshua dutifully reminds the people that the way they "shall know the living God is among" them, and know that He will drive out the Canaanites and other peoples from the land before them, is "when the soles of the feet of the priests bearing the ark of the Lord, the Lord of all the earth, shall rest in the waters of the Jordan, the waters of the Jordan shall be cut off from flowing, and the waters coming down from above shall stand in one heap" (Joshua 3:10–13).

As promised, when the priests step into the river, "the waters coming down from above stood and rose up in a heap very far away" (Joshua 3:16), even though at that time the Jordan was overflowing all its banks because it was harvest time (Joshua 3:15). The Israelites then pass over on dry ground into Canaan. Tremper Longman describes this event as "a reactualization of the miracle at the Red (Reed) Sea, showing that the God who defeated Egypt is still with them as they face an even greater enemy."[35]

God appears before Joshua in battle as "the commander of the army of the Lord" (Joshua 5:14). When the Israelites obey God's precise commands, they summarily conquer Jericho. But after they disobey His order not to take any of the booty from the vanquished people there (Joshua 6:18), they are defeated at the city of Ai, again illustrating God's sovereignty alongside the people's accountability. After this setback the Israelites press forward and triumph, as detailed in Joshua 12. They are not permitted to fully complete their occupation of the land, however, because they have broken their covenant with God by making covenants with the Canaanites and failing to tear down their pagan altars. So the Angel of the Lord tells the people at Bochim, "I brought you up from Egypt and into the land that I swore to give to your fathers. I said, 'I will never break my covenant with you, and you shall make no covenant with the inhabitants of this land; you shall break down their altars.' But you have not obeyed my voice. What is this you have done? So now I say, I will not drive them out before you, but they shall become thorns in your sides and their gods shall be a snare to you" (Judges 2:1–3).

The second half of the Book of Joshua sets forth the distribution of the newly conquered land to the tribes of Israel. In the final chapters (23–24), God reminds the people that He has been faithful to His promises and admonishes them not to intermarry with the remnant of the conquered peoples. If they disobey He will no longer drive the nations out and they will "be a snare and a trap for you." He also sternly warns them against serving and worshipping other gods. Joshua then gathers the people and, speaking on God's behalf, reviews their God-orchestrated history, beginning with Abraham and continuing through their time in Egypt, their exodus, and their conquering of the land (Joshua 24:1–13). Joshua closes by telling them they must make a choice between the false gods and the one true God. "But as for me and my house, we will serve the Lord," he affirms (Joshua 24:15). The people then renew their covenant with God, after which Joshua dies and is buried.

TIME OF JUDGES

The Book of Judges, which records Israel's history from Joshua's death until Samuel emerges on the scene, chronicles how the people break their renewed covenant with God, God's consequent punishment, their repentance, and God's deliverance—over and over. Fallen man is habitually sinful, but God is long-suffering and forgiving. The period in which we see this cyclical pattern has been described as the "Dark Ages" of the Hebrew people's history. It is a time of apostasy and disobedience, when the stubbornly independent people repeatedly defy God's commands not to adopt the practices and beliefs of the pagan people who remain among them.[36] The theme of the book, accordingly, is captured in a short statement repeated throughout its pages: "The people of Israel did what was evil in the sight of the Lord" (2:11, 3:7, 3:12, 4:1, 6:1, 10:6, 13:1). By ignoring God's order to wholly eradicate the Canaanites, the Hebrew people set a trap for themselves because they inevitably intermingle with the Canaanites and adopt their idolatrous practices.

The term "judges" is a bit misleading from our perspective because the so-called judges are mostly military leaders, not arbiters of judicial disputes, though some also perform in a judicial capacity. But they don't make laws, as God has already given them the Law, and they are powerless to interpret laws because that responsibility falls to the priests.[37] A total of twelve judges are named in the book, including Deborah, the female warrior, and Samson, the legendary strong man. The judges are not kings who can pass on their power to their heirs, impose taxes, or negotiate treaties with other nations. They have no armies of their own, but depend on Israel's tribal leaders for military actions. They are not royalty and have none of its trappings, but more closely resemble regular citizens specially empowered by God to redeem the people from their oppressors on His behalf.[38]

The people at this time are still under God's rule—a theocracy—though they often resist Him and long for an earthly king. The period of the judges is chaotic, at times bordering on anarchy, but from God's sovereign perspective, it is anything but random—a cohesive pattern of events is playing out. God is nothing if not consistent and dependable in His dealings with His people. This dark history involves a recurring, four-stage cycle, memorably referenced by this alliterative construct: sin, servitude, sorrow and supplication, salvation.[39] The four-fold pattern is:

1. The people sin, especially through idolatry (Judges 3:6) and intermarriage (Judges 3:6).
2. God punishes them by sending a nation to oppress them.
3. The people repent and pray for deliverance.
4. God raises up a judge to defeat the oppressor (Judges 2:18).[40]

Let's look at how the Bible describes this pattern.

They sin. Not only does God want His chosen people to remain separate from other nations; He insists they serve only Him, worship only Him, and not idolize false gods, as emphasized in His first two commandments. God's commands, as always, are for the good of His people,[41] but they disobey anyway—they "served the Baals" (Judges 2:11) and "abandoned the Lord, the God of their fathers, who had brought them out of the land of Egypt. They went after other gods, from among the peoples who were around them, and bowed down to them. And they provoked the Lord to anger" (Judges 2:12).

God gives them over to servitude: "And he sold them into the hand of their surrounding enemies, so that they could no longer withstand their enemies" (Judges 2:14).

The people respond in sorrow and supplication, praying to God for His deliverance: "And they were in terrible distress" (Judges 2:15).

God mercifully provides for their salvation: "Then the Lord raised up judges, who saved them out of the hands of these raiders" (Judges 2:16). Nehemiah would later write that the people ignored God's warnings not to sin. Yet after punishing them, He always came to their rescue. "Therefore, you gave them into the hand of the peoples of the lands. Nevertheless, in your great mercies, you did not make an end of them or forsake them, for you are a gracious and merciful God" (Neh. 9:30–31).

God's punishment is not just punitive but corrective. As we are told in Proverbs, "Do not despise the Lord's discipline or be weary of his reproof, for the Lord reproves him whom he loves, as a father the son in whom he delights" (3:11–12); (cf. Hebrews 12:5–10). His punishment is meant to prevent the Israelites from falling into greater depravity. They always begin following the judge, but man's fallen condition being what it is, they can't hold on to the blessings, and within a generation or two descend again into their sinful practices. In the end, however, God is always there to correct, redeem, and improve them. The period is, to be sure, a turbulent one for the people of Israel, but also, in the words of Roy Gingrich, it represents "an age of learning through experience. Israel as an adolescent received many wisdom bumps."[42] Later, Gingrich notes, Israel would be taught by oral and writing prophets.

Occurring during the period of the judges, the events described in the Book of Ruth give us a view of the social conditions existing among the Hebrew people at the time. This book, writes J. W. Reed, "gleams like a beautiful pearl against a jet-black background."[43] Ruth doesn't just shine in its content, but also in its literary magnificence. German writer and poet Johann Wolfgang von Goethe believes that Ruth was "the loveliest complete work on a small scale."[44]

Ruth herself stands out as an example of faithfulness and right living, showing that even during Israel's ebbs, God is present in the lives of the faithful. The book depicts individuals who live with restraint and responsibility—the antithesis of the spirit of permissiveness and reckless independence prevailing at the time. Though Ruth is a Moabitess and not a Hebrew, she comes to have faith in the true God Who accepts and blesses her, vindicating the wisdom of following God and not idols, and demonstrating that Gentiles are included in God's redemptive plan.

UNITED KINGDOM

The United Kingdom period marks a radical departure from previous historical eras for the Hebrews because they transition from a collection of disorganized, non-cohesive tribes to a united nation under a single king. This transformation is overseen by Samuel, the last of the judges. He is one of the four central figures of this period, the others being the three kings of the United Kingdom—Saul, David, and Solomon.[45] Samuel is involved in virtually every important aspect of history during his lifetime. Credited with founding the United Kingdom, Samuel is arguably the greatest Israelite since Moses.[46]

There are three major godly offices held by the Israelites: prophet (2 Samuel 7:2), priest (1 Samuel 30:7), and king (2 Samuel 5:3).[47] The occupants of these offices, which would later be united in Jesus Christ,[48] are customarily consecrated by anointing with oil.[49] In essence, Samuel occupies each of these offices. He serves not only as leader (judge) of Israel, but also as its leading priest (even though he is not in Aaron's priestly line) and as a prophet. Men who preceded Samuel had the prophetic gift and served in the capacity of prophet, but Samuel is the first to occupy the prophetic office.[50] Samuel is believed to have established schools for prophets (1 Samuel 10:5, 19:20) who would be exceedingly influential over Israel's future kings.[51]

Kings Saul, David, and Solomon each serve forty years. This is Israel's golden age, the people having become a united nation with a king and a central government. Though the period doesn't last much more than a century, by the time it reaches its peak under Solomon's reign the nation is stronger and more prosperous than ever. Nearly every aspect of national life improves—economic, educational, political, social, and religious.[52] Additionally, the Hebrews vastly expand their land—when Saul became king they only occupied about half of Canaan, but by the time of Solomon's death the kingdom covers approximately fifty thousand square miles, from Mesopotamia to Egypt and from the desert to the Mediterranean Sea.[53]

The neighboring Philistines are particularly aggressive toward the end of the period of the judges, constantly attacking Israel. After one victory, the Philistines even steal the Ark of the Covenant (1 Samuel 4:5–11), which holds the Ten Commandments. The persistent threat from the Philistines in the west and from the Ammonites, who are east of the Jordan River, provoke the Israelites to demand a king to organize and lead their defenses. When Samuel resists, the people respond, "But there shall be a king over us, that we also may be like all the nations, and that our king may judge us and go out before us and fight our battles" (1 Samuel 8:19–20).

Samuel warns that a king will oppress the people with onerous taxes, take their land, and virtually enslave many of them (1 Samuel 8:10–18). But having lost faith in God, the people persist, and Samuel finally yields when it becomes apparent that his own sons are not fit to succeed him as judge. He prays to God, who tells him to grant the people's wish because they have rejected His theocratic rule (1 Samuel 8:1–9). Note, however, that God had always planned an eventual kingship for Israel, even if He was disappointed with Israel's premature timing (Gen. 17:6).[54]

As for anointing a king, God tells Samuel he should choose Saul, whom He will send from the land of Benjamin and who "shall save my people from the hand of the Philistines" (1 Samuel 9:15–16). Samuel then informs the people they will have a king but he also rebukes them, saying, "Today you have rejected your God, who saves you from all your calamities and your distresses, and you have said to him, 'Set a king over us'" (1 Samuel 10:19). Shortly after he becomes king, Saul leads an army of 330,000 men and defeats the Ammonites, which inspires confidence in his leadership and cements his kingship (1 Samuel 11:8–15).

After these events Samuel bids farewell to the people, again cautioning them to remember all the times God helped them and rescued them.

Though they responded with ingratitude by asking for an earthly king, says Samuel, in the end, the overall relationship between them and God would not change, for God remains sovereign regardless of the kingship. "If you will fear the Lord and serve him and obey his voice and not rebel against the commandment of the Lord, and if both you and the king who reigns over you will follow the Lord your God it will be well," Samuel affirms. "But if you will not obey the voice of the Lord, but rebel against the commandment of the Lord, then the hand of the Lord will be against you and your king" (1 Samuel 12:14–15).

During this period the Israelites are still threatened by the Philistines, who are emboldened by their monopoly on iron smelting in Palestine.[55] The Philistines jealously protect this monopoly "lest the Hebrews make themselves swords or spears" (1 Samuel 13:19). Consequently, the Israelites depend on the Philistines for their plowshares and other tools (1 Samuel 13:20). The Philistines' dominance over the Israelites, however, would end later in this period, under the rule of King David.[56]

Two years into his reign Saul vanquishes a Philistine garrison at Geba, but the enemy responds by assembling thousands of chariots, horsemen, and troops. The Israelites then "hid themselves in caves and in holes and in rocks and in tombs and in cisterns" (1 Samuel 13:6). Earlier, when he had prophesied these events, Samuel told Saul that when they came to pass he should wait seven days for Samuel to come to him and present sacrifices to God (1 Samuel 10:8). But a fearful and anxious Saul makes the offerings before Samuel arrives. Sternly admonishing him for disobeying God's command, Samuel tells Saul this mistake will cost him his kingdom: "But now your kingdom shall not continue. The Lord has sought out a man after his own heart, and the Lord has commanded him to be prince over his people, because you have not kept what the Lord commanded you" (1 Samuel 13:14).

Later, after Saul defeats the Amalekites, he again disobeys God's commands by sparing their king, Aga, and saving the best of his cattle. He compounds his sin by lying about these acts to Samuel. After being reprimanded Saul remains defiant, claiming he's done as God commanded by destroying the Amalekites, and that he only kept the "spoils" to sacrifice them to God.

Samuel then issues a crucial response: "Has the Lord as great delight in burnt offerings and sacrifices, as in obeying the voice of the Lord? Behold, to obey is better than sacrifice, and to listen than the fat of rams. For rebellion is as the sin of divination, and presumption is as iniquity and idolatry. Because you have rejected the word of the Lord, he has also rejected you from being king" (1 Samuel 15:22–23). God, speaking through Samuel, is not condemning the very system of sacrifices He had instituted. He is pointing out that sacrifice means nothing if one merely goes through the motions without a repentant spirit. In other words, it is far more important to obey God than to sacrifice. Jesus would later echo this principle: "And if you had known what this means, 'I desire mercy, and not sacrifice,' you would not have condemned the guiltless" (Matt. 12:7).

"Clearly the Torah integrated sacrifice into the life of obedience to God," Old Testament Professor Robert D. Bergen writes, "however, it never envisioned it as a substitute for obedience."[57] Indeed, Saul's presumptuous acts are tantamount to idolatry—because Saul is acting as his own god. Estranged from this point forward, Samuel and Saul never see each other again (1 Samuel 15:35).

In the meantime, God tells Samuel He regrets making Saul king because Saul had turned his back on Him and had not performed His commandments (1 Samuel 15:10). He orders Samuel to anoint one of the sons of Jesse the Bethlehemite to be king. This leads to David's anointing (1 Samuel 16:13), though his reign doesn't formally begin until after Saul's death some fifteen years later.[58] Initially unaware that David has been chosen as his successor, Saul warmly accepts him into his court as a lyre player: "And Saul loved him greatly, and he became his armor-bearer" (1 Samuel 16:21).

But sometime after David slays Goliath and becomes a hero to the people, Saul's attitude toward him changes. He perceives David as a grave threat and is consumed with jealousy. Instead of tending to his kingdom and dealing with Israel's enemies, he grows obsessed with pursuing and killing David. Saul is thwarted at every turn, however, sometimes due to the intervention of his son Jonathan, who has become David's dear friend.

Ultimately, it is God's sovereign hand that protects David, who obediently allows God's plan to unfold and even repeatedly spares Saul's life when he could have killed him. In the midst of all these events, Samuel dies (1 Samuel 25:1), dealing a major blow to the people. The Philistines later critically wound Saul in battle, and his armor-bearer, at his direction, finishes the job. Three of his four sons and all his men die along with him (1 Samuel 31).

David is then anointed king of the tribe of Judah (2 Samuel 2:4), a public reconfirmation of his private anointing by Samuel (1 Samuel 16).[59] Meanwhile, for a brief time Saul's surviving son Ishbosheth reigns as king of the tribes east of the Jordan and over some of the tribes in "all Israel" (2 Samuel 2:9). Upon the death of Ishbosheth, David becomes king over all of Israel, north and south (2 Samuel 5:1–5).

David chooses the strategically located city of Jerusalem ("Jebus") as his new capital, calling the stronghold the City of David (2 Samuel 5:9). When David settles there, he focuses on finding a proper place for housing the Ark of the Covenant. He tells Nathan the prophet, "See now, I dwell in a house of cedar, but the ark of God dwells in a tent" (2 Samuel 7:2). Though Nathan is initially delighted with this idea, God tells him that night that the building of a temple is in His divine plan— but it would not be built by David. Instead, He would build David a different kind of "house"—the dynastic House of David. Here God unveils what has come to be called the "Davidic Covenant," which, notes Professor Roy B. Zuck, underlies all God's dealings with the monarchy after David as well as with the eschatological 'David.'"[60] We deal with the Davidic Covenant in greater detail in Chapter 6.

God instructs Nathan to tell David, "The Lord declares to you that the Lord will make you a house. When your days are fulfilled and you lie down with your fathers, I will raise up your offspring after you, who shall come from your body, and I will establish his kingdom. He shall build a house for my name, and I will establish the throne of his kingdom forever" (2 Samuel 7:11–13). The promise of the Davidic kingdom reaffirms the promise of the Abrahamic Covenant that the patriarchs would be the fathers of kings (Gen. 17:6, 16, 35:11). That is, in the words of Craig A. Blaising, "the final fulfillment of the Abrahamic promise of blessing in the Promised Land will take place under the rulership of a

Davidic king.... The Davidic covenant provides the *means* by which the Abrahamic blessing will be fulfilled for all descendants."[61] This, incidentally, is further proof God always intended a king for Israel—in His time.

David, as attested by his psalms, understands the theological implications of God choosing him to be a key part of the messianic line that would result, ultimately, in a divine Descendant and King—Jesus Christ. (Psalms 2:6–7, 110). Other Old Testament prophets also announce that the Messiah would come from the Davidic line (Isaiah 9:1–7, 11:1–5; Jer. 30:4–11; Ezek. 34:23–24, 37:24–25; Amos 9:11–15).[62] R. E. Clements observes, "Clearly if there is one passage in the Old Testament which can deserve the title of the seed-bed of the messianic hope it is that of 2 Sam. 7:1–17 and especially v. 16 itself."[63] (God's message to David in verse 16 reads, "'And your house and your kingdom shall be made sure forever before me. Your throne shall be established forever.'")

David would be Israel's greatest king, but his reign is characterized by ups and downs, from his triumph to his tragic fall brought on by his sins that damage him, his family, and his whole nation.[64] He falls into sin through a flagrantly adulterous act with his neighbor Bathsheba, which begins with a simple glance in her direction. His sin leads to other sins—covetousness, bearing false witness, stealing, and eventually murder. Enabled by David's idleness while away from his troops, his affair with Bathsheba results in her pregnancy. He then recalls her husband Uriah from the battlefield to be with Bathsheba in a failed attempt to cover up his transgression. Plotting Uriah's death, David commands that he be placed on the front lines—and His evil plan succeeds. Though he may believe he's getting away with murder, the Bible makes clear that nothing misses the ubiquitous eyes of God: "But the thing that David had done displeased the Lord" (2 Samuel 11:27).

Sent by God to rebuke David, Nathan relates to him a parable of a rich man who exploits a poor one. David is outraged at the rich man's behavior, declaring, "The man who has done this deserves to die." Nathan jolts him with his reply: "You are the man.... You have struck down Uriah the Hittite with the sword and have taken his wife to be your wife and have killed him with the sword of the Ammonites" (2 Samuel 12:1–9). Speaking on behalf of God, Nathan then announces David's punishment: "Now, therefore the sword shall never depart from your house, because you have despised me...I will raise up evil against you out of your own house" (2 Samuel 12:10–11). Note that God regards David's sin as a transgression against Himself. He is God. He is the Lawgiver.

David responds with humility and contrition, refusing to evade responsibility or make excuses. God continues to love David, "a man after God's heart," but does not exempt him from judgment. Repentance restores our right relationship with God, but we still have to suffer the consequences of our sin. As such, David's child with Bathsheba dies. To comfort Bathsheba, David fathers another child with her—Solomon—who would be David's successor.

Meanwhile, David has trouble with his sons Amnon and Absalom. Amnon rapes his half-sister Tamar, and Absalom eventually avenges her by murdering her killer. Absalom then flees to escape David's punishment. Subsequently, while Absalom is leading a failed rebellion against his father, David's men kill him despite David's orders to spare his life. So in the end, as Nathan warned (2 Samuel 12:10), David, as a result of his sin, loses a newborn baby and two sons, and his daughter is raped. This is a stark lesson about the consequences of sin. Roy Matheson explains the key spiritual principles we should learn:

1. "God is not mocked: For whatever one sows, that will he also reap" (Gal. 6:7).
2. "For the Lord disciplines the one he loves" (Heb. 12:6 and Prov. 3:12).

God forgives the past, but He does not undo it. God forgives David's sins, but they plague him the rest of his life.[65]

Despite his shameful sins, David acts as an exemplar of graciousness throughout this narrative, repeatedly forgiving those who wrong him, as he'd done with Saul. As such, David fits perfectly Paul's teachings on leaving judgment to God and overcoming evil with good. "'Vengeance is mine, I will repay, says the Lord.' To the contrary, 'if your enemy is hungry, feed him; if he is thirsty, give him something to drink; for by so doing you will heap burning coals on his head'" (Romans 12:19–20).[66]

Toward the end of 2 Samuel, David recites a poem of praise to God and delivers his final address to his people, affirming the importance of a king ruling justly over men and expressing his gratitude for God's everlasting covenant with his house. Before David dies he enjoins his son and successor, Solomon, to obey God's laws, vowing that as long as he walks before God in faithfulness, God will honor His covenant with David to keep him on the throne (1 Kings 2:1–4). After serving forty years, David dies and Solomon assumes power.

Early on, God appears to Solomon in a dream and invites him to make a request. In humility, Solomon responds that God has made him king, but that he hasn't the faintest idea how to govern. "I am but a little child," Solomon exclaims. "I do not know how to go out or come in" (1 Kings 3:7). He asks God for the wisdom to govern God's people and to discern between good and evil, acknowledging that only God has such wisdom to impart (1 Kings 3:9). It deeply pleases God that instead of asking for riches or divine retribution against his enemies, Solomon asks God for "understanding to discern what is right" (1 Kings 3:11). Fittingly, God grants him "a wise and discerning mind, so that none like you has been before you and none like you shall arise after you" (1 Kings 3:12). He also gives him riches and honor, promising that if he will walk in His ways and keep His laws, He will lengthen his days.

Solomon soon has a chance to demonstrate his unique wisdom in the legendary story of two prostitutes coming before him, both claiming to be the birthmother of the same baby. Solomon flushes out the imposter by offering to divide the child in half and give each woman her own half, at which point the real mother identifies herself by offering to give the child to the imposter to save the child's life (1 Kings 3:16–27).

Solomon distinguishes himself in governance, and his kingdom prospers. His wisdom exceeds that of every other person on earth. He speaks three thousand proverbs and writes 1,005 songs. He has detailed knowledge of nature, both plant and animal life, and people travel from afar to soak up his wisdom (1 Kings 4:29–34).

Once Solomon establishes his kingship, he undertakes the formidable project of building the Temple. God assures Solomon that if he is faithful and obedient, He will bless his kingdom and continue to dwell among His people (1 Kings 6:11–13). After seven years of construction, a Temple is completed that is twice the size of the portable Tabernacle—though it's not particularly big by today's standards.[67]

It may seem odd that the Bible talks about an omnipresent God dwelling anywhere, much less in a small temple. The idea of dwelling, however, wasn't a matter of confining God, but recognizing that He had especially chosen His people and that He would superintend His salvation history through them. The Temple symbolizes God's dwelling place. It is a place for worship and a reminder of God's presence, blessing, and protection.[68] God makes clear that He is not in any sense constrained: "Heaven is my throne and the earth is my footstool; what is the house that you would build for me, and what is the place of my rest?" (Isaiah 66:1). Solomon has no illusions about this, which he emphasizes at the dedication of the Temple. "But will God indeed dwell on the earth?" he asks. "Behold, heaven and the highest heaven cannot contain you; how much less this house that I have built!" (1 Kings 8:27).

He goes on to clarify what God's dwelling there actually entails. "Yet have regard to the prayer of your servant and to his plea, O Lord my God, listening to the cry and to the prayer that your servant prays before you this day, that your eyes may be open night and day toward this house, the place of which you have said, 'My name shall be there,' that you may listen to the prayer that your servant offers toward this place. And listen in heaven your dwelling place, and when you hear, forgive" (1 Kings 8:28–30). Roy Matheson provides a useful analogy, explaining that just as God's presence was manifested in Solomon's Temple, the Holy Spirit resides in our bodies today and manifests Himself through us.[69]

Perhaps the Israelites don't realize that their chosen status does not immunize them from responsibility, and may actually increase it. Thus Solomon, despite his unprecedented knowledge, begins to fall away from God, proving that superior knowledge alone, including knowledge of God, is no guarantee of a close relationship with Him. How could this wisest of all men have become so foolish? Perhaps it is because he abandons the formula for acquiring wisdom laid down in Proverbs, much of which he is believed to have penned himself: "The fear of the Lord is the beginning of knowledge (wisdom)" (1:7).

Solomon loses sight of God and succumbs to the trappings of power and greed, acquiring an obscene abundance of material pleasures, horses and chariots, and wives (700) and concubines (300), many of them foreign. This directly violates God's command, "You shall not enter into marriage with them, neither shall they with you, for surely they will turn away your heart after their gods" (1 Kings 11:2; Exodus 34:16). And this is precisely what happens, for when he grows old these wives turn his heart after other gods and he turns away from his God (1 Kings 11:4).

Solomon's brazen idolatry kindles God's wrath. He tells Solomon He will take his kingdom away but, for David's sake, He will not do it during Solomon's lifetime. He further explains that He will not destroy the entire kingdom but only part of it. Solomon dies after a forty-year reign and is replaced by his son Rehoboam (1 Kings 11:34). At the time of his death, Solomon's kingdom is severely strained largely due to the foreign adversaries God has raised up against him in judgment for his transgressions (1 Kings 11:14).

As we'll see in the next chapter, Israel's United Kingdom does not remain united for long. It splits into two divisions, each of which, in turn, eventually succumbs to foreign powers because of its disobedience. But as we shall also see, God does not permanently forsake His people. Where there is despair, there is always hope from their loving, faithful God.

CHAPTER 4

OLD TESTAMENT HISTORY
DIVIDED KINGDOM THROUGH RESTORATION

*During the divided kingdom, many of the kings of Israel
acted evilly, culminating with Ahab. First Kings 16:33 says
"Ahab did more to provoke the Lord God of Israel to
anger than all the kings of Israel who were before him."*

—R. L. DROUHARD[1]

DIVIDED KINGDOM

As God promised, when Solomon dies the United Kingdom dies with him. "Solomon was a double-minded man," argues Roy Matheson. "It is evident that he was trying to serve two masters, and this was his downfall. His dual allegiance was reproduced in his kingdom. A divided heart resulted in a divided kingdom."[2]

After Solomon's death, the people of the ten Northern tribes, through Jeroboam (a man who had fled to Egypt after leading a failed rebellion against Solomon), plead with the new king Rehoboam to reduce the onerous tax burden introduced by Solomon. "Whereas my father laid on you a heavy yoke, I will add to your yoke," King Rehoboam arrogantly replies. "My father disciplined you with whips, but I will discipline you with scorpions" (1 Kings 12:11). So the people revolt, killing Rehoboam's messenger Adoram. Barely escaping alive, Rehoboam flees to Jerusalem. The ten Northern tribes make Jeroboam king over the Northern Kingdom (Israel) while Rehoboam remains king of the two southern tribes, which become the Southern Kingdom (Judah). Encompassing 9,500 square miles, Israel is almost three times larger than Judah, though Judah houses the capital city of Jerusalem as well as the Temple, along with most of the nation's treasures from David's and Solomon's reigns.[3]

Aiming to recapture the Northern tribes, Rehoboam assembles his warriors. But God instructs the prophet Shemaiah to warn Rehoboam not to pursue his plan, "for this thing is from me" (1 Kings 12:24). The people listen to God and return to their homes, thus finalizing the Israelites' division between Israel and Judah.

Fearing his people will become loyal to Rehoboam if he allows them to make pilgrimages to the Temple in Jerusalem, Jeroboam decides on the worst possible response—he makes two golden calves, placing one in Bethel and the other in Dan. He blasphemously encourages the people to worship these idols as their gods, insisting it was these idols that delivered them from Egyptian slavery (1 Kings 12:28). Jeroboam also places false temples on high places, appoints priests who are not from the priestly line of the Levites, and establishes new holy days and feasts.

Early in his reign, a chilling thing happens to Jeroboam. As he is standing by his fraudulent alter to make offerings, a "man of God" approaches him and says, "O altar, altar, thus says the Lord: 'Behold, a son shall be born to the house of David, Josiah by name, and he shall sacrifice on you the priests of the high places who make offerings on you, and human bones shall be burned on you.' . . . Behold, the altar shall be torn down, and the ashes that are on it shall be poured out'" (1 Kings 13:1–3). This prophecy is one of the most amazing of the entire Bible, for some three hundred years later, it is fulfilled by King Josiah (2 Kings 23:15–20).

The Bible narrative then shifts back and forth between the two kingdoms and their respective rulers. Though the Southern Kingdom is certainly no model of faithfulness,[4] the Northern Kingdom's dissipation at this time is far worse—each of the Northern Kingdom's nineteen kings follows Jeroboam's pattern of idolatry. The results are devastating—seven of these kings are assassinated, one commits suicide, one dies in battle, one dies of injuries from a fall, and another is taken into captivity when the kingdom falls. Only eight of the nineteen die natural deaths.[5]

During this dark period, a major biblical figure makes his appearance in the Northern Kingdom of Israel. Elijah is a man of such remarkable faith that he raises a widow's son from the dead (1 Kings 17:17–24). As God's true spokesman he comes forth to challenge the moral order of the day. He chastises King Ahab—among the worst of Israel's kings, in no small part due to his evil wife Jezebel—for abandoning God's commandments and for making Baal worship, introduced to Israel by Jezebel, Israel's official religion. Elijah instructs Ahab to gather all the people of Israel to meet him at Mount Carmel along with the 450 prophets of Baal and the four hundred prophets of Asherah, another false god (1 Kings 18:18–19). Meeting there, he challenges the false prophets to summon their god to bring fire to burn wood for a sacrifice. These prophets call upon Baal for hours and nothing happens. Elijah responds by preparing an offering and calling to God, "O Lord, God of Abraham, Isaac, and Israel, let it be known this day that I have done all these things at your word. Answer me, O Lord, answer me, that this people may know that you, O Lord, are God, and that you have turned their hearts back" (1 Kings 18:36–37). God immediately brings forth fire that consumes the offering, at which point all the people fall on their faces and worship the one true God.

Ahab's son Ahaziah continues his father's idolatrous ways, worshipping Baal and angering the Lord. After a severe injury from a fall he sends messengers to the temple of Baal-Zebub in the town of Ekron to find out if he will recover—a stunning rejection of God. After informing Elijah about this, the Angel of the Lord directs him to tell the messengers that Ahaziah will never recover and will die in his bed. The prophecy shortly comes to fruition (2 Kings 1:17).

Elijah is one of only two men in the Bible to have been taken from the earth without dying. As he is walking down the road from Gilgal with his successor-to-be Elisha, he asks if Elisha is aware that God will take him away that day. When they reach the Jordan River, Elijah takes his cloak, rolls it up, and strikes the water, causing the water to part and allowing both of them to walk over on dry ground (2 Kings 2:8). This is reminiscent of Moses' parting of the Red Sea (Exodus 14:21–22) and of the previous parting of the Jordan River as the Israelites crossed into Canaan (Joshua 3:14–17). Old Testament professor Dale R. Davis contends that Elijah's parting of the Jordan shows that "the God of 1400 BC is just as mighty in 850 BC. His arm has not atrophied." The same holds true for us today, notes Davis, because God is timeless and "is still saving and sanctifying his people, still keeping them from the evil one, and the Holy Spirit is still leading wandering Christians to repent and to renew their obedience.... The historical God is also the contemporary God."[6]

Once they cross, Elijah asks Elisha what he can do for him. Elisha responds, "Please let there be a double portion of your spirit on me." Elijah says his wish shall be granted if he sees Elijah being taken up by God (2 Kings 2:9–10). While they are talking, chariots of fire and horses of fire separate them, and Elijah is taken up into heaven by a whirlwind (2 Kings 2:11): "And Elisha saw it and he cried, 'My father, my father! The chariots of Israel and its horsemen!' And he saw him no more" (2 Kings 2:12). Back in Jericho, the sons of the prophets immediately recognize Elisha's new power, declaring, "The spirit of Elijah rests on Elisha."

There are different interpretations of what Elisha means when he asks for a double portion, but most commentators agree he isn't seeking a material blessing—he asks for a double portion of Elijah's *spirit*, after all. Some believe Elisha's request is granted in that his ministry lasts twice as long as Elijah's and he performs twice as many miracles.[7] And indeed, Elisha becomes an influential spiritual man, performing more than fifteen miracles.[8] Moreover, just as Elijah had "troubled" King Ahab and held him accountable, Elisha would trouble King Jehoram for his lack of faithfulness.[9]

Another reasonable interpretation is that Elisha is so respectful of Elijah's spirit and so uncertain of his own abilities that he asks to be given special spiritual power to help him meet the awesome responsibility of replacing Elijah.[10] As such, he would need twice as much power to be able to perform close to Elijah's level. Some scholars have likened this passing of the torch from Elijah to Elisha to the transition of power from

Moses to Joshua, "portraying Elisha as a new Joshua destined to win decisive new victories for Israel."[11]

Returning to our historical timeline, we note that around 750 BC the Assyrian empire extends its control into Palestine and within a few short decades Israel becomes its vassal state.[12] In fact, both the Northern and Southern Kingdoms place their trust in foreign alliances instead of in God, eventually leading to the demise of both kingdoms.

Hoshea, the last king of Israel, ignores God's prophets and continues apostate worship. He attempts to preserve his kingdom by swearing allegiance to the Assyrian king Tiglath-pileser. But when Tiglath-pileser dies in 727 BC, Hoshea tries to assert his independence and withholds his annual tribute money to Assyria. Shalmaneser, the new ruler, coerces him to resume his tribute. Desperate to free his country from Assyria, Hoshea makes an alliance with King So of Egypt and again withholds tribute to Assyria. Invading and besieging Israel for several years before conquering it completely in 722 BC, Shalmaneser exiles thousands of Israelites throughout the Assyrian empire—Assyrian records indicate that 27,290 people are taken into captivity, and there are probably many more.[13]

Assyria follows its customary policy of deporting the best of the defeated people and repopulating the conquered land with foreigners (2 Kings 17:24). In Israel, the newcomers eventually intermarry with the remaining Israelites, thus giving rise to the Samaritans, who are mentioned in the New Testament.[14] Samaritans mix some Hebrew beliefs into their polytheistic religion, "so they feared the Lord but also served their own gods, after the manner of the nations from among whom they had been carried away" (2 Kings 17:33).

The Bible explains that Israel's fall and exile occur "because the people of Israel had sinned against the Lord their God...and had feared other gods and walked in the customs of the nations whom the Lord drove out before the people of Israel, and in the customs that the kings of Israel had practiced.... They despised his statutes and his covenant that he made with their fathers and the warnings that he gave them.... [And] they abandoned all the commandments of the Lord their God" (2 Kings 17:7–16). Because the sins of the Southern Kingdom are not yet as severe, God preserves it—for the time being.

SURVIVING KINGDOM: JUDAH

After Israel is conquered, Judah becomes more vulnerable to the Assyrians, though it survives another 140 years. God will allow Assyria to victimize Judah but will ultimately thwart its plan to conquer Judah entirely because He intends to use another foreign nation to do so. In Jerusalem, the prophet Isaiah tries to alert Judah of God's coming judgment.[15] "O, Assyria, the rod of my anger; the staff in their hands is my fury!" he cries. "Against a godless nation I send him, and against the people of my wrath I command him, to take spoil and seize plunder, and to tread them down like the mire of the streets" (Isaiah 10:5–7). Assyria itself, Isaiah declares, will not be spared His judgment: "When the Lord has finished all his work on Mount Zion and on Jerusalem, he will punish the speech of the arrogant heart of the king of Assyria and the boastful look in his eyes" (Isaiah 10:12).

King Hezekiah, son of Ahaz, comes to the throne of Judah a few years after Israel's fall and quickly establishes himself as a godly king. He immediately orders that the Temple, which Ahaz has locked, be opened and cleansed of filth (2 Chron. 29:3–5). He restores worship, reinstitutes the sacrificial offerings (2 Chron. 29:20–24), and in general, "he did what was right in the eyes of the Lord.... He removed the high places and broke the pillars and cut down the Asherah.... He trusted in the Lord, the God of Israel, so that there was none like him among all the kings of Judah after him, nor among those who were before him.... And the Lord was with him" (2 Kings 18:3–7).

About midway through Hezekiah's twenty-nine-year reign, Assyria attacks and conquers Judah except for the fortified city of Jerusalem. Hezekiah pleads with Assyrian King Sennacherib to lift the siege, offering him great tribute including all the silver in the Temple. Sennacherib, through his messengers, taunts Hezekiah, warning that his God won't be able to save him, just as the gods of all Assyria's other conquests failed to save them (2 Kings 18:26–35). Distressed, Hezekiah turns to Isaiah for reassurance. Isaiah instructs Hezekiah's servants to tell Hezekiah not to be afraid of Sennacherib because God will "put a spirit in him, so that he shall hear a rumor and return to his own land, and I will make him fall by the sword in his own land" (2 Kings 19:7). After Hezekiah prays for deliverance, God, through Isaiah, promises He will indeed deliver Judah and that Sennacherib will not conquer Jerusalem. God acts quickly, for "that night the angel of the Lord went out and struck down 185,000 in the camp of the Assyrians.... Then Sennacherib king of Assyria departed and went home and lived at Nineveh. And as he was worshipping...his sons...struck him down with the sword" (2 Kings 19:35–37).[16]

Shortly thereafter, when Hezekiah becomes gravely ill, Isaiah tells him to get his house in order because he will not recover. But after Hezekiah prays to God to be healed, God extends his life for fifteen years. Soon, however, Hezekiah has an uncharacteristic lapse of faith. When Merodach-baladan, son of Babylonian King Baladan, sends envoys and a gift to Hezekiah, Hezekiah puffs up with pride and shows them all his treasures: "There was nothing in his house or in all his realm that Hezekiah did not show them" (2 Kings 20:15). Isaiah admonishes him, warning that in the coming days the Babylonians will capture Judah, take some of Hezekiah's sons captive, and carry off all the treasures he had shown them—a prophecy that will be fulfilled with Babylon's conquest and exile of Judah.

Hezekiah is succeeded by his son Manasseh, who is as spiritually depraved as Hezekiah was faithful. Turning away from the Lord and from proper spiritual practices, he erects alters for Baal and worships idols (2 Kings 21:3). God then reiterates His vow that Judah, because of its persistent idolatry and other evils, will fall.

When Manasseh dies his son Amon takes over, continuing his father's evil ways and idol worship. After ruling only two years his servants kill him, after which Amon is succeeded by his eight-year-old son Josiah, a godly king unequaled in his zeal for the Law (2 Kings 23:25). Despite Josiah's holiness, however, God renews His promise to discipline Judah due to the egregious sins of Manasseh and some of his predecessors. What's more, though Josiah cleanses the land of idolatry and restores proper worship, his reforms don't take hold among the people. Borrowing from Jesus' parable of the sower (Mark 4:1–20; Matt. 13:1–23), nineteenth-century German theologian John Peter Lange explains, "The good soil was wanting for the seed, and hence his reformation was but a sowing among thorns. He had cleansed the land but not the hearts of the people and after his death the weeds shot forth again in full luxuriance."[17]

During the eighteenth year of his reign Josiah arranges for the Temple to be repaired. During this project Hilkiah the priest finds the Book of the Law hidden in rubble. Though this book was available to the kings of Israel and Judah previously, it had apparently been lost or hidden during the reign of the apostate King Manasseh.[18] Scholars disagree on the contents of the book—some believe it is the entire Pentateuch (the first five books of the Bible) while others claim it is less comprehensive. Still, most agree it at least contains all or a substantial part of the Book of Deuteronomy.[19]

Regardless of the precise contents, God's providential hand is undoubtedly at work. Josiah is disturbed by what the Scriptures say, suddenly realizing how far his people have deviated from God's commands. Josiah, whose shocked reaction indicates Judah had not consulted the Law for a long time and that he may not have known all the Lord's requirements,[20] then orders Hilkiah and other servants to ask the Lord how to interpret these passages. They appeal to Huldah the prophetess, who responds, "Thus says the Lord, 'Behold I will bring disaster upon this place and upon its inhabitants, all the words of the book that the king of Judah has read. Because they have forsaken me and have made offerings to other gods, that they might provoke me to anger with all the work of their hands, therefore my wrath will be kindled against this place, and it will not be quenched'" (2 Kings 22:15–17). But the Lord assures Josiah that because of his penitent heart and humility, He will gather him to his grave in peace so that he will "not see the disaster that I will bring upon this place" (2 Kings 22:20).

Summoning all the inhabitants of Judah and Jerusalem, Josiah reads the Book of the Law to them, after which he and his people make a covenant with God to keep His commandments (2 Kings 23:1–3). Josiah then commands Hilkiah and the other priests to purge the Temple of vessels made for Baal and other idols, which are burned in the fields outside Jerusalem. Pagan shrines in other cities are torn down, and Josiah even destroys the altar at Bethel where King Jeroboam had placed an idolatrous golden calf three hundred years before (2 Kings 23:15). As mentioned earlier, this is in spectacular fulfillment of a prophecy delivered to Jeroboam foretelling that a future king from the line of David named Josiah would sacrifice and burn the bones of the priests on his altar (1 Kings 13:1–3).

After Josiah is killed by the Egyptian pharaoh Neco in 609 BC, there are only four more kings of Judah: Jehoahaz, Jehoiakim, Jehoiachin, and Zedekiah. These are the last kings in the Davidic line in Old Testament times. The end of Judah unfolds according to the predictions of Old Testament prophets who foretold that the Judeans would be held in captivity in Babylon for seventy years and then return to the land. For example, Jeremiah proclaimed, "This whole land shall become a ruin and a waste, and these nations shall serve the king of Babylon seventy years" (Jer. 25:11). He added, on the Lord's behalf, "When seventy years are completed for Babylon, I will visit you, and I will fulfill to you my promise and bring you back to this place" (Jer. 29:10).

The Babylonians' conquest of Judah is preceded by their capture of Assyria in 606 BC, when the Assyrians fall victim to a siege by Nabopolassar, viceroy of Babylon, who leads a combined army of Chaldeans and Medes.[21] This fulfills the prophecy of Nahum, who foretold that Nineveh would fall and Judah would rejoice (Nahum 1:15–3:19). The prophet Habakkuk, whose Old Testament book discusses why God would use a wicked nation like Babylon for His divine purposes, testifies that the Babylonians are much crueler and more barbaric than the Assyrians: "They are dreaded and fearsome; their justice and dignity go forth from themselves" (Hab. 1:7).

Shortly after Assyria's fall, Babylon begins a long process of enslaving the Judeans. In 605 BC Babylonian King Nebuchadnezzar defeats the Egyptians and establishes the Babylonians as the supreme power in the Near East.[22] He attacks Judah that same year and deports some Judeans, including the prophet Daniel, to Babylon (Daniel 1:1–3). In 597 BC Nebuchadnezzar raids Judah again, taking an additional ten thousand Judean captives to Babylon, including King Jehoiachin and the prophet Ezekiel (2 Kings 24:14–15). Nebuchadnezzar replaces Johoiachin with Johoiachin's uncle Mattaniah, whose name he changes to Zedekiah (2 Kings 24:17). After Zedekiah rebels against Babylon about a decade into his reign, Nebuchadnezzar defeats his army and destroys Jerusalem and the Temple in 586 BC. He blinds Zedekiah and forces him, along with most of the remaining Judeans, into exile in Babylon (2 Kings 25:1–7). The prophet Jeremiah is among the remnant left in Judah (Jer. 40:1–6), though a final, relatively small deportation occurs in 582 BC (Jer. 52:30).

The prophecy that the Babylonian captivity would last seventy years is actually fulfilled in two ways. First, there is around seventy years between the first deportation of Jews in 605 BC and the end of captivity sometime in 538–536 BC, when the Persian king Cyrus, after conquering Babylon, issues a proclamation allowing the Judeans to return to their land and rebuild the Temple (2 Chron. 36:22–23; Ezra 1:1–4). Second, there are seventy years between Jerusalem's fall (586 BC) and the completion of the rebuilding of the Temple in 516 BC (2 Kings 25:1–7; Ezra 6:15).

BABYLONIAN CAPTIVITY

The Babylonian exile is the culmination of a grim period of Judah's history when we finally see God's long-withheld judgment being implemented. Bible scholar J. Sidlow Baxter describes the heartbreaking period leading up to the captivity as "the most tragic national record ever written. The elect people, through whom the gracious purposes of God were to have been developed for the enlightenment and regeneration of the whole race, become more and more steeped in infidelity and moral degradation, until finally the measure of their wickedness is full, judgment falls, pitiless foes wreak vengeance on them, and drag them from their own land into humiliating captivity."[23]

Roy Gingrich finds it fitting that some 1,300 years earlier, Abraham had accepted God's call and left Babylonia in faith and obedience, but now his descendants are returning to that same land due to their unbelief and disobedience.[24] God had promised He would disperse His people in judgment, but He also assured them it would not be permanent, unlike His judgment on the sinful nations He had used to punish His people. "Fear not, O Jacob my servant, declares the Lord, for I am with you," God proclaimed through Jeremiah. "I will make a full end of the nations to which I have driven you, but of you I will not make a full end.

I will discipline you in just measure, and I will by no means leave you unpunished" (Jer. 46:28).

Relatively little is known of the Judeans during this period either in Babylon or in their homeland. Most of our information about these times is from the Books of Daniel, Jeremiah, and Ezekiel and from 2 Kings 24.[25] From what we can tell, life is difficult in Judah for those who remain there or have returned after taking refuge elsewhere during the conflict.[26] According to nineteenth-century biblical scholar Alfred Edersheim, only the poorest in the land are left in Judah to be husbandmen and vinedressers, to keep the soil cultivated in anticipation of future colonizers from Babylon.[27]

The exiles in Babylon seem to be treated better than the Israelite captives were in Assyria.[28] In fact, it seems to be a relatively peaceful and prosperous time for them.[29] They are placed in or near the capital city of Babylon, some on a rich plain by the Chebar canal (Ezek. 1:1). Granted a substantial amount of freedom, they are largely permitted to manage their own affairs. They apparently enjoy some level of religious freedom, though their leaders are made to conform to the kingdom's religious practices, as demonstrated by the saga of Daniel and his friends discussed below. Babylonian records indicate that the Babylonians treated the Judeans relatively well, even releasing King Jehoiachin from prison and giving him court apartments.[30] Another possible testament to their favorable treatment is that when King Cyrus of Persia permits them to return to Jerusalem, many Judeans remain in Babylon.[31] The exiles there who love God, however, still consider these decades as punishment, as expressed poignantly in the Book of Lamentations.

Meanwhile, false prophets are telling the exiles their captivity won't last long, so Jeremiah sends a letter to the exiles from Jerusalem delivering God's message that they should not be deceived—they will be there seventy years, and they should settle down, build houses, plant gardens, and multiply. God wants them to be cohesive and to await their return to their land as He had promised (Jer. 29:1–10).

Daniel was among the first group of Israelites taken to Babylon in 605 BC. The first half of his book describes his experiences and those of three friends, Shadrach, Meshach, and Abednego, in captivity, illustrating how faithful they remain to God and how God rewards them by giving Daniel favor and compassion in the sight of the chief of the eunuchs (Daniel 1:8–9). The story shows that even in the midst of punishing His people for their rebellion, God is still there to protect them. He also demonstrates this when Nebuchadnezzar has Daniel's three friends thrown into a fiery furnace for refusing to worship his gods. God intervenes to protect the trio from the flames, which so moves Nebuchadnezzar that he decrees that all who speak against the Hebrews' God will be torn limb from limb and have their houses destroyed. He also promotes the three within the province of Babylon (Daniel 3:29–30).

A similar incident occurs involving Daniel himself shortly after the Persians conquer Babylon. Persian King Darius appoints Daniel as one of three high officials who oversee the 120 satraps (governors) of his kingdom. Aware that Daniel is faithful to God and won't worship pagan idols, the satraps, who are jealous of Daniel's position, successfully conspire to have the king decree that anyone who prays to any god or man other than the king should be cast into the den of lions. Despite the decree, Daniel continues to pray to God. Though Darius wants to spare Daniel, he is bound to apply the law (Daniel 6:1–13). When he reluctantly orders Daniel to be cast into the lions' den, he tells Daniel, "May your god, whom you serve continually, deliver you" (Daniel 6:16). And as was the case with Daniel's friends, God intervenes to protect Daniel from certain death, this time by sending an angel to shut the lions' mouths.

The ministries of many prophets occur during the Babylonian exile, a phenomenon also witnessed during the Assyrian captivity. Like Jeremiah, Ezekiel mostly ministers in Babylonia. Ezekiel, who was exiled along with King Jehoiachin in 597 BC, begins his ministry in 593 BC,[32] inspiring his people with his messages and warning them against abandoning God for paganism.[33]

God directs Ezekiel to speak both to the Israelites in captivity and those remaining in the homeland, many of whom will later be exiled upon the sacking of Jerusalem in 586 BC.[34] But Ezekiel's warnings to the stubbornly unfaithful often fall on deaf ears, as Judah is "a rebellious house" (Ezek. 2:6, 3:26, 12:3). With their continued disobedience and apostasy, the remnants in Judah are effectively begging to be vanquished and taken captive themselves, as they unrepentantly blame their ancestors for their predicament (Ezek. 18:2). Rejecting their scapegoating,

God clarifies that they are being punished for their own sins. "The soul who sins shall die," He says. "The son shall not suffer for the iniquity of the father, nor the father suffer for the iniquity of the son. The righteousness of the righteous shall be upon himself, and the wickedness of the wicked shall be upon himself" (Ezek. 18:20).

There is a silver lining to the Babylonian captivity. In fact, according to P. A. Beaulieu, the exile is the defining moment in the formation of Judaism.[35] At first many Judean exiles are discouraged, believing God had failed them and had been defeated by the Babylonian god Marduk.[36] And sadly, many continue their sinful ways in Babylonia. But others realize their predicament is God's just punishment for their wicked acts.[37] With the encouragement of the prophets, they become even more faithful to God and confident He will protect them in captivity, eventually return them to the land, and help them rebuild the Temple. Furthermore, though the Judeans cannot observe the sacrifices, this constraint sparks their renewed appreciation for the Law.[38]

Indeed, as Dr. Foakes-Jackson argues, "The captivity of Judah is one of the greatest events in the history of religion.... With the captivity the history of Israel ends, and the history of the Jews commences."[39] Surrounded by hostile and heathen neighbors in Babylonia, they cling to the faith of their fathers and grow more cohesive as a people. "Being without a country, without a ritual system, without any material basis for their life as a people," T. Nicol writes, "they learned as never before to prize those spiritual possessions which had come down to them from the past."[40] They begin to meet for group worship, and this, many scholars believe, is the genesis of the synagogues that would spring up in the land after the people's return from captivity.[41] (Interestingly, the synagogue services were the model for the type of church service we have today.)[42] Never again, notes Larry Richards, would the Jews worship false gods after they are returned to their land.[43]

As for the Judean remnant left in the land after the destruction of Jerusalem, we get some important details from Jeremiah 40–44. When Judean leaders meet with Gedaliah, the governor of Judah, he reassures them of their security, saying, "Do not be afraid because of the Chaldean officials. Live in the land and serve the king of Babylon, and it shall be well with you" (2 Kings 25:24). Nevertheless, the people later rebel and assassinate Gedaliah along with some Babylonian soldiers (Jer. 41:2–3). The people then consider going to Egypt in fear of retaliation. Asked by Jeremiah for direction, however, God declares that the Judeans should remain in the land and that He will deliver them from the king of Babylonia. He also warns that if they defy Him and go into Egypt they will die by the sword and by famine. But they disobey anyway and even force Jeremiah to go to Egypt with them, leaving few Judeans in the land.[44]

The Bible records no direct fulfillment of Jeremiah's prophecy that those who fled to Egypt would perish, but Bible prophecy scholar John Walvoord explains that this is, in fact, what happened to them.[45] As for Jeremiah, his fate is unknown. Some believe he eventually returned from Egypt to Judah, others maintain he went to Babylon and died there, and still another tradition holds that he was stoned in Egypt.[46]

RESTORATION

This period spans from the return of the Jews from Babylonian exile to their homeland during Nehemiah's second governorship (roughly 538 BC to 423 BC) to the accession of Persian King Darius II (Neh. 12:22), which is the last event referred to in the Old Testament. The Books of Ezra and Nehemiah contain much of the Bible's historical record of this restoration period.

The Jews return to the land in three waves over almost a century, the first two described in the Book of Ezra and the third in Nehemiah. Each wave involves a similar pattern of God initiating the return and reconstruction efforts, relentless opposition arising to these efforts, and the eventual completion, with God's help, of the reconstruction projects. The author uses language reminiscent of the Exodus Period—such as "go up"—to draw a connection between the returning, post-exilic community and their ancestors in the land prior to the Assyrian and Babylonian captivities. This highlights the continuity between all the periods of Old Testament history from the patriarchs forward, and the notion that the returning Jews are heirs of God's covenants with their ancestors.[47]

The first return is under Zerubbabel (Ezra 1–6), the second under Ezra (Ezra 7–10), and the third under Nehemiah (Neh. 1:7). The returns fulfill God's prophecy made through Jeremiah prior to the Babylonian captivity (Jer. 18:1–6), in which Jeremiah watched a potter break a vessel while reworking it into another vessel. The prophecy illustrates how God will deal with Israel: God is the potter, and Israel is the vessel that God breaks (with the captivity) and then remakes and restores.[48]

The prophet Isaiah miraculously predicted the seminal event that would launch this period of return and restoration. More than one hundred fifty years beforehand he wrote, "The Lord says of Cyrus, 'He is my shepherd, and he shall fulfill all my purpose'; saying of Jerusalem, 'She shall be built,' and of the temple, 'Your foundation shall be laid'" (Isaiah 44:25). In the next chapter (45), Isaiah mentioned Cyrus again by name, referring to him as the Lord's anointed and saying, "I have stirred him up in righteousness, and I will make all his ways level; he shall build my city and set my exiles free" (Isaiah 45:13).

Ezra records the fulfillment of this prophecy at the beginning of his book, reporting the proclamation of Cyrus in his first year as king of Persia: "That the word of the Lord by the mouth of Jeremiah might be fulfilled, the Lord stirred up the spirit of Cyrus king of Persia, so that he made a proclamation throughout all his kingdom and also put it in writing: 'Thus says Cyrus king of Persia: The Lord, the God of heaven, has given me all the kingdoms of the earth, and he has charged me to build him a house at Jerusalem, which is in Judah. Whoever is among you of all his people, may his God be with him, and let him go up to Jerusalem, which is in Judah, and rebuild the house of the Lord, the God of Israel—he is the God who is in Jerusalem'" (Ezra 1:1–4).

The first return is in 538 BC, when Zerubbabel and others lead the people, fifty thousand strong (Ezra 2:64–65), back to the land, bringing with them the vessels from the Temple that the Babylonians had carried away years before. They resettle in their own towns in Jerusalem and throughout Judah (Ezra 1:5–2:2), finding that Jerusalem's walls and the Temple lie in ruins.[49] Not long after their return, the people gather in Jerusalem, build an altar to God, and present burnt offerings on it (Ezra 3). After about a year they lay the foundation for a reconstructed Temple. Almost as soon as they begin this work, however, they encounter fierce opposition from those who had remained in the land during the exile.

The adversaries had first offered to help in the project, but Zerubbabel rejected them, believing it was the sacred duty of the returning people to rebuild the Temple. The opponents then begin criticizing the project, discouraging and scaring those involved in it, and bribing counselors to frustrate it (Ezra 4:1–6). As a result, the Temple work is suspended for some sixteen years.

At that point the builders resume the project, with the encouragement of the prophets Haggai and Zechariah. Opponents try to stop the project again, but the builders remain committed. After confirming the existence of King Cyrus' decree authorizing the Temple's reconstruction, Cyrus' successor Darius issues another decree authorizing a resumption of the project. Following its sixteen-year hiatus, the project is completed in just five years and the people formally dedicate the Temple to God. The builders had been spurred to work fast by Haggai's rebuke of the people's laziness and apathy.[50] Just consider this stinging barb: "Thus says the Lord of hosts: These people say the time has not yet come to rebuild the house of the Lord.... Is it a time for you yourselves to dwell in your paneled houses, while this house lies in ruins?" (Haggai 1:2–5).

Years later, in 458 BC, a second return wave occurs under the leadership of the Jewish scribe Ezra. This takes place on the order of Persian King Artaxerxes, who also allows Ezra to appoint magistrates and judges for the land who are versed in the Law of Moses and are tasked with reinstituting the Law (Ezra 7:21–25). So this second return is accompanied not by a building reconstruction project, but a reconstruction, of sorts, of the community as grounded in Mosaic Law. Throughout this period, successive pagan rulers consistently support the rebuilding and restoration projects even against fierce opposition, which clearly illustrates God's sovereign will that the Temple be rebuilt and the people be restored to the land in furtherance of His outworking of salvation history.

Despite the restoration, however, the people continue to sin by intermarrying with other peoples. Ezra takes firm action, ordering the people to "make confession to the Lord, the God of your fathers and do his will. Separate yourselves from the peoples of the land and from the foreign wives" (Ezra 10:11). This time, the people comply (Ezra 10:16).

The third return wave occurs in 444 BC under Nehemiah, who is appointed governor of Judah and is tasked with reconstructing Jerusalem's walls and reordering the people's social and economic lives.[51] Like clockwork, opposition to the projects materializes. Sanballat, with his brothers and the army of Samaria, mocks the "feeble" Jews and their reconstruction efforts. "Yes, what are they building—if a fox goes up on it he will break down their stone wall!" remarks one of the critics (Neh. 4:3). Nehemiah responds in earnest prayer to God, and he and his people continue, in faith, with the rebuilding.

This angers opponents, who plot new efforts to thwart the project. In response, Nehemiah arranges for the people to guard the wall day and night. Half the people work on construction and the other half is armed with spears, shields, bows, and coats of mail. With dogged determination, the people complete the wall in just fifty-two days (Neh. 6:15). This success strikes fear in their foreign enemies, who know that God has superintended the project (Neh. 6:16).

The people's work is still not complete, however. Ezra brings the Law of Moses before the people and reads it from morning until noon: "And the ears of all the people were attentive to the Book of the Law" (Neh. 8:3). The people respond by worshipping God, showing they had heard, understood, absorbed, and responded obediently to the message. They confess their sins (Neh. 9), and remember God's dealings with them, including their disobedience that led to the captivity. They recognize God's faithfulness, His righteousness, and His grace (Neh. 9:33), and reaffirm their commitment to Him (Neh. 9:38).

In the meantime, having gone back to Persia, Nehemiah returns to Jerusalem and discovers the people are not upholding their covenant with God. In fact, Tobiah, a notorious enemy of the people, is living in the Temple. Nehemiah throws all of Tobiah's furniture out of the Temple and orders that its vessels be brought back inside. He immediately takes further steps to repurify the Temple and reestablish the holy practices of the priests and Levites. The Old Testament history ends here, and God's salvation history is not resumed until the Gospel record begins more than four hundred years later.

I included this rather extensive review of Old Testament history for a specific reason. When I was first studying the Bible many years ago, I found myself floundering when trying to get a handle on the major events. With my confusion on the historical timeline blurring the Bible's message, I looked for an accessible summary of the history. What I found, however, was either too extensive or too general and neither served my purposes. So I hope that the above summary struck the right balance by relating most of the major events without drowning you in minutiae. I'm not suggesting that any events recorded in the Bible are unimportant, only that it's unnecessary to get bogged down in every detail when your purpose is to grasp the grand sweep of this history. I found that once I understood the history's general flow, I could focus more clearly on God's inspired message, centering on Jesus Christ, that was built into that history. I sincerely hope these summaries enhanced your overall comprehension as well.

Having finished this historical review, we're now in a better position to examine the principal subject at hand: the many ways that Christ is foreshadowed in the Old Testament.

CHAPTER 5

ALL ROADS LEAD TO CHRIST
BIBLICAL COVENANTS, PART 1

Christ dominates the whole revelation [of the Bible].
This is not imaginative, but real; it is not a wishful
theory, but a satisfying fact. The evidence of the fact
is manifold, and can be presented in various ways.

—W. GRAHAM SCROGGIE[1]

CHRIST THEMES

The Bible is Christ and Christ is the Bible. He is in it from first to last, and it is all about Him. Indeed, due to the overwhelming and multi-faceted presence of Jesus Christ in the Old Testament, various Bible scholars emphasize different ways the Old Testament points to Christ. I will share a number of these because each is instructive, many are overlapping, and they are not inconsistent.

According to Graham Scroggie, "Christ is predicted in the Old Testament, present in the Gospels, proclaimed in the Acts, possessed in the Epistles, and predominant in the Revelation."[2] This description is similar to one by Roy Gingrich, who argues that in the Old Testament, "He is coming;" in the Gospels, "He is here;" in the Book of Acts, "He came [Jesus was the Messiah];" in the Epistles, "He came for certain reasons

[He came to reveal God to man by His life and to redeem man to God by His death];" and in the Book of Revelation, "He is coming again."[3]

Each part of the Old Testament—Law, History, Poets, and Prophets—anticipates Christ, and each part of the New Testament actualizes Him.[4] The Old Testament Law lays the foundation for Christ's coming: "So then, the law was our guardian until Christ came, in order that we might be justified by faith" (Gal. 3:24). It informs us about sin and our need for Christ, without Whom we will die in our sins. "The trouble with people who are not seeking for a Savior, and for salvation," writes Dr. Martin Lloyd-Jones, "is that they do not understand the nature of sin. It is the peculiar function of the Law to bring such an understanding to a man's mind and conscience."[5] The Apostle Paul writes in a similar vein, "Yet if it had not been for the law, I would not have known sin" (Romans 7:7). He adds, "It was sin, producing death in me through what is good, in order that sin might be shown to be sin, and through the commandment might become sinful beyond measure" (Romans 7:13). The Old Testament prepared us for Christ, among other ways, by showing God's exemplary dealings with Israel, which also demonstrates our need for a Savior. Old Testament poetry anticipated Christ, and the prophets foretold of His coming.[6]

Saints longed for a redeemer in the Old Testament, and this savior is foreshadowed throughout its books. As Job exclaims, "Oh, that I knew where I might find him, that I might come even to his seat!" (Job 23:3). Naturally, the New Testament disciples are ecstatic upon finding Him, with Philip telling Nathanael, "We have found him of whom Moses in the Law and also the prophets wrote, Jesus of Nazareth, the son of Joseph" (John 1:45).[7] James E. Smith notes that "the Old Testament can be likened to a mighty river flowing toward the ocean. Remove Christ and there is no place for the river to go. It simply is swallowed up by the sands of time like a river that flows into a desert."[8]

Before tracing Christ's foreshadowing and actual presence in each book of the Old Testament, let's look at some of the methodologies and thematic approaches scholars and other Christian writers have employed to demonstrate the dominant Christ-centeredness of Scripture.

Some critics object that enthusiastic commentators find Christ too easily in the Old Testament. But we should recognize that, conversely, certain liberal critical scholars, with their presuppositions against miracles or other supernatural occurrences, make it difficult to see Christ—or God at all—when a fair reading indicates that it is He to Whom Scripture is pointing. Those scholars, for example, who believe that the Hebrews borrowed their monotheistic ideas from pagan cultures, or that they evolved gradually into them from a polytheistic beginning, are almost guaranteed *not* to see Christ because, in essence, they reject the inspiration of Scripture. If God did not inspire the Old Testament, then we can hardly expect foreshadowings of Christ anywhere in its books. After all, apart from God's inspiration, how would finite men living in Old Testament times have acquired such an accurate picture of the nature and life of the coming Messiah? But if we are open to the notion that Scripture was breathed into the human writers, we will have little difficulty believing that God progressively revealed His truths to man, as Jesus Christ validated in His Emmaus road discourse.

So read the Old Testament with an aggressively skeptical eye if you must. But I suggest that if you open yourself slightly to the possibility that Christ did in fact say what the New Testament records Him as saying, and that He could not have been mistaken because He is God, the Old Testament may just come alive to you like never before. You will begin to see Christ in places you hadn't noticed before—for I believe it is Christ's intent that we all be blessed by His Emmaus road revelation. The two men He encountered on the road to Emmaus, and a number of His apostles shortly thereafter, are perhaps the only ones He enlightened during His incarnation with specific details about His permeation of the pages of the Old Testament. With His words recorded for us in the New Testament, however, we are all beneficiaries of that experience and, with the aid of the Holy Spirit, we're able to glean a great deal of what Christ said to those men.

As the editors of the ESV Study Bible observe, when the Bible records that Jesus opens the Scriptures to the Emmaus road travelers and shortly thereafter opens the minds of His disciples to understand the Scriptures, "it cannot mean just a few scattered predictions about the Messiah. It means the Old Testament as a whole, encompassing all three of the major divisions of the Old Testament that the Jews traditionally recognized.... The Old Testament as a whole, through its promises, its symbols, and its pictures of salvation, looks forward to the actual accomplishment of salvation that took place once for all in the life, death, and resurrection of Jesus Christ."[9]

We will now briefly examine the various ways the Old Testament points to the Person and Work of Jesus Christ. We should know that the Bible's Christ-centeredness is not merely a matter of disjointed Old Testament themes or threads, such as isolated prophecies, types, and symbols pointing to Christ, but involves an integrated unity. As Dr. Norman Geisler explains, Christ is the content of the whole canon and the unifying theme within each book of the Bible[10]—that is, Christ gives the Bible its structure. In studying these various threads pointing to Christ, we'll demonstrate how they frame Christ as the center of all Scripture. We will identify these Christ-directed themes and threads, provide examples, and then discuss more in-depth examples, when helpful, in the succeeding chapters detailing how each individual book of the Old Testament points to Christ. These threads are:

- God's promise-plan.
- God's major covenants with His people.
- Gospel portraits.
- The doctrine of the Lamb.
- The Old Testament offices of prophet, priest, and king.
- Christ's actions as creator and sustainer of His creation.
- Titles of and references to Christ in the Old Testament.
- Christ's saving activity in the Old Testament.
- The Christophanies (appearances) of Christ in the Old Testament.
- Old Testament typology pointing to Christ.
- The messianic prophecies of the Old Testament.
- Christ seen through God's dealings with Israel.

GOD'S PROMISE-PLAN

I argue that Jesus Christ is the focal point of all history, prophecy, and type. "Both parts of the Revelation meet in Him; the one part as preparation, and the other, as realization," Graham Scroggie contends. "All parts of the Bible...constitute a divine progressive revelation of redeeming love; God and man meet in the one who is the God-Man."[11] Salvation history, in its entirety, points to Christ, and in Christ, all fulfillment comes.

While all the various Christ-oriented themes discussed here are quite real and important, I suspect that when Christ explains to the Emmaus road travelers and His disciples how the Old Testament points to Him, He does far more than just unveil to them the messianic prophecies and the persons, places, institutions, and ceremonies prefiguring Himself. He surely reveals for them an all-encompassing theme, running from Genesis to Malachi, that foretells of Him. That unifying theme is God's promise of a coming Messiah Who would bless all mankind through His gift of salvation for all who will place their faith in Him (trust in Him for their salvation). So as we look at these various themes and examples pointing to Christ, let's be mindful that there is one central promise coursing through God's revelation, and that all other themes and symbols pointing to Christ are integrally related to that promise.

Old Testament scholar Walter Kaiser describes this central, unifying promise as God's "promise-plan":

> The promise-plan is God's word of declaration, beginning with Eve and continuing on through history, especially in the patriarchs and the Davidic line, that God would continually *be* in his person and *do* in his deeds and works (in and through Israel, and later the church) his redemptive plan as his *means* of keeping that promised word alive for Israel, and thereby for all who subsequently believed. All in that promised seed were called to act as a light for all the nations so that all the families of the earth might come to faith and to new life in the Messiah.[12]

I believe Kaiser is saying that Scripture is tied together by God's promise that He will provide a Messiah Who will offer redemption to all mankind. While there are many pointers to Christ in the Old Testament, they can all be understood in the context of God's promise-plan.

If we understand that God's central promise of a coming, redeeming Messiah is the focal point of the Old Testament, we will begin to see Christ in its pages in ways we never considered. We can view God's promise-plan as the glue that holds all Scripture together as a singular thematic work centered in Jesus Christ.

Consider, for example, the messianic prophecies, which we discuss below as one of the many threads that lead to Christ. These prophecies clearly illustrate the centrality of God's promise-plan. Without question, the messianic prophecies are nothing short of miraculous, but we shouldn't become so mesmerized by the stunning accuracy of these predictions that we lose sight of how they fit into God's promise-plan. These prophecies, as Kaiser notes, are not just random predictions in the Old Testament, included merely to demonstrate the supernatural inspiration of Scripture, as important as that is. Rather, says Kaiser,

> it is amazing how the depictions concerning the coming Messiah and his work comprised one continuous plan of God. Each aspect was linked into an ongoing stream of announcements beginning in the prepatriarchal period, supplemented by the patriarchal, Mosaic, premonarchial, monarchial, and prophetic periods, down to the postexilic times of Israel's last leaders and prophets. The promise was a single one; yet it was cumulative in its net results. Indeed its constituent parts were not a collection of assorted promises about a Messiah who was to come: instead, they formed one continuous pattern and purpose placed in the stream of history.[13]

Kaiser's point here, I think, is that we must distinguish between the many scattered predictions and what he calls "one all-embracing divine word of promise." This promise is actually God's guarantee that He will redeem fallen mankind. God initially makes this promise in broad terms, with few details, when He assures Adam and Eve in the Garden of Eden that Eve's "seed" would crush Satan's head (Gen. 3:15). We have already identified this passage as both the first messianic prophecy and the first announcement of the Gospel—for Eve's "seed" is to be understood as the coming Messiah. As Scripture unfolds, God continues to renew and amplify this promise through other promises, including His covenants.

God renews and expands on this promise when He tells Abraham, among other things, that He will make him into a great nation and bless all peoples and nations of the earth through him and his nation (the Abrahamic Covenant, which we'll examine further below). Set apart as a holy nation, Israel would be a blessing to all people because the Messiah would come from it and would offer salvation to all.[14]

God further amplifies the promise through the other patriarchs and through Moses, King David, other prophets, and biblical writers throughout the remainder of the Old Testament. "The promise-plan of Messiah was not concluded when the days of the covenant promises made to Eve, Shem, Abraham, Isaac, Jacob, and David were over," Kaiser explains. "On the contrary, these same promises began to proliferate and blossom beyond anything anyone could have imagined once we arrive at the writing of the . . . prophets. In their writings, the doctrine of the Messiah and his work, as outlined in the writings already covered, became the constant basis of their appeals for what God was doing and was going to do."[15] The New Testament writers also treat the promise-plan as the unifying thread of the Old Testament and as "the way to trace the continued advancement and development of the metanarrative of the future work of God."[16] When we discuss God's major covenants below, we will see how God expands on His central messianic promise with each successive covenant in furtherance of His promise-plan.

God also expands on His promise through His various prophecies. According to Kaiser, God's major promise of a coming Messiah is worked out in a series of successive promises that are fulfilled along the way, and each fulfillment demonstrates God's faithfulness and takes mankind one step closer to the fulfillment of the ultimate promise of the Messiah. So when He promises, for example, that the Messiah will come through the line of David, each time a new king in the Davidic line assumes the throne we have a partial fulfillment of the promise that is an essential link in the chain leading to the ultimate fulfillment in Christ.

These partial fulfillments, Kaiser argues, can be seen as down payments on the fulfillment of God's promise-plan.[17] He says the writers of Scripture employ a "now" along with a "not-yet" aspect to many of their predictions about the future, in which they encapsulate "contemporary fulfillments of their predictions into the ultimate and final fulfillment of the climactic work of God in the last day."[18] That's because they see many of these events as part of a series of causes that are all related to the coming Messiah. "Thus, each chosen son of each of the three patriarchs and each successive king in the Davidic line of Judah is at once a fulfillment of the promise of the Messiah (in the sense that he is an earnest down payment on what God will ultimately do) and a further prediction that the Messiah will yet come."[19]

As I believe Kaiser is correct that God's promise-plan can be seen as the primary unifying thread of Scripture, I thought it appropriate to mention it first among the various Christ-pointing threads. Before considering each of the threads individually, I wanted to illustrate how collectively they can be understood as various subsets of God's promise-plan. For example, the gospel portraits and the doctrine of the Lamb each point to God's promise-plan of a coming Redeemer, as do all the other threads we'll discuss.

God's major covenants, the next of these threads that we'll explore, are especially to be understood in the context of God's promise-plan. They are a series of successive promises and agreements He enters into with Israel that all serve to actualize God's promise-plan. I think of them as the series of renewals and amplifications of God's central promise to bless all mankind through the coming Messiah, Jesus Christ.[20] As we'll see, each and every covenant God makes advances His salvation history toward fulfillment of His promise-plan.

Now let's turn to the major covenants in the Bible. All of God's covenants involve His promises, and sometimes the people's reciprocal promises and obligations. So let's keep in mind, as we examine these covenants, that they are themselves unified and progressive, and that they fall within the larger rubric of God's promise-plan.

THE BIBLICAL COVENANTS

The Bible records God's sovereign dealings with man in the context of His salvation history. We've seen that some scholars reduce salvation history to a simple, three-point outline:

- Generation: God's creation of man in His image and placing Him in paradise.
- Degeneration: man sins and loses his place in paradise (the fall).
- Regeneration: man's regaining of paradise.

God's series of covenants with man is the means by which He works out His sovereign plan for man's redemption and unfolds His promise-plan. Every period of salvation history involves God's covenantal dealings with man.[21]

The term "covenant" generally means a binding commitment agreed upon through negotiations between two or more autonomous parties. But when God is a party to a covenant with man, He defines the obligations of both sides because He is sovereign.[22] Accordingly, theologian Wayne Grudem defines a covenant between God and man in Scripture as "an unchangeable, divinely imposed legal agreement between God and man that stipulates the conditions of their relationship."[23]

God's commitments in His covenants with man are generally in the form of His promises, His blessings, and His curses. Some of His promises are absolute and unconditional while others are conditioned on man's performance of his obligations under the covenant. The primary element underlying all the covenants is God's promise that "I will be their God and they shall be my people."[24] New Testament Scholar Simon Kistemaker describes these words as "a golden thread that God has woven into his Word from beginning to end."[25]

Kistemaker further notes that God first invokes a form of the commitment in Genesis 17:7: "And I will establishment my covenant between me and you and your offspring after you throughout their generations for an everlasting covenant, to be God to you and to your offspring after you." Then He reaffirms it in Exodus 6:7: "I will take you to be my people, and I will be your God, and you shall know that I am the Lord your God, who has brought you out from under the burdens of the Egyptians." He repeats the promise in Leviticus 26:12; Jeremiah 7:23, 11:4, 24:7, 30:22, 31:33; Ezekiel 11:20, 14:11, 36:28, 37:26–27; 2 Corinthians 6:16; Revelation 21:3; and in numerous other passages.

To be sure, with these words God is declaring His divine covenantal election of Israel.[26] But as the above citations show, He carries the same assurance into the New Testament, and Paul repeats it to the Corinthians (2 Cor. 6:16). This reinforces a point we made in our discussion of the Exodus Period in Chapter 3: God's election of Israel was not primarily for the sake of Israel, but to use it as a vehicle to enable the salvation of all people, thereby blessing all nations through Abraham, as He promised. God is the God of the Jews, with whom He made a series of special covenants, but He is also the God of the Gentiles, with whom He shares the covenant blessings.

Providing the framework for God's saving activities on behalf of humanity, the covenants also unify the events in the Bible concerning God's interactions with human beings.[27] All God's covenants are related, building upon each other in furtherance of God's ultimate promise to bring salvation to mankind. In this way we can understand them as the specific outworking of God's overall promise-plan.

Crucially, every biblical covenant culminates in the Person and work of Jesus Christ.[28] Indeed, the obligations of both parties under each covenant—God and man—point to Christ. God's promises and blessings contained in these covenants, even if they involve other people, events, or institutions initially, all point to Christ, as He is the ultimate fulfillment of the promises and the source of the final blessings. The curses likewise presage Christ because He will eventually endure the curse on our behalf, and because He will be the active agent Who executes judgment on sin. But Christ is also the key figure in fulfilling man's side of the bargain, because He is the One Who lives a perfectly obedient and sinless life and otherwise accomplishes what man, in his fallen and sinful state, cannot achieve on his own.[29]

Let's now examine the major biblical covenants and see how Christ fulfills each of them as the culmination of salvation history. All of God's covenantal promises are perfectly fulfilled in Christ, even as some of those promises are partially fulfilled in other individuals as salvation history unfolds (e.g., each successive king in the Davidic dynasty represents a partial fulfillment of the Davidic Covenant). I will first summarize the major covenants in the next few pages and then explore each in more detail.

Keep in mind that the Bible doesn't label these covenants as we are labeling them here. Yes, God clearly makes these covenants, but their identifying names come from theologians and Bible scholars after the fact. So, for example, while we'll see that God makes a covenant with Abraham, the Bible does not call it the "Abrahamic Covenant." Nevertheless, these names are helpful for Bible students and will assist us as we examine the major elements of these covenants. We should also note that the promises contained in the various covenants are often repetitive and overlapping. This is because they are all related, cumulatively building upon one another and serving to advance God's salvation history.

A historical examination of the Bible's major covenants begins with God's charge to Adam in the Garden to be fruitful and multiply, and His permission for Adam to eat from every tree in the Garden except for one lest he die. This is known as the Edenic Covenant (Gen. 2:16). God's implied promise of life and blessing is conditioned on Adam and Eve's obedience. Since they disobey, they forfeit the promised blessing and the story of humanity could have ended there. But instead, God, in His unfathomable grace, gives Adam and Eve (and thereby mankind) His first promise of a Redeemer—the Adamic Covenant (Gen. 3:15).

The next covenant accompanies God's judgment of the flood against man's pervasive wickedness, whereby He promises Noah that He will preserve humankind—the Noahic Covenant (Gen. 6:5–18, 9:8–17). God becomes more specific in His next covenant when He calls Abram (later Abraham) to leave his homeland in Ur of the Chaldeans and go to the land He would show him—Canaan. Abram is to receive divine blessings, some for himself and his people and others for all mankind, which include promises of land, offspring, and personal, national, and universal blessings—the Abrahamic Covenant (Gen. 12:2, et seq.). This is a pivotal moment in God's salvation history because with Abraham the history of redemption becomes grounded in the covenant.[30]

Next, God enters into a covenant with the people by giving Moses the Law, which contains many rules along with blessings for their obedience and curses for their disobedience—the Mosaic Covenant (Exodus 19:5). This covenant, however, by no means abrogates the grace God irrevocably bestowed on Israel with the Abrahamic Covenant and those preceding it[31]—that is, just because the Mosaic Covenant involves many laws and rules for the Israelites, it does not negate His unconditional, eternal promise of blessing in the Abrahamic Covenant.

Subsequently, through the Palestinian Covenant, God reaffirms the land promise of the Abrahamic Covenant (Deut. 28–30:3). The Palestinian covenant emphasizes the importance of the land in relation to Israel.[32] God later renews and further defines His earlier covenants by promising David and his descendants an eternal kingship over Israel—the Davidic Covenant (2 Sam. 7:16). Finally, God introduces the last covenant—the New Covenant—to Jeremiah, telling him that one day He will replace the "old" covenant (the Mosaic Covenant) with a better one that will bring far greater blessings (Jer. 31:31–34; Heb. 8:6–8).[33]

The Edenic Covenant and the Mosaic Covenant are conditional covenants, i.e., God's promises of blessings are conditioned on man fulfilling certain requirements. When man fails, he will sometimes lose the special blessings available through that covenant and often be punished.[34] This is not to imply, however, that God's Law is suspended upon the failure of Israel to live up to its obligations. The Law remains in effect even when Israel sometimes forfeits its blessings.

All the other major covenants are unconditional, whereby God agrees to bestow the promised blessings irrespective of man's response. God may impose conditions attendant to His promises, but He does not condition their fulfillment on man's performance. Now let's examine the major covenants in greater detail.

THE EDENIC COVENANT

With the Edenic Covenant God charges man to "Be fruitful and multiply and fill the earth and subdue it, and have dominion over the fish of the sea and over the birds of the heavens and over every living thing that moves on the earth" (Gen. 1:28). Man is given permission to eat from every tree of the garden except from the tree of the knowledge of good and evil, the eating from which would lead to his death (Gen. 2:16–17). The Edenic Covenant is not referred to as a covenant per se in Genesis, but Hosea 6:7 makes it clear that it is: "But like Adam they transgressed the covenant; there they dealt faithlessly with Me."

God's promise here to Adam, and through him to all mankind, is of life and blessing, even if implied rather than explicitly expressed—for when God tells Adam that he will surely die if he disobeys, He means that he will live if he obeys. Disobedience will result in physical death as well as spiritual death—the separation of soul and spirit from God.[35] The Edenic Covenant has been referred to as a "Covenant of Works" because the keeping of the covenant depends on Adam's merit—his obedience to the terms of the covenant. Some scholars don't include this in their discussion of the covenants, and others include it in tandem with the Adamic Covenant. But few would deny that it's an important first link in the redemptive chain because its outworking—Adam's failure— demonstrates man's incapability of sustaining a proper relationship with God even when situated in paradise.[36]

Man's resulting fall has disastrous consequences for the human race because Adam's sin spreads to all men (Romans 5:12). But the fall lays the groundwork for God's gracious plan of redemption, which will unfold with the later covenants and culminate with Jesus Christ's death on the cross. As Paul underscores, "All who rely on works of the law are under a curse" (Gal. 3:10). However, "Christ redeemed us from the curse of the law by becoming a curse for us— for it is written, 'Cursed is everyone who is hanged on a tree'—so that in Christ Jesus the blessing of Abraham might come to the Gentiles, so that we might receive the promised Spirit through faith" (Gal. 3:13–14).

We also turn to Paul to see how Christ succeeds (and gives life) where Adam failed (and brought death). Paul describes Christ as "the last Adam," contrasting him with "the first man Adam" and pointing to His redemptive work. "For as in Adam all die, so also in Christ shall all be made alive" (1 Cor. 15:22). He adds, "The first man Adam became a living being; the last Adam became a life-giving spirit" (1 Cor. 15:45). Furthermore, "Just as sin came into the world through one man, and death through sin, and so death spread to all men because all sinned.... For if, because of one man's trespass, death reigned through that one man, much more will those who receive the abundance of grace and the free gift of righteousness reign in life through the one man Jesus Christ" (Romans 5:12–17).

Theology Professor Sung Wook Chung notes that though "the first Adam" failed to fulfill the commission and mandate God gave him through the Edenic Covenant, Jesus Christ, as "the last Adam," fulfills both. First, when He was on earth, observes Chung, "Jesus Christ as the King of kings exercised dominion over the entire creation," mainly through His miracles. "Second, Jesus Christ as the High Priest loved God with all his heart, all his mind, all his soul, and all his power. His love for God was demonstrated through his perfect obedience to the Father's will, even up to death on the cross. Whereas the first Adam obeyed Satan and disobeyed God, the last Adam obeyed God and rejected Satan's temptations. Through his love for, and obedience to, God, the last Adam began to fulfill what the covenant of Genesis 2:16–17 required not only of the first Adam but also of all humanity.... Jesus Christ revealed God's plan and will for the redemption of fallen humanity and the restoration of cursed cosmos."[37]

THE ADAMIC COVENANT

As noted in our discussion of the Primeval Period (the first period of Old Testament history), God initially announces the Gospel, albeit in shadowy form, in the third chapter of Genesis along with His infliction of punishment for Adam and Eve's sin (3:14–19). What a God of grace!

God delivers the transgressors' consequences in the order they defected: He first curses the serpent and then the woman and man, telling the woman she will suffer painful childbirths and the man that he will have to toil throughout his life.[38] The ground is cursed and will bring forth thorns and thistles. Because of man's sin, he will die both spiritually and, in time, physically.

But in the very process of administering these judgments, God announces His future blessing on mankind: "Because you have done this, cursed are you above all livestock and above all beasts of the field.... I will put enmity between you and the woman, and between your offspring and her offspring; he shall bruise your head, and you shall bruise his heel" (Gen. 3:14–15). Paul confirms that Christ is the One referred to here as the woman's offspring in Galatians 4:4: "But when the fullness of time had come, God sent forth his Son, born of a woman, born under law, to redeem those who were under the law, so that we might receive adoption as sons."

Though Satan had tempted Adam and Eve, leading to their sin and the fall of the entire human race, and he would later "bruise" the *heel* of the woman's offspring Jesus Christ (causing Him to suffer), Jesus will bruise Satan's *head* (destroying him completely). Paul seemingly alludes to this passage when he tells his fellow Christians in Rome, "The God of peace will soon crush Satan under your feet. The grace of our Lord Jesus Christ be with you" (Romans 16:20). The Book of Revelation describes Satan's fate, in fulfillment of God's promise: "And the devil, who had deceived them was thrown into the lake of fire and sulfur where the beast and the false prophet were, and they will be tormented day and night forever and ever" (20:10).

I find it fascinating that while Satan does cause Christ to suffer, even physical death, He only succeeds in injuring Christ because Christ allows him to do so. And this is key: the reason Christ allows him to is that He loves us. Christ inflicts this punishment on Himself in order to redeem us from our sins, wholly thwarting Satan on multiple levels. It is ironic that Christ uses this same suffering to redeem us and give us life. So not only is Satan's bruising of Christ non-fatal in a permanent sense, that very bruising leads to our redemption, which illustrates just how lopsided this battle is and how impotent Satan is in relation to Christ. Indeed, Christ becomes man for the express purpose of defeating Satan, sin, and death, and to redeem us with the gift of life. The Apostle John puts it simply, "The reason the Son of God appeared was to destroy the works of the devil" (1 John 3:8).

THE NOAHIC COVENANT

In the days of Noah, man has become so wicked that God vows to wipe out the human race and the animal kingdom (Gen. 6:5–7). Despite this rampant evil, however, God will not allow His sovereign plan of redemption to be thwarted. Finding Noah to be righteous, God preserves him, his three sons (Shem, Ham, and Japheth), and their wives, as well as representatives of the animals. After the waters recede from the flood, God instructs Noah and his family to come out of the ark along with the creatures, and to be fruitful and multiply (Gen. 8:16–17). In reverential appreciation, Noah "built an altar to the Lord and took some of every clean animal and some of every clean bird and made burnt offerings on the altar" (Gen. 8:20). God then makes His covenant with Noah: "I will never again curse the ground because of man, for the intention of man's heart is evil from his youth. Neither will I ever again strike down every living creature as I have done" (Gen. 8:21–22). Blessing Noah and his sons, God repeats His command to be fruitful and multiply and fill the earth (Gen. 9:1), reaffirming that they will again have dominion over all other creatures.

To emphasize the dignity of man created in His image, God tells Noah, "Whoever sheds the blood of man, by man shall his blood be shed, for God made man in his image" (Gen. 9:6). God further declares, "I establish my covenant with you and your offspring after you…that never again shall all flesh be cut off by the waters of the flood, and never again shall there be a flood to destroy the earth" (Gen. 9:11). He also tells Noah that the rainbow would serve as a sign of the covenant (9:13–17). In this way, God reestablishes His kingdom after the pattern of His original creation in Eden.[39] This covenant with Noah also enshrines the principle of human government—the rule of man over other men (Gen. 9:5, 6).[40]

Through Noah, God curses Ham's son Canaan, saying he will be a servant to Noah's sons Shem and Japheth. He also declares that Shem will have a special relationship to God (Gen. 9:26–27).[41] As such, God will form a nation from the Semites and will entrust the Law to them, and through them will bring forth His Messiah, Who will bless all nations. Abraham (Abram), as a Semite and a descendent of Shem, is thus an heir of the Noahic covenant,[42] and also becomes part of a special covenant with God.

Shem's special relationship with God can be seen as a continuation of the relationship Adam had with God before the fall, a relationship that is restored by God's grace.[43] Shem, writes Old Testament Professor Gerard Van Groningen, "is to be the specific channel through which the Lord is to work out his restoration program…. He is to provide the eventual royal agent of redemption, a Hebrew, a descendant of the Semites."[44] Jesus validates this arrangement with His exclamation that "salvation is from the Jews" (John 4:22). Christ, as the greatest "son" of Shem, fulfills God's promise to Noah concerning His special relationship with Shem.[45] Van Groningen cogently summarizes the messianic import of the Noahic Covenant: "God revealed himself and his grand plan for the full and complete restoration of the cosmos and fallen royal mankind.... Indeed, as Noah prophesied the word of the Lord, he also confessed it as a glorious, life-giving, covenant-maintaining, and kingdom-restoring word of God."[46]

THE ABRAHAMIC COVENANT

Chapter 12 of Genesis records a major turning point in Old Testament history. "The most crucial event in the Bible between the fall of Adam and the birth of Christ occurs in Genesis 12," writes Mark Dever. "The Lord calls Abram (12:1–3). This call sets off the story of the rest of the Bible."[47] After all, notes Dever, this is the precise point in history that God puts in motion the redemptive work He promised in Genesis 3:15.

We discussed the Abrahamic Covenant earlier, but to recapitulate, God calls Abraham out of his land, telling him to go to the land He would show him. God promises Abraham He will make his name great and bless him (and bless those that bless him and curse those that curse him), make a great nation out of him, give his nation the land as an everlasting possession, and bless all nations and all the families of the earth through his offspring (Gen. 12:1–4, 13:14–17, 15:1–7, 17:1–8, 22:17–18). Abraham—the son of Terah, who is a descendant of Shem— becomes God's representative to continue the promised blessings.[48] One can begin to see here the successive covenants building on each other toward ultimate fulfillment in Christ.

This covenant eminently points to Christ, for it is through Christ, who comes out of the Hebrew nation and is a descendant of Abraham, that all nations and peoples will be blessed—through faith in Him. The Apostle Peter comments on this theme in his second sermon in Acts, in which he identifies Jesus as the Servant God raised up to turn Israel away from its sinfulness and back to God. "All the prophets who have spoken from Samuel and those who came after him, also proclaimed these days," Peter states. "You are the sons of the prophets and of the covenant that God made with your fathers, saying to Abraham, 'And in your offspring shall all the families of the earth be blessed.' God, having raised up his servant, sent him to you first, to bless you by turning every one of you from your wickedness" (3:24–26). According to Craig Blaising, "Peter's sermon confirms that the blessings of the Abrahamic covenant are mediated by the Christ."[49] Paul is also clear on this point, emphasizing that the blessing is for the Gentiles as well as the Jews, through faith in Jesus Christ: "In Christ Jesus the blessing of Abraham might come to the Gentiles, so that we might receive the promised Spirit through faith" (Gal. 3:14). So, while the covenant was given to Abraham and his offspring, it would eventually benefit and bless all believers.

I believe the Abrahamic Covenant is unconditional, though scholars have differing opinions on this, and it does not serve our purposes here to delve deeply into this debate. But the covenant is expressly stated to be eternal, and it is often repeated by God and sometimes enlarged. Historically, when two parties entered into a covenant, they would both walk together between two pieces of a sacrificed animal.[50] But God formally solemnizes this covenant through a ceremony He performs alone while Abraham is asleep (Gen. 15:12–21), thus signifying that the agreement is unilateral and its validity is not dependent on Abraham's obedience. God even reaffirms His commitment to the promise after Abraham disobeys Him in certain respects, as if to say, *I'm going through with this despite your disobedience and rebelliousness.*

The writer of Hebrews affirms that the promise is set in stone: "For when God made a promise to Abraham, since he had no one greater by whom to swear, he swore to himself, saying, 'Surely I will bless you and multiply you.'…So when God desired to show more convincingly to the heirs of the promise the unchangeable character of his purpose, he guaranteed it with an oath, so that by two unchangeable things, in which it is impossible for God to lie, we who have fled for refuge might have strong encouragement to hold fast to the hope set before us. We have this as a sure and steadfast anchor of the soul" (Heb. 6:13–19).[51] We see here that not only is God's promise binding, but He gives it to us so that we can have "strong consolation" and a "sure and steadfast anchor" for our soul.

The Abrahamic Covenant contains promises that are further developed by later covenants: the promise of land undergirds further promises concerning land in the Palestinian Covenant; the promise of blessing is the cornerstone for aspects of the Mosaic and New Covenants; and the promise of seed (descendants) is foundational to the promise of kingly descendants in the Davidic Covenant.[52]

It is probably no overstatement to say that the Abrahamic Covenant provides a unifying theme for the Bible. It is, at a minimum, foundational to God's promise-plan. Its principal message is that God's redemptive plan of grace is available to mankind through faith in His Son, Jesus Christ. "The choice of Abraham and the unconditional promises of land and nationhood have as their ultimate goal the blessing of all the earth's communities," contends William LaSor. "The beginning of redemptive history offers a word about its end. The salvation promised Abraham would ultimately embrace all humankind. God has not dismissed the human family in wrath forever, but now acts to mend the breach that sin has placed between Him and His world. This promise stands as a key to understanding all of Scripture."[53]

THE MOSAIC (SINAITIC) COVENANT

The Mosaic Covenant is struck when God gives His divine Law to Moses on Mount Sinai. In addition to instituting these laws, this covenant reaffirms many of the promises of its Abrahamic predecessor. With the Mosaic Covenant, God promises to bless Israel (Lev. 26:4–12; Deut. 7:13–15, 28:3–12) and multiply the nation (Lev. 26:9; Deut. 6:3, 8:1, 28:11); give Israel the land (Lev. 26:5; Deut. 6:3, 8:1, 9:4, 28:11); make it a great nation (Deut. 7:14, 28:1, 3); be Israel's God—and they would be His people (Lev. 26:11–12; Deut. 7:6–10, 28:9–10); and confirm His covenant with the Israelites of that generation (Lev. 26:9).[54]

While these reaffirmed promises are couched in similar terms in the Abrahamic and Mosaic Covenants, the promised blessings in the former were unconditional and were to materialize in the indefinite future. By contrast, in the Mosaic Covenant God offers a particular generation of Abraham's descendants the chance to enjoy these blessings in the present. But these blessings are conditioned on Israel's obedience to God and to the Law He handed down as part of the covenant. The Israelites' disobedience would not only remove the blessing but would bring God's curse and punishment (Exodus 15:25–26, 19:3–8, 26:3–36; Deut. 28).[55] Roy Zuck captures the continuity between the Abrahamic Covenant and the Mosaic Covenant while emphasizing the latter's more particular and conditional nature: "That Israel was (and still is) the people of God is a matter of unqualified divine initiative; that Israel was to function in a special way as the people of God would now rest in Israel's free choice."[56]

In several ways, the Mosaic Covenant advances certain promises of the Abrahamic Covenant. Whereas the Abrahamic Covenant absolutely and permanently guaranteed Israel the Promised Land, it was not specific as to when this promise would come to fruition. The Mosaic Covenant empowers Israel to partially realize that promise so long as it is obedient, but among the curses for its disobedience is its removal from the land and exile.[57] Whereas the Abrahamic Covenant promised, generally, that all nations would be blessed through Israel, the Mosaic Covenant establishes Israel as a kingdom of priests and a holy nation, thereby placing it in a position to bless the nations (Exodus 19:4–6). Affirming this point, Roy Zuck writes, "Israel's value as God's possession lay precisely in her function as a holy kingdom of priests."[58]

God outlines His purpose for the Covenant by telling Moses, "You yourselves have seen what I did to the Egyptians, and how I bore you on eagles' wings and brought you to myself. Now therefore, if you will indeed obey my voice and keep my covenant, you shall be my treasured possession among all peoples, for all the earth is mine; and you shall be to me a kingdom of priests and a holy nation" (Exodus 19:4–6). The people of Israel accept the terms of the covenant, vowing, "All that the Lord has spoken we will do" (Exodus 19:8).[59]

God's promises to make Israel His treasured possession, a kingdom of priests, and a holy nation underscore our earlier point that God is not solely concerned with Israel. The primary function of a priest, writes Zuck, is to mediate and intercede. "A priest stands between God and a person (or persons) who is in need of making contact with God," he explains. "So Israel must be viewed as bearing mediatorial responsibility, of serving as an intercessor between a holy God and all the peoples of the earth."[60] While I agree that God loves all His people and primarily called Israel for its priestly role, I want to reiterate here my belief that Scripture suggests God does have a special love for Israel that goes beyond its mediatorial role.

Pursuant to this covenant, God provides Israel with three types of law—moral, civil, and ceremonial—that span across 613 specific commandments. The moral law comprises the Ten Commandments (Exodus 10:2–17; Deut. 5:6–21), which govern the Israelites' lives and their relationship with God. The civil law consists of many specific laws set out in Exodus 21:1–24:18 and in Leviticus and Deuteronomy. These are detailed rules and instructions to govern the civil and social life of the nation. Scripture refers to these laws as the "Book of the Covenant" (Exodus 24:7). The ceremonial law, which can be found in Exodus 25:1–40:38 and in Leviticus and Deuteronomy, sets forth the rules concerning the Tabernacle, the ceremonies, the priests' clothing and functions, and the sacrifices and offerings, all given for the purpose of teaching the people how to purify themselves in order to approach their holy God, which they could not do, in any event, without a mediator.[61]

A key element of the Mosaic Law is the blood sacrifice, which is set out in Leviticus 17:11: "For the life of the flesh is in the blood; and I have given it to you upon the altar to make atonement for your souls: for it is the blood that makes atonement by reason of the life." J. Vernon McGee writes, "The life is in the blood. This is a great, eternal truth. This explains why Abel's sacrifice was acceptable and Cain's was not. It is the blood that maketh an atonement for the soul."[62] The writer of Hebrews confirms, "Without the shedding of blood there is no forgiveness of sins" (Heb. 9:22).

The sacrifices established under this system are not meant to permanently remove the people's sins, as the Hebrew word for "atonement" means the covering of sin, not its removal.[63] According to the writer of Hebrews, "For since the law was but a shadow of the good things to come instead of the true form of these realities, it can never, by the same sacrifices that are continually offered every year, make perfect those who draw near. Otherwise, would they not have ceased to be offered? ...For it is impossible for the blood of bulls and goats to take away sins" (10:1–4).

Only the blood of Jesus Christ can permanently remove sin. But these Old Testament sacrifices foreshadow Christ's one-time, perfect sacrifice. As described in the Book of Hebrews, Christ, the perfect High Priest, "entered once for all into the holy places, not by means of the blood of goats and calves but by means of his own blood, thus securing an eternal redemption" (9:11–12). The writer also declares, "For it was indeed fitting that we should have such a high priest, holy, innocent, unstained, separated from sinners, and exalted above the heavens. He has no need, like those high priests, to offer sacrifices daily, first for his own sins and then for those of the people, since he did this once for all when he offered up himself" (7:26–27). As Vern Poythress explains, "The Old Testament thus reaches out in longing for Christ who brings an end to its frustrations and brings to accomplishment its promises. Christ is the final offering to which all the animal sacrifices look forward."[64]

Again, the Mosaic Covenant does not replace or supersede the Abrahamic Covenant, which is unconditional and permanent. It was never intended to set aside God's promises from that covenant, but to reinforce and complement them. In Galatians Paul confirms that the Mosaic Covenant, coming 430 years after the Abrahamic Covenant, does not annul it and is distinct from it (3:17–19, 4:24).

Overall, the Abrahamic Covenant should be understood as the "theological backbone" undergirding the Mosaic Covenant. God adds the Mosaic Covenant alongside its predecessor to provide guidelines for the people of Israel on how to conduct their lives and how to be protected—while still fully under the Abrahamic Covenant. This situation is meant to last until the coming of the Messiah[65] ("until the offspring should come to whom the promise had been made"), when the Old Testament system of sacrifices would no longer be necessary (Gal. 3:19). "It was the means by which the goal of the promise would be advanced in and through Abraham's national descendants (Gen. 12:2; cf. 18:18–19)," notes Paul Williamson.[66] Craig Blaising and Darrell Bock agree, noting that the Mosaic Covenant "set up an arrangement by which God would relate to the descendants of the patriarchs as a nation, distinguishing them from other nations on earth.... It provided the means for blessing an entire nation and, through them, all peoples on the earth."[67]

Further, the Law is not given as a means to salvation; to the contrary, part of its purpose is to show people just how desperately incapable they (and we) are of living holy, sinless lives on their own. As stated in Galatians, "The law was our guardian until Christ came, in order that we might be justified by faith" (3:24). It's meant to show their inability to save themselves and their consequent need for a Savior (Gal. 3:19). "The spirit of the Law condemns us," maintains Charles Spurgeon. "And this is its useful property. It humbles us, makes us know we are guilty, and so we are led to receive the Savior."[68] Spurgeon adds, "Lower the Law and you dim the light by which man perceives his guilt; this is a very serious loss to the sinner rather than a gain; for it lessens the likelihood of his conviction and conversion. I say you have deprived the gospel of its ablest auxiliary [it's most powerful weapon] when you have set aside the Law. You have taken away from it the schoolmaster [guardian] that is to bring me to Christ."[69]

No, the Law cannot bring salvation. Salvation has always been attained by faith in Christ—and in the Old Testament it was gained by faith in the coming Messiah (Gen. 15:6). The laws given under the Mosaic Covenant serve as the constitution of Israel, and the covenant is given to these people who are already in a relationship with God; it is not given to place them in that relationship, but to show those already in that relationship how to live.[70]

The covenant further helps to reveal God's holiness, the standards of righteousness He requires for a proper relationship with Him, and the means of purification to satisfy those standards (Lev. 11:44, 19:1–2, 37; 1 Peter 1:15–17). The Law also helps the Hebrews remain set apart as a distinct people designated by God for His holy purposes (Lev. 11:44–45; Deut. 7:6, 14:1–2).

Jesus Christ, representing Israel as God's Son and Servant, is the substance of all the covenant shadows. He fulfills the Mosaic Covenant wholly and perfectly by living a sinless life and bearing its curse for our failure to do so, thereby making a perfect sacrifice.[71] As Paul writes to the Romans, "There is therefore now no condemnation for those who are in Christ Jesus. For the law of the Spirit of life has set you free in

Christ Jesus from the law of sin and death. For God has done what the law, weakened by the flesh, could not do. By sending his own Son in the likeness of sinful flesh and for sin, he condemned sin in the flesh in order that the righteous requirement of the law might be fulfilled in us, who walk not according to the flesh but according to the Spirit" (Romans 8:1–4).

Christ fulfills the covenant by becoming the final and perfect Mediator. It is worth repeating that the Mosaic Covenant makes clear that blood is vitally important to worshipping a holy God and to our relationship with Him. Our sin cannot be expiated and we cannot approach God without blood. Christ's blood on the cross is the consummate fulfillment of the covenant's blood requirement, prefigured by the Mosaic animal blood sacrifices.

What, then, is the status of the Mosaic Covenant today? The answer is that it has been wholly fulfilled in Christ and so it has passed away. This does not mean the Ten Commandments of the Law are invalidated—the New Testament restates almost all of them, though the specified penalties for violation and the promises attached to them are sometimes different. For example, notes Dr. Norman Geisler, the Mosaic penalty for committing adultery is capital punishment, whereas under the New Covenant it is excommunication. And while the Mosaic promise attached to the commandment to honor one's parents is that one would live long in the land that God was giving him (Exodus 20:12), the New Covenant promise accompanying this command is "that it may go well with you and that you may enjoy a long life (Eph. 6:3).[72]

As we are in the Church age, which is an age of grace rather than the theocracy of Mosaic times, we are no longer under the Law as such. Dr. Geisler cogently summarizes these distinctions: "While the basic moral principles, reflective of God's moral nature, embedded in the theocratic construct of Old Testament Israel, are the same immutable principles expressed in the context of grace for the New Testament church, nevertheless, church-age believers are not under Mosaic Law, which has been fulfilled and passed away."[73]

I must briefly acknowledge that some theologians seem to disagree with this description of the relationship between the Law and the Gospel or the Law and grace, at least in a technical sense. Kaiser urges that we reject the idea that the Law ceases to be valid just because Jesus fulfilled its requirements for all believers. The Law itself is still valid, he claims, it's just that we are empowered to obey it through faith. Kaiser is not arguing that we are saved by obeying the Law, as our salvation is purely from our faith in Christ and His finished work on the cross. He seems to be saying, however, that it still remains the perfect standard for holiness—and who can argue with that? He cites Paul, who asks, "Do we then overthrow the law by this faith? By no means! On the contrary, we uphold the law" (Romans 3:31).[74] As I will discuss further in the next chapter in connection with the New Covenant, we can all acknowledge that God's Law is perfect because its Maker is perfect. It was never intended, however, to impart life (Gal. 3:21).

CHAPTER 6

ALL ROADS LEAD TO CHRIST
BIBLICAL COVENANTS, PART 2

*Theologians of all kinds focus on Christ as the
key to understanding the biblical covenants.*

—LARRY PETTEGREW[1]

THE PALESTINIAN COVENANT

s part of the Abrahamic Covenant, God guaranteed to Israel
the Promised Land as an everlasting possession. The Palestinian Covenant (Deut. 28–30:20) reaffirms and further devel-
ops that guarantee. Like the Abrahamic Covenant it amplifies, it is
eternal and unconditional, securing Israel's title deed to the Promised
Land and its future and final restoration and conversion.[2] Theologian
C. I. Scofield explains that the Palestinian Covenant contains seven
elements:

1. Israel's dispersion from the land for disobedience (Deut.
   28:63–68, 30:1).
2. The future repentance of Israel while in the dispersion
   (Deut. 30:2).
3. The return of the Lord (Deut. 30:3; Amos 9:9–14; Acts
   15:14–17).

105

4. Restoration to the land (Deut. 30:5; Isaiah 11:11, 12; Jer. 23:3–8; Ezek. 37:21–25).

5. National conversion (Deut. 30:6; Romans 11:26, 27; Hosea 2:14–16).

6. The judgment of Israel's oppressors (Deut. 30:7; Isaiah 14:1, 2; Joel 3:1–8; Matt. 25:31–46).

7. National prosperity (Deut. 30:9; Amos 9:11–14).[3]

Neither the Abrahamic Covenant nor the Palestinian Covenant guarantee Israel immediate and continuous possession of the land, though they do promise full, complete, and permanent possession of it in the future. In fact, writes Walter Kaiser, "Sixty-nine times, the writer of Deuteronomy repeated the pledge that Israel would one day 'possess' and 'inherit' the land promised to her."[4] God promises Israel, "If you diligently obey the voice of the Lord your God...the Lord your God will set you high above all the nations of the earth" (Deut. 28:1). This means if Israel is obedient it will occupy the land, be prosperous there, and enjoy safety and protection (Deut. 28:3–7).[5]

When Israel doesn't obey, it is subject to God's curses and punishments (Deut. 28:15–68). Although these censures include God's dispersion of Israel among foreign nations, the covenant also promises the eventual regathering of the people to the land, where they will live prosperously and faithfully, while He will punish their enemies.[6] "God takes Israel's relation to the land as a matter of extreme importance," argues Dwight Pentecost. "God not only guarantees its possession to them, but obligates Himself to judge and remove all Israel's enemies, give the nation a new heart, a conversion, prior to placing them in the land."[7]

It may seem contradictory to describe this covenant as unconditional yet acknowledge that God made the Israelites' blessings for the land conditional on their obedience and even inflicted punishment on them for disobedience. A simple explanation is that while enjoyment of the land (possession) is conditioned on obedience, ownership of the land is unconditional.[8] So with this covenant, God, through His prophets, specifies that He will remove Israel from the land when it is disobedient. But He also promises it will eventually be restored in the future—in what some scholars refer to as the "millennial kingdom."[9] Before the

Palestinian Covenant will be completely fulfilled, however, Israel must come to repentance and turn to the Messiah (Zech. 12:10–14). Jesus Christ, then, is integrally and foundationally connected to this covenant as well, for it will reach its fulfillment through Christ when He returns and reigns over Israel, which will then be fully restored to the land.

I also think it worthwhile to repeat a point I made in *Jesus on Trial* because I find it probative of God's promises and, in this particular case, His faithfulness to Israel. Though today Israel does not yet occupy the land fully, the nation has returned there. This was foretold about 2,500 years ago by the prophet Jeremiah (Jer. 31:38–40), while Isaiah (Isaiah 11:11–13) and Ezekiel (37:21–28) also prophesied that Israelites would be regathered in their homeland "from the four corners of the earth." These prophecies were made before the Jews were dispersed in Babylon (beginning in 586 BC), and even more amazingly, before they were dispersed again for almost two thousand years by Rome (in 70 AD).

Yet in 1948, the nation was reconstituted and millions of Jews have now returned to the land. When David Ben-Gurion, Israel's principal founder, announced on May 14, 1948, that the new Jewish homeland would be called "Israel," he cited Ezekiel's prophecy. Even if the prophecy has not yet been completely fulfilled, it is utterly remarkable that a nation dispersed for two millennia would retain its identity and regather in the very land it left, and to which God said it would eventually return. Highlighting the astounding nature of these events, Josh McDowell observes that throughout history, every other nation that left its homeland lost its national identity within about five generations.[10] Pastor Tony Evans further notes that no other nation in history vanquished from its land for fifty years or more has ever returned speaking the same language.[11]

THE DAVIDIC COVENANT

The Davidic Covenant, originally announced by the prophet Nathan, is God's promise to David that his descendants will rule in Israel forever, and that He will elevate the nation of Israel to a kingdom under the rule of kings in David's line (2 Samuel 7:5–16; 1 Chron. 17:10–14, 23–27; 2 Chron. 6:10, 15–17, 42, 7:17–18, 13:8, 23:3).[12] As part of this covenant, David shall have a "house" (a royal dynasty), a throne (the symbol of royal authority), and a kingdom (a sphere of rule) in perpetuity. Disobedience will bring judgment and chastisement, but not the annulment of the covenant.[13] The psalmist is unequivocal on this point: "If they violate my statutes and do not keep my commandments, then I will punish their transgression with the rod and their iniquity with stripes, but I will not remove from him my steadfast love or be false to my faithfulness. I will not violate my covenant or alter the word that went forth from my lips. Once for all I have sworn by my holiness; I will not lie to David. His offspring shall endure forever, his throne as long as the sun before me. Like the moon it shall be established forever, a faithful witness in the skies" (Psalms 89:30–37).

This covenant is the source of the Davidic dynasty and of the promise for a temple, which would become Solomon's Temple.[14] This is referenced in Psalm 132, in which the psalmist pleads with God to remember that David had bemoaned the fact that he had a house when God didn't, and so he asked God's permission to build His Temple. The psalmist then reminds God of His covenant with David, which stipulates that He would place one of David's heirs on the throne forever in Israel.

The Davidic Covenant includes these provisions:

1. God promises David, like He did Abraham, that He will make his name great (2 Samuel 7:9).
2. David will have a son who will succeed him as king, and God will establish his kingdom (2 Samuel 7:12).
3. This son will build the Temple (2 Samuel 7:13).
4. This kingdom, the throne, and the Davidic line will continue forever (2 Samuel 7:13).
5. God will center this dynasty in the Promised Land and provide His people rest and peace (2 Samuel 7:10).
6. God's love will remain on this house forever, even when it sins (2 Samuel 7:15). Note that this is not hyperbolic language. By "forever," God has His Son Jesus Christ in mind, Who will be the fulfillment of all these promises and will reign forever.[15]

This covenant constitutes an integral part of God's salvation history. It is not explicitly referred to as a covenant when it is announced (2 Samuel 7:5–16), but that is made clear in 2 Samuel 23:5: "For does not my house stand so with God? For he has made with me an everlasting covenant, ordered in all things and secure." Psalms 89:3 confirms this—"I have made a covenant with my chosen one"—as does Psalms 132:11–12—"The Lord swore to David a sure oath from which he will not turn back: One of the sons of your body I will set on your throne. If your sons keep my covenant and my testimonies that I shall teach them, their sons also forever shall sit on your throne."

The covenant is unconditional for David, but not for his offspring[16]— that is, it is unconditional in terms of its ultimate fulfillment, but it does not guarantee that every occupant of the throne in David's line will enjoy its blessings, as sin and faithlessness will assuredly interrupt it.[17] As noted earlier, though God's sovereign plans will always proceed, He will also make human beings accountable. Thus, the unbroken succession of kings in David's line from generation to generation will depend on the particular king's faithfulness, as later passages specify (1 Chron. 28:7; 1 Kings 2:3–4, 3:14).[18] But God's plan for the Davidic line to continue forever shall not be thwarted (2 Samuel 7:16; Jer. 33:17) and, as the New Testament confirms, will ultimately be fulfilled in Christ: "He will be great and will be called the Son of the Most High. And the Lord God will give to him the throne of his father David, and he will reign over the house of Jacob forever, and of his kingdom there will be no end" (Luke 1:32–33).

The unconditionality and eternality of this covenant become clear when you consider that God announces the covenant with full knowledge that David will soon commit adultery and murder[19]—though David, a man after God's heart, is repentant and appreciative of God's faithfulness to His promises despite David's disobedience, which David acknowledges with his dying breaths, quoted above in 2 Samuel 23:5.

God is clear that there will always be a descendant of David's qualified for Israel's throne, and that one of his descendants will eventually rule over an everlasting kingdom. While this kingdom is certainly an earthly kingdom, it also has an important spiritual dimension. "The kingdom of Israel was not only a geo-political entity," John Barry writes, "it was *God's* kingdom, responsibility for which was vested in the line of David."[20]

During the glory days of the United Kingdom, though the Temple is built under Solomon and the Davidic Covenant is partially fulfilled, the kingdom descends into a prolonged period of division and decline (1 Kings 12). Later, the prophets would announce a New Covenant that would continue and restore the Davidic Covenant, as explained below (Jer. 33:14–26; Isaiah 9, 11, 55:3; Ezek. 37:15–28).[21]

In the meantime, however, after the fall of Jerusalem and during the Babylonian Captivity and beyond, one would think that the later writers of the Old Testament would be concerned that the Davidic Covenant is in jeopardy. After all, even the greatest kings, David and Solomon, were seriously flawed. "Yet future expectation and the hope for a better world did not die;" write Craig Evans and Peter Flint, "instead, the horizon shifted to the end times and a golden age of peace, righteousness, and prosperity."[22] The prophets begin to frame the fulfillment of the covenant as being sometime in the future when a new David would come to power and usher in this golden era. In other words, they begin to associate the covenant with their expectation of a Messiah—the "anointed one"— Who will deliver Israel in the last days. In this way, the Davidic Covenant becomes the conceptual framework for Jewish messianic anticipations, which are voiced both in the Old Testament and other Jewish writings that precede the New Testament.[23]

One of the main themes of the gospels is that Jesus Christ fulfills God's promises contained in the Davidic Covenant. Indeed, the very first verse of the New Testament introduces this theme: "The book of the genealogy of Jesus Christ, the son of David, the son of Abraham" (Matt. 1:1). This motif continues through the Gospels, as Jesus is referred to as the son (descendant) of David and as the eternal righteous king God promised in the covenant (see Matt. 9:27, 12:23; Mark 10:48, 12:35; Luke 18:38–39, 20:41).[24] The idea is carried forward into Revelation, the last book of the Bible, in which John, in his opening vision, describes the reigning Christ as "the Lion of the tribe of Judah" and "the Root of David" (5:5). Enhancing the theme, John quotes Jesus identifying Himself as "the root and the descendant of David, the bright morning star" (Rev. 22:16).

So in the very first verse of the New Testament, five verses from the end of the New Testament, and countless times in between, Christ is identified as David's reigning descendant. Let me suggest that this becomes an even more amazing demonstration of biblical continuity, unity, and divine intervention in history when you consider that God's promise of a royal dynasty of kings was originally made to Abraham way back in the early chapters of Genesis (17:6, 11, 35:11). More astounding still is Jacob's prophetic blessing to his son Judah of a coming ruler who would come out of his tribe. Significantly, Judah, the fourth son of Jacob's wife Leah, is the first of Jacob's sons in this series of blessings to receive nothing but praise from Jacob.[25] Jacob tells Judah,

> Judah, your brothers shall praise you; your hand shall be on the neck of your enemies; your father's sons shall bow down before you. Judah is a lion's cub; from the prey, my son, you have gone up. He stooped down; he crouched as a lion and as a lioness; who dares rouse him? The scepter shall not depart from Judah, nor the ruler's staff from between his feet, until tribute comes to him; and to him shall be the obedience of the peoples. Binding his foal to the vine and his donkey's colt to the choice vine, he has washed his garments in wine and his vesture in the blood of grapes. His eyes are darker than wine, and his teeth are whiter than milk (Gen. 49:8–12).

Gordon Johnston observes, "By divine design this enigmatically worded oracle speaks not only of the rise of the first historical king from the tribe of Judah (David), but also the ultimate eschatological [future] King (Jesus, who is the Christ)."[26] There you have it, God's promise to David of eternal divine kingship through his descendants in the land of Israel appears at the very beginning of the Bible and at the very end of the Bible; and at the very beginning of the New Testament and at the very end of the New Testament. Who can reasonably doubt that these are divinely placed bookends, crafted by our wondrous creator before time began?

Just for good measure, let me leave you with one final prophecy on this subject that involves Balaam, a Mesopotamian seer.[27] Moab's King

Balak, fearful of the strength of the Israelites who were encamped in Moab and ready to enter the Promised Land, sends for Balaam to come to Moab to curse Israel (Num. 22:1–6). After initially refusing to come—because the true God of the Bible forbids him to go and prohibits him from cursing the blessed Israelites (Num. 22:12)—he ends up going and blessing Israel four times through four oracles (Num. 23–24). In his fourth and final oracle, Balaam, purporting to speak on behalf of the God of the Bible (Yahweh), declares, "The oracle of Balaam, the son of Beor...who hears the words of God, and knows the knowledge of the Most High, who sees the vision of the Almighty, falling down with his eyes uncovered: I see him, but not now; I behold him, but not near: a star shall come out of Jacob, and a scepter shall rise out of Israel; it shall crush the forehead of Moab and break down all the sons of Sheth. Edom shall be dispossessed; Seir also, his enemies, shall be dispossessed. Israel is doing valiantly. And one from Jacob shall exercise dominion and destroy the survivor of cities!" (Num. 24:15–19). Referring to this prophecy, D. Stuart Briscoe affirms, "Though there is disagreement on details there has been agreement for centuries that this is a prediction of the arrival of the Messiah."[28]

Is it not stunning that a pagan diviner of a foreign land is prevented from cursing God's people, then transforms into a prophet for the true God to confirm that the Messiah will come from the tribe of Jacob? I think you'd have to be willfully blind not to see this as a messianic prophecy. But to add some heft to my conclusion, let me share Old Testament scholar Eugene Merrill's observation: "The truth Balaam saw concerned primarily a star and a scepter that would originate in Israel in the future. Since poetically the star is parallel to the scepter [see our discussion on parallelism in Chapter 13], the star must also refer to royalty. This has now been strikingly confirmed in the prophetic texts from Mari (an ancient, influential city-state situated on the bank of the Euphrates in eastern Syria), which describe various kings by the epithet 'star.' The connection of this prophecy to that of Jacob, in which he predicted that a ruler over Israel would come from Judah (Gen. 49:10), is unmistakable."[29]

Jesus Christ, Who in His humanity is a descendant of David, will ultimately fulfill the Davidic Covenant by sitting on the throne during

His one-thousand-year reign and then for eternity.[30] As the angel Gabriel tells Mary, "And behold, you will conceive in your womb and bear a son, and you shall call his name Jesus. He will be great and will be called the Son of the Most High. And the Lord God will give to him the throne of his father David and he will reign over the house of Jacob forever, and of his kingdom there will be no end" (Luke 1:31–33). Jesus Himself confirms that "when the Son of Man comes in his glory, and all the angels with him, then he will sit on his glorious throne" (Matt. 25:31).

As an interesting, faith-building sidebar, I'd like to point out that Old Testament critics sometimes seek to diminish the uniqueness of God's sovereignty by alleging that the Mesopotamians and Babylonians also viewed their gods as proactively involved in the history of their people through their appointed rulers. But Carl F. H. Henry argues that these comparisons are superficial at best. The God of the Bible creates the universe and mankind out of nothing by His Word, and He "ongoingly preserves life, intervenes in nature and history for redemptive ends, and sustains and protects the nation for a preannounced purpose. The Hebrews do not impose upon their wars the polytheistic speculations concerning a struggle between the gods." It's not just that the God of the Bible is superior in every way to these unsophisticated "deities" described in Babylonian and similar writings, but the Bible presents prophecy and its fulfillment as a distinctive feature throughout the Old Testament. "Yahweh's special relation to the Hebrew people through the [Mosaic] covenant, reaffirmed in the Davidic covenant, goes beyond any conception of divine covenant found outside Israel," says Henry. "Among Yahweh's incomparable activities is that he speaks before he acts and then vindicates in history his unique position and relation to his chosen people (cf. Deut. 33:29; 1 Samuel 2:2; Psalms 19:7; Isaiah 46:9)."[31]

THE NEW COVENANT

Explicitly identifying His body and blood as the New Covenant promised by the Old Testament prophets, Jesus proclaims, "This cup that is poured out for you is the new covenant in my blood" (Luke 22:20; 1 Cor. 11:25). Thus, God's series of progressive covenants is capped off by His New Covenant, which He first announces through the prophet Jeremiah:

> Behold, the days are coming, declares the LORD, when I will make a new covenant with the house of Israel and the house of Judah, not like the covenant that I made with their fathers on the day when I took them by the hand to bring them out of the land of Egypt, my covenant that they broke, though I was their husband, declares the LORD. For this is the covenant that I will make with the house of Israel after those days, declares the LORD: I will put my law within them, and I will write it on their hearts. And I will be their God, and they shall be my people. And no longer shall each one teach his neighbor and each his brother, saying, "Know the LORD," for they shall all know me, from the least of them to the greatest, declares the LORD. For I will forgive their iniquity, and I will remember their sin no more.... Behold, the days are coming, declares the Lord, when the city shall be rebuilt for the Lord...It shall not be plucked up or overthrown anymore forever (Jer. 31:31–34, 38, 40; see also 50:4–5).

It was this profound Old Testament passage that motivated Church Father Origen to designate the last twenty-seven books of the Bible "the New Testament."[32] Jeremiah 31:31–34 is also the longest section of continuous text quoted in the New Testament—in Hebrews 8:8–12 and partially repeated in Hebrews 10:16–17.[33]

God likewise promises and further expands upon the New Covenant through the prophet Ezekiel. God tells Israel that to vindicate the holiness of His great name, which Israel and the other nations have profaned, He will gather the Israelites from the other nations to which they had been dispersed and bring them back to their own land: "I will sprinkle clean water on you, and you shall be clean from all your uncleannesses, and from all your idols. I will cleanse you. And I will give you a new heart, and a new spirit I will put within you. And I will remove the heart of stone from your flesh and give you a heart of flesh. And I will put my Spirit within you, and cause you to walk in my statutes and be careful to obey my rules. You shall dwell in the land that I gave to your fathers, and you shall be my people, and I will be your God" (Ezek. 36:25–28).

Isaiah also refers to this covenant: "'And a Redeemer will come to Zion, to those in Jacob who turn from transgression,' declares the Lord. 'And as for me, this is my covenant with them,' says the Lord: 'My Spirit that is upon you, and my words that I have put in your mouth, shall not depart out of your mouth, or out of the mouth of your offspring, or out of the mouth of your children's offspring,' says the Lord, 'from this time forth and forevermore'" (Isaiah 59:20–21).

As laid out by Jeremiah, Ezekiel, and the New Testament writers, the New Covenant is to be different from the Old or Mosaic Covenant, which the Israelites broke. The main provisions of the New Covenant are:

1. Regeneration: the people will be given new hearts and God's Law will be internalized in their minds and hearts.
2. National restoration: God will be their God, the nation of Israel will be His people, and the nation of Israel will have an endless existence.
3. A comprehensive knowledge of and personal relationship with God through the personal ministry of the indwelling Holy Spirit: they will all be taught personally and individually by God Himself.
4. Full justification and forgiveness: their sins will be wholly removed.
5. Jerusalem will be rebuilt and shall remain intact forever.[34]

God specifies that this covenant is unconditional in spite of Israel's disobedience. (Note how He repeats the promise "I will" as He spells out the covenant's stipulations in Ezekiel 36:23–36.)[35] The covenant is unconditional because it is being instituted not for Israel's sake, but for the sake of God's holy name (Ezek. 36:21–22). Furthermore, God declares the covenant to be everlasting (Jer. 32:40; Ezek. 16:60, 37:26; Isaiah 61:8–9).[36]

Dr. Norman Geisler succinctly captures the differences between the Old Covenant and the New. The Old Covenant, he explains, is temporal while the New is everlasting; the Old is written in stones, the New on hearts; the Old involves the blood of animals, the New involves the blood of Christ; the Old entails many sacrifices, the New involves one permanent sacrifice; the Old is mediated by Moses, the New by Jesus Christ; the Old anticipates forgiveness, in the New forgiveness is realized through the cross; in the Old there is no permanent indwelling of the Holy Spirit, as is guaranteed for believers in the New; in the Old God is approached through Aaron the high priest and his successors, in the New Christ is our High Priest; and the Old Covenant is celebrated by sacrifices that anticipate the cross while the New Covenant is celebrated by Communion—looking backward to the cross.[37]

In his announcement of the New Covenant, Jeremiah promises that one day God will replace the Old Covenant—the Mosaic Covenant—with a better one. The writer of Hebrews avers, "But as it is, Christ has obtained a ministry that is as much more excellent than the old as the covenant he mediates is better, since it is enacted on better promises.... In speaking of a new covenant, he makes the first one obsolete" (8:6, 13). The New Covenant is superior, among other reasons, because it cannot be broken and because it brings immediate access to God's presence for believers in Jesus Christ, as the writer of Hebrews attests. Another priest has arisen, he says, "who has become a priest, not on the basis of a legal requirement concerning bodily descent, but by the power of an indestructible life.... For on the one hand, a former commandment is set aside because of its weakness and uselessness (for the law made nothing perfect); but on the other hand, a better hope is introduced, through which we draw near to God.... For those who formerly became priests were made such without an oath, but this one was made a priest with an oath by the one who said to him: 'The Lord has sworn and will not change his mind, "You are a priest forever."' This makes Jesus the guarantor of a better covenant" (7:16–22). The writer also encourages believers to approach God with confidence: "Let us then with confidence draw near to the throne of grace, that we may receive mercy and find grace to help in time of need" (4:16). He later relates that this New Covenant is also superior to the Old because it is established by the blood that Christ shed for us once for all times (7:27).

The Mosaic Covenant gives people rules showing what they ought to do but provides no means by which they, as fallen human beings, can wholly obey those rules. The New Covenant is different, explains Roy Zuck, though "the difference would not lie in the basic demand of the covenant itself but in the people's capacity to obey it."[38] Christians are empowered to obey its commands because Christ has given believers the Holy Spirit (Acts 1:8; 1 Cor. 12:13; 2 Cor. 3:4–18). He has put His Law into our minds and written the Law on our hearts (Heb. 8:10). Moreover, the New Covenant is eternal (Heb. 13:20), and through it we may have a permanent personal relationship and fellowship with God—and "He shall be our God, and we shall be His people."[39] The New Covenant, as God promised, guarantees believers that they will experience a change of heart based on the new spirit within them (the indwelling of the Holy Spirit). This change of heart will reach perfection for believers when they meet Jesus in the afterlife, when they will be glorified and freed from the presence of sin (Romans 8:18–30).[40]

Finally, the spiritual blessings of the New Covenant are far superior to all preceding covenants because Jesus died and atoned for our sins (Heb. 9:24–28). He reveals God to us through Himself "as the radiance of the glory of God and the exact imprint of His nature" (Heb. 1:3; John 14:9). The New Covenant involves the finished work of Christ on the cross in order that believers may, through faith in Him, appropriate His work and be legally declared righteous so that when God looks on believers, He doesn't see our wretched sinfulness. As Charles H. Spurgeon argues, "If the Holy One of Israel shall look upon us as we are He must be displeased; but when He sees us in Christ Jesus He is well pleased.... When the Lord looks this way we hide behind the veil, and the eyes of the Lord behold the exceeding glories of the veil, to wit the person of His own dear Son, and He is so pleased with the cover that he forebears to remember the defilement and deformity of those whom it covers. God will never strike a soul through the veil of His Son's sacrifice. He accepts us because He cannot but accept His Son, who has become our covering."[41] Through faith in Jesus Christ, we experience the New Covenant promise that our sins will be completely forgiven and we will receive eternal life in the Son.

While the New Covenant is better than the Old, let's not assume that is because our perfect and holy God didn't get it right the first time. The trouble with the Mosaic Covenant, says Dr. Walter Kaiser, was not the fault "of the covenant-making God nor with the moral law or promises reaffirmed from the patriarchs and included in that old covenant." No, "the problem was with the *people*."[42] It's important, argues Kaiser, that we don't make the Law the scapegoat for our problem with sin because "the law itself is 'holy,' 'righteous,' 'good,' and 'spiritual' (Romans 7:7; 12:14)."[43] Wayne Strickland, likewise, observes that the Mosaic Law "is a reflection of the moral perfection of its Giver."[44] As the psalmist affirms, "The law of the Lord is perfect, reviving the soul" (Psalms 19:7)—and as Robert Mounce reminds us, "Since the law is God's law, it must of necessity be consistent with his holy nature (Isaiah 6:3)."[45]

Kaiser notes that both Jeremiah and the writer of Hebrews agree that the fault is with the people and not the Law. Jeremiah "points the finger," says Kaiser, when he says, "they broke my covenant, though I was a husband to them." The writer of Hebrews adds, "For he finds fault with them when he says: 'Behold, the days are coming, declares the Lord, when I will establish a new covenant with the house of Israel and the house of Judah...for they did not continue in my covenant" (Hebrews 8:8–9).[46]

If there is a virtual consensus that the Law itself is holy, good, and even perfect, why couldn't it suffice to bring an end to man's sin? Paul explains that it is simply impossible for the Law to do so: "If a law had been given that could give life, then righteousness would indeed be by the law" (Gal. 3:21). Paul is saying that no law can give life; that's not its purpose. The Law sets the standard but, as discussed above, it doesn't animate fallen human beings to obey it. The New Covenant, however, changes our hearts and empowers us to live more righteously.

In the above passage, note that Paul homes in on the idea of "life" in connection with the infusion of righteousness. This says it all, doesn't it? Isn't Paul giving us here a thumbnail sketch of the Gospel? Life doesn't come through a thing, but through a Person, Jesus Christ, Who *is* capable of obeying the Law and did so, in order that through His sinless life and sacrificial, substitutionary death, those with faith in Him could have life and have it abundantly. So let's not blame the Law for our own depravity. The Mosaic Law, writes Rev. H. D. Spence, "had a perfectness of its own. If there had been a Law fitted to give life...it would have been the Mosaic Law. It was raised above all mere human law.... That it did not actually effect righteousness was simply because that was impossible."[47]

We must think of the New Covenant as the consummation of its predecessor covenants and thus the capstone of salvation history. O. Palmer Robertson validates this point: "Because of its unique role in gathering together the various strands of covenantal promise throughout history, this last of God's covenants appropriately may be designated as the covenant of consummation. This covenant supersedes God's previous covenantal administration."[48] Unarguably the New Covenant completely fulfills the Old, as is conveyed in Dr. Geisler's contrasts of the two, related above. Consider also this statement by the writer of Hebrews: "For if the blood of goats and bulls, and the sprinkling of defiled persons with the ashes of a heifer, sanctify for the purification of the flesh, how much more will the blood of Christ, who through the eternal Spirit offered himself without blemish to God, purify our conscience from the dead works to serve the living God. Therefore he is the mediator of a new covenant, so that those who are called may receive the promised eternal inheritance, since a death has occurred that redeems them from the transgressions committed under the first covenant" (9:13–15).

The New Covenant fulfills the other covenants of salvation history.[49] It restores and completes the Davidic Covenant because, as noted, Jesus is in the line of David and He will assume, for eternity, kingship over Israel and the heavenly Jerusalem (Heb. 12:22–24). Craig Blaising and Darrell Bock note that "the most well known fact of the New Testament proclamation of Jesus, namely that He is the Christ, is a proclamation that He is the Davidic king, the King of Israel."[50] Jesus fulfills the Adamic Covenant as the new Adam (Romans 5:12–21), Who transforms believers into a new creation (2 Cor. 5:17; Gal. 6:15). Scott Hahn summarizes, "The notion of covenant reaches its zenith in Christ, who fulfills the divine covenants not only in who He is, as the eternal Son of the Father, but by what He accomplishes in causing us to share in the grace of His own divine sonship (1 John 3:1–2). The new covenant of

Christ ends up fulfilling the old covenant in a way that surpasses the greatest hopes of ancient Israelites, even as it will exceed our own expectations (1 Cor. 2:9)."[51]

Additionally, the New Covenant fulfills that component of the Abrahamic Covenant whereby God promised to bless all nations and people through Abraham (Gen. 12:3, 17:4), a promise whose specifics were shrouded in mystery until the New Testament revelation. The matter is clarified in Paul's letter to the Ephesians in which he describes the mystery of the Church, which was not mentioned in the Old Testament: "For this reason I, Paul, a prisoner for Christ Jesus on behalf of you Gentiles— assuming that you have heard of the stewardship of God's grace that was given to me for you, how the mystery was made known to me by revelation, as I have written briefly. When you read this, you can perceive my insight into the mystery of Christ, which was not made known to the sons of men in other generations as it has now been revealed to his holy apostles and prophets by the Spirit. This mystery is that the Gentiles are fellow heirs, members of the same body, and partakers of the promise in Christ Jesus through the gospel" (Eph. 3:1–6).

Like the previous covenants, God makes this New Covenant with Israel. In fulfillment of the Abrahamic Covenant, however, some promises of the New Covenant—the ones involving spiritual blessings, mainly forgiveness of their sins (and thus their redemption)—apply to all believers in Jesus Christ.[52] We are all recipients of God's blessings promised to Abraham—for Jesus Christ, who descended from Abraham, died for our sins and brings the blessing of eternal life for all those with faith in Him.

Old Testament scholar Walter Kaiser comments that the New Covenant indeed fulfills the spiritual promises made to Abraham's seed for Gentiles as well as Jews.[53] As Paul explains, the Gentiles were at one time "separated from Christ, alienated from the commonwealth of Israel and strangers to the covenants of promise, having no hope and without God in the world. But now in Christ Jesus you who once were far off have been brought near by the blood of Christ.... For through him we both have access in one Spirit to the Father. So then you are no longer strangers and aliens, but you are fellow citizens with the saints and members of the household of God" (Eph. 2:12–13, 18–19). In his letter to the

Galatians, Paul expands on the point, making it quite clear that all believers, including Gentiles, are Abraham's offspring for purposes of the covenant promises: "For in Christ Jesus you are all sons of God, through faith. For as many of you as were baptized into Christ have put on Christ. There is neither Jew nor Greek, there is neither slave nor free, there is no male and female, for you are all one in Christ Jesus. And if you are Christ's then you are Abraham's offspring, heirs according to promise" (Gal. 3:26–29).

As is true for all the covenants beginning with the Abrahamic, God establishes the New Covenant with Israel, thus guaranteeing the permanency of the nation and of the city of Jerusalem. But I want to acknowledge there are at least two schools of thought on whether the covenant still applies to Israel. Roughly summarizing, Dispensationalists believe the covenant still applies to Israel (some even argue there are two separate new covenants)[54] but that some of its blessings also apply to all believers, i.e., to the New Testament Christian Church. That is, though the initial promises and blessings were made specifically to the Jews and not the Gentiles, the Gentiles are nevertheless the beneficiaries of some of those blessings—namely the spiritual blessings, especially the promise of salvation. Covenant theologians, on the other hand, argue that Israel forfeited its blessings under the covenant through its rebellion and unbelief,[55] and that the Church now stands in its place as the spiritual Israel.[56]

This issue is too complex to explore in depth here, but I do want to make a few important points. I believe the New Covenant was made with Israel and continues to apply to Israel. Let us never forget that God loves Israel, which is "precious" and "honored" in His eyes (Isaiah 43:4). In addition, when God articulates these promises through Ezekiel, He is quite explicit that He will fulfill the promises for the Israelites (Ezek. 36:16–20). Furthermore, while some of the covenant's promises are spiritual in nature (e.g., the provision of a new heart and the indwelling of the Holy Spirit) and apply to Gentiles and Jews alike, other promises are material and specific to the nation of Israel.[57]

As Renald Showers observes, these promises are not being fulfilled in connection to the Church. For example, one of the promises is that the future nation will no longer be threatened by other nations. Obviously, the Church has been persecuted throughout history and continues to be to this day. As such, it is clear that those promises have not yet been fulfilled, but will be in the future with the nation of Israel. Paul adds heft to this idea, explaining that the New Covenant promises would be fulfilled for Israel at Christ's second coming (Romans 11:25–29). Take special note how Paul says that God will not change His mind on this: "For the gifts and calling of God are irrevocable" (Romans 11:29). The teachings of the Old Testament are wholly consistent with this notion (Isaiah 59:20–21; Jer. 32:37–44, 50:4–5; Ezek. 36:22–38, 37:21–28).[58]

In addition, I am convinced that Christian believers, including Jewish converts to Christianity, are also beneficiaries of God's promises of spiritual blessings, initially through the Abrahamic Covenant, even though the Old Testament is silent regarding the relationship between the Church and the New Covenant.[59] Note that when Jesus institutes the service of Communion He declares, "This cup is the new covenant in my blood" (Luke 22:20). Paul quotes Jesus on this point, thereby confirming that the Church is under the New Covenant umbrella.[60] Taken in context, Jesus is saying that the New Covenant promised to Israel by the Old Testament prophets also applies to the Church, and it would be commemorated by the Communion service. He speaks of *the* New Covenant, as if there were only one such covenant, and that makes sense because God, through His Old Testament prophets, only promised one New Covenant. At the time He makes the statement, Jesus is surrounded by Jewish men who would understand Him to be referring to that one and only New Covenant.[61]

Renald Showers offers another reason to conclude that the same New Covenant applies to the Church, which is that the New Testament applies the very same spiritual blessings to believers who make up the Church. Believers are spiritually regenerated (Titus 3:5), and they receive forgiveness of their sins (Eph. 1:7, 4:32; Col. 1:14; John 2:12), receive an indwelling of the Holy Spirit (1 Cor. 6:19), and receive a new nature because the Law is written on their hearts (Rom. 7:22; 2 Cor. 3:3; 2 Peter 1:4).[62] One last and compelling reason to believe the New Covenant blessings apply to the Church is that Paul states that the apostles of the Church are "ministers of a new covenant" (2 Cor. 3:6).[63]

Since many—probably most—Covenant theologians believe the Church has become the spiritual Israel and replaced literal Israel as the beneficiary of the New Covenant, it follows that they believe there never will be a fulfillment of the New Covenant for literal Israel. But Dispensationalists see no conflict between the New Covenant applying to the Church now, and the notion that the fulfillment of its promises for Israel will occur in the future. "The Abrahamic Covenant's promise that all nations would be blessed through its provisions (Gen. 12:3) does not in any way annul the other provisions (e.g., the land promise) to Abraham and his physical descendants," claims Dr. Norman Geisler. "Jesus inaugurated a spiritual (mystery) form of the kingdom in Matthew 13; there is still a political messianic form to come."[64] When it's all said and done, this is the crux of the disagreement between Dispensationalists and Covenant theologians on the New Covenant—the former believe its promises are still applicable to Israel and the latter do not.[65]

In summary, most conservative theologians, including both Dispensationalists and Covenant theologians, believe that many of the promises of the New Covenant apply to the Church, whether or not those promises are a result of the Church becoming a "spiritual Israel" (Covenant view), or a result of a separate new covenant (some Dispensationalists), or of the Church being grafted into the blessings of the New Covenant (most Dispensationalists). Concerning this "grafting in," Paul warns the Gentiles not to be arrogant about the unbelief of the Jews: "But if some of the branches were broken off, and you, although a wild olive shoot, were grafted in among the others and now share in the nourishing of the olive tree, do not be arrogant toward the branches. If you are, remember it is not you who support the root, but the root that supports you" (Romans 11:17–18).

All camps also seem to agree that the New Covenant has not been fulfilled by Israel, though they disagree over whether it ever will. Generally speaking, Dispensationalists believe it will and Covenant theologians believe it will not.

If you want to clear your head of all the confusion, don't worry about Dispensationalist or Covenant theology—let the theologians debate that among themselves. Just understand that almost all Bible-believers agree that the spiritual promises contained in the New Covenant (as opposed to the material and national ones that by their terms could only apply to Israel) apply to the Church—to believers in Jesus

Christ—whether or not they think there is a separate new covenant applying to them. And how could we believe otherwise, as the spiritual promises are nothing less than the Gospel itself: forgiveness of sins, spiritual regeneration, and indwelling of the Holy Spirit for all who place their saving faith in Jesus Christ? Thus we see the exquisite unity of the Bible from the beginning of the Old Testament through the end of the New in the outworking of God's promise-plan through His progressive covenant promises in His salvation history. The Bible, from first to last, is about our Savior, Jesus Christ!

God's covenants constitute a progressive thread running through the Bible and through God's salvation history that leads to and achieves finality in Jesus Christ. "The heart of this consummative realization consists of a single person," says O. Palmer Robertson. "As fulfiller of all the messianic promises, he achieves in himself the essence of the covenantal principle: 'I shall be your God and you shall be my people.' He therefore may be seen as the Christ who consummates the covenant."[66] Note that this echoes my earlier argument that the primary element underlying all the covenants—a golden thread that God has woven into His Word from beginning to end—is God's promise, "I will be their God and they shall be my people."

Robertson continues, "In this single person all of God's purposes find climactic fulfillment. He is the head of God's kingdom and the embodiment of God's covenant.... Because the various strands of hope for redemption converge on this single person, he becomes the unifying focus of all Scripture.... In the person of Jesus Christ, the covenants of God achieve incarnational unity.... He himself guarantees the unity of the covenants, because he himself is the. heart of each of the various covenantal administrations."[67]

Now that we have a good grasp of the relationship between the various biblical covenants and Jesus Christ, in the next chapter we'll take a look at some of the other signs of Jesus—some big, some small—that fill the pages of the Old Testament.

CHAPTER 7

ALL ROADS LEAD TO CHRIST
PORTRAITS, OFFICES, CREATION, AND SALVATION

The prophets searched. Angels longed to see. And the disciples didn't understand. But Moses, the Prophets, and all the Old Testament Scriptures had spoken about it—that Jesus would come, suffer, and then be glorified. God began to tell a story in the Old Testament, the ending of which the audience eagerly anticipated. But the Old Testament audience was left hanging. The plot was laid out, but the climax was delayed. The unfinished story begged for an ending. In Christ, God has provided the climax to the Old Testament story.

—IAIN DUGUID AND MATTHEW HARMON[1]

GOSPEL PORTRAITS

A
s the overarching theme of the Bible and its history revolve around God's redemptive plan for mankind, it stands to reason that Jesus Christ, the only One through Whom we can attain salvation, is the focal point of Scripture. "It follows that if the purpose

of Scripture is to guide men to the Lord and if the only way to the Lord is through the redemption of the Lord Jesus Christ," contends Old Testament Professor Michael Barrett, "then the revelation of Christ should be the grand and predominant theme of the Scripture. Indeed it is. All revealed truth in one way or another relates to and is ultimately defined by the central truth of the Messiah, the Christ, the anointed."[2]

As the New Testament writers taught, Christ is the key that unlocks all the mysteries of the Old Testament.[3] It is neither speculation nor hyperbole to say that all Scripture centers on the *Person* of Jesus Christ. Christians are certainly instructed to learn *about* God and glean everything we can from His revealed Word to better understand His nature, but ultimately we must get to *know* God through Jesus Christ. Paul captures the essence of it when he writes to the Corinthian Church, "And I, when I came to you, brothers, did not come proclaiming to you the testimony of God with lofty speech or wisdom. For I decided to know nothing among you except Jesus Christ and him crucified" (1 Cor. 2:2).

Now that we've examined God's promise-plan of redemption and the major covenants by which He implemented that plan, we will turn to some of the other evidence of Christ in the Old Testament, first looking at what Pastor Kurt Strassner refers to as "gospel portraits" of Jesus. In his book *Hints and Signs of the Coming King: Pictures of Jesus in the Old Testament*, Strassner notes that in the Bible, particularly in the Old Testament, God sometimes paints word pictures—metaphoric ways of describing spiritual concepts—because He knows this sort of visualization can enhance our understanding. One example we've noted is John 1:29: "Behold, the Lamb of God who takes away the sin of the world." Jesus' parables showcase other examples, such as "the kingdom of heaven is like a mustard seed" (Matt. 13:31).

In addition, Strassner posits, it's not just in the Bible's teaching that we see metaphors, but in biblical events, too. Sometimes God "has worked out biblical history to *show* us (as in the Passover Lamb of Exodus 12)."[4] I am quite receptive to that idea. As I remarked earlier, I believe that God, in addition to His other methods of instructing us in Scripture, teaches us through events He sovereignly orchestrates in history and reveals to us in Scripture.

Strassner cites eight examples of gospel portraits. I'd like to summarize a few of them to illustrate how God uses these Old Testament events to point to Christ and His saving work on our behalf. I won't dig deep into these but would encourage you, if you are interested, to read Strassner's book to get a more complete picture.

The first portrait is of Noah's ark, "aboard which we may climb, escaping the flood waters of God's judgment." The flood was God's ordained judgment on mankind due to his sinfulness. This event truly happened in history and, as Strassner points out, will happen again, though next time God's judgment will be administered by fire instead of water (2 Peter 3:5–7). But just as God provided an escape for the righteous (Noah and his family), He has provided a way for all who believe in Him to be saved from present and future judgments on sin. Like the ark, says Strassner, faith in Jesus is the one and only remedy that will hold up on the Day of Judgment.

Here are some other Strassner gospel portraits:

- *The passionate love* King Solomon has for his wife, a simple village girl (Song 1–8), which reflects Christ's infinite love for mankind.
- *A ram* (Gen. 22) that God allows Abraham to use instead of his son Isaac as a sacrifice, which points to Christ laying down His life for our sins.
- *A bronze serpent* (Num. 21), which God instructs Moses to make and set on a pole so that each person who was bitten by actual fiery serpents, "when he sees it, shall live," and which points to Christ's work on the cross.

We will examine some of these foreshadowings of Christ in detail when we discuss how events in each Old Testament book point to Christ. For now, I just wanted to share Pastor Strassner's helpful insight that God uses word pictures in actual historical events as one of many ways He demonstrates the centrality of Christ to the Old Testament and to all of Scripture.

THE DOCTRINE OF THE LAMB AND
PROGRESSIVE REVELATION

One of my favorite Christian writers is Australian pastor and theologian J. Sidlow Baxter. I first came across his work more than twenty years ago when I bought his classic *Explore the Book*, a 1,760-page tome that examines every book of the Bible. I was particularly impressed with Baxter's illuminating insights at a time when, as a fairly unknowledgeable Christian, I was seeking to accelerate my learning curve on the Bible and Christianity. I have discovered that Baxter's writing is not just accessible for the beginning Christian, but also enlightening for those who have more than a few hours of study under their belts.

Some people have a unique gift for grasping biblical truths and communicating them, and Baxter is among the best. That's why I was pleased when, doing my research for this book, I came across another work of his that seemed relevant to my inquiry, *The Master Theme of the Bible*.[5] In this book, Baxter looks at two Christ-centered threads running through the Bible that demonstrate its God-inspired unity: the Lamb of God and the Cross of Christ. I want to briefly address the first of these because I find Baxter's discussion to be fascinating and unique.

In his introduction to the topic, Baxter writes, "To my mind, the most satisfying proofs that the Bible is divinely inspired are not those which one 'reads up' in volumes of religious evidences or Christian apologetics, but those which we discover for ourselves in our own study of the Book. To the prayerful explorer the Bible has its own way of revealing its internal credentials." In *Jesus on Trial* I made a similar observation: "Indeed, for me, theology and the Bible are the best apologetic of all. As I've said throughout this book, I find Christ's teachings, the letters of the New Testament writers, and the history and teachings in the remainder of the Bible intellectually, emotionally, and spiritually attractive, and probative of the truth of Christianity."[6]

In introducing his thesis on the Lamb, Baxter discusses progressive revelation, which I touched on earlier. Generally, this is the idea that God reveals in Scripture His message and plan for humanity in stages. This is one of the things Bible teachers mean when they say God sometimes presents shadows and types of truths in the Old Testament that become much clearer as God's revelation progresses through Old Testament Scripture into the New Testament. As R. C. Sproul puts it, "The revelation within Scripture unfolds in an ever-deepening and broadening way."[7] Remarkably, not only does God reveal His truths progressively through the Bible, He actually revealed these truths progressively in history. So the Bible, in recording and conveying that history, reflects its progressive nature.

My favorite quote explaining progressive revelation is by Sidney Greidanus. In his book *Preaching Christ from Ecclesiastes*, he relates that when one of his colleagues saw the title of his manuscript he accused him, lightheartedly, of "trying to find Christ under every rock." Greidanus later explained, "It's not a matter of trying to find Christ under every rock but it's a matter of connecting the dots—the dots that run from the periphery of the Old Testament to the center of God's revelation in Jesus Christ. Redemptive-historical progression is the basic, foundational way of connecting the dots. Because redemptive history progresses from its earliest beginnings after the Fall into sin (Gen. 3:15), through God's dealings with Israel, to the incarnation of Christ, his life, death, resurrection, and ascension, and finally to his Second Coming, Christian preachers must understand an Old Testament passage in the light of redemptive history."[8]

Baxter refers to progressive revelation as the "progress of doctrine." He is quick to point out that the progressive nature of revelation doesn't mean God's truth ever changed or was improved upon; only that He revealed it to us more clearly as He went along. When we speak of this, says Baxter, "we do not mean…a groping progress from error to truth…. We mean…progress from the dimness of dawn to the brightness of the noon. It is the same divine light which shines through all the pages, but the degree of the light increases as the revelation unfolds."[9] He observes that teachings that first appear in Scripture are often repeated in subsequent pages, their meaning and significance developing with each additional reference until they reach their full fruition in the New Testament, "in which there is either a classic summary or a completive culmination."

When these subjects are first mentioned, they don't necessarily seem to be incomplete or require further development, nor do the Old Testament writers seem to have any awareness that the revelation entrusted to them for transmission to us is, in any way, unfinished or part of a progressive unfolding. This fact, notes, Baxter, "only makes such progress of doctrine the more obviously supernatural and fascinating."[10] Chew on that for a moment and you'll see what he means. The biblical writers are relating their stories and prophecies in ways that make sense to them, perhaps having no idea that years, centuries, or even a millennium later, another biblical author will expound on the earlier revealed doctrine in a way that elucidates it—without nullifying it—for current readers and for posterity.

Baxter then explains the Bible doctrine of the Lamb as an outstanding example of progressive revelation, the highlights of which I will share with you because this is the very type of thing Jesus might have explained on the road to Emmaus.

There are ten passages in the Bible in which the Lamb is conspicuously mentioned, writes Baxter. The first is Genesis 4:3–7, which relates the story of Cain offering God "the fruit of the ground" while Abel offers Him the firstborn of his flock and their fat portions. Cain's offering is beautiful but bloodless, so God rejects it while accepting Abel's. Among other things, notes Baxter, this shows the *necessity* of the Lamb.

The next passage is Genesis 22, where Abraham, after God releases him from the command to sacrifice Isaac, immediately sees a ram in the thicket that he can offer instead. Here the emphasis shifts from the necessity of the lamb to God's *provision* of it. (Through Jesus Christ, God *provided* the Ultimate Sacrifice for us.)

Next is Exodus 12, where God instructs all His people to slay a lamb without blemish and put some of its blood outside the doors of their houses. When God passes through the land of Egypt to strike all the firstborn, He passes over those houses that show the blood. The stress here is on the *slaying* of the lamb because the lamb, no matter how perfect, would be of no sacrificial use unless it was slayed and its protective blood administered to the house.

Baxter then takes us to Leviticus which, as we indicated earlier, is a worship manual of sorts that contains instructions on administering sacrifices, the feasts, and other things. Throughout the book, he says, the focus is on the *character* of the lamb, noting that it is stated some twenty times that the offerings must be "without blemish." The Hebrews are not permitted to offer flawed animals, as that would not be a true sacrifice: "To be accepted it must be perfect; there shall be no blemish in it" (Lev. 22:21).

Isaiah 53 is one of the most famous messianic prophecies (prophecies pointing to Christ) in the Bible. This short section from that chapter makes the point: "All we like sheep have gone astray; we have turned—every one—to his own way; and the Lord has laid on him the iniquity of us all. He was oppressed, and he was afflicted, yet he opened not his mouth; like a lamb that is led to the slaughter, and like a sheep that before its shearers is silent, so he opened not his mouth. By oppression and judgment he was taken away; and as for his generation, who considered that he was cut off out of the land of the living, stricken for the transgression of my people?" (53:6–8). This rendering of the Lamb shows a monumental progression, for in the previous examples "Lamb" always signified an animal, but now we learn that the Lamb that God provides is a *person*.

Moving on to the New Testament, Baxter starts with John 1:29, where John the Baptist, recognizing Jesus coming toward him, declares, "Behold the Lamb of God, who takes away the sin of the world!" Here, argues Baxter, we see that the Lamb is not just any person, but he is *that* person: Jesus Christ. The next day, John sees Jesus again and exclaims, "Behold the Lamb of God!" (John 1:35). So now we know, says Baxter, "*who* is the typified Lamb."

Now on to the Book of Acts—the history of the early Christian Church—to the scene where the evangelist Philip gets instruction from an Angel of the Lord to help an Ethiopian eunuch, who is an official of Queen Candace, understand parts of chapter 53 of Isaiah. The eunuch reads verses 7 and 8: "Like a sheep he was led to slaughter and like a lamb before its shearer is silent, so he opens not his mouth. In his humiliation justice was denied him. Who can describe his generation? For his life is taken away from the earth?" When the eunuch asks who is being described here, "Philip opened his mouth, and beginning with this Scripture he told him the good news about Jesus" (Acts 8:35).

Now we can see, notes Baxter, that Jesus the Lamb is the promised *Christ*.

Next, moving into the epistles, specifically 1 Peter, we read this passage: "Knowing that you were ransomed from the futile ways inherited from your forefathers, not with perishable things such as silver or gold, but with the precious blood of Christ, like that of a lamb without blemish or spot. He was foreknown before the foundation of the world but was made manifest in the last times for the sake of you who through him are believers in God, who raised him from the dead and gave him glory, so that your faith and hope are in God" (1:18–21). Baxter says this is a pivotal passage in the progressive doctrine of the Lamb, which looks both backward and forward.

What he means is that Peter summarizes the different aspects of the Lamb that had been previously revealed in Scripture and then "adds a startling new truth which points us on to wonderful consummations in the future." Peter reaffirms the *necessity* of the lamb ("not with perishable things"), the *provision* ("He was foreknown before the foundation of the world"), the *slaying* ("the precious blood of Christ"), the *character* ("without blemish or spot"), and that He is a *person*, specifically *Christ* (whom Peter explicitly identifies in this passage). Here we see a summary of progressive and cumulative revelation at its finest, as a foundation to the next revelation, the *resurrection* of the slain Lamb ("God...raised him from the dead and gave him glory"). This was a new revelation, for while there were hints at the resurrection in the Old Testament, it was nowhere clearly revealed. Baxter says that with the concept of the *resurrection* Peter also introduced the accompanying feature of *hope* ("God raised him...so that your faith and hope are in God"). "So," asks Baxter, "what is this new hope?" The answer, he says, is in the next revelation.

That is in Revelation 5, where we see the *enthronement* of the Lamb in heaven: "And between the throne and the four living creatures and among the elders I saw a Lamb standing, as though it had been slain, with seven horns and with seven eyes, which are the seven spirits of God sent out into all the earth. And he went and took the scroll from the right hand of him who was seated on the throne. And when he had taken the scroll, the four living creatures and the twenty-four elders fell down before the Lamb, each holding a harp, and golden bowls full of incense, which are the prayers of the saints" (5:6–8). The Lamb now sits on the throne of heaven—the throne of the entire universe, the significance of which is revealed in the final revelation in this series.

Revelation 21–22, the last two chapters of the New Testament, reveal the climax of biblical salvation history: "No longer will there be anything accursed, but the throne of God and of the Lamb will be in it, and his servants will worship him. They will see his face, and his name will be on their foreheads. And night will be no more. They will need no light of lamp or sun, for the Lord God will be their light, and they will reign forever and ever" (22:3–5).

Though Baxter doesn't reprint the following passage, I think it adds immeasurably to his point. Going back to the beginning of chapter 21, John relates his vision of a new heaven and a new earth, "for the first heaven and the first earth had passed away, and the sea was no more. And I saw the holy city, new Jerusalem, coming down out of heaven from God, prepared as a bride adorned for her husband. And I heard a loud voice from the throne saying, 'Behold, the dwelling place of God is with man. He will dwell with them, and they will be his people, and God himself will be with them as their God. He will wipe away every tear from their eyes, and death shall be no more, neither shall there be mourning, nor crying, nor pain anymore, for the former things have passed away'" (21:1–4). This final revelation, affirms Baxter, demonstrates Christ's everlasting *kingship*.

Do you see how this kingship remarkably corresponds to the promise of the everlasting kingship in the covenants—beginning with the Abrahamic and through the Davidic to the New Covenant? When you put this string of revelations together, you see that even before creation, God knew we would sin and that He'd send His Son Jesus Christ, Who would spill His blood in substitutionary propitiation for our sins, then conquer death through His resurrection and sit on the throne of heaven everlastingly, where He joins saved sinners who will enjoy His presence forever.

Baxter goes on to show the expansive nature of the progressive revelations, but it is beyond my purposes to further explore that. His analysis, which I have attempted to summarize here, amply demonstrates the inspiration of God's Word and the sheer beauty and genius of progressive revelation therein, which reflects God's gracious, redemptive activity in history, from beginning to end, motivated by His incomparable love for us and by His plan to exhibit His glory.

PROPHET, PRIEST, AND KING

God's redemptive work began before Adam sinned—in fact, before he was even created—and has continued throughout history. God, one imagines, could have just zapped mankind into a redemptive state, but in His infinite wisdom, He determined that this would either not get the job done or was vastly inferior to the method He chose. God created man in His image, which necessarily means He gave man free will. God doesn't force people to love Him, and throughout all of history some have rejected Him. Love must be freely given, and simply zapping us into heaven would be inconsistent with our free will.

Additionally, we see in all of salvation history and repeatedly in the Bible's teaching that man learns through his experiences, grows stronger through adversity, and with the proper mindset draws closer to God in the process. Old Testament scholar Iain Duguid comments that God's "redemptive pathways" don't lead us around conflict, hardship, and suffering. "Instead, his perfect plan for our lives often takes us right through the eye of the storm, where our dysfunction and sin, along with that of our families and friends, is on full and tragic display, so that the gospel of his powerful grace and sovereign mercy can be equally power-fully on display."[11] We have already seen in the potter's wheel analogy that throughout history God used this process to mold and refine the nation of Israel, and we learn through its example.

Indeed, while Christ's crowning redemptive acts of His sacrificial death and resurrection are the crux of salvation history, they are not the entire story, and in this book I aim to tell the rest of that story. Professor W. Stanford Reid explains that "a long time of preparation preceded [Christ's death and resurrection], and a period of explanation and inter-pretation" followed them.[12] Christ, says Reid, has been active in history to bring people to faith in Himself, both before and after His culminating redemptive acts.

To fully understand the totality and significance of Christ's redemptive activities in history, it helps to view His work in a systematic manner.[13] One of the ways theologians have facilitated men's understanding of this is to look at Christ's work through the prism of His offices of prophet, priest, and king. These were the three major offices among the Israelites in Old Testament times.

The prophet, beginning with Moses, communicates God's message to the people; the priest, beginning with Aaron (Exodus 29:9), acts as intermediary and offers sacrifices and prayers to God for the people; and the king, best exemplified by David (2 Samuel 5:3), rules over the people.[14] These three offices are distinct, yet sometimes certain people, as we have seen, serve more than one function. Though priests generally mediate between God and His people, prophets (and less frequently, kings) sometimes mediate between God and Israel as well. But priests are different from prophets because priests bring the people into God's presence while prophets bring God and His Word to the people.[15]

The officeholders, being members of the fallen human species, perform their duties imperfectly and incompletely, yet we can see, in retrospect, that each of them is a prefiguring of Jesus Christ[16]—for in the outworking of His redemptive activities, Christ combines in one person all three Old Testament offices, serving as the consummate prophet, priest, and king.[17] "Christ is prophet in that He perfectly reveals God to us," writes Richard D. Phillips. "He is priest in offering himself for our sins, cleansing us, and interceding for us with God. He is our king, reigning now in heaven and ruling over us as our Sovereign Lord."[18]

These comparisons are not latter-day contrivances. Bible interpreters as far back as Church Father Eusebius, bishop of Caesarea (260–340 AD), have regarded Christ's ministry in terms of these three Old Testament offices. This is a logical association because, among other reasons, the Messiah is the Anointed One, and all three Old Testament officeholders are anointed into their positions: the prophets (1 Kings 19:16; Isaiah 61:1), priests (Exodus 30:30, 40:13), and kings (1 Samuel 10:1, 15:1; 1 Kings 19:15–16).[19]

As Eusebius explains, "And we have been told also that certain of the prophets themselves became, by the act of anointing, Christs in type, so that all these have reference to the true Christ, the divinely inspired and heavenly Word, who is the only high priest of all, and the only King of every creature, and the Father's only supreme prophet of prophets. And a proof of this is that no one of those who were of old symbolically anointed, whether priests, or kings, or prophets, possessed so great a power of inspired virtue as was exhibited by our Savior and Lord Jesus, the true and only Christ."[20] Eusebius bases his conclusion, in part, on three Old Testament passages:

1. "I will raise up for them a prophet like you from among their brothers. And I will put my words in his mouth, and he shall speak to them all that I command him" (Deut. 18:18). This passage shows God telling Moses that another prophet like him will later arrive.
2. "The Lord has sworn and will not change his mind, You are a priest forever after the order of Melchizedek" (Psalms 110:4).
3. "It is he who shall build the temple of the LORD and shall bear royal honor, and shall sit and rule on his throne. And there shall be a priest on his throne, and the counsel of peace shall be between them both" (Zec. 6:13).[21]

Now let's look in turn at each of the three offices.

PROPHET

A fuller context of the above passage on Moses is that Moses is telling the people, "The Lord your God will raise up for you a prophet like me from among you, from your brothers—it is to him you shall listen.... And the Lord said to me, '...I will raise up for them a prophet like you from among their brothers. And I will put my words in his mouth, and he shall speak to them all that I command him'" (Deut. 18:15, 18). Based on this promise, the Israelites are waiting on God to raise up a prophet Who will be like Moses but much greater, and will deliver Israel into a new era.[22] Again, the writer of Hebrews affirms the superiority of Jesus to Moses: "For Jesus has been counted worthy of more glory than Moses—as much more glory as the builder of a house has more honor than the house itself.... Now Moses was faithful in all God's house as a servant, to testify to the things that were to be spoken later, but Christ is faithful over God's house as a son" (Heb. 3:3, 5–6).

Unmistakably serving as a prophet during his earthly ministry, Jesus was often recognized as such by His disciples and others. Here are some examples: when Jesus makes His Triumphal Entry into Jerusalem the crowds exclaim, "This is the prophet Jesus, from Nazareth of Galilee" (Matt. 21:11); the chief priests and Pharisees are furious at Him when they hear about His parables, for they figure He is condemning them, but they dare not arrest Him because they fear the people who regard Him as a prophet (Matt. 21:46); when He encounters the woman of Samaria at the well, she perceives Him to be a prophet (John 4:19); when He feeds the five thousand with five loaves of bread and two fish, the people cry out, "This is indeed the Prophet who is to come into the world!" (John 6:14); when He raises a widow's son, the crowd of people exclaim, "A great prophet has arisen among us!" and "God has visited his people!" (Luke 7:16); Jesus is well aware of His calling as a prophet (Luke 4:24, 13:33); and in His prophetic role He explains the significance of the Law (Matt. 5:17–18), continually preaches about the kingdom of God (Matt. 24:14; Mark 1:14–15; Luke 22:18), and, like the Old Testament prophets, foretells the future (Matt. 24:2–31; Luke 19:41–44).[23]

Illustrative of the theme of salvation history culminating in Jesus Christ, we see that Jesus is not just a prophet, but the consummate Prophet. And illustrative of the notion of progressive revelation, the New Testament clearly affirms what the Old Testament only points to, noting Jesus' prophetic superiority precisely because He is the Son of God. He doesn't just speak on God's behalf like other prophets. He *is* God, speaking for the Father and for Himself. "Long ago, at many times and in many ways, God spoke to our fathers by the prophets," declares the writer of Hebrews. "But in these last days he has spoken to us by his Son, whom he appointed the heir of all things, through whom also he created the world. He is the radiance of the glory of God and the exact imprint of his nature, and he upholds the universe by the word of his power" (1:1–3).

PRIEST

Priests served the functions of representing men in their relations with God, and offering gifts and sacrifices for sins (Heb. 5:1). The priestly work of Christ, the perfect priest, includes His activities of atonement and intercession.[24] As we indicated earlier, the priests were incapable of making lasting sacrifices due to their own weaknesses, necessitating that they make sacrifices for their own sins as well (Heb. 5:2–3). Additionally, there was no perfect offering they could make to God that would satisfy His holy requirements for justice, "for it is impossible for the blood of bulls and goats to take away sins" (Heb. 10:4). But Jesus, as completely sinless, is fully capable of offering a perfect sacrifice and permanent atonement because He is the perfect *Offeror* of sacrifices, having no weaknesses Himself, and is also the perfect *Offering*. The Old Testament priests offer animals as sacrifices while Christ offers Himself as the spotless Lamb of God. According to the writer of Hebrews, "Every priest stands daily at his service, offering repeatedly the same sacrifices, which can never take away sins. But when Christ had offered for all time a single sacrifice for sins, he sat down at the right hand of God, waiting from that time until his enemies should be made a footstool for his feet. For by a single offering he has perfected for all time those who are being sanctified" (10:11–14).

Through Christ's offering God's wrath is satisfied, we are forgiven and liberated from sin, and we are restored into intimate fellowship with God.[25] Christ's work of atonement is accompanied by His further work on our behalf, as intercessor. "Consequently, he is able to save to the uttermost those who draw near to God through him, since he always lives to make intercession for them" (Heb. 7:25). This intercession, like His sacrifice, is perfect, active, and ongoing. "For Christ has entered, not into holy places made with hands, which are copies of the true things, but into heaven itself, now to appear in the presence of God on our behalf" (Heb. 9:24). Paul adds, "Who is to condemn? Christ Jesus is the one who died—more than that, who was raised—

who is at the right hand of God, who indeed is interceding for us" (Romans 8:34). The apostle John affirms this truth: "My little children, I am writing these things to you so that you may not sin. But if anyone does sin, we have an advocate with the Father, Jesus Christ the righteous" (1 John 2:1).

The writer of Hebrews explains, "For every high priest chosen from among men is appointed to act on behalf of men in relation to God, to offer gifts and sacrifices for sins.... And no one takes this honor for himself, but only when called by God, just as Aaron was. So also Christ did not exalt himself to be made a high priest, but was appointed by him who said to him, 'You are my Son, today I have begotten you'; as he says also in another place, 'You are a priest forever, after the order of Melchizedek'" (5:1, 4–6). According to Carl F. H. Henry, "Everywhere the New Testament writers affirm a religion that centers in the mediator.... (John's) Gospel unqualifiedly declares Jesus to be 'the way, the truth, and the life' (14:6)."[26]

Jesus is the perfect priest, like no other before Him and vastly superior to Aaron in numerous ways. Aaron doesn't just offer sacrifices for the people's sins, but for his own as well because he, too, is a sinner. Christ, however, is sinless and atones for the people alone; Aaron performs his priestly duties in the manmade and perishable Tabernacle, but Christ appears directly to the Father on our behalf, in heaven (Heb. 9:1, 24); Aaron offers the blood of animals as sacrifice, Christ offers His own blood; and perhaps most important, Aaron's sacrificial work is temporary and has to be repeated, but Christ's is once and for all (Heb. 9:25).[27]

KING

The psalmist tells us that "the Lord swore to David a sure oath from which he will not turn back: One of the sons of your body I will set on your throne" (Psalms 132:11). Similarly, the prophet Nathan says to David, "The Lord declares to you that the Lord will make you a house. When your days are fulfilled and you lie down with your fathers, I will raise up your offspring after you, who shall come from your body, and I will establish his kingdom" (2 Samuel 7:11–12). This promise of an eternal king from David's line is to be fulfilled in Christ, as noted in our discussion of the Davidic Covenant. Paul records the fulfillment of this promise: "Concerning his Son, who was descended from David according to the flesh and was declared to be the Son of God in power according to the Spirit of holiness by his resurrection from the dead, Jesus Christ our Lord" (Romans 1:3). Paul writes again, in 2 Timothy, "Remember Jesus Christ, risen from the dead, the offspring of David" (2:8. See also Matt. 19:28, 25:31; Luke 1:32; Acts 2:30, 13:23; Romans 1:3; 2 Tim. 2:8; Heb. 1:8, 8:1, 12:2, Rev. 22:1).

Christ is the perfect and everlasting King of all creation, whereas His predecessors are imperfect mortals, no matter what level of earthly greatness they may achieve. Solomon is the wisest man in the world, but Christ *is* Wisdom—the One who answers Solomon's prayer for wisdom. David is a man after God's heart, but Christ *is* God: "And the angel said to her, 'Do not be afraid, Mary, for you have found favor with God. And behold, you will conceive in your womb and bear a son, and you shall call his name Jesus. He will be great and will be called the son of the Most High. And the Lord God will give to him the throne of his father David, and he will reign over the house of Jacob forever, and of his kingdom there will be no end" (Luke 1:30–33).

Through Jesus, we shall also fulfill God's command to Adam that he have dominion over His created world. Scripture seems to indicate that while God is and will always be sovereign and supreme, we will get a little taste of reigning alongside Him and enjoying His kingdom. "If we have died with him," writes Paul, "we will also live with him; if we endure, we will also reign with him" (2 Tim. 2:11–12). John affirms, "And you have made them a kingdom and priests to our God, and they shall reign on the earth" (Rev. 5:10). Let's not forget that Christ was not only present and active in the creation, but unlike the fictitious god of the Deists who abandons his creation after he sets it in motion, Jesus Christ, by His sovereign power, sustains the universe with His loving hands, which is a further manifestation of His everlasting kingly reign. As the writer of Hebrews puts it, "He upholds the universe by the Word of His power" (1:3). We'll explore this further below.

CHRIST'S ACTIONS AS CREATOR

The Bible is clear that God created the universe—it did not spring into existence from purely materialistic causes, as many insist. Most Christians probably think of creation as being exclusively by the Father, but Scripture clearly points to all three Persons of the Godhead being active in that work. "The work of creation 'is always applied in Scripture not partially but to the whole, entire, full, complete Godhead,'" notes theologian Thomas Oden.[28] Furthermore, the Nicene Creed attributes the work of creation to all three Persons of the Trinity.[29] As St. Thomas Aquinas affirms, "The power of creation...was common to the three Persons.[30]

Concerning the Holy Spirit, we remember the words in the Bible's second verse: "The earth was without form and void, and darkness was over the face of the deep. And the Spirit of God was hovering over the face of the waters" (Gen. 1:2). Likewise in Job we read, "The Spirit of God has made me, and the breath of the Almighty gives me life" (Job 33:4). And the psalmist says, "When you send forth your Spirit, they are created" (Psalms 104:30; see also Isaiah 40:12–13).

Paul acknowledges the Father's (and Christ's) work in his first letter to the Corinthians: "For us there is one God, the Father, from whom are all things and for whom we exist, and one Lord, Jesus Christ, through whom are all things and through whom we exist" (1 Cor. 8:6). For his part, John stresses the Son's (Christ's) role: "All things were made through him, and without him was not any thing made that was made" (John 1:3). Referring partly to this verse, Oden observes, "The evangelist could not make any more dramatic affirmation than to identify Christ with the Word present in creation, by whom the world was made."[31] John further contends, "He was in the world, and the world was made through him, yet the world did not know him" (John 1:10). In Colossians, Paul is even more emphatic about Christ's role: "For by him all things were created, in heaven and on earth, visible and invisible, whether thrones or dominions or rulers or authorities—all things were created through him and for him" (1:15–16).

CHRIST AS PRESERVER AND SUSTAINER OF HIS CREATION

Christ proactively superintends His creation. He sustains it, holds it together, and as noted previously, He tends to it with loving care. "He is the Creator of the universe and its Sustainer," David MacLeod writes. "He is the one who in the end, will reconcile the universe. As Jensen says, Jesus Christ is 'creation's past, present, and future.'"[32] Paul writes in the same vein to the Colossians, "And he is before all things, and in him all things hold together" (Col. 1:17; see also Heb. 1:3). John Walvoord points out that the Bible is replete with evidence of the providence of God. "Providence," in this context, means God's care for His creatures.[33] Hundreds of passages could be cited, Walvoord says, but usually the names of God that are used are not specifically associated with just one Person of the Trinity. When this occurs, he continues, we may fairly say that the work of the triune God is also a work of Christ.[34] Crucially, Christ was demonstrably involved in the preservation and guidance of Israel. References to the Angel of Jehovah (God) acting in that capacity are references to Christ that constitute "monumental proof that the Son of God preserved and guided Israel."[35] We'll look at this more closely below, in the discussion of Christophanies.

Further, there are many references to Jehovah as the Shepherd of Israel. These, says Walvoord, "may be taken as specific references to Christ." See, for example, Genesis 49:24: "Yet his bow remained unmoved; his arms were made agile by the hands of the Mighty One of Jacob (from there is the Shepherd, the Stone of Israel)"; and Psalms 23:1: "The Lord is my shepherd; I shall not want." Similar references include Psalms 80:1; Isaiah 40:11; Jeremiah 31:10; and Ezekiel 34:11–12, 23; 37:24. Walvoord reasons that while these references to "shepherd" could refer only to the triune God, Christ's reference to Himself as the good Shepherd in John 10 would justify concluding that the references are to Christ. The same reasoning applies to the references in Psalm 22 (the good Shepherd died for His sheep); in Hebrews 13:20 (the great Shepherd); and in 1 Peter 5:4 (the chief Shepherd). Additionally, Isaiah 63:9 refers to the Son of God as "the angel of his presence" who saved God's people, further demonstrating Christ's work of providence and preservation in Old Testament times.

Finally, Psalm 72 indicates that God's continued purpose is to bring all creatures of the earth under Christ's authority. "Give the king your justice, O God, and your righteousness to the royal son! ...May he have dominion from sea to sea, and from the River to the ends of the earth! ...May all kings fall down before him, all nations serve him" (Psalms 72:8, 11). Skeptics might argue this passage refers to an earthly king, but as Dr. Donald Williams notes, no earthly king could hope to fulfill this vision, and so the passage is clearly prophetic and messianic.[36] This theme is carried forward into the New Testament, with Jesus declaring, "All authority in heaven and on earth has been given to me" (Matt. 28:18). In Philippians Paul echoes this sentiment: "Therefore God has highly exalted him and bestowed on him the name that is above every name, so that at the name of Jesus every knee should bow, in heaven and on earth and under the earth, and every tongue confess that Jesus Christ is Lord, to the glory of God the Father" (2:9–11).

THE SAVING ACTIVITY OF CHRIST IN THE OLD TESTAMENT

I stated earlier that unless you believe in the inspiration of Scripture you will probably not acknowledge shadows of Christ in the Old Testament. If you believe the book was written by human beings unaided by God, then you are unlikely to believe there were any hints of Christ, much less divinely placed prophecies, in the Hebrew Scriptures. This holds true for the doctrine of salvation (the doctrine of Christ's work in salvation)[37] in the Old Testament. "One of the major difficulties in the discussion of the Old Testament doctrine of salvation," John Walvoord writes, "is that modernism and evolution have relentlessly invaded Old Testament teachings. If the primary religion of early man was polytheistic, animistic or reduced to a fetishism and totemism, obviously we shall look in vain for any true revelation of salvation.... (But), if the Scriptures are accepted as infallible, the revelation of salvation is not a late development of prophetic writers but a primary and basic revelation of God to the first man and succeeding generations."[38]

Due to the punishment of death that God administers against mankind following Adam's sin in the Garden, man is lost and in need of salvation. One of the most transcendent lessons of the early pages of Genesis and throughout all Scripture is that man is depraved and helpless apart from God. His efforts to go his own way and become his own god began in the Garden and continue to this day. This is the essence of the conflict between biblical Christianity and secular humanism.[39]

As noted earlier, however, at the same time God pronounces judgment on Adam and Eve, He also promises them—in rather shadowy terms—that He will provide a means of salvation, when He says the seed of the woman will bruise the head of the serpent (Gen. 3:15). With the benefit of hindsight, and especially through subsequent Old Testament and New Testament revelations, we can see, without much difficulty, that God is promising a Savior Who will come from a woman and not a man, i.e., a suggestion of the virgin birth (Isaiah 7:14; Matt. 1:21–22).[40] I'm certainly not contending that readers of the Scriptures in Old Testament times could have readily understood the full ramifications of these revelations. As Dr. Walvoord explains, "The gospel of grace was given to Paul as *new* revelation (Romans 1:2–4). God does not hold the Old Testament saints to account for revelation given in the New Testament.... As the exact character and work of the Deliverer is only gradually unfolded in the Old Testament, faith took the form of trust in Jehovah Himself without necessarily specific knowledge of the way by which Jehovah was to provide an adequate salvation."[41] But we are not living in Old Testament times, and there is no excuse for our blindness to New Testament revelation.

In fact, the writer of Hebrews reveals that Moses, in effect, has faith in Christ: "By faith Moses, when he was grown up, refused to be called the son of Pharaoh's daughter, choosing rather to be mistreated with the people of God than to enjoy the fleeting pleasures of sin. He considered the reproach of Christ greater wealth than the treasures of Egypt, for he was looking to the reward. By faith he left Egypt, not being afraid of the anger of the king, for he endured as seeing him who is invisible. By faith he kept the Passover and sprinkled the blood, so that the Destroyer of the firstborn might not touch them" (11:24–28). Moses in this situation can be likened to Paul, who says, "Indeed, I count everything as loss because of the surpassing worth of knowing Christ Jesus my Lord. For his sake I have suffered the loss of all things and count them as rubbish, in order that I may gain Christ and be found in him" (Philip. 3:7–8). Similarly, Peter writes, "If you are insulted for the name of Christ, you are blessed, because the Spirit of glory and of God rests upon you" (1 Peter 4:14). Most important, be aware that Christ Himself delivers a substantively identical message in the Beatitudes: "Blessed are you when others revile you and persecute you and utter all kinds of evil against you falsely on my account. Rejoice and be glad, for your reward is great in heaven, for so they persecuted the prophets who were before you" (Matt. 5:11–12).

Again, reading the Old Testament alone, without the benefit of later revelation, we would have no way of knowing that Moses in any way looks to Christ, but Hebrews is pretty clear on the point. Additionally, if you believe that "All Scripture is breathed out by God and profitable for teaching, for reproof, for correction, and for training in righteousness" (2 Tim. 3:16), then it should be easy to believe that the writer of Hebrews isn't placing his own thoughts into the mind of Moses and reporting them as revelation. Instead, the Holy Spirit inspired him to report what lay behind Moses' actions. Leon Morris observes that the writer of Hebrews sees Christ to be the same yesterday as he is today (Heb. 13:8), meaning the writer probably thinks of Him as being identified with Israel in Old Testament times.[42] Consider also Paul's affirmation concerning the Israelites: "All were baptized into Moses in the cloud and in the sea, and all ate the same spiritual food, and all drank the same spiritual drink. For they drank from the spiritual Rock that followed them, and the Rock was Christ" (1 Cor. 10:2–4).

Whether or not the writer of Hebrews intends to convey that Moses sees the full picture of Christ's role in salvation, we are clearly meant to understand that Christ was guiding and interacting with Moses and superintending Israel's salvation from Egypt—and that is exciting. After all, God is the same and unchanging now and forever. The Savior of the Old Testament *is*—not *might be*—the Savior of the New Testament.[43] It's also clear that in the quote above, Paul contends that Christ accompanied the Israelites in the desert and was the source of the supernatural water that sprang from the rock, as we'll explore more fully later.[44] Paul, you will note, doesn't say, "and the Rock was *like* Christ," but "the Rock *was* Christ." Also consider that in the Old Testament "rock" is often used to mean God, such as the "the Rock of Israel" referenced in Genesis 49:24; Moses' depiction of God as a rock (Deut. 32:4, 14, 18, 30, 31); and the psalmist's depiction of the same (Psalms 18:31, 62:2, 78:35, 89:26, 95:1). More significant, the term "rock" is sometimes associated in the Old Testament with Christ's redemptive work, such as the rock of salvation (Deut. 32:15; Psalms 62:2, 95:1, 89:26), the rock as Redeemer (Psalms 78:35); and the rock who gave you birth (Deut. 32:18).[45] As we can see, Christ's role in man's salvation in Old Testament times was not limited to His work in redeeming man from sin, but also involved delivering God's people from Egypt and from other dangers of all sorts.

CHAPTER 8

ALL ROADS LEAD TO CHRIST
TITLES, CHRISTOPHANIES, TYPOLOGY, PROPHECY, AND ANALOGY

Jesus did not arrive unannounced; his coming was declared in advance in the Old Testament—not just in explicit prophecies of the Messiah, but also by means of the stories of all the events, characters, and circumstances in the Old Testament. God was telling a larger, overarching, unified story. From the account of creation in Genesis to the final stories of the return from exile, God progressively unfolded his plan of salvation. And the Old Testament account of that plan always pointed in some way to Christ.

—IAIN DUGUID[1]

TITLES AND REFERENCES TO CHRIST IN THE OLD TESTAMENT

C hrist is given many titles throughout the Bible, and here we'll focus on those given to Him in the Old Testament. Bible scholars have long noted that the names of God both identify and describe—that is, they are more than arbitrary labels used to designate God. They also reveal something about God's character and His work. This holds true for the biblical titles of Jesus Christ.

Titles applied to Christ in the Old Testament include Jehovah, Elohim, Adonai, Son of God, the First Begotten, and the Angel of Jehovah.[2] Let's briefly consider some of these names. The word "Jehovah" is based on the Hebrew term for the God of the Hebrews, "Yahweh." It is usually rendered in English Bibles as LORD in small caps. Many conservative theologians recognize that the term Jehovah typically applies to the Triune God collectively. But it also sometimes refers to the individual Persons of the Trinity, including Christ.

In a well-known messianic prophecy in Zechariah, Jehovah (rendered in our translations as "LORD") is speaking and says, "when they look on me, on him whom they have pierced, they shall mourn for him, as one mourns for an only child, and weep bitterly over him as one weeps over a firstborn" (Zech. 12:10). In essence, this is Jehovah calling Himself "Christ," as it is Christ Who is pierced. Revelation 1:7 makes this clear: "Behold, he is coming with the clouds, and every eye will see him, even those who pierced him, and all tribes of the earth will wail on account of him." Jeremiah, just as directly, identifies Christ as Jehovah, for after declaring that God will raise up for David a righteous Branch—a clear reference to Christ—He says, "And this is the name by which he will be called: The Lord (Jehovah) is our righteousness" (Jer. 23:5–6). Paul echoes this language to the Corinthians: "And because of him you are in Christ Jesus, who became to us wisdom from God, righteousness and sanctification and redemption" (1 Cor. 1:30).

Christ, notes Walvoord, is also designated in the Old Testament as the Jehovah of the Temple: "Behold, I send my messenger, and he will prepare the way before me. And the LORD whom you seek will suddenly come to his temple" (Mal. 3:1). In his gospel, Matthew removes any doubt this is a reference to Christ: "And Jesus entered the temple and drove out all who sold and bought in the temple, and he overturned the tables of the money-changers and the seats of those who sold pigeons. He said to them, 'It is written, "My house shall be called a house of prayer," but you make it a den of robbers'" (21:12–13).

We cannot overstate the significance of the term Jehovah being applied to Christ, because Jehovah is the holiest of names applied to God in the Old Testament. Jews would not even say the name (originally YHWH, or Yahweh) aloud when reading the Scriptures, but would substitute another name for God in its place. That the term Jehovah was used of Jesus Christ "affirms beyond any question the deity of Jesus Christ and with this all the attributes of God."[3]

Christ is also identified as Elohim, another name for God, in the Old Testament. In fact Isaiah 40:3 uses both "Jehovah" and "Elohim" to describe the same Person: "A voice cries: In the wilderness prepare the way of the LORD (Jehovah); make straight in the desert a highway for our God (Elohim)." Mark cites this passage as explicitly referring to Christ (Mark 1:2–3). Isaiah refers to Elohim again in 9:6: "For to us a child is born, to us a son is given; and the government shall be upon his shoulder, and his name shall be called Wonderful Counselor, Mighty God (Elohim), Everlasting Father, Prince of Peace." It's hard to deny this signifies Christ and that, in addition to the other descriptions and titles given to Him in this passage, He is called "Elohim"—Mighty God. If Christ is indeed Elohim of the Old Testament, notes Walvoord, then He is the One introduced in Genesis 1:1 as the God of creation, which is consistent with our previous discussion of Christ's involvement in the creation.[4]

The Old Testament features many other names and titles for Christ beyond those designated above, such as "Messiah" or "Anointed One" (Daniel 9:24); Branch (Jer. 23:5; 33:15; Isaiah 4:2, 11:1); "Immanuel" (Isaiah 7:14); and "Holy One" (Psalms 16:10, 22:3, 89:18). In his first sermon in Acts, Peter quotes Psalms 16:10, clearly indicating it points to the resurrected Christ, about Whom Peter is preaching. Other Old Testament titles for Christ include "King of Glory" (Psalm 24); "Man of Sorrows" (Isaiah 53:3); "Precious Cornerstone" and "Sure Foundation" (Isaiah 28:16); "The Stone the Builders Rejected" (Psalms 118:22); "Prince of Princes" (Daniel 8:25); "Root of Jesse" (Isaiah 11:10); "Ruler" (Micah 5:2); "Seed" (Gen. 3:15, discussed above in the Covenants section); and "Star Out of Jacob" (Num. 24:17, also referred to earlier).

New Testament writers often identify Jesus as the God of the Old Testament by applying Old Testament texts to Christ that were originally written as applying to the God of the Old Testament. In the Old Testament Joel writes, "And it shall come to pass that everyone who calls on the name of the Lord shall be saved" (Joel 2:32). While teaching that salvation comes by faith in Jesus Christ, Paul writes in his letter to the Romans, "For everyone who calls on the name of the Lord will be saved" (10:13). In the Old Testament Isaiah writes, "To me every knee shall bow, every tongue shall swear allegiance" (45:23). Addressing the same subject, Paul writes to the Philippians, "So that at the name of Jesus every knee should bow, in heaven and on earth and under the earth, and every tongue confess that Jesus Christ is Lord, to the glory of God the Father" (Philip. 2:10).

Similarly, in the Old Testament Jeremiah writes, "Let him who boasts boast in this, that he understands and knows me, that I am the Lord who practices steadfast love, justice, and righteousness in the earth. For in these things I delight, declares the Lord" (Jer. 9:24). Paul, in his first letter to the Corinthians, applies this passage to Christ, writing, "So that, as it is written, 'Let the one who boasts, boast in the Lord'" (1 Cor. 1:31). In the Old Testament the psalmist declares, "You ascended on high, leading a host of captives in your train and receiving gifts among men, even among the rebellious, that the Lord God may dwell there" (Psalms 68:18). Paul tells the Ephesians, "Therefore it says, 'When he ascended on high he led a host of captives, and he gave gifts to men" (Eph. 4:8). In 2 Samuel it is written, "The Lord repay the evildoer according to his wickedness!" (3:39), and Paul writes of Alexander the coppersmith who did Paul "great harm," "The Lord will repay him according to his deeds" (2 Tim. 4:14).[5] There are many other examples as well.

CHRISTOPHANIES

A theophany is a visual manifestation of God to human beings.[6] Old Testament theophanies involving Christ are called "Christophanies." So a Christophany is a particular kind of theophany that involves a preincarnate appearance of Christ in human form. It does not include visions of God or metaphors involving God, but actual, temporary appearances of God in the form of a human being.[7] In the Old Testament Christ appeared in His preincarnate state. But in the New Testament, God appears not as a temporary human being but as one Who is entirely permanent in the God-man, Jesus Christ.[8]

As Old Testament scholar G. Henton Davies notes, "In reality there are no true [Christophanies] in the New Testament, for their place is taken by the manifestation of God in Christ (John 1:14; Col. 1:15: Heb. 1:1–3)."[9] The incarnation of Christ, explains Dr. J. Oliver Buswell, differs from the Christophanies because when Jesus is born in Bethlehem, He takes to Himself a permanent and genuinely human nature. In the Old Testament Christophanies He appears as a man at certain times and places but is not actually a member of the human race.[10]

There is another distinction, however, which is that the incarnation involves "a permanent union between God and complete manhood."[11] Jesus, as we know, is fully God and fully man. Therefore, the incarnation is completely distinct from the Christophanies. So think of these Christophanies as occasions when the Second Person of the Holy Trinity appears as a man but is not actually a man—that is, He takes the form of a man, but is not in the nature of a man. In His incarnation, however, Christ becomes a man while retaining His full deity.[12]

Christophanies are a valuable component of God's progressive revelation because they are a clear method for God to make Himself known while introducing the only Person of the Triune Godhead in Whom the invisible God would be visible. Not only do the Christophanies reveal information to man about God, His nature, His works (as a prophet, priest, and king), and His dealings with man, but they also set the stage for the actual bodily appearance of Christ as a human being (and as a God) in His incarnation.[13]

The most prominent Christophanies in the Old Testament involve the Angel of Jehovah (Angel of the Lord)—sometimes called "Messenger of the Lord"—which is the Son of God appearing as an angel.[14] Not every Christophany invokes the Angel of the Lord, but every time the Angel of the Lord is mentioned, it refers to Christ.[15] The Old Testament repeatedly records such appearances—a quick electronic search for "Angel of the Lord" in the Old Testament yields fifty-six examples from Genesis 16:7 to Zechariah 12:8. The Angel is especially prominent during the wilderness wanderings, during which God accompanies Israel as a cloud (Exodus 40:38) and a pillar (Exodus 33:9–23).[16] Most Christophanies, however, involve short-term appearances.[17]

Let's look at a few familiar examples. The Angel of the Lord appears to Abraham and tells him not to sacrifice his son Isaac (Gen. 22:11); the Angel appears to Moses from the burning bush (Exodus 3:2); and the Angel strikes down 185,000 Assyrians to protect Jerusalem and Judah (2 Kings 19:35). Additionally, there are other Christophanies in which the manifested God seems to be the Angel of the Lord, though He's not expressly identified as such. Many scholars, for example, believe the "man" who wrestles Jacob is the Angel; after the struggle, the man blesses Jacob, and Jacob names the place Peniel, or "Face of God," saying, "For I have seen God face to face, and yet my life has been delivered" (Gen. 32:30). Though in the Genesis account Jacob doesn't specifically refer to God as the Angel of the Lord, the prophet Hosea does identify Jacob's opponent as the Angel (Hosea 12:4).

We should note that most conservative scholars, who are in accord with the most ancient view of the Church fathers, believe that all the Old Testament theophanies involve the appearance of the Son of God exclusively, not the Father or the Holy Spirit—thus under this view they are all accurately described as Christophanies. Justin Martyr, Irenaeus, Clement of Alexandria, Theophilus, Tertullian, Cyprian, Cyril, Hilary, and Chrysostom all believed the preincarnate Christ was the one Who appeared.[18]

Some critics dismiss the idea that these appearances were by the Second Person, the Son of God, as "mere conjecture," maintaining there is no conclusive evidence for the Trinity in the Old Testament.[19] But if we can show that the Old Testament strongly suggests the plurality of the Godhead—that it is not reckless conjecture—then it is much easier to see how these appearances were actually Christ, in His preincarnate state.

Although the doctrine of the Trinity is not explicitly expressed in the Old Testament, James Borland convincingly argues it is strongly suggested by various references to multiple Persons of the Godhead, such as in Psalms 2:7 ("You are my Son; today I have begotten you") and in Psalms 45:6–7 ("Your throne, O God, is forever and ever. The scepter of your kingdom is a scepter of uprightness; you have loved righteousness and hated wickedness. Therefore, God, your God, has anointed you with the oil of gladness beyond your companions.") The writer of Hebrews points to the second example as a clear reference to the Father and Son (1:8).

There are many other examples as well, such as Psalms 110:1 ("The Lord says to my Lord"); after speaking of God's various activities in creation, the psalmist Agur asks, "What is his name, and what is his son's name?" (Proverbs 30:4); the prophet Jeremiah says the Lord will raise up for David a righteous Branch who will be called, "The Lord is our righteousness" (Jer. 23:5–6); Isaiah 48:16 states, "The Lord God has sent me, and his Spirit"; and Isaiah 61:1 says, "The Spirit of the Lord God is upon me," which Jesus quotes and identifies Himself as "me" (Luke 4:18–21). Additionally, it is hard to deny that Isaiah 63:9–10 refers to all three Persons of the Godhead: "The angel of his presence saved them; in his love and in his pity he redeemed them... but they rebelled and grieved his Holy Spirit." According to Borland, "his presence" refers to the Father, "the angel" is the Son, and the "Holy Spirit" completes the Godhead.[20]

Borland also provides several examples of New Testament writers referring to the Jehovah or "Messenger of Jehovah" of the Old Testament as Christ. These instances are not only Christophanies, but are further examples of the Old Testament pointing to the Trinity. These involve the activities of the Messenger of Jehovah, who is sent by Jehovah—a distinct Person. One example is Hebrews 12:18–26, read in tandem with Haggai 2:6, in that the former shows Jesus shaking Mount Sinai and the latter attributes it to Jehovah. Borland provides numerous other examples (compare 1 Cor. 10:4 with Heb. 11:26; and John 12:38–41 with Isaiah 6; and lastly, see Luke 1:15–17).[21]

Professor Michael Barrett agrees that the Old Testament suggests the Trinity, specifically in relation to some of the Christophanies. He notes that "the person of the Christophany is God, and yet He is distinct from God." As proof, he says the Angel sometimes speaks *as* Jehovah in the first person, but also speaks *of* Jehovah in the third person—such is the wondrous mystery of the Trinity. Barrett cites Genesis 16:11 as an example: "And the angel of the LORD said to her,

'Behold, you are pregnant and shall bear a son. You shall call his name Ishmael, because the LORD has listened to your affliction.'" Here, the Angel is telling Hagar what He, as God, will do. But He also says that "the Lord has listened to your affliction," referring to God in the third person. A similar occurrence can be found in Genesis 21:17: "And God heard the voice of the boy, and the angel of God called to Hagar from heaven and said to her, 'What troubles you, Hagar? Fear not, for God has heard the voice of the boy where he is.'" Further, in Genesis 22:12 the Angel tells Abraham, "For now I know that you fear God, seeing you have not withheld your son, your only son, from me"—we see the suggestion of both first and third person here.[22] These allusions to the Trinity are powerful evidence of Christ radiating forth from the pages of the Old Testament.

Borland advances five other lines of evidence to demonstrate Christ is the sole agent involved in the Christophanies:

1. The Second Person of the Triune Godhead is the manifestation of God in the New Testament via the Incarnation. Thus, it stands to reason that the same Person would be involved in God's manifestations in the Old Testament.

2. The Messenger [or Angel] of the Lord from the Old Testament never appears again, as such, after the Incarnation, which warrants the inference that He is the same Person.

3. It is the Father who sends both the Angel of the Lord and Christ, which indicates it is either Christ or the Holy Spirit Who is sent, because the existence of a Sender implies there is another distinct Person in the Godhead Whom He sent.

4. John 1:18 reads, "No one has ever seen God; the only God, who is at the Father's side, he has made him known." When John asserts that no one has ever seen God, he is referring to God the Father, says Borland, which is clear from the second part of the verse. As God appears in the Old Testament Christophanies and was seen by people, it is obvious that God, in these cases, is not the Father but the Son, Who is seen during the Incarnation. The Holy

Spirit, being Spirit, has not been seen as a person, but only in the form of a dove. (See also John 6:46 and 16:27–28).

5. There are parallels between the types of functions and loving services performed by the Old Testament "Messenger of the Lord" and by Christ in His incarnation.[23]

Finally, we should note that the Christophanies impart a vital lesson about God: He is a personal Being, not some abstract force of energy. God's appearances to man in the Old Testament demonstrate His personal and relational nature and His loving-kindness toward man. "These Christophanies introduce to man extremely profound theology concerning Christ and His place in the Trinity," Professor Barrett writes. Then he reminds us, "And this is the Old Testament."[24]

OLD TESTAMENT TYPOLOGY POINTING TO CHRIST

Typology has been defined as "a method of biblical interpretation by which a person, event, or institution ('type') in the Old Testament corresponds to another one ('antitype') in the New Testament within the framework of salvation history."[25] This means that God uses the Old Testament type in some redemptive activity for His people, and it foreshadows or prefigures what He would perfectly fulfill in Christ. What God partially accomplishes through the type corresponds to what He will fully accomplish through Christ, so that the fulfillment is superior to the type.[26] In short, the type is the *shadow* of Christ and the antitype is the *substance* of Christ in the fulfillment.[27] The Old Testament sacrifices, for example, are a type of Christ, but were vastly inferior and temporary. So these persons, events, or things in the Old Testament, while possessing true historical validity in themselves, also function as divinely appointed illustrations of what was yet to come.[28]

Some scholars believe "types" also rightly include situations in which persons, events, or institutions in the Old Testament correspond to those in other parts of the Old Testament—not just in the New Testament.[29] Some of the most widely known examples of Old Testament types used by other Old Testament writers are those of the exodus from Egypt (Isaiah 51:9–11, 52:7–12), Sodom and Gomorrah (Jer. 23:14), and Eden as a type of future blessings (Ezek. 36:33–35).[30] Many writers insist that types include not just persons, events, and institutions, but also ceremonies, among other things.[31]

In this book we are more interested in situations in which an element found in the Old Testament prefigures Christ and His salvation work in the New Testament. There are many that fit this description.[32] Consider Jesus telling Nicodemus, "And as Moses lifted up the serpent in the wilderness, so must the Son of Man be lifted up, that whoever believes in him may have eternal life" (John 3:14). Jesus here is referring to the event recorded in Numbers 21:9. Moreover, the Passover lamb in Exodus (12:1–13, 49) is a type of Christ (1 Cor. 5:7), as is the rock that Moses strikes in the wilderness to produce water for the people (Exodus 17:6), which anticipates Christ providing spiritual drink from the Spiritual Rock (1 Cor. 10:3–4). Such types of Christ are scattered throughout the biblical record, especially in Hebrews.

It's important to distinguish between typology and allegory. Typology, as noted, involves a person, event, institution, or ceremony in the Old Testament as a foreshadowing or prefiguring of something in the New Testament. Both events are historical. Allegory, by contrast, is when a feature of Scripture is used as a symbol of some general spiritual truth.[33] So allegories generally spiritualize Bible history,[34] for example, Paul's discussion of Sarah and Hagar in Galatians 4:21–31, in which he likens the two Old Testament women to "two covenants."[35] Concerning types, scholars generally believe that God superintended the placement of types in history and, correspondingly, in the biblical text as part of His progressive revelation.

Admittedly, some Bible students avoid delving too deeply into types, believing it is too subjective—they say some people, including some of the early Church fathers, see types in everything, warranted or not. This area of study has indeed been tainted a bit, Professor Barrett admits, because some readers of Scripture "take the most obscure or seemingly theologically meaningless texts they can find and then preach or teach from them the most wonderfully profound themes of the gospel, declaring that those obscure statements are types of Christ." Barrett used to wonder why he hadn't seen the types in such examples until it dawned on him "that they are not there. Types do not exist just because someone thinks he discerned something in the text that reminds him about Christ when he thinks about it hard enough." He cautions that typology is not a technique of interpretation that one can arbitrarily impose on an Old Testament text just to rescue it for Christian relevance.[36]

Due to these concerns, typology has become one of the most neglected areas of theological study.[37] It's unfortunate that some are gun-shy on this subject because it can produce rewarding insights. One technique Barrett suggests using to avoid interpretive errors is to study the use of types by New Testament writers not as an exhaustive list of legitimate types, but for insight into the proper way to identify and interpret them.[38] Dr. Norman Geisler points out there are many fitting pictures of Christ in the Old Testament that should not technically be classified as types, but which are appropriately applied to Christ. In succeeding chapters, I will cite more examples of prefigurings of Christ that don't strictly satisfy the definition of "type." These are fascinating to consider even if they don't meet the narrow criteria of some theologians.

MESSIANIC PROPHECIES OF THE OLD TESTAMENT

Messianic prophecies are passages in the Old Testament that predict a future Messiah.[39] In his classic *Messiah in Both Testaments*, Fred John Meldau relates this wonderful quote by British pastor D. M. Panton:

> The most amazing drama that ever was presented to the mind of man—a drama written in prophecy in the Old Testament and in biography in the four Gospels of the New Testament— is the narrative of Jesus the Christ. One outstanding fact, among many, completely isolates Him. It is this: that one man only in the history of the world has had explicit details given beforehand of His birth, life, death and resurrection; that these details are in documents given to the public centuries before He appeared, and that no one challenges, or can challenge,

that these documents were widely circulated long before His birth; and that anyone and everyone can compare for himself/herself the actual records of His life with those ancient documents, and find that they match one another perfectly.[40]

As we go through the books of the Old Testament individually, I will cite both the Old Testament messianic prophecies and the New Testament passages recording their fulfillment. I hope this will convey the sheer enormity and specificity of this amazing phenomenon. For a striking visual side-by-side, see the chart of messianic prophecies and their fulfillment in the appendix on page 337.

Please keep in mind that many of the prophecies are promises made by God. This is only natural, as biblical prophecies are not really predictions like a typical human being would make—they are statements from God's spokesmen (prophets). They are more than mere predictions because there is no uncertainty about their fulfillment. The prophecies are actually divine *guarantees* that certain things will take place in the future, both because in His sovereignty God is the Active Agent in fulfilling His promises, and because the mind of God is infinite; He exists outside of time. He sees the future as clearly as if it has already transpired.

CHRIST SEEN THROUGH GOD'S DEALINGS WITH ISRAEL

Another helpful way to see Christ's footprints in the Old Testament is by observing God's instructive dealings with Israel and then examining the uncanny parallels between the lessons God imparts to His people and the teachings of Christ to His people, i.e. the Church. Likewise, there are instructive parallels between God's promises to Israel and Christ's promises to the Church, and between the Law that God commands Israel to follow and the demands Christ makes on His Church.[41]

For example, God vows to give His people the Promised Land of Canaan as an everlasting possession, but this transaction involves more than a promise. As we've seen, He also demands that they claim the land for themselves—which they initially resist doing out of fear of the Canaanites—and that they conquer it wholly and completely. To preserve the purity of Hebrew worship, they are to leave no remains of the religious practices or rituals of the conquered peoples and are forbidden to intermarry with them. Just as God commands the Hebrews to wholly possess Canaan, by analogy, Jesus Christ requires His Church to "make disciples of all nations, baptizing them in the name of the Father and of the Son and of the Holy Spirit, teaching them to observe all that I have commanded you" (Matt. 28:18–20).

God's dealings with His people and Christ's dealings with His Church are sometimes quite different, which logically follows in the context of God's progressive revelation. God institutes the requirement of circumcision among His people for every male, but that requirement becomes moot upon Christ's death and resurrection, after which baptism emerges as the sign of covenant membership for the Church. The contrast between these two practices is wholly a result of the work of Jesus Christ and His once and for all blood sacrifice,[42] and it is in this contrast that we are better able to see Christ's perfection and His infinite love for us, and the imperative of our saving faith in Him.

Having examined the various Old Testament threads pointing to Christ, we now turn our attention to the Christ-centeredness of each specific book of the Bible.

CHAPTER 9

CHRIST IN EVERY BOOK
GENESIS

*Jesus gave [His disciples] an Old Testament sermon that
started with the writings of Moses (the first five books
of the Bible) and continued through all the prophets (the
rest of the Old Testament), showing them how the pattern of suffering followed by glory is continually interwo-
ven through the threads of the history of God's people. If
they had understood the Old Testament better, the death
and resurrection of Jesus would not have come as such a
shock. They would have been better equipped to face the
tough realities of life with an unshakable faith in God.*

—IAIN DUGUID[1]

CHRIST IN EVERY BOOK OF THE BIBLE

In an eloquent passage, Pastor M. R. DeHaan passionately argues
that the Bible is about Jesus Christ throughout:

If we search long enough we shall find upon every page of
Scripture, standing somewhere in the shadow, the outline of
the central Person of the Book—the Lord Jesus Christ, both
the object and end of all Scripture. The last book of the Bible
opens with the words, "The Revelation of Jesus Christ," and
this is not only the title of the last book of the Bible, but it may

well be taken as the title of all the books of the Bible, for it is truly the "revelation of Jesus Christ". Every incident recorded in the Scriptures has a bearing directly or indirectly upon this theme, "revealing Jesus Christ". A godly minister, now gone to be with the Lord, said to me early in my ministry, "Son, you have never found the true interpretation of any passage of the Scriptures until you have found in it somewhere a reference to the Lord Jesus Christ. If you search long enough you will find Him standing somewhere in the background, sometimes clear and unmistakable, sometimes faintly and dimly, but He is there."[2]

In the remainder of this book I will endeavor to show that Pastor DeHaan is correct and that every book of the Old Testament includes numerous and varied prefigurings of Christ.

Before proceeding, let's remember that Christ affirms the historicity, inspiration, inerrancy, and infallibility of all Scripture. If we consider the possibility that Scripture really is inspired by God, we will treat the entire Bible with the greatest reverence and respect, and it will not be difficult to see Christ on every page—of both Testaments. I firmly believe Christ's Emmaus road revelations are intended not only for his two interlocutors, but to open all our eyes to His centrality to Scripture, thereby quickening our understanding of His Word and deepening our knowledge of and relationship with Him.

Throughout the New Testament, Jesus repeatedly and emphatically confirms the Old Testament's legitimacy. In His High Priestly Prayer to His Father, He says, "Your word is truth" (John 17:7); on a separate occasion He declares, "The Scripture cannot be broken" (John 10:35); and He affirms the Pentateuch (the first five books of the Bible) by proclaiming, "For truly, I say to you, until heaven and earth pass away, not an iota, not a dot, will pass from the Law until all is accomplished" (Matt. 5:18). Furthermore, when the Pharisees and scribes ask Jesus why His disciples broke their traditions by not washing their hands when they ate, He replies, "And why do you break the commandment of God for the sake of your tradition? ...So for the sake of your tradition you have made void the word of God" (Matt. 15:3, 6).

Jesus, as noted, also validates many specific events recorded in the Old Testament. When asked about the permissibility of divorce, He cites Genesis 22:23–24: "Have you not read that he who created them from the beginning made them male and female, and said, 'Therefore a man shall leave his father and his mother and hold fast to his wife, and the two shall become one flesh?' So they are no longer two but one flesh. What therefore God has joined together, let not man separate" (Matt. 19:4–5). He also confirms, as historical and not merely allegorical, the stories of the creation of Adam and Eve, Jonah and the great fish, the flood, the slaying of Abel, the miracles of Elijah, and many more.[3]

Numerous liberal critics today discount Scripture as the actual Word of God and simply read out of the text whatever parts they find disagreeable. The account in Genesis of man's fall, however, contains a stern warning against disrespecting God's Word. The story begins when God unambiguously tells Adam, "You may surely eat of every tree of the garden, but of the tree of knowledge of good and evil you shall not eat, for in the day that you eat of it you shall surely die" (Gen. 2:16–17). The serpent questions Eve about this command, cleverly undermining her certainty of what God had actually said. When Eve responds that God had commanded they not eat the fruit of the tree of knowledge of good and evil or they would die, the serpent retorts, "You will not surely die" (Gen. 3:4). The serpent knowingly contradicts God, insisting He had only issued the command because He didn't want Adam and Eve to become God-like themselves by recognizing good and evil. The serpent finally convinces Eve to eat the forbidden fruit, and afterward Adam eats it as well. So you see, the very fall of mankind, it can be fairly said, resulted, in part, from man's failure to take God at His Word.

Few lessons from Genesis are more important than the admonition to take God's Word—which centers on Jesus Christ—seriously and reverently. Pastor DeHaan writes that behind Satan's cleverly concealed concern for Adam and Eve "was a plan to cast doubt upon the plain, literal, unmistakable meaning of *thus saith the Lord*."[4]

GENESIS

Let us also be mindful that the Bible is a story demonstrating God's inestimable love for the beings He created in His image. Genesis, of course, is the beginning of the story, but it also tells, in general terms, how the story will end—for in the book God, through Moses, tells of man's creation in a state of innocence and in the presence of God, his tragic fall into a sinful state leading to separation from God, and finally God's plan to redeem man. So this first Book of Books describes not only man's creation and his fall, but as earlier noted, God's first promise of the Gospel: God's plan to redeem man and reconcile man to Himself.

The ultimate message, then, is not one of despair but of hope. Recall that God created man knowing he would sin and that his redemption would require God to send and sacrifice His Son. Therefore, regardless of certain Old Testament stories that may make God seem harsh or forbidding, we must remember that this is essentially a love story—and it is centered on Jesus Christ, Who created us to redeem us. God didn't need to create the universe and man—He chose to, primarily as an expression of His unbounded love.

As Christ, the Second Person of the Godhead, is a being of eternal existence Who is at the very heart of Scripture, it is hardly surprising that His footprint is seen throughout the Bible. As we've already seen, He is right there at the beginning of Genesis, as a prime mover in the creation (John 1:1–3, 10; 1 Cor. 8:6; Col. 1:15–16).

THE IMPORTANCE OF GENESIS 1–11 AND OF GOD'S SELECTION OF ISRAEL

Though we've covered some aspects of early biblical history, I want to emphasize the role of the first eleven of the fifty chapters of Genesis. God calls Abraham in chapter 12 to begin the process of establishing the Hebrew nation, but many foundational events occur prior to that, including the creation, the fall, judgment, the first announcement of the Gospel, Cain and Abel, the flood, God's sparing of humankind through Noah, and the dispersion of mankind at Babel. The abbreviated history told in these first eleven chapters powerfully showcases the depravity of man apart from God. Man left to his own devices can produce nothing but chaos, destruction, and death.

This fact—the reality of sin—must not be brushed over lightly, because all of mankind's problems arise from man's sin and separation from God. As sin separates us from God, making provision for our sin is a necessary condition to reuniting us and restoring our relationship with Him. The Christian Church must not drop its constant focus on man's sin lest we lose sight of our helplessness and emptiness apart from God and our dire need for a Redeemer. Without these first eleven chapters we wouldn't understand the necessity for God's redemptive plan, which is outlined from chapter 12 through the remainder of the Bible. "The doctrines of creation, the Fall, judgment, the progress of evil, the exhibition of God's grace, election, covenant, sovereignty and salvation history all have their beginnings here," observes Graeme Goldsworthy. "Suffice it to say…that Genesis 1–11 provides the rationale and backdrop to the calling of Abraham and the covenant of grace that God establishes with the patriarch of Israel. The terms of God's covenant with Abraham in Genesis 12:1–3 do not make a lot of sense apart from the account in the previous chapters."[5]

But why does God establish and take special sovereign control of just one relatively tiny nation to use as His vehicle to accomplish His redemptive plan in salvation history? Why does God choose Israel as His "firstborn son" (Exodus 4:22; Deut. 33:17; Psalms 89:27; Jer. 31:9) and make the Israelites His chosen people and His treasured possession (Deut. 14:2)? God's assertion that He has a "filial relationship with Israel" is "an astonishing concept," writes Eugene Carpenter. "Thus [God] bears the relationship of a Father toward His people—before the exodus, before the [Mosaic Covenant].... He is a *Father*."[6]

Just look at all the special ways God sets Israel aside. According to Paul, "They are Israelites, and to them belong the adoption, the glory, the covenants, the giving of the law, the worship, and the promises. To them belong the patriarchs, and from their race, according to the flesh, is the Christ, who is God over all, blessed forever. Amen" (Romans 9:4–5). Referring to these verses, J. A. Witmer lists the "seven spiritual privileges" that God gives to Israel as His chosen nation: the adoption of sons, the divine glory, the covenants, the receiving of the Law, the temple worship, the promises (especially of the coming Messiah), and the patriarchs (from whom will come the Messiah "who is God over all").[7] All these privileges contribute to God's ultimate purpose of bringing salvation to all mankind.

Recall that Israel is assigned a special role as a "kingdom of priests" (Exodus 19:6). To understand that charge, we must understand the priesthood.[8] The priesthood, says Daniel Juster, "brings the people to God and God to the people." In its priestly role, Israel serves "to illustrate God's truth;" to act "as a testimony to the nations by exhibiting Israel's quality of life, a result of its submission to the Torah, the instruction of God;" and "as a witness to the power of God in the midst of Israel and his ultimate place as Lord over all the earth."[9]

Juster maintains that we cannot fully appreciate the biblical concept of priesthood unless we comprehend the principle of representational righteousness. "Because God sees humanity as a whole," he explains, "the righteousness of a few may stave off judgment for the many." We see this in the Sodom and Gomorrah narrative and elsewhere in the Bible, but the culmination of representational righteousness is Jesus Christ, "whose individual sacrifice atones for the whole human race."[10] Note, however, that this does not alter the fact that God judges us each individually. We are all separately accountable to God, and while Christ's sacrifice atones for the sins of the entire human race, one must appropriate His sacrificial work, through faith in Him, to be redeemed.

As we acknowledged, God could have just zapped people directly into heaven, but He chose to place us on earth and enabled our salvation instead. The reason why is a mystery, but I believe it's related, at least in part, to His creation of mankind as free beings. Further, Scripture is quite clear that God refines us through our experiences—our hardships and sufferings—so that we undergo a spiritual maturation process. He uses our experiences to build our character, to impart wisdom to us, and to draw us to Him by showing us our inadequacies apart from Him and our need to rely on Him and place our faith in Him. This is what He did with the nation of Israel, as related in Isaiah: "Behold, I have refined you, but not as silver; I have tried you in the furnace of affliction" (48:10). The Book of Jeremiah contains a similar declaration: "Behold, I will refine them and test them, for what else can I do, because of my people?" (9:7). And this is what He does for all of us: "We rejoice in our sufferings, knowing that suffering produces endurance, and endurance produces character, and character produces hope, and hope does not put us to shame because God's love has been poured into our hearts through the Holy Spirit who has been given to us" (Romans 5:3–5).

Iain Duguid calls this refining process "God's training program of suffering." He illustrates the principle by citing the life of Joseph. This man was a type of Christ, though he didn't begin that way. First, observes Duguid, God had to do work in Joseph's heart because he was not yet ready to be a leader:

> He was a brash, overconfident, self-centered young man.... Joseph would be prepared through trials, temptations, and suffering until God decided he was ready to step onto the stage in his service. The path of spiritual growth for Joseph involved abuse and mistreatment, separation from home and family, having his character dragged through the mud, and finally, being neglected and forgotten for years by the very people he had helped. But this training process was necessary to make him into the person God was calling him to be. It was precisely these trials and difficulties that would show Joseph his weakness as well as his strength, and cast him back repeatedly on his need to rely on God. These were lessons that he could never learn while sitting at home comfortably in his father's house, dressed in his fancy coat.[11]

We learn much about this maturation process through Israel's experiences. By choosing one nation as the medium through which to bring salvation to all mankind, and then recording Israel's complex and very human relationship with God throughout biblical history, God shows us, by example, the consequences of living obediently versus those of disobedience. He demonstrates the indispensability of our drawing closer to Him if we are to have meaning and fulfillment in our lives. G. Campbell Morgan captures the rich ways Israel serves as an example to the nations:

> The Divine intention was the creation of a people who under His government should reveal in the world the breadth and beauty and beneficence of that government; a people who, gathered in their national life about His throne and His altar, obeying His commands and worshipping Him, should reveal to outside nations the meaning of the Kingship of God. It was not the selection of a pet, but the creation of a pattern. The story, then, of the nation is that of the creation of a testimony, and the Divine ensurance of its proclamation through both the failure and the success of the people. The method [seems to human beings to be] a long and tedious one, but it is the only one possible. It is that which God has ever followed. He constantly embodies a truth in an instrument; either a man, a society, or a nation; in order that other men, other societies, other nations may understand it. The responsibilities of the races, in the midst of which the testimony is borne, are created and limited by that testimony.[12]

Don't overlook those last few sentences. Morgan is saying God doesn't just teach us propositional truths, he *shows us* those truths in history. Thus, God chooses a single nation to bring salvation to all mankind because it is the only possible method, even though it's a "long and tedious one." It is God's way. He shows us through examples in history and especially through the example of His chosen nation.

Israel's experiences not only illustrate the importance of obedience and establishing a right relationship with God, but also the necessity of having a mediator to bring us nearer to Him. These experiences model the concept of representational righteousness that Jesus will fulfill for us. God's selection of one nation, I believe, also brings order to His redemptive plan. Working through this one nation in a designated piece of real estate, God always centers His focus on that people and on that land, even through the end of history—though all peoples of the earth, as noted, share the blessings of God's gift of salvation through faith in Christ.

God sometimes punishes the Israelites for their flaws and disobedience, but He never abandons them. "It is one of the marvels of God's grace," writes Graeme Goldsworthy, "that it continues unabated within the life of a people that is full of ambivalence, rebellion, and evil. But then, of course, the thing that makes grace gracious is that it is undeserved mercy to those who deserve only the judgment of condemnation."[13] Indeed, God still pours out His grace on Israel, and He will continue to do so as history marches toward its redemptive conclusion. He does the same for us; but in the end, we must place our faith in Him.

We see God's grace throughout all of biblical history. We can view this history as an hourglass, with the first eleven chapters of Genesis involving all peoples and not just the Hebrew nation, which had not yet been established.[14] Then, beginning with chapter 12, the focus narrows when Abraham is called and God begins to take us through the history of His chosen people. This continues until the life, death, and resurrection of Jesus Christ, when the scope expands again to include the entirety of mankind.

During the long period when the Bible focuses exclusively on Israel, God's purpose never changes. His abundant grace cannot be restrained. The idea from the beginning is to provide a means of salvation for all people, but the process involves a narrowing of the biblical and historical focus until the time is ripe for God to become Man and unite both Jews and Gentiles in His salvation plan, as the Apostle Paul confirms: "For he himself is our peace, who has made us both one and has broken down in his flesh the dividing wall of hostility by abolishing the law of commandments expressed in ordinances, that he might create in himself one new man in place of the two, so making peace, and might reconcile us both to God in one body through the cross, thereby killing the hostility" (Eph. 2:14–16). He reiterates the point in Colossians: "Here there is not Greek and Jew, circumcised and uncircumcised, barbarian, Scythian, slave, free; but Christ is all, and in all" (3:11). What begins as bliss for mankind in the Garden of Eden, writes Goldsworthy, will "return to Edenic bliss in the new Jerusalem at the center of the new creation."[15]

There's an important distinction we should make, however, between man in his original state of paradise in Eden, and man in the new Jerusalem in his redeemed state based on Christ's work on the cross. British preacher Charles Spurgeon, whose brilliant biblical insights transcend time, invites us to speculate as to the state in which mankind would exist had Adam never sinned. At this moment we would be unfallen beings—not yet afflicted with the taint of original sin—but we would be in constant jeopardy because at any moment Adam might transgress and bring us down with him. Even the passing of a thousand years wouldn't release us from this perpetual state of probation because the original covenant had no time limit.

Spurgeon is doubtlessly correct. If you recall, the Edenic Covenant had an absolute prohibition against eating from that one tree. There was no expiration date. "You and I therefore would be holding our happiness by a very precarious tenure;" writes Spurgeon, "we could never glory in absolute security and eternal life as we now do in Christ Jesus." However, as "we have now lost everything in Adam, and the uncertain tenure has come to an end, our lease of Eden and its joys has altogether expired; but we that believed, have obtained an inheritance which we hold by an indisputable and never-failing title which Satan himself cannot dispute; . . . The lord Jesus Christ has finished the work by which His people are saved, and that work has been certified by His resurrection from the dead. There are no 'ifs' in the covenant now; . . . no chances of failure caused by unfinished conditions can be found in it. . . . 'There is therefore now no condemnation to them that are in Christ Jesus.' Thus we have obtained a surer standing than we could have had under the first Adam."[16]

In summary, while conceding that the strict historical focus of the Bible, with the exceptions of Genesis 1–11 and portions of the New Testament, is on Israel, we must not conclude that salvation history is separate from secular history—for as Goldsworthy writes, "even if Israel had a very limited perception of the nations among whom [God] would act, all the nations of the world are implied. The biblical view is comprehensive: all nations belong to the one world history that finds its meaning in Jesus Christ."[17]

TYPES AND PICTURES OF CHRIST IN GENESIS

Let us now turn to types (foreshadowings) and pictures of Christ in Genesis, starting with the creation. The book's third verse reads, "Then God said, 'Let there be light,' and there was light."[18] That is historically true, but it can also be tied, allegorically, to a New Testament truth: Jesus is repeatedly called, or calls Himself, "the light." He is the light of men (John 1:4), the light of the world (John 8:12, 9:5, 12:46), and in the transfiguration "his face shone like the sun, and his clothes became white as light" (Matt. 17:2). The Old Testament repeatedly reiterates the theme: "The Lord is my light and my salvation" (Psalms 27:1); "For with you is the fountain of life; in your light do we see the light" (Psalms 36:9); "The people who walked in darkness have seen a great light" (Isaiah 9:2).

Interestingly, when Paul is instructing Christians on how to conduct their lives to become more Christ-like, he tells them to distinguish themselves "in the midst of a crooked and twisted generation" as "lights in the world, holding fast to the word of life" (Philip. 2:15–16). This metaphor continues through the Book of Revelation, where we read that "the city has no need of sun or moon to shine on it, for the glory of God gives it light, and its lamp is the Lamb. By its light will the nations walk, and the kings of the earth will bring their glory into it, and its gates will never be shut by day—and there will be no night there" (21:23–25). I hardly think it's a stretch to imagine that the picture of light presented in the creation account is a hint of the Light of the world—the Lamb of God— Who is fully revealed to us in the New Testament.

Pastor DeHaan sees a picture of Christ in Genesis 2:21 when, while Adam is sleeping, God takes his rib from his wounded side and creates Eve, who is part of Adam, thus implying a wounding and shedding of blood. "Then the man said, 'This is the bone of my bones and the flesh of my flesh; she shall be called Woman, because she was taken out of Man.' Therefore a man shall leave his father and his mother and hold fast to his wife, and they shall become one flesh" (Gen. 2:23–24). We can only see the full significance of this, says DeHaan, with Paul's illumination of the passage: "For no one ever hated his own flesh, but nourishes and cherishes it, just as Christ does the church, because we are members of his body. 'Therefore a man shall leave his father and mother and hold fast to his wife, and the two shall become as one flesh.' This mystery is profound, and I am saying that it refers to Christ and the church" (Eph. 5:30–32).

DeHaan suggests that Adam is a picture of Christ, who left His Father's house to get His bride at the cost of His own life: "Jesus, the last Adam, like the first, must be put to sleep to purchase His Bride, the Church, and Jesus died on the cross and slept in the tomb for three days and three nights." His side was also opened after He'd fallen asleep, and from His wounded side redemption came and the Church was born. The Church, like Eve, was a new supernatural creation, coming from His side. At the very dawn of creation then, says DeHaan, "we have an implied reference to a new creature taken from the side of a man and becoming a part of him, even of his flesh, and of his bones."[19]

ADAM

Genesis is rich with types of Christ, as the New Testament confirms. The first type, of course, is Adam, whom Satan tempted, just as he tempted Jesus.[20] But the two men react differently—Adam succumbs and Jesus resists—so the typology is more by way of contrast. Because Adam represents the sinner and Christ the Conqueror of sin, Adam is not a type of Christ in the sense of someone we should emulate, but in the sense that, like Christ, he was man's representative and what he did affected all human beings.[21] "The resemblance, on account of which Adam is regarded as a type of Christ, consists in this," argues Everett F. Harrison, "that Adam communicated to those whom he represented what belonged to him, and that Christ also communicated to those whom he represented what belonged to him."[22]

Paul, in his letter to the Romans, expands on this relationship, showing how death is ushered into the world through Adam's sin and conquered by Christ's life, death, and resurrection: "Therefore, just as sin came into the world through one man, and death through sin, and so death spread to all men because all sinned.... Yet death reigned from Adam to Moses, even over those whose sinning was not like the transgression of

Adam, who was a type of the one to come" (5:12–14). Paul next points out, though, how much greater God's grace is than Adam's trespass, "For if, because of one man's trespass, death reigned through that one man, much more will those who receive the abundance of grace and the free gift of righteousness reign in life through the one man Jesus Christ. Therefore, as one trespass led to condemnation for all men, so one act of righteousness leads to justification and life for all men" (5:17–18). Along the same lines Paul teaches the Corinthians, "The first man Adam became a living being; the last Adam became a life-giving spirit.... The first man was from the earth, a man of dust; the second man is from heaven" (1 Cor. 15:45, 47).

Paul closes out this section with a profound declaration that is illustrated through this contrasting typology: "As was the man of dust, so also are those who are of the dust, and as is the man of heaven, so also are those who are of heaven" (1 Cor. 15:48). This, to me, is a clear statement of the life-and-death consequences of faith in Christ. Forcing us to reckon with ourselves and to take personal inventory, Paul reminds us that we have to make a choice or it will be made for us. We either appropriate, through faith, Jesus Christ's finished work on the cross and have life in Him, or we choose the way of Adam and return to dust in our sins. The next verse expands the idea further: "Just as we have borne the image of the man of dust, we shall also bear the image of the man of heaven" (1 Cor. 15:49). Paul here affirms the theology he taught elsewhere in his epistles—that with faith in Christ we shall be born again, become new creatures, and be conformed to His image (Romans 8:29). As David Murray avers, God "set up Adam as a representative man, who sadly chose death, so that we will grasp Jesus' representative work that brings life."[23]

There is another verse related to Adam that may be much more meaningful than it appears. In Genesis 3:9 God asks Adam, "Where are you?" I believe that God doesn't simply mean *Where are you physically?* Instead, He is declaring, *Where are you in your relationship with Me? Don't hide from me or you will defeat the purpose for which I created you.* If you think about it, in this verse God might also be speaking to all of us individually about this decision that will affect *our* eternal destiny.[24] Augmenting this point is God's prohibition against eating from the tree of the knowledge of good and evil. God issues this injunction to Adam and Eve not because, as the serpent insidiously suggests, if they partake of it they would be like God; rather, if they touch or eat from it, they would be engaging in disobedience and acting as their own gods, trying to sever the cord of dependence from Him.[25]

Looking back on this event through the prism of New Testament revelation, we realize that we should cherish our dependence on God—regardless of contrary viewpoints that increasingly dominate our culture. Fearing the Lord (in the sense of having reverential awe) is the beginning of wisdom and of forming a proper relationship with God. It is fitting that the very sin that led to the fall is the direct antithesis of the attitude that brings our redemption and restoration. We acknowledge our sin and our utter helplessness apart from God to live rightly and to save ourselves. Accepting our dependence on Jesus Christ is a 180-degree turn from Adam's actions that led to our death—and this dependence brings us eternal life with God. Viewed in this way, God's prohibition against eating from the tree was an act of abounding grace that was rejected and whose consequences can only be reversed through the blood of our Savior.

ABEL AND HIS OFFERING

God rejects Cain's sacrifice because it doesn't involve blood. Abel's offering is a type of Christ because it is an innocent, living creature—a lamb, without spot or blemish—whose blood is spilled in sacrifice. Cain represents a religion of works in that he offers "fruit of the ground" that is the product of his own labor. Abel, by contrast, represents a religion of faith, established in blood.[26] Cain's offering also fails, it's worth noting, because it does not involve a substitutionary death of an innocent victim.[27]

Further, Abel is a type of Christ in that he makes his offering to God in his capacity as a shepherd (Gen. 4:2)—just as Jesus, the Good Shepherd, "lays down his life for the sheep" (John 10:15). Abel's brother hates him for no reason, just as many of Christ's brethren despise Him without cause (John 15:25). Cain kills Abel out of envy and jealousy, just as

Christ is delivered up out of envy (Matt. 27:18). Christ is killed by His brethren, as Abel is killed by his brother.[28]

On the other hand, there are also contrasts distinguishing Abel and his offering from Christ. Abel's blood demands vengeance on the murderer, but Christ's blood is ultimately about mercy, atonement, and pardon. Additionally, Abel's sheep die for Abel, but Christ dies for His sheep (John 10:15). Finally, there is a contrast in Cain's attitude and Christ's—Cain scoffs at the notion of being his brother's keeper whereas such selfless service defines Jesus' work.[29]

NOAH AND THE ARK

Noah is not specifically identified in the New Testament as a type of Christ,[30] but he points to Christ in foreshadowing our redemption. He is saved because of his faith in God's promise to spare him and his family, which prefigures the believer's salvation in Christ through faith. Noah has been called a "second Adam" because, in a sense, all living human beings come from him, just as they come from Adam, while Christ earns the same moniker because eternal life can only be found in Him. Interestingly, though not something that can strictly be called a type, the ark has only one door and is controlled solely by God, just as Jesus is the only Door through which man may enter into eternal life: "I am the door. If anyone enters by me, he will be saved and will go in and out and find pasture" (John 10:9).

The ark provides refuge for all creatures, just as Christ's Church provides salvation for all human beings, Jews and Gentiles. J. P. Lange likens Noah to Christ because Noah is not only saved, but he is, in a sense, "the savior or the mediator of the divine salvation for his house. He was a type of Christ, the absolute mediator."[31] Other comparisons include Noah offering a blood sacrifice (Gen. 8:20) and Christ offering His own blood in sacrifice;[32] and the ark coming to rest on the mountains of Ararat on the seventeenth day of the Jewish month of Nisan, the same date often cited as the day of Christ's resurrection.[33]

English biblical scholar Arthur Pink points us to Genesis 6:8, reporting the first words God speaks to Noah: "But Noah found favor in the eyes of the Lord." Note that only Noah finds favor, not even his family members. "He is the one in whom the heart of the Father delighted," writes Pink. God's words here resemble those the Father speaks to Jesus at the commencement of his public ministry: "This is My beloved Son, in whom I am well pleased" (Matt. 3:17). Pink further observes that Noah builds the ark alone,[34] which means, symbolically, that Noah alone provides the means of securing the lives that God entrusts to him. This prefigures the sole and complete work of Christ: "He himself bore our sins in his body on the tree" (1 Peter 2:24). Furthermore, in doing this work, Noah acts in total obedience to God—"He did all that God commanded him" (Gen. 6:22)—just as Jesus keeps His Father's commandments (John 15:10).[35]

MELCHIZEDEK

Genesis 14 introduces us to a great man, Melchizedek, king of Salem (Jerusalem) and "priest of God Most High," who brings bread and wine to Abraham after Abraham returns from defeating the kings. He then blesses Abraham on behalf of God, and Abraham gives him a tenth of everything he owns. Skipping forward to Psalms 110:4, we find a prediction that Christ will be a priest forever after the order of Melchizedek. Referring to this verse, the writer of Hebrews supplies more information about this mysterious man, including that his name means "king of righteousness" and that he is a king of peace. Some scholars believe Melchizedek is an angel, some that he is a Christophany,[36] and others, like John Walvoord, that he is a type of Christ because he is both a king and a priest.[37]

ISAAC AND THE RAM

Some see Abraham's son Isaac as a type of Christ because God commands Abraham to sacrifice him. But when God sees that Abraham passes the test of faith and is willing to offer up Isaac, God spares

Isaac and sovereignly arranges for a ram to be substituted for him, thereby making the ram a type of Christ as well (Gen. 22:13). Thus God provides the sacrifice, just as He provides His Son as the ultimate and final sacrifice for us. Marveling at the divinely arranged specificity of the prefiguring in this sacrifice, John MacArthur remarks, "Did you know that Isaac bore his own wood to his own execution? And Jesus did too or the type would have been destroyed; Jesus fulfilled it to the very letter. This is divine inspiration.... This is how verbal and typical prophecy predicted to the very tiniest point the death of Jesus Christ."[38] Isaac is further like Christ in his miraculous birth, having been born to a hundred-year-old man and a ninety-year-old woman (Gen. 17; Gal. 4:21–31).[39]

JOSEPH

Joseph is authentically a type of Christ. Though the New Testament nowhere designates him as such,[40] there are abundant comparisons. Like Christ, Joseph is born by God's supernatural action—he is born to Rachel, who had been unable to conceive (Gen. 30:22–24); is especially loved by his father (Gen. 37:3); is mistreated by his brothers (Gen. 37:4); is in constant turmoil and is rejected as a ruler over his brothers (Gen. 37:8); has his robe taken away from him (Gen. 37:23); is conspired against by those who want to kill him (Gen. 37:18); is rescued from prison (as Christ is resurrected from death) and allowed to reign and rule (Gen. 41:39–41); is sold for silver (Gen. 37:28); becomes a servant (Gen. 39:4); is condemned despite being innocent (Gen. 39:11–20); is later received by his brothers and exalted as a savior and deliverer (Gen. 45:1–15); and uplifts his brothers to places of honor and safety (Gen. 45:16–18).[41]

In his speech in the Book of Acts, Stephen proclaims, "And the patriarchs, jealous of Joseph, sold him into Egypt; but God was with him and rescued him out of all his afflictions and gave him favor and wisdom before Pharaoh, king of Egypt" (Acts 7:9–10). Luke offers a similar description of Christ: "And Jesus increased in wisdom and in stature and in favor with God and man" (Luke 2:52).[42] What's more, in a passage suggestive of Jesus, Joseph becomes a savior to all people despite being left for dead: "All the earth came to Egypt to Joseph to buy grain, because the famine was severe over all the earth" (Gen. 41:57).[43]

BENJAMIN

Rachel dies giving birth to her son, whom she called Ben-Oni, but Jacob, the baby's father, calls him Benjamin (Gen. 35:18). Ben-Oni means "son of my sorrow," and Benjamin means "son of the right hand."[44] Some see a connection between these names and Christ. In the New Testament, the death of Mary's Son Jesus causes her unbearable sorrow: "And Simeon blessed them and said to Mary his mother, 'Behold, this child is appointed for the fall and rising of many in Israel, and for a sign that is opposed (and a sword will pierce through your own soul also), so that thoughts from many hearts may be revealed'" (Luke 2:34–35). So Jesus was first the Son of Sorrow, but would later sit at the right hand of the Father (Luke 22:69).[45]

JACOB'S LADDER

Jacob dreams of a ladder that reaches from earth to heaven. The angels of God are ascending and descending on it, and God reiterates to Jacob some of the promises He had made to Abraham (Gen. 28:10–17). Many see Jacob's ladder as a type of Christ in that it makes heaven visible (John 1:51; Matt. 3:16); reaches to earth (John 12:46); reaches to God (1 Peter 3:18); happens in a place of blessing (Eph. 1:3); is a gate of heaven (John 10:9; Romans 5:2); and involves a commitment to tithing by Jacob (Gen. 28:22; Acts 2:44–45, 4:32).[46] The angels going up and down the ladder also resemble a saying of Jesus: "Truly, truly, I say to you, you will see heaven opened, and the angels of God ascending and descending on the Son of Man" (John 1:51; see also Heb. 1:6; Luke 2:9, 18).

ADAM'S CLOTHING

Genesis records that after the fall, God graciously clothes Adam and Eve (3:21). This is more than God merely tending to their physical needs. As John Walvoord contends, God is representing to them that He would supply a righteous covering for their naked sin.[47] Scripture carries forward this theme: "I put on righteousness, and it clothed me; my justice was like a robe and a turban" (Job 29:14); "Let your priests be clothed with righteousness" (Psalms 132:8); "I will greatly rejoice in the Lord; my soul shall exult in my God, for he has clothed me with the garments of salvation; he has covered me with the robe of righteousness" (Isaiah 61:10); and "It was granted her to clothe herself with fine linen, bright and pure" (Rev. 19:8). Charles Spurgeon comments on the stark contrast between the covering represented by Adam's fig leaves and the righteousness of Christ: "Adam went to the fig tree for garments, and fig leaves yielded him such covering as they could. But we come to Christ and we find, not fig leaves, but a robe of righteousness that is matchless for its beauty, comely in its proportions, one which will never wear out, which exactly suits to cover our nakedness from head to foot, and when we put it on makes us fair to look upon, even to Christ himself."[48]

THE SABBATH

Though I haven't found a great deal written about this (apart from the writings of John Calvin and H. A. Ironside),[49] it seems reasonable to conclude that the Sabbath is a prefiguring of Christ for two reasons. The first is because we find our ultimate rest in Christ. The second is this declaration by Paul: "Therefore let no one pass judgment on you in questions of food and drink, or with regard to a festival or a new moon or a Sabbath. These are a shadow of things to come, but the substance belongs to Christ" (Colossians 2:16–17).

As we've seen, the Book of Genesis, from its accounts of creation to the life of Joseph, is replete with divinely inspired types and foreshadowings of Christ, whose shadowy forms become crystal clear in the light of New Testament revelation. Next we turn to the Book of Exodus, where we'll see a similar abundance of such prefigurings.

CHAPTER 10

CHRIST IN EVERY BOOK
EXODUS

Is there in all history a more amazing spectacle than the
Exodus?—a more august and solemn revelation of God
than at Sinai?—a more significant piece of architecture than
the Israelite Tabernacle?—a greater human figure than the
man Moses—a more influential national epoch than the
founding of the Israel theocracy? All these are found in this
second book of Scripture. It is the...very fount and origin
of the national life, law, and organized religion of Israel.

—J. SIDLOW BAXTER[1]

E xodus is central to the Old Testament, and its abundant foreshadowings of the New Testament make it a crucial part of the entire
Bible. Christian imagery and symbolism course through the
book, from Moses as a "type" of Christ, to the Passover, to the exodus
event, to the construction of the Tabernacle with all its God-ordained
furnishings. This ancient document points to so many significant events
of the New Testament, especially in the way its types prefigure the consummation of God's salvation history in Christ. A few short verses in
the second chapter of Exodus, and repeated many times thereafter, show
there is no interruption here in God's redemptive plan. Just as the Mosaic
Covenant described in Exodus continues and enhances the Abrahamic
Covenant from Genesis, these verses show a distinct continuity in God's
relationship with His people through the Bible's first two books: "During those many days the king of Egypt died, and the people of Israel
groaned because of their slavery and cried out for help. Their cry for

rescue from slavery came up to God. And God heard their groaning, and God remembered his covenant with Abraham, with Isaac, and with Jacob. God saw the people of Israel—and God knew" (2:23–24).

God, being omniscient, is incapable of forgetting His covenant or of failing to hear the Israelites' cries. So why state the obvious? I believe this language (here and elsewhere in Scripture) is meant to assure us that God does not change; He is not aloof; He hears the cries of His people and takes their pain seriously. His initial commitments to Israel, as promised to Abraham, were indeed unconditional and eternal, so they would not be diminished by what He is about to do. The language shows that while delivering Israel and entering into the Mosaic Covenant with them, God's original promise-plan remains in full force and effect. Professor Walter Kaiser emphasizes the significance of this event. "The loyal love and dependable grace of this covenant-making God to His promises dominated the transition between these ages," writes Kaiser. "He had heard Israel's groaning in Egypt, and His interest in them and action on their behalf were summed up as a 'remembering of His covenant with Abraham, Isaac, and Jacob. The God of the deliverance was one and the same as the God of your fathers' (Exodus 3:13); 'the God of Abraham, the God of Isaac and the God of Jacob.'"[2] God would deliver His people from bondage, formalize His special relationship with them, and continue to superintend their unique stewardship role in salvation history.

The essential theme of Exodus—God's deliverance of the people and their redemption—points to Jesus Christ. As we mentioned, it is where God begins to actualize His promise to redeem mankind. The book leaves us with no doubt that our God is sovereign and is faithful to His promises, especially His promise to redeem us.

Redemption is not presented as a theological doctrine in Exodus, but we see it represented thematically in the book's narrative arc. Egypt symbolizes the world—that is, the venue sinners inhabit before they are saved. In pharaoh we see the devil—the adversary who rebels against God and is the conniving enemy of His people, whom he seeks to keep from God's deliverance. Israel, during its bondage in Egypt, represents man in his fallen state and in need of redemption. The people's enslavement is a metaphor for the cruel bondage of sin. The groaning of the Israelites can be analogized to the spiritual agony of sinners as they recognize their sinful and lost condition. God's plagues on Egypt demonstrate the sovereign power of the Redeemer. God's provision of the Passover and the sacrificial system reveal that redemption must be purchased by blood. Moses is a type of Christ, who delivers his people. The exodus event signifies the sinner's liberation from sin, and the crossing of the Red Sea prefigures our union with Christ in His sacrificial death and resurrection.

God's laws and guidelines show the necessity of the people's obedience and how they can maintain a right relationship with Him.[3] God is not interested in our one-time redemption; He wants to bring us into an ongoing relationship with Him, as Moses underscores directly to Him: "You have led in your steadfast love the people whom you have redeemed; you have guided them by your strength to your holy abode" (Exodus 15:13).

The trials and tribulations the Israelites experience are emblematic of the struggles of all individuals. The giving of the Law imparts the necessity of our obedience to God. And the Tabernacle, as we'll soon see, is a multifaceted type of Christ in a remarkable number of ways.[4] Indeed, the exodus narrative gives us encouragement and hope. As Paul explains, "For whatever was written in former days was written for our instruction, that through endurance and through the encouragement of the Scriptures we might have hope" (Romans 15:4).

The redemption motif is also strikingly pictured by types and symbols. Hinting at Christian doctrines that would be revealed more clearly in the New Testament,[5] these illustrations indicate what is to come. The prefigurings of Christ in Exodus are robust and exciting, as conveyed by Pastor Donald Fortner, who tells of his experience listening to one of his pastors preach from the Old Testament: "He made those types and pictures seem to dance with life before my mind…as he expounded their meaning in light of the New Testament…. The facts and laws, ceremonies and rituals of the Mosaic economy became vibrant, bursting with life."[6]

TYPES AND PICTURES OF CHRIST IN EXODUS

There are so many prefigurings of Christ in Exodus that it's difficult to do them all justice. The following are types or pictures of Christ, some of which we'll just briefly mention and others we'll examine in more detail.

MOSES

With his messianic character, Moses is a special type of Christ. He is strong yet humble, obedient, pure of heart, and compassionate, as when he pleads with God to spare the people even after their debauchery with the golden calf (Exodus 32:11–13).[7] Moses is the only biblical figure besides Christ to fill the three offices of prophet, priest, and king (or ruler in Moses' case), though others came close, as we've seen (Exodus 34:10–120, 32:31–35, 33:4, 5).[8]

Moses tells his people, "The Lord your God will raise up for you a prophet like me from among you, from your brothers—it is to him you shall listen" (Deut. 18:15). Jesus also refers to Himself as a prophet (Mark 6:4; Luke 13:33), and the people in His time are expecting God to bring them one, as seen when they ask John the Baptist whether he is "the prophet" (John 1:21, 25). As we have seen, the people acknowledge Jesus is in fact the prophet when He feeds the five thousand, when He asserts His own deity (John 8:58), and when He otherwise speaks as one with authority (John 6:14, 7:40).

There are many Old Testament prophets between Moses and Christ, so what distinguishes Moses as a type of Christ in his role as a prophet? Some suggest it's that Moses is a unique type of prophet in that he doesn't merely speak the words of God like all the other prophets; he has a special fellowship with God.[9] This can be seen in Moses going alone to meet God up on the mountain to receive the Law (Exod. 24:15–18), and God's speaking there to Moses directly and entrusting His commandments to him (Deut. 22–27). "If there is a prophet among you, I the Lord make myself known to him in a vision; I speak with him in a dream," God tells Moses. "Not so with my servant Moses. He is faithful in all my house. With him I speak mouth to mouth, clearly, and not in riddles, and he beholds the form of the Lord" (Num. 12:6–8). Exodus also relates that God speaks to Moses "face to face" (Exodus 33:11). These are powerful statements from God, especially considering that no one can look directly at Him and live (Exodus 33:20).[10] Though God's statement that Moses "beholds the form of the Lord" doesn't mean Moses literally sees Him, it suggests an intimate relationship not enjoyed by any other prophet before or since, except for Jesus, Who is God.

In his prophetic role, Moses is a unique type of Christ, but most of the typology concerning him is based on important events in his life that prefigure Christ.[11] Both are in danger but rescued in childhood (Exodus 2:1–10; Matt. 2:14–15); both are chosen to be saviors and deliverers of their people (Exodus 3:7–10; Acts 7:25); both are rejected by their people (Exodus 2:11–15; John 1:11; Acts 7:23–28, 18:5–6); after being separated from his people, Moses returns to deliver Israel, just as Scripture promises God will return to deliver Israel (Exodus 4:19–31; Romans 11:24–26; Acts 15:14, 17); both have to do battle with Satan or his forces (Exodus 7:11; Matt. 4:1); both fast forty days (Exodus 34:28); both take control of the sea (Exodus 14:21; Matt. 8:26); both feed the multitudes (Exodus 16:15; Matt. 14:13–21); the faces of both radiate with God's glory (Exodus 34:35; Matt. 17:2); Moses is a leader of his people and Jesus is the King (Deut. 33:4–5; John 1:49); both are distrusted and challenged by their immediate families (Num. 12:1; John 7:5); both advocate for their people (Exodus 32:32; John 2:1–2, 17:9); both intercede for their people (Exodus 17:1–6; Heb. 7:25); about seventy people (Jesus had seventy-two) are appointed to help each of them (Num. 11:16–17; Luke 10:1); both establish days of commemoration to the Lord (Exodus 12:14: Luke 22: 19); both engage in healing ministries, specifically for leprosy (Num. 12:10–13; Matt. 8:2–3); both choose twelve messengers (Num. 13:2–16; Matt. 16:17–19; Mark 3:16–17); both perform significant historical events on a mountain (Exodus 19:20; Deut. 6:5–25; Matt. 5:1–12); God's voice is heard when a cloud overshadows Moses, Aaron, and Miriam, just as His voice is heard when a cloud overshadows Peter, James, John, and Jesus (Num. 12:5–8; Matt. 17:1–5);[12] and both reappear after their physical deaths, albeit in different forms (Matt. 17; Acts 1:3).[13]

There are even more analogies. Moses, like Christ, humbly and quietly suffers for his people's sins. Even when Miriam and Aaron speak against him, He remains silent (Num. 12).[14] Indeed, despite his position as leader and his intimate relationship with God, Moses "was very meek, more than all people who were on the face of the earth" (Num. 12:3).

Moses is called the servant of the Lord (Deut. 3:24, 34:5), as is Christ (Rev. 15:3). Moses dies so that his people can enter into the Promised Land (Deut. 1:37, 4:21–22), while Jesus dies so that we can enter into life.[15] Moses, like Christ, is also a priest (Psalms 99:6; Heb. 7:24) and, like Christ, his work as a priest is interrelated with his role as a prophet.[16] Moses, like Christ, was a shepherd (Exodus 3:1; John 10:11–14) and is faithful (Heb. 3:5), obedient, and mighty in word and deed (Acts 7:22; Mark 6:2).[17]

God singles out Moses as a mediator between Himself and the people because He cannot look upon sin (Hab. 1:13). No impurity can be in His presence. In view of this, Pastor Timothy Keller observes that our idea of God's holiness is inadequate. "We have a Hallmark-greeting-card understanding of God," writes Keller. "To us, holy means reverent and inspiring and organ music in the background." But this doesn't capture the infinite contrast between God and mankind. When Moses encounters God at the burning bush, Keller continues, God doesn't say, "Come in Moses, I'd like to give you a hug." He says, "Stop! Come no closer." Moses, says Keller, was rightfully scared because "if even a cow touched" that holy ground "it died because of the otherness of God, because of the transcendence of God, because of the magnitude of God." Yet Moses occupies that sacred ground without being harmed, much less being wholly consumed. This is only possible, argues Keller, because "the Angel of the Lord was in the bush.... It's the Angel of the Lord who is mediating the presence of God."[18] Of course, we understand from our previous discussion that the Angel of the Lord is Christ in His preincarnate form (a Christophany). So while Moses is a type of Christ in his mediatorial role on behalf of his people, even he, in that very moment, also needs a mediator, and that mediator is Jesus Christ.

Savor that: Moses, the quintessential mediator, himself needs a mediator. This underscores Charles Spurgeon's point that "we must approach the Lord through a Mediator: it is absolutely necessary."[19] This Mediator walks among and on behalf of His people, just as Moses did. As Spurgeon observes, "Moses was truly one of the people, for he loved them intensely, and all his sympathies were with them. They provoked him terribly, but still he loved them. We can never admire that man of God too much when we think of his disinterested love to that guilty nation."[20] The most striking parallel I see between Moses and Christ is that they are both unique bridges to God because of their special relationship with their people *and* their special relationship with God. Each of them, in a sense, has a foot in both worlds—the human and the divine. And though Moses pales greatly in both capacities in comparison with Christ, Moses more closely resembles Him in this respect than any other person and thereby prefigures Him.

THE PASSOVER

When none of the first nine plagues moves pharaoh to liberate the people (in fact, each plague merely hardens pharaoh's heart), God pulls out all the stops. He would not only attack Egypt, but pharaoh specifically. He would bring death to the firstborn of all Egyptians but spare the Israelites (Exodus 11:5–7). God institutes the Passover as His means of setting apart the firstborn of the Israelites for salvation.

The Passover is strikingly typical of Christ and His sacrificial and saving work. Like our salvation in Christ, the Passover is a function of God's sovereign and gracious will. It is an illustration, in real-life history, of how God saves sinners through the shedding of blood. The Passover story probably has as much New Testament symbolism as any event in the Old Testament. This episode and its subsequent commemoration unmistakably point to the cross.

God tells Moses to instruct His people to set aside lambs without defects. The animals are to be slaughtered at twilight and their blood is to be applied to the sides and tops of the doorframes of their houses (Exodus 12:5–7). God reveals that on that same night He will "pass through" Egypt and strike down every firstborn man and animal, bringing judgment on Egypt and her gods. The lambs' blood will be His sign to "pass over" the houses of the Israelites who will thereby avoid the plague (Exodus 12:12–13). God also commands them to commemorate this event for posterity by celebrating it as a festival to the Lord (Exodus 12:14). The Israelites obey God's instructions and, as promised, are spared the plague.

The symbolism and even language of the Passover event is emphasized in the New Testament—just as the Passover blood spares and redeems the Hebrews, the blood of Christ redeems Christians from their sinful state. For example, Paul tells the Romans that God presented the sacrifice of Christ "to demonstrate his righteousness, because in the forbearance of God, he passed over the sins previously committed" (Romans 3:25). The selection of the lamb is particularly meaningful. Note John the Baptist's proclamation about Jesus, "Behold, the Lamb of God, who takes away the sin of the world!" (John 1:29), as well as Paul's description of Christ as "our Passover lamb, [Who] has been sacrificed" (1 Cor. 5:7). Moreover, the Passover lambs must be without defect, just as Christ, in His sinlessness, lived without defect. Peter makes the connection: "knowing that you were ransomed from the futile ways inherited from your forefathers, not with perishable things such as silver or gold, but with the precious blood of Christ, like that of a lamb without blemish or spot" (1 Peter 1:18–19).

In describing the sacrificial lamb, God tells Moses, "You shall not break any of its bones" (Exodus 12:46). This admonition connects to Christ's crucifixion: "But when they came to Jesus and saw that He was already dead, they did not break his legs. But one of the soldiers pierced his side with a spear, and at once there came out blood and water. He who saw it has borne witness—his testimony is true, and he knows that he is telling the truth—that you also may believe. For these things took place that the Scripture might be fulfilled: 'Not one of His bones will be broken'" (John 19:33–36).

To be spared God's tenth plague, the Israelites have to take specific action—anyone failing to apply blood to his doorframe would meet the fate of the Egyptians. Thus, the Passover also teaches that in order to avail oneself of God's saving work, you have to appropriate it for yourself—you have to smear the blood on your door, metaphorically, by placing your saving faith in Jesus Christ. "The provision must be applied personally," Dr. Roy Matheson writes. "It is not enough that the provision was made at Calvary for my sins. I must appropriate and apply this provision by trusting Christ in a personal way."[21] This points to God's requirement that Christ's blood, in order to effect our individual salvation, must be appropriated by each of us and applied personally by our faith, trusting in Him and His redemptive shedding of blood. The late Pastor Ray Stedman put it well: "The Passover is a beautiful picture of the cross of Christ.... But the Israelites—those who, by a simple act of faith, took the blood of a lamb and sprinkled it on the doorposts and lintels of their houses—were perfectly safe. Then and now, salvation is accomplished by the simple act of faith, a trusting response to God's loving provision of a Savior who has settled our guilt before God. Then and now, the angel of death passes over those who are covered by the blood of the Lamb."[22]

THE EXODUS

"The exodus," writes Tremper Longman, "was the most important salvation event of the Old Testament. God rescued his people from Egyptian bondage by miraculous and extraordinary means."[23] It is a redemptive event at the beginning of Israel's history different from all other events in Scripture. "It was a stupendous happening," marvels Gerard Van Groningen, "promised by God to Abraham (Gen. 15:16), a central theme of Moses' farewell address.... [I]t was a significant point in Joshua's final rehearsal of God's covenantal faithfulness to the victorious Hebrews (Josh 24:5–7)." It was also often sung by the psalmists and invoked by later prophets, both Major and Minor.[24]

The delivery of Israel out of Egypt and into the Promised Land points to the work of Christ in salvation, representing judgment on the wicked world[25] and salvation for God's people. Describing the exodus as a key messianic event, Van Groningen outlines the many separate redemptive events included in the story: Israel's bondage; Egypt's cruel treatment of Israel; the people's anguished cries for deliverance; the unique preparation and calling of Moses as the delivering agent; Moses' confrontations with Egypt's self-described deified ruler; the plagues; Israel's departure; the destruction of Egypt's armies and Israel's safe passage to liberty; God's providential provisions for Israel in the wilderness; the formalizing of the covenant; the military organization of the people; and the people's tutelage in worship practices.[26]

Van Groningen, however, cautions that the exodus is not "*the* messianic event per se for all times and all places." The exodus, along with the wilderness experiences, brings redemption and freedom, but it largely matters because it "was a necessary preliminary event which set the stage for the new, full, and complete exodus.... The first exodus, effectual and productive as it was, was a type; its antitype, Christ's redemptive work, the new exodus, made this type effectual."[27]

The exodus, says J. Sidlow Baxter, means four essential things for Israel: a new life, a new liberty, a new fellowship, and a new assurance. "All of this has its counterpart in the Gospel of Christ," he argues. "The exodus under Moses is indeed a *type* of that which Christ has wrought for us." And just as the exodus represents these four essential things for Israel, "so the Gospel of Christ means all this to the believer."[28] Naturally, the event means something dramatically different for Egypt—the exodus exposes the falseness of idolatry and the impotence of false gods, the futility of rebelling against God and resisting His will, and the notion that Egypt belongs to "the world" apart from God.[29]

MANNA

Shortly after being delivered from Egypt, the people begin grumbling in the wilderness, asking why God had liberated them if He's just going to let them starve (Exodus 16). God then tells Moses He will rain bread from heaven. God gives them just enough to get by on each day so they will realize they are dependent on Him for their daily sustenance, which is to send the greater message that they are dependent on Him for spiritual sustenance.

The manna signifies the presence of the Lord with His people and His shepherding care. It typifies Christ because, like Christ, it is all the people need.[30] The manna is practically the sole nourishment the Israelites have until they enter Canaan (Josh 5:12). "So Christ is the food of the soul during its entire pilgrimage through the wilderness of this world, until it reaches the true Canaan, heaven," states Rev. H. D. Spence. "The Israelites were in danger of perishing for lack of food—they murmured—and God gave them the manna. The world was perishing for lack of spiritual nourishment—it made a continual dumb complaint—and God heard, and gave his own Son from heaven. Christ came into the world, not only to teach it, and redeem it, but to be its 'spiritual food and sustenance.' He feeds us with the bread of life. He gives us his own self for nourishment. Nothing else can truly sustain and support the soul."[31]

In later times, when the Jews remind Jesus that Moses had provided manna in the wilderness and ask what signs Jesus could give them that He is the Lord, Jesus replies with the stunning revelation that He Himself is the manna: "Truly, truly, I say to you, it was not Moses who gave you the bread from heaven, but my Father gives you the true bread from heaven. For the bread of God is he who comes down from heaven and gives life to the world" (John 6:30–33).

WATER FROM THE ROCK

Not long after God provides the manna, the people test Him by quarreling with Moses and demanding he give them water to drink. Moses, at God's command, strikes the rock at Horeb and water flows from it (Exodus 17:1–7). In another incident, God commands Moses to speak to the rock but he strikes it instead (Num. 20:11). Though water comes out, God is displeased by Moses' lack of trust and bars him from entering the Promised Land.

The rock in these events represents Christ because, like the rock, Christ is struck with divine judgment—His crucifixion—and because He flows with the water of life, as shown in John 4:14: "Whoever drinks of the water that I will give him will never be thirsty again. The water that I will give him will become in him a spring of water welling up to eternal life." When Paul declares, "That rock was Christ," he is confirming that Christ is our provider, protector, and always-present Lord.[32] Furthermore, in the Old Testament God is frequently identified as a rock (Gen. 49:24; Deut. 34:4, 15, 18, 30, 31; Psalms 18:31, 62:2, 78:35, 89:26, 95:1), and the term is associated, typically, with Christ, often in connection with His redemptive work (Deut. 32:15; Psalms 62:2; 95:1; 89:26; 78:35; Deut. 32:18).[33]

THE TABERNACLE

At the same time that God gives Moses the Law, He also gives him directions for building the Tabernacle, a portable shrine the Israelites would use for worshipping in the wilderness.[34] The Tabernacle is a prefiguring of the heavenly temple.[35] The instructions for building it are curiously interrupted in the biblical record by the story of Israel breaking its covenant and making the golden calf at the foot of Mt. Sinai. After retelling that event, the narrative returns to the Tabernacle. Roy Matheson notes that this juxtaposition of the golden calf story emphasizes Israel's desperate need for a means to approach God. "Israel has just been given the law and has promised to keep it," writes Matheson. "But as soon as the opportunity arises, Israel is pictured as breaking the first two of the Ten Commandments at the base of the mountain. By doing so they demonstrate they will not be able to keep the commandments and thus need a means of approach to God. The Tabernacle provides such an approach. It is a demonstration of the grace of God even under the law."[36] Philip Jenson argues, alternatively, that the instructions are given twice because "it reinforces the significance and importance of the action and the reality of the divine dimension being approached."[37]

God "walked" with Adam in the Garden and spoke to the patriarchs, but the Tabernacle is His first dwelling place on earth.[38] Of course, God is always present, but the Tabernacle assures the Israelites of His presence.[39] The Tabernacle is in the form of a tent, ten cubits wide and thirty cubits long. (A cubit is about eighteen inches.)[40] Like the more

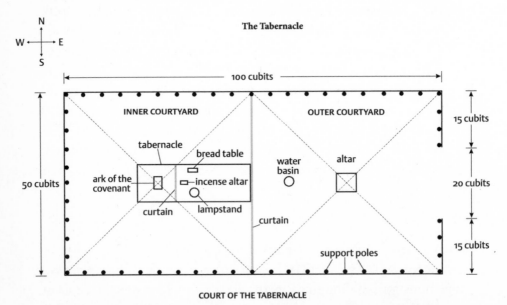

COURT OF THE TABERNACLE

Image used by permission: T. B. Dozeman, Commentary on Exodus *(Grand Rapids, MI; Cambridge, UK: William B. Eerdmans Publishing Company, 2009), page 608.*

Reconstruction of the Israelite Tabernacle and its court. The court was formed by curtains attached to erect poles. Before the tent was placed the Altar of Burnt Offerings and the Laver. The Tabernacle was always erected to face the east, so this view is from the northeast.

Image used by permission: Holman Book of Charts, Maps and Reconstructions *(Nashville, TN: B&H Publishing Group, 1993), page 144.*

permanent Temple to follow, it is divided into two compartments separated by a curtain or veil. The outer compartment, called the Holy Place, is the main chamber in which priests perform their routine duties. The inner sanctuary, called the Most Holy Place or the Holy of Holies, can only be entered by the high priest, and only on one day a year—the Day of Atonement, discussed below.[41] The Tabernacle is surrounded by a spacious courtyard that is one hundred cubits long, fifty cubits wide, and is enclosed by a fence five cubits high. The Tabernacle structure is in the western half of the courtyard while the eastern half contains the bronze altar and the laver (water basin).[42]

The only entrance to the Tabernacle courtyard is through the gate on its eastern side. This is significant because it seems that Cain and Abel brought their offerings to the east gate of the Garden of Eden, before the flaming sword.[43] To prevent Adam and Eve from returning to the Garden after their expulsion, God "placed the cherubim and a flaming sword that turned every way to guard the way to the tree of life" (Gen. 3:24).[44] With the Tabernacle, God is allowing Israel to enter His presence through the eastern gate. (Incidentally, the design of Solomon's Temple also echoes imagery of the Garden of Eden, as the Temple's eastern gate models the gate of the garden.)[45] The preceding illustrations show the Tabernacle's layout.[46]

The Tabernacle prefigures individual Christians, argues David Levy. "Paul said, 'Know ye not that your body is the temple [sanctuary] of the Holy Spirit who is in you, whom ye have of God, and ye are not your own?' (1 Cor. 6:19). As a sanctuary where the Spirit of God dwells, believers are not at liberty to allow their bodies to be used outside of His designed purposes for them."[47] The Tabernacle and the more permanent Temple were also types of Jesus Christ, Who "became flesh and dwelt among us" (John 1:14). Notice how this theme is advanced in Revelation as God tells us about the new heaven and the new earth: "Behold, the dwelling place of God is with man. He will dwell with them, and they will be his people, and God himself will be with them as their God. He will wipe every tear from their eyes, and death shall be no more, neither shall there be mourning, nor crying, nor pain anymore, for the former things have passed away" (Rev. 21:3–4).

The Tabernacle in the wilderness is the foreshadowing of Christ dwelling with us, putting an end to our sorrow, and bringing us everlasting joy. "By all the complex tabernacle operations, the sacrifices, and the ceremonies, God is picturing what Christ will do," contends Michael Barrett. "These pictures are full of Christ and therefore are a key place that we must search for him."[48] Also note, in the Revelation passage cited above, God's reiteration of the key element of the covenantal promise that we looked at earlier, which is now carried forward to the very end of the New Testament: "And they shall be my people, and I will be their God" (Ezek. 11:20; cf. Gen. 17:7).

THE FURNISHINGS

God provides detailed instructions for the sanctuary's furniture. Each of the furnishings points distinctly to Christ.

1. The brazen altar in the outer court, where animals are sacrificed, typifies Christ's work on the cross to save all

who place their faith in His blood shed on our behalf (Romans 3:24–25). No Israelite can come into God's presence without sacrificing at the brazen altar, just as today no sinner may come into communion with God except through Jesus and the cross.[49] The altar typifies the Atonement of Christ.[50]

2. The laver is also in the outer court, between the brazen altar and the Tabernacle. This water basin is solely for the priests, who are required to wash before entering the Tabernacle. Prefiguring the Christian's need for purification, the laver speaks of Christ as our sanctification (Romans 6:1–9). It is a shadowy image of the work of the Holy Spirit, applying the redemptive work of Christ.[51] Christians, while they are forgiven for salvation purposes, need to continue to walk with God on their path to sanctification. "The continual cleansing each of us needs is provided in Christ, and pictured in the laver before the tabernacle entrance," notes Larry Richards. "Purified, we can freely enter the presence of our God."[52]

3. The Table of Showbread, which holds twelve loaves of bread—one for each of Israel's twelve tribes—is in the Holy Place. It foreshadows Christ as our spiritual sustenance. As Jesus proclaims, "I am the bread of life; whoever comes to me shall not hunger" (John 6:35, 48).

4. The lampstand fills the Holy Place with light, providing illumination for the priest as he ministers.[53] It speaks of Christ as "the light of the world" (John 8:12), typifying our spiritual illumination. Remember that not everyone avails Himself of the Light of the world: "And this is the judgment: the light has come into the world, and people loved the darkness rather than the light because their works were evil. For everyone who does wicked things hates the light and does not come into the light, lest his works should be exposed. But whoever does what is true comes to the light, so that it may be clearly seen that his works have been carried out in God" (John 3:19–21). The

light from the lampstand, then, is a picture of Christ's holiness[54]—as recorded in 1 John, "God is light, and in him is no darkness at all" (1:5). Indeed, Christ's light is so radiant that by itself it will illuminate the new Jerusalem for all eternity (Rev. 21:23).

5. The Altar of Incense (Exodus 30:1–10), which stands in front of the curtain or veil in the Holy Place, represents the prayers of God's people constantly arising in His presence. Intended to remind the high priest of the need for prayer in the presence of God (Rev. 8:3–4), it symbolizes prayer with Christ as our intercessor and high priest (Heb. 7:25; John 17:9). Christians should be aware of Christ's work on our behalf as high priest, Who intercedes in prayer for us, for His Church, and with the Father. We should especially familiarize ourselves with John chapter 17, which contains the High Priestly Prayer, in which Christ prays to the Father on our behalf. We are to see His prayers rise up like the smoke of incense as a pleasing aroma to the Father.

I think we should look at this prayer in the context of the foregoing discussion of the Tabernacle as a prefiguring of Christ dwelling with us into eternity. In this prayer Jesus asks the Father to prepare us for that everlasting fellowship we shall enjoy with Him, thus showing us what are Jesus' priorities and concerns for us.[55] Jesus further prays that we would be filled with His joy (John 17:13) and protected from Satan (John 17:15); for our sanctification and growth in the Word and the truth (John 17:17); and for believers to become one, as a united Church, just as He and the Father are One (John 17:20–23).[56]

We should study this remarkable prayer, described by some as the true Lord's prayer and by Warren Wiersbe as "the greatest prayer ever prayed."[57] In this prayer Jesus asks the Father to glorify Him, which is a remarkable assertion of deity, as no one other than God Himself would have been so bold. Moses, you'll recall, merely asked to see God's glory (Exodus 33:18), but would never have presumed to become part of it. In the prayer Jesus initially prays for Himself, but nevertheless in a selfless way, for He is facing the cross and is praying for the strength to complete the task that leads to our redemption. As Wiersbe explains, "The glorification of Jesus Christ meant the completion of the great work of salvation."[58] Jesus' very words confirm this: "Father, the hour has come; glorify your Son that the Son may glorify you, since you have given him authority over all flesh, to give eternal life to all whom you have given him" (John 17:1–2). Even at the height of His agony, Jesus is thinking about us and our eternal destiny.

6. The Ark of the Covenant—the only piece of Tabernacle furniture in the Holy of Holies—is covered with a gold "mercy seat," which is literally translated as "atonement covering."[59] The ark, which is symbolic of God's throne and presence, is the most sacred item of furniture in the Tabernacle. Indeed, the Tabernacle is built specifically to house the ark, so that God can dwell among His people.[60] The ark holds the stone tablets engraved with the Ten Commandments, which is why it is sometimes called the Ark of the Testimony. The priest also spreads the blood of the sacrifice on it.

   The ark is one of the most distinct types of Christ in the entire Bible. Its acacia wood typifies Christ's life and ministry. It beautifully portrays the humanity of Christ, Who came from "a root out of a dry ground" (Isaiah 53:2) and was wholly sinless in His birth (Luke 1:35) and His life (1 Peter 1:19, 2:22). The gold in the Table of Showbread represents Jesus' deity,[61] and the ark represents Christ as the full satisfaction for our sins (1 John 2:2).

The priesthood plays a key role in ceremonies at the Tabernacle and later at the Temple. The sacrifice has to be made by the high priest on behalf of everyone else, and ultimately, God is not approachable except through the priestly caste. But the substitutionary death of Christ, our High Priest, changes that exclusivity, allowing us all to approach God through Jesus Christ. Note that at the precise moment Jesus dies,[62] completing His work on our behalf on the cross, the veil of the Temple that separated the Holy Place from the Holy of Holies "was torn in two, from top to bottom" by a supernatural act of God (Matt. 27:51). As a result, any man at any time by faith in Christ might enter directly into God's presence.[63] Lest there be any doubt, the writer of Hebrews assures us, "Therefore, brothers, since we have confidence to enter the holy places by the blood of Jesus, by the new and living way that he opened for us through the curtain, that is, through his flesh, and since we have a great priest over the house of God, let us draw near with a true heart in full assurance of faith, with our hearts sprinkled clean from an evil conscience and our bodies washed with pure water" (10:19–22).

Jesus' work for us culminates here. He died so that we may have an everlasting relationship with Him, separated by no curtain, separated by nothing. Christ "is the mediator of a new covenant, so that those who are called may receive the promised eternal inheritance, since a death has occurred that redeems them from the transgressions committed under the first covenant" (Heb. 9:15). Ray Stedman explains, "The blood of Jesus, the perfect sacrifice of the God-Man upon the cross, completes what the blood sacrifices of the Old Testament only symbolized. Through the perfect sacrifice of Jesus, we now have access to the presence of God, which was forbidden to the common people in the days of Moses."[64] Stedman adds that because of Christ's death for us, the Temple is no longer needed, because our bodies are God's temple (1 Cor. 3:16) and Christ dwells in all believers through His Holy Spirit. "The great truth for us here," notes Stedman, "is that God has completely settled the problem of sin in us—absolutely and completely settled it!"[65] As Paul writes in the Book of Romans, "There is therefore now no condemnation for those who are in Christ Jesus. For the law of the Spirit of life has set you free in Christ Jesus from the law of sin and death" (8:1).

This tearing of the veil not only signifies that we can go directly into God's presence through Jesus Christ, writes Pastor Timothy Keller, but it also means that His glory is now in the Church: "Christ says, 'Little flock, I have given you the kingdom.' Now our lives are transformed because that kingdom power that was in the garden of Eden and then was in the tabernacle is now out in our lives."[66]

MESSIANIC PROPHECIES IN EXODUS

We already discussed the messianic prophecies related to Christ as the Passover Lamb, particularly God's instructions that the bones of the sacrificial lambs shall not be broken, just as none of Christ's bones were broken when He was sacrificed on the cross. But Exodus offers another intriguing messianic prophecy—this one related to God's instructions to Moses to consecrate to Him all the firstborn of both man and beast (Exodus 13:1–2; Num. 8:17). In the New Testament, Luke reports that Jesus was Mary's firstborn son (Luke 2:7), and "when the time came for their purification according to the Law of Moses, they brought him up to Jerusalem to present him to the Lord (as it is written in the Law of the Lord, 'Every male who first opens the womb shall be called holy to the Lord')" (Luke 2:22–23). Elsewhere, the New Testament refers to Christ as the "only begotten" (John 1:14, 18, 3:16, 18) and the "firstborn" Son of God (Romans 8:29; Col. 1:15, 18).

The firstborn eldest son had substantial advantages in Hebrew culture. For example, he came ahead of his younger brothers according to his birthright, the firstborn being "preeminent in dignity and preeminent in power" (Gen. 43:33, 49:3). He was also entitled to a double portion of his father's estate (Deut. 21:15–17). The pecking order was not absolute, however, as the firstborn could, through misconduct, forfeit his prerogatives. The father could also sometimes deviate from the rule, as when David chose his younger son Solomon, in obedience to God (1 Kings 1:12–30).

God instructs Moses to tell pharaoh that Israel is His firstborn son, and that he must "Let my son go that he may serve me. If you refuse to let him go, behold, I will kill your firstborn son" (Exodus 4:22). This passage is rich with meaning, indicating that God claims Israel as His special, privileged, and preeminent people—His chosen servants who will represent Him among the nations. Israel, as firstborn of God, also has certain duties, including to "Be holy, for I the Lord your God am holy" (Lev. 19:2). The firstborn—Israel, in this case—must be respectful, grateful, and obedient.[67] Just as God instructs Israel to consecrate their firstborn males once they were brought out of Egypt (Exodus 13:2), Israel's firstborn status must be consecrated, which is among the reasons God instructs Israel to keep that status holy (as we'll see in our discussion of Leviticus). God makes it clear that if pharaoh doesn't release His "firstborn" from captivity, He will take pharaoh's firstborn. Thus the concept of the "firstborn son" is integrally tied to God's redemptive plan, and He will tolerate no interference with it.[68]

When the New Testament writers identify Jesus as God's firstborn and only Son, they are endorsing the idea that the firstborn son introduced in the Old Testament reaches its fulfillment in Christ. "The firstborn typified Christ;" argues Gerard Van Groningen, "more so, the firstborn was a direct antecedent of Jesus the Christ, God's only, firstborn son."[69] Walter Kaiser says that the terms used in the Old Testament concerning firstborn "were used of Jesus the Messiah.... He too was delivered out of Egypt and was given the same familial term, 'my son' (Matthew 2:15; cf. Hosea 11:1). Moreover, He was God's 'firstborn,' (Romans 8:29; Col. 1:15, 18; Heb. 1:6; Rev. 1:5)." Kaiser adds, "The continuity of terms, identities, and meanings throughout both Testaments is more than a mere accident. It is a remarkable evidence of a single planned program and a unified single people of God."[70]

Exodus gives us a beautiful picture of Christ's redemptive activities to come. We turn next to the Book of Leviticus, which points to the believer's personal relationship with Jesus Christ and the pathway to holiness flowing from it.

CHAPTER 11

CHRIST IN EVERY BOOK
LEVITICUS THROUGH DEUTERONOMY

The Law, holiness, the sacrifices, the tabernacle—all the essential elements of Leviticus—find their meaning in Christ, who uniquely fulfilled the law, lived a perfect, sinless life, died as a sacrifice for sins, and was the presence of God incarnate. These themes are like streams that flow through biblical history as well as through the rest of the pages of Scripture until they converge in the person of the Messiah, Jesus Christ. Thus Leviticus, like the Bible as a whole, is about the person and work of Jesus Christ and finds its ultimate meaning in him. To ignore this section of the Word of God is to diminish our understanding of the long-anticipated one who has now brought us our great salvation!

—MARK ROOKER[1]

LEVITICUS

◇◇◇◇◇◇◇◇◇◇◇◇◇◇◇◇◇◇◇◇

The Book of Leviticus chronologically and logically follows Genesis and Exodus. Genesis tells of man's fall and God's promise to redeem him, Exodus begins God's actual plan of redemption, and Leviticus features God's instructions to Israel as to how man can develop a relationship with Him. The narrative in Leviticus begins where Exodus leaves off, with God instructing Moses from the entrance to the Tabernacle.

While Exodus describes Israel's redemption from her Egyptian slavemasters, Leviticus involves liberation from an even more daunting oppressor: sin. The bondage of sin is particularly pernicious because it interferes with God's primary purpose in creating mankind: having a loving relationship with Him. Sin, because it is mainly an offense against God, keeps us from being in His presence and communing with Him. When we are marching to the steps of a different master we are not following God. As we read in Luke, "No servant can serve two masters, for either he will hate the one and love the other, or he will be devoted to the one and despise the other" (16:13). In Leviticus, therefore, God shows Israel how it can begin to atone for its sins and enter into the presence of God.

God, having vowed to mold Israel into a nation of priests through whom He would eventually bring His promise of salvation to all other nations (Exodus 19:6), must now implement His promise to set that nation apart. That means God has to teach the Israelites how to be His chosen vehicle and be fully devoted to Him. Accordingly, Leviticus sets forth God's instructions to Israel as to how to become that special, holy nation of priests, which is why some scholars have referred to the book as God's worship manual for Israel.[2]

Leviticus 10:10–11 defines the crux of the priestly ministry: "You are to distinguish between the holy and the common, and between the unclean and the clean, and you are to teach the people of Israel all the statutes that the LORD has spoken to them by Moses." Roy Zuck observes, "Israel, then, was a people separated to [God] from among all nations of the earth. Her lifestyle and, indeed, her very character must advertise to all peoples the meaning of that identity and mission."[3] Ray Stedman adds, "Because the sacrifices, rituals, and ceremonies of Leviticus are a foreshadowing of Jesus and His saving work, this book can teach us a great deal about how Jesus Christ can meet our needs now. This is not just a historical book. It is a tremendously practical manual on how to live the Christian life."[4]

The book may initially seem tedious, but on closer examination it is a fascinating preview of God's ultimate plan for the blood sacrifice of His only Son in total satisfaction of man's sin. All the sacrificial offerings and holy festivals point to Christ. As such, in addition to their immediate function of maturing Israel for her elective task, they provide invaluable insights for New Testament believers. Rev. Joseph Exell captures the book's significance:

> The historical importance of the Book of Leviticus is very great. One might as well expect to understand the history of Greece, while remaining in ignorance of philosophy and art, or of England, while knowing nothing whatever of parliament and the constitution as to understand the history of Israel without a knowledge of the Hebrew ritual. Think how much labor is spent in the study of the classical mythology at our schools and universities, not for any value there is in itself, but for the light it throws upon classical literature; and yet how little do Christian people realize the importance of studying the modes of worship among the Jews, in order to understand their literature, which is our Bible! And besides, not only is the knowledge of the Tabernacle worship necessary in order to understand the sacred literature, but it is of real value in itself; not merely of antiquarian and psychological value, like the ancient mythologies, but of present practical value, as throwing light upon the New Testament and illustrating that gospel on which our hopes are founded.[5]

Central to the book's theme is God's oft-repeated no-nonsense charge to Israel: "Be holy, for I am holy" (Lev. 11:44, 11:45, 19:2, 20:7). God is telling Israel that as His chosen nation, specially selected to model and disseminate the Gospel to all other peoples, it must be spiritually and morally pure after the pattern of God Himself.

Scholars tend to agree that Leviticus contains two main sections. The first discusses the means of approach and access to a perfectly holy

God in order to establish a proper relationship with Him, including God's prescribed methods of sacrifice. The second section imparts instructions on how to maintain fellowship with God, including laws pertaining to cleanliness, regulations on holiness, and teachings about the religious feasts. As some have noted, the structure of the book prefigures the Christian's walk. Once a person becomes a Christian he has access to God, but his spiritual maturation is just beginning—he finds himself in a continuing battle between his sinful nature and his new, spirit-filled nature. The idea is that by practicing the spiritual disciplines—Bible study, prayer, worship, etc.—he will become more holy and more Christ-like.

The first section of Leviticus shows that for man to gain access to God there must be both an offering and an offeror, or priest.[6] Therefore God specifies the types of acceptable sacrifices and also establishes the priesthood. Theologian Richard Niebuhr once wrote that the watered down Christian theologies of today tend to believe in "a God without wrath who took man without sin into a kingdom without righteousness through the ministrations of a Christ without a cross."[7] In other words, many seem to want an easy, feel-good religion that requires no sacrifice. But unsanitized Christianity teaches that God's justice requires that payment be made for man's sin. Sacrifice is the currency for this transaction—it is the God-given vehicle through which sinful men can approach their holy God. The Old Testament system of sacrifice entails the death of the sacrificial victim (an animal) as a foreshadowing of the ultimate sacrificial death of Jesus Christ. As the writer of Hebrews states, "For by a single offering he has perfected for all time those who are being sanctified" (Heb. 10:14).

While Leviticus formalizes and details this intricate sacrificial system, the practice predates the book. God had made it clear to Cain and Abel that He requires blood sacrifice when He approved Abel's offering and disapproved Cain's. Old Testament scholar Robert Harris observes that the "doctrine of the typological blood of the sacrifices and the efficacious blood of Christ...has often been called the scarlet line of redemption that begins in Abel's sacrifice in Genesis and climaxes in the blood of the Lamb slain from the creation of the world in Revelation (13:8)."[8] As Jesus Himself proclaims, "I lay down my life for the sheep" (John 10:15).

But the Old Testament animal sacrifices were imperfect, serving to cover up sins rather than wash them away. That is why they had to be repeated day after day and year after year. "By itself, the bringing of sacrifices could never save the sinner," Warren Wiersbe explains. "There had to be faith in God's Word, for it is faith that saves the soul. David knew that sacrifices alone could never take away his sins. (Ps. 51:16–17); the prophets also made this clear (Isa 1:11–24). However, when the sinner came with a contrite heart, putting faith in God's Word, then his sacrifice was acceptable to God."[9] The perfect sacrifice of Christ only had to be done once. In fact, further sacrifices beyond Christ's would be to insult, injure, and crucify Him all over again. The Book of Hebrews, which has been called the New Testament's commentary on Leviticus,[10] illuminates the point:

> For since the law has but a shadow of the good things to come instead of the true form of those realities, it can never, by the same sacrifices that are continually offered every year, make perfect those who draw near. Otherwise, would they not have ceased to be offered, since the worshipers, having once been cleansed, would no longer have any consciousness of sins? But in these sacrifices there is a reminder of sins every year. For it is impossible for the blood of bulls and goats to take away sins. Consequently, when Christ came into the world, he said, "Sacrifices and offerings you have not desired, but a body have you prepared for me; in burnt offerings and sin offerings you have taken no pleasure. Then I said, 'Behold, I have come to do your will, O God, as it is written of me in the scroll of the book.'" When he said above, "You have neither desired nor taken pleasure in sacrifices and offerings and burnt offerings and sin offerings" (these are offered according to the law), then he added, "Behold, I have come to do your will." He does away with the first in order to establish the second. And by that will we have been sanctified through the offering of the body of Jesus Christ once for all. And every priest stands daily at his service, offering repeatedly the same sacrifices, which can never take away sins. But when Christ had offered for all

time a single sacrifice for sins, he sat down at the right hand of God, waiting from that time until his enemies should be made a footstool for his feet. For by a single offering he has perfected for all time those who are being sanctified. And the Holy Spirit also bears witness to us; for after saying, "This is the covenant that I will make with them after those days, declares the Lord: I will put my laws on their hearts, and write them on their minds," then he adds, "I will remember their sins and their lawless deeds no more." Where there is forgiveness of these, there is no longer any offering for sin" (10:1–18).

Though Leviticus has no messianic prophecies, it is a treasure trove of types, pictures, and foreshadowings of the spiritual realities to be consummated in Christ. "Here is the New Testament gospel for sinners stated in Old Testament language and enshrined in the ritual of sacrifice," James E. Smith avers. "The Old Testament offerings, appointed times, priestly consecration, and office of high priest, were all designated by God to portray the spiritual realities of the Christian Age."[11]

THE OFFERINGS

There are five main types of offerings prescribed in the first seven chapters of Leviticus: the burnt offering, the grain (meal) offering, the peace offering, the sin offering, and the trespass offering. Each of these sacrifices points to Christ and His ultimate sacrifice.

The Burnt Offering. This can be made with a bull (Lev. 1:5), a sheep or goat (Lev. 1:10); or a bird (Lev. 1:14). The offering has to be a male without defect. The species that is offered depends on the wealth of the person on whose behalf the sacrifice is made. The offeror is required to "lay his hand on the head of the burnt offering, and it shall be accepted for him to make atonement for him" (Lev. 1:4). By laying his hand on the offering, the offeror identifies with the offering and avails himself of the benefits of its substitutionary sacrifice on his behalf. The offering is then completely consumed on the altar (Lev. 1:9).[12] Being wholly consecrated to God, it depicts Christ's complete consecration in death.[13]

The Grain (Meal) Offering. This is mixed with oil but not yeast (Lev. 2:4). Since yeast is a symbol of sin, the offering depicts Christ's sinlessness and His sinless service.[14] This is the only sacrifice permitted that does not involve the shedding of blood, though it is associated with the burnt offerings or peace offerings that do involve blood.[15] It is not an exception to the requirement for blood sacrifice, then, because it is never brought as an offering by itself. Once the blood sacrifice has been made, this offering becomes acceptable to God.[16]

The Peace (Fellowship) Offering. This closely resembles the burnt offering in that the animal has to be without blemish or defect (Lev. 3:1) and the offeror is required to lay his hand on the animal to identify with it (Lev. 3:2). But it differs from the burnt offering in that only the best of the animal—the fat—is sacrificed (Lev. 3:3–5), and the offeror can eat what is left. This offering symbolizes the peace and communion resulting from Christ's death—that is, His sacrificial death (the burnt offering) and His sinless life (the meal offering) lead to peace with God (the peace offering).[17] Note that Isaiah foretells that Christ would be chastised for our peace (Isaiah 53:5), and Paul writes in Colossians that Christ made peace by the blood of His cross (Col. 1:20). In addition, Ephesians 5:2 can be seen as referring to the peace offering: "And walk in love, as Christ loved us and gave himself up for us, a fragrant offering and sacrifice to God."[18]

The Sin Offering. This is made on behalf of those who have sinned unintentionally (Lev. 4:2). "Even sins done unknowingly," writes Robert Vasholz, "must be atoned for in regards to the sanctity of God's house."[19] Once again, an animal without blemish or defect must be used, and the offeror must place his hands on it (Lev. 4:3–4). The fat is to be burned on the altar, but the remainder of the animal is burned in a wood fire outside the camp in a place that is ceremonially cleaned (Lev. 4:12).

Hebrews specifies the New Testament significance of this procedure: "For the bodies of those animals whose blood is brought into the holy places by the high priest as a sacrifice for sin are burned outside the camp. So Jesus also suffered outside the gate in order to sanctify the people through his own blood" (13:11–12). This sacrifice depicts Christ as bearing our sin: "He Himself bore our sins in his body on the tree, that we might die to sin and live to righteousness" (1 Peter 2:24). English theologian Andrew Jukes makes the important point that human beings have a sin nature, or an evil nature, from which our sins or trespasses proceed. God knows we are evil and makes provision for it. So there's a distinction, Jukes argues, between the sin offering and the trespass offering described below: "One is for sin in our nature, the other for the fruits of it."[20] Edward Hindson, in the KJV Bible Commentary, explains why this offering is applied to unintentional sins: "The sin offering was for the guilt and defilement of the sin nature. It had to do with our natural depravity as the sons of Adam, hence the aspect of sins done in ignorance."[21] British evangelist John Stott depicts Christ as the ultimate sin offering: "By sending his own Son in the likeness of our sinful nature to be a sin offering, he actually condemned our sin in the human Jesus. It was only because he was condemned that we could be justified."[22]

The Trespass Offering. This is made on behalf of those who have sinned intentionally such as through deceit, fraud, lying, or stealing (Lev. 6:2–3). It can also be made for certain sins that could be unintentional, namely those related to the Lord's holy things—these include improper use of sacrificial flesh eaten by worshippers after a peace offering, and misuse of "most holy" portions of the grain, sin, or guilt offerings that are reserved for priests alone (Lev. 5:14–15).[23] (Note that no provisions are made in the sacrificial system for certain kinds of intentional sins, i.e., defiant sins [Numbers 15:30–31].)[24] In addition to offering the animal, the wrongdoer has to make restitution amounting to the original value plus one-fifth (Lev. 5:16).

This sacrifice depicts Christ as redeeming us by paying the ransom price for our sins: "you were ransomed from the futile ways inherited from your forefathers, not with perishable things such as silver or gold, but with the precious blood of Christ, like that of a lamb without blemish or spot"(1 Peter 1:18–19). Similarly, the letter to Ephesians informs us we are dead in our trespasses and sins, "But God, being rich in mercy, because of the great love with which he loved us, even when we were dead in our trespasses, made us alive together with Christ—by grace you have been saved—and raised us up with him and seated us with him in the heavenly places in Christ Jesus, so that in the coming ages he might show the immeasurable riches of his grace in kindness toward us in Christ Jesus. For by grace you have been saved through faith" (2:4–8).

AARON AND THE PRIESTHOOD

God establishes the priesthood in order to allow the people to approach Him through an intermediary. The priesthood signifies that God has a personal relationship with human beings.[25] It testifies to Israel's unique relationship with God and its quality of life as a result of submitting to and living under the Law. The priesthood is also a witness to God's power and His particular dwelling in the midst of His chosen nation.[26]

God appoints Aaron as the high priest, consecrating (purifying) him and his sons through a ceremony in which the priest's ear is consecrated with blood so that he will understand what the other parts of his body (feet and hands) must do. The priests first offer sacrifices for themselves—as they, too, are human and sinners—and then make sacrifices on behalf of the people. The priesthood is based on the principle of representational righteousness alluded to earlier.[27] Throughout the Bible we see God's willingness to spare people because of the righteousness of others, such as His response to Abraham's pleading for the deliverance of Sodom because of a few righteous men. The priests, likewise, could function as the people's representatives in atoning for their sins before God.

This concept of representational righteousness, it seems, is a prefiguring of Christ's ultimate representational (and substitutionary) sacrifice on behalf of all those who appropriate, through faith, His finished work on the cross. The priests serve on behalf of the Israelites, and the nation of Israel itself serves as a nation of priests in a representational capacity to bring the promised covenantal blessings to all mankind.

In the end, however, Aaron's priesthood is imperfect and limited because it can't provide access to God. "The one thing men needed most," writes John MacArthur, "couldn't be provided by Aaron. Therefore, there had to come another priest who could bring access to God, a priest after a different order, and that is Jesus Christ.... And so Christ has come and provided the access that Aaron couldn't provide."[28]

In other respects, however, Aaron actually typifies Christ: He ministers in sacred things (Heb. 5:1), he is made a priest by God Himself (Heb. 5:4–10), and he is a true mediator.[29] But whereas Aaron ministers in the earthly sphere, Christ serves as our high priest in heaven. So

Aaron serves as a copy and shadow of the heavenly things (Heb. 8:5), whereas Christ "has obtained a ministry that is as much more excellent than the old as the covenant he mediates is better, since it is enacted on better promises" (Heb. 8:6).

THE DAY OF ATONEMENT

The Day of Atonement, which occurs once a year, is the most solemn Old Testament ritual. God's instructions for it are given in Leviticus 16. On this day the people fast, the Tabernacle is purified, and atonement is made for the high priest and the people for sins committed over the previous year.[30] It is the only day that the high priest may enter into the Holy of Holies.

This day and its sacrifices and procedures are a pattern of Christ's work. Unlike the high priest, however, Jesus did not have to make atonement for His own sins, because He was sinless.[31] Hebrews tells us, "For Christ has entered, not into the holy places made with hands, which are copies of the true things, but into heaven itself, now to appear in the presence of God on our behalf" (9:24). On the Day of Atonement, the Aaronic high priest carries the sacrificial blood into the Holy of Holies, but Christ, writes James Hastings, "entered heaven 'through his blood' having obtained eternal redemption (Heb. 9:12).... Unlike the [Israelites]...who were unable to partake of the sin-offering offered on the Day of Atonement, Christians may partake of Christ."[32]

THE FEASTS

Leviticus 23 outlines seven feasts that help the Israelites to maintain their relationship with God. During these observances, which are designated by God Himself, the people assemble at the sanctuary (the Tabernacle and later the Temple) to meet with God. They are not allowed to do regular work on those days.[33] These occasions allow the Israelites to renew their allegiance to God and to promote their national unity.

The act of expressing their devotion to God for His graciousness toward them serves to unite the people.[34] The feasts include:

Passover (Lev. 23:4–5). Marking the deliverance of Israel from Egypt, this feast is observed for seven days. The event, as we've already seen, typifies Christ, Who is our Passover (1 Cor. 5:7).

The Feast of Unleavened Bread (Lev. 23:6–8). Observed the day after the Passover, this commemorates the Israelites' hasty departure out of Egypt—the people had no time to put leaven in their bread when they consumed their final meals as captives in Egypt.[35] This feast speaks of Christ as the bread of life. Paul compares this to the Christian life, saying that we must "Cleanse out the old leaven that you may be a new lump, as you really are unleavened. For Christ, our Passover lamb, has been sacrificed" (1 Cor. 5:7–8). According to John Walvoord, the prohibition against work during the feast also typifies the walk of the believer in Christ, who has not been saved as a result of his own works, but by grace through faith.[36] It bears repeating that Christ was crucified on the eve of the Passover, and that in his Gospel, John states that the Romans did not break His legs in accordance with their usual practice, which mirrors God's instructions that the Passover lambs' legs were to remain intact (19:31–37).

The Feast of Firstfruits (Lev. 23:9–14). This involves the Israelites offering the first products of the harvest to God, and the priests waving a sheaf of grain before Him, as symbols of Israel's gratitude and dependence on the Lord.[37] It is the first token of a new life, with an indication of more to come. Again, Paul analogizes this to Christ's resurrection:[38] "But in fact Christ has been raised from the dead, the firstfruits of those who have fallen asleep. For as by a man came death, by a man has come also the resurrection of the dead. For as in Adam all die, so also in Christ shall all be made alive. But each in his own order: Christ, the firstfruits, then at his coming those who belong to Christ" (1 Cor. 15:20–23). The feast occurs the day after the Sabbath (Lev. 23:11), which is the first day of the week, just as Christ was raised on the first day of the week.

The Feast of Pentecost (or Feast of Weeks) (Lev. 23:15–21). Occurring fifty days after the Feast of the Firstfruits, this celebrates the end of the grain harvest. Two baked loaves of new, fine, leavened flour are brought out of people's dwellings, and the priest waves them before the Lord, along with the animal sacrifice offerings for the sin and peace offerings (Lev. 23:17–20). Christians revere Pentecost because it is the day, as described in the Book of Acts, when the Holy Spirit was poured out on the people and the Church was formed. The two loaves in the original ceremony are believed to prefigure that both Jews and Gentiles would come together in Christ.[39]

The Feast of Trumpets (Lev. 23:23–25). This is a day for solemn rest and holy convocation that falls on the first day of the seventh month of the Jewish year. Signaling to the Israelites that they are beginning a sacred month, this feast encourages them to reflect on the harvest as well as the sins that had accumulated during the previous year.[40] Trumpets are sounded on the first day (Lev. 23:24) as a triumphant memorial to God's gracious provision for His people with the Mosaic Covenant.[41] In the Bible, trumpets are often used to announce God's presence.[42] In fact, Jesus foretold that the judgment of mankind would be announced by a blast of trumpets (Matt. 24:31), and Paul similarly taught that the day of resurrection will be introduced by trumpets (1 Cor. 15:52; 1 Thess. 4:16). This feast is also believed to be a picture of the regathering of Israel, because at the second coming of Christ to earth, Israel will respond to the sound of a trumpet and will be regathered to the land (Matt. 24:31; Isaiah 27:13).

The Day of Atonement. As discussed above, this points to Christ's work on the cross as an act of atonement, which was the final, once-and-for-all entering of the actual Holy of Holies—heaven. As Christ perfectly fulfilled the Day of Atonement, no further acts of atonement are necessary.[43]

The Feast of Tabernacles (Booths) (Lev. 23:33–44). This involves the Israelites leaving their homes and living in tents throughout the feast. It's a time for the people to rejoice in the completion of their harvest (Exodus 23:16)[44] and also a solemn reminder of their wilderness wanderings. It anticipates the time when they will enjoy lasting rest with God when the Messiah will reign on earth and in heaven.[45] Indeed, the last day of this feast is filled with joy and celebration as the people come out of their booths (tents) and anticipate their eternal rest.[46]

NUMBERS

The Book of Numbers records the Israelites' wilderness wanderings and their journeys from Sinai eventually to the Plains of Moab, where they await permission to enter the Promised Land. The book's main theme is that God's people must walk by faith and trust in His promises, or they will not make progress in their walk.[47] As I've mentioned, the Old Testament points to Christ in its progressive revelation of salvation history steadily marching toward the culmination of history in the perfect God/man Jesus Christ, and in its instructional revelations concerning God's dealings with His chosen people. God's relationship with Israel in recorded biblical history also points to Christ because it teaches Christians critical lessons about developing a relationship with God and the importance of faith, of walking with God, of obedience, of "fearing" God, and of trusting His promises. It also teaches us that there are real consequences for disobedience, idolatry, and trying to live independently of God under the illusion that we can be self-sufficient.

Numbers shows that apart from God, His people are "sojourners" wandering aimlessly through life without stability, direction, or purpose. Without Christ, we too are aimless wanderers in the wilderness of the world, impotent to save ourselves, successfully restrain our sinful nature, or conduct our lives in a meaningful way. Likening us to sojourners, Peter warns us of the pitfalls of living apart from God: "Beloved, I urge you as sojourners and exiles to abstain from the passions of the flesh, which wage war against your soul" (1 Peter 2:11).

So while Leviticus instructs the Israelites how to approach God through priestly intercessors and points to the work of Jesus Christ as our high priest Who eliminates the need for middlemen in accessing God, Numbers describes the Israelites' walk with God, anticipating the Christians' walk with God once they have placed their faith in Christ.

So we must read Numbers, like the rest of the historical books, not just to learn the history of God's people, but also to profit from their experiences and especially to learn from their mistakes. Because of our sin nature, walking with God is not as easy as it seems. But the consequences of falling away are always destructive. In relative terms, the

Israelites don't have far to go to get to Canaan, and the reason they get lost is not because they have no compasses. They choose to wander off course—to abandon God—and they pay the price.

I don't believe we should be discouraged by this message because, while a generation of Israelites forfeits the opportunity to see the Promised Land, during this interval God molds the people and teaches them the importance of obedience, faith, and trust. While they abandon Him, He most certainly does not abandon them, and though He does punish them for their disobedience, it isn't just about punishment—as noted, God disciplines those He loves for their own good. Similarly, Christians learn from adversity, which is why Paul exhorts us to "rejoice in our sufferings, knowing that suffering produces endurance, and endurance produces character, and character produces hope, and hope does not put us to shame because God's love has been poured into our hearts through the Holy Spirit who has been given to us" (Romans 5:3–5).

God could have miraculously transported the Israelites to Canaan and skipped the wandering, but that wouldn't have helped them because they weren't ready. He kept them in the wilderness, in my view, not just for punitive purposes, but to teach them indispensable lessons about the importance of maintaining a proper relationship with Him and walking by faith instead of by their own unaided devices. As believers armed with these scriptural lessons, we should be better equipped to avoid the disobedience that will result in us wandering in the spiritual wilderness.

We must keep our eyes on the prize—and that is Christ. As Stephen Kaung observes,

> God's purpose for us is to move forward towards His ultimate end and purpose, and that is Christ and His riches; for Canaan, spiritually speaking, betokens the riches of Christ because Canaan was a land flowing with milk and honey. Spiritually speaking, it is an environment that is not lacking in anything, for Canaan symbolically speaks of the unsearchable riches of Christ. God's purpose for His people is always that. He does not want to barely save us, like a brand plucked out of the fire (see Amos 4: 11; Zechariah 3: 2; Jude 23; I Corinthians 3: 15). Rather, God wants to save us abundantly

into experiencing the unsearchable riches of Christ, and He is always moving forward towards that end. He is always leading us in that way and it is our responsibility to move on with Him, from station to station, until we enter into the fullness of Christ.[48]

One of the main themes of Numbers is found in a single verse in the Book of Hebrews that refers to the wandering Israelites: "So we see that they were unable to enter because of unbelief" (3:19). Indeed, Numbers teaches us, first and foremost, that faith leads to obedience, a proper relationship with God, and life, while unbelief leads to rebellion, alienation from God, and death. Even as believing Christians, we must discipline ourselves to walk with Christ and to grow, because our spiritual growth is never automatic. We don't want to ignore God, neglect the spiritual disciplines, and end up wandering in our own type of wilderness as uncommitted believers communing with God only on Sundays and special occasions. Otherwise, the rest of the time, we'd be struggling in the wilderness, where we are considerably more vulnerable to the allures of the world, apart from Christ.

The writer of Hebrews admonishes us not to "harden your hearts as in the rebellion, on the day of testing in the wilderness, where your fathers put me to the test and saw my works for forty years.... They always go astray in their heart; they have not known my ways.... They shall not enter my rest.... Take care, brothers, lest there be in any of you an evil, unbelieving heart, leading you to fall away from the living God. But exhort one another every day...that none of you may be hardened by the deceitfulness of sin" (3:8–13).

While recognizing these warnings, we should not overlook the constructive messages in the book's next chapter. Chapter 3 of Hebrews warns of the consequences of unbelief, but chapter 4 emphasizes the positive, exhorting us to learn from the mistakes of the Israelites and do better. That is the point, after all, is it not? The writer of Hebrews tells us we must take to heart God's promise of the good news that the Israelites heard but did not heed, "because they were not united by faith with those who listened" (4:2). He adds, "Let us therefore strive to enter that rest, so that no one may fall by the same sort of disobedience.

For the word of God is living and active, sharper than any two-edged sword, piercing to the division of the soul and of spirit, joints and marrow, and discerning the thoughts and intentions of the heart." Because we have a "great high priest who has passed through the heavens, Jesus, the Son of God, let us hold fast our confession. For we do not have a high priest who is unable to sympathize with our weaknesses, but one who in every respect has been tempted as we are, yet without sin. Let us then with confidence draw near to the throne of grace, that we may receive mercy and find grace to help in time of need" (4:11, 12, 14–16).

TYPES, PICTURES, AND PROPHECIES OF CHRIST IN NUMBERS

In addition to these important messages for the Christian, Numbers has several important prefigurings of Christ. Here's one briefly alluded to earlier: on their journey, God's people complain about the lack of food and water. God sends fiery serpents among them, which bite them and cause many to die. When the people repent to Moses and ask that he pray to God to remove the serpents, Moses complies. God hears his prayer and tells Moses, "Make a fiery serpent and set it on a pole, and everyone who is bitten, when he sees it, shall live" (Num. 21:8). Moses does so and, thereafter, "if a serpent bit anyone, he would look at the bronze serpent and live" (Num. 21:9).

We have it on no less an authority than Jesus Himself that this is a prophecy or type pointing to Him, for He tells us, "And as Moses lifted up the serpent in the wilderness, so must the Son of Man be lifted up, that whoever believes in him may have eternal life" (John 3:14–15). Gary Staats notes, "Those who look to Christ, lifted up on the cross and in His ascension, are rescued from the venomous poison of sin and are brought into eternal life through faith in him."[49] In this type, he declares, we see "a stunning picture of the Crucifixion."[50]

Also in Numbers we read the story of Balaam, the Mesopotamian sorcerer who prophesied of Jesus, "A star shall come out of Jacob, and a scepter shall rise out of Israel; it shall crush the forehead of Moab and break down all the sons of Sheth. Edom shall be dispossessed; Seir also, his enemies, shall be dispossessed. Israel is doing valiantly. And one from Jacob shall exercise dominion and destroy the survivors of cities!" (24:17–19). As we've seen, this prophecy was fulfilled, as Christ descended from the line of Jacob (Luke 3:23–34), and when he was born, wise men from the east came to Jerusalem, declaring, "Where is he who has been born king of the Jews? For we saw his star when it rose and we have come to worship him" (Matt. 2:2).

In addition, the offer of the red heifer "without defect or blemish" in chapter 19 can be seen as representing salvation through Jesus' offering of Himself (see Heb. 9:13–14).[51] Furthermore, Christ's presence is in the pillar of cloud and fire leading the Israelites throughout their journeys (Exodus 33:9–23, 40:38).

Some scholars point to Aaron's rod, in chapter 17, as prefiguring Christ's resurrection. When Aaron's leadership is challenged, God orders him and all the tribal leaders to put their staffs in the Tabernacle. The next day only Aaron's staff "had sprouted and put forth buds and produced blossoms, and it bore ripe almonds" (Num. 17:8).[52]

Finally, the Mosaic Law establishes six cities of refuge, on each side of the Jordan River, to provide protection for anyone who has unintentionally killed another (Num. 35). The refugee is safe as long as he remains in the city, and he is allowed to return home once the high priest dies (Num. 35:28). If he leaves the city before then, the "avenger of blood" is permitted to execute him (Num. 35:27).

Some scholars believe that even if the cities of refuge aren't technically a "type," they point to Christ because it is in Christ that we find refuge from judgment and are made free by the death of the High Priest. Francis Schaeffer notes that the cities are "a strong illustration of the work of Christ" because they are in central locations on both sides of the river and therefore easy for everyone to reach. Additionally, they are open to all, and according to historical custom, the great doors of these cities are never locked. Moreover, the cities are stocked with food to ensure not only the refugee's legal protection but also his physical needs. Lastly, the Bible tells us that if a killer does not flee to a city of refuge, there is no help available to him—which points to Jesus as the only way to salvation.[53]

DEUTERONOMY

The name of this book is widely believed to derive from the Greek expression for "second law," though that is a misnomer, probably based on an early mistranslation in Deuteronomy 17:18, which actually reads "copy of this law." The book indicates that the Law is not new, but is a restatement of the original Law God gave to Moses at Sinai.[54]

The people have just emerged from thirty-eight years in the wilderness and are about to enter Canaan. Moses is intent on impressing the Law on their minds again, as their disobedience had largely caused their wandering in the first place. He has already accepted that Joshua, rather than he, will lead the people into the land, and he knows their success depends on their obedience to God and His Law. Accordingly, the book is a series of addresses by Moses on the east side of the Jordan as the people await entry into the land. In keeping with the biblical theme of remembrance, Moses rehearses the people's history in the wilderness to remind them how they went wrong and encourage them to proceed on a new path of obedience.

This emphasis on remembering, as noted, is a universal lesson and one that Christians must take to heart, because one gains biblical wisdom by a process of trial and error and learning from one's mistakes. Christians must remember the lessons of Old Testament history, including the Israelites' abandonment of the Law, and incorporate those lessons into their own lives of faith by re-dedicating themselves to God's Word, reading it and studying it diligently, and consistently profiting from its wisdom. It is indispensable for our relationship with God, for it is in the Word that we primarily hear His message for us and that we are reminded of His character, His grace, His faithfulness, and His love and salvation plans for us. It is imperative that the Israelites learn the consequences of their disobedience and idolatry, and it is equally important that we learn from their transgressions.

Albert Baylis expands on the idea of remembering: "If a mutual love relationship with Yahweh is the engine that powers the response of obedience, then memory is the fuel." Both Testaments of the Bible, he says, motivate through hope and memory, "focusing on God's promise for the future and remembering God's activities in the past."[55] As Israel is about to enter into Canaan to experience another phase of God's promise to Abraham, the people need to remember the past in order to avoid displeasing God and losing possession of the land—for the land is central to God's purposes for His people, and in the end, for us.

The land always has significance for the Israelites and for God's covenantal relationship with them, as described by theologian Walter Brueggemann: "Land is history with Yahweh. It is never contextless space. It is always a place where memories of slavery and manna are recalled and where hopes of fidelity and well-being are articulated. Land is always where Israel must come to terms with the Lord of memories and hopes."[56] The people ignore that at their peril because if they believe possession of the land comes without responsibility and they turn from God, they will lose the land, as history repeatedly demonstrates.

With more than eighty citations, Deuteronomy is one of the most frequently quoted books in the New Testament.[57] Jesus quotes more from Deuteronomy than any other Old Testament book.[58] He directly ties Deuteronomy to the New Testament when He proclaims that the essence of the entire Old Testament Law and prophets could be summed up by the commandment to love God with all your heart, soul, and mind, and to love your neighbor as yourself (Matt. 22:37; Deut. 6:5, 10:19).[59] Additionally, each time He is tempted by Satan in the wilderness, He responds with Scripture from Deuteronomy (Matt. 4:4, 7, 10; Luke 4–12; Deut. 8:1–3, 6:1–13, 16).

The Law and the Mosaic Covenant, as we've seen, are not inconsistent with the other covenants, including that which God made with Abraham. Remember: the Law was never provided as a means to salvation. To the contrary, it was a schoolmaster teaching man's need for Jesus Christ. The Law sends us into the arms of Christ because it teaches us that we are incapable of saving ourselves or of following the Law on our own power. When Christ says that we must be perfect as God is perfect, He is telling us, essentially, that we need to place our trust in Him, for without Him we can never reach that standard of perfection on our own. We must appropriate His finished work on the cross to have His perfect righteousness imputed to us.

In another significant Deuteronomy passage, Moses tells his people that the Law he is restating is not far away from them. It is not in heaven and it is not beyond the sea, "But the word is very near to you. It is in your mouth and in your heart, so that you can do it" (Deut. 30:14). In his letter to the Romans, Paul recalls that passage and applies it to the New Covenant in Jesus Christ as the complete fulfillment of the Law: "But the righteousness based on faith says, 'Do not say in your heart, "Who will ascend into heaven?"' '(that is, to bring Christ down)' or "Who will descend into the abyss?"' (that is, to bring Christ up from the dead). But what does it say? 'The word is near you, in your mouth and in your heart' (that is, the word of faith that we proclaim); because if you confess with your mouth that Jesus is Lord and believe in your heart that God raised him from the dead, you will be saved" (Romans 10:6–9).[60]

We have already discussed the messianic prophecy in which Moses says that God will raise up a prophet like himself. There is another messianic prophecy in Deuteronomy: "And if a man has committed a crime punishable by death and he is put to death, and you hang him on a tree, his body shall not remain all night on the tree, but you shall bury him the same day, for a hanged man is cursed by God" (21:22–23). Paul paraphrases this verse in his letter to the Galatians: "Christ redeemed us from the curse of the law by becoming a curse for us—for it is written, 'Cursed is everyone who is hanged on a tree'—so that in Christ Jesus the blessing of Abraham might come to the Gentiles, so that we might receive the promised Spirit through faith" (Gal. 3:13–14).

This completes our review of the Christ-centeredness of the Pentateuch. In the next chapter we'll begin with the Book of Joshua, which serves as a link between the Bible's first five books and the Old Testament's other historical books. Joshua takes the baton from Moses and leads the Israelites into a new period in their history revolving around the land, which they will finally come to possess.

CHAPTER 12

CHRIST IN EVERY BOOK
JOSHUA THROUGH ESTHER

This is the greater Joshua, Jesus Christ. The One who died so that men can escape judgment will be the One who will be the judge. And it is this Christ who stood before Joshua as the captain of the host of the Lord.

—FRANCIS SCHAEFFER[1]

JOSHUA

Joshua is a transitional book that bridges the writings of Moses with the remainder of Scripture.[2] It records Israel's history from the death of Moses to the time of the judges. I find it fascinating that Moses, the great lawgiver, is denied permission to take God's people into the Promised Land. Instead, God chooses Joshua, whose name means "The Lord Saves."[3] Ray Stedman suggests this name anticipates the New Testament revelation that God's promises cannot be fulfilled by the Law, but only by Jesus Christ.[4]

God had been preparing Joshua for years for this task. Having been a slave in Egypt who served as a minister for Moses, Joshua had later led the army in battle against Amalek (Exodus 17).[5] He was one of the two spies who trusted God to take the people into Canaan when all the others caved in fear.

The Book of Joshua relates Israel's entrance, conquest, and occupation of Canaan. Thus, writes J. Sidlow Baxter, its central message is the victory of faith. "In this, the Book of Joshua stands in sharp contrast to the Book of Numbers where we see the failure of unbelief—failure to enter (Num. 14:2–4), failure to overcome (Num. 14:44, 45), and failure to occupy (Num. 14:28–34). Spiritually interpreted, the exploits of Israel under Joshua proclaim the great New Testament truth—'This is the victory that has overcome the world—our faith' (1 John 5:4)." Baxter writes that each Israelite triumph is meant to show that victory comes from faith in God, not man's self-reliance. "To quailing unbelief," he maintains, "the overthrow of giants and great cities was an *impasse*, but to the eye of faith it was a *fait accompli*."[6] Baxter is obviously correct. As they move into Canaan, the Israelites prevail over their enemies when they obey God, but when they disobey they suffer defeats. For example, they are defeated at Ai because one man—Achan—defies God by taking spoils that were meant to be destroyed as a devotional act to the Lord (Joshua 6:17–18, 21).

That defeat was preceded by a victory at Jericho that included a compelling Christophany: as Joshua is preparing to attack the town, he sees a man standing before him with a drawn sword in his hand. The man identifies himself as the commander of the army of the Lord—it is Jesus Christ in one of His preincarnate appearances. After telling Joshua to remove his sandals because he's standing on holy ground, the Lord delivers Jericho into Joshua's hands (Joshua 5:13–6:27).

The Israelites' crossing of the Jordan and entrance into the land are prefigurings as well, though scholars disagree on the particulars, with some seeing the land as a type of heaven and others viewing it differently. John Walvoord says the better view is to see Canaan as "the believer's present sphere of conflict and possession in Christ.... The experiences of Joshua have their parallel in Ephesians in the New Testament. The believer gains spiritual possessions by faith in Christ, by crucifixion with Christ and by the mighty power of God."[7]

JOSHUA AS A TYPE OF CHRIST

Joshua's name—"The Lord Saves"—is significant in that Joshua becomes a type of Christ who brings salvation. The writer of Hebrews contrasts the temporary rest that Joshua provides to his people through his military victories, with the permanent rest found in Jesus Christ: "For if Joshua had given them rest, God would not have spoken of another day later on. So then, there remains a Sabbath rest for the people of God, for whoever has entered God's rest has also rested from his works as God did from his. Let us therefore strive to enter that rest, so that no one may fall by the same sort of disobedience" (4:8–11). Gary Staats explains that as believers in Christ, we rest in His finished work—the work that Joshua typified. We don't work to gain our salvation, but our works flow from it. Our works only follow as a result of having entered into the finished work of Christ, through faith in Him.[8]

Joshua is a type of Christ in these additional respects: He is a self-described servant (Joshua 24:15) as is Jesus (Luke 22:27; John 13:1–17; Philip. 2:7); as Joshua succeeds Moses, Christ succeeds the Law; Joshua gives Israel what Moses couldn't (the Promised Land), and Christ gives us what the Law couldn't (God's salvation) (Romans 8:2–4; Gal. 3:23–25); in a time of conflict and defeat both Joshua and Christ intercede for their people (Joshua 7:5–9; Luke 22:32; 1 John 2:1)[9]; and Joshua is governor of Israel and commander of its armies, who is qualified for these positions because of his wisdom, courage, and integrity, just as Christ is the king of saints, the leader and commander of the people, and the captain of our salvation.[10]

Further, Joshua parts the Jordan River so that Israel could cross over (Joshua 3:7–17), as Christ walks on water and calls others to come over to Him (Matt. 14:25–29); Joshua leads God's people into the Promised Land (Joshua 1:2–3) and into their rest (Joshua 21:44), as Jesus leads His people into God's promised inheritance (Matt. 25:34; Eph. 1:13–14) and into rest in the new creation (Heb. 4:1); Joshua's army is arrayed in earthly armor (Joshua 6:9) and pulls down earthly strongholds (Joshua 6), while

Jesus' army is arrayed in spiritual armor (Eph. 6:10–17) and pulls down spiritual strongholds (2 Cor. 10:3–5).[11]

JUDGES

Despite suffering some setbacks because they disobey God, the Israelites steadily advance across the land in fulfillment of God's sovereign plan. In the Book of Judges, however, we see that after entering into Canaan, "everyone did what was right in his own eyes" (Judges 21:25), which plunges the people into turmoil. This results in the fourfold cycle of judges we discussed earlier—sin, servitude, sorrow and supplication, and salvation—in which God repeatedly raises up a judge to lead the people out of their decadence.

Though Judges contains no messianic prophecies, it does thematically point to Christ in that the judges anticipate Him as Savior and King of His people.[12] Moreover, some commentators suggest that the announcement to Samson's mother that her future son would lead Israel is a foreshadowing of God's announcement to Mary that she would give birth to the Messiah.[13]

The book demonstrates God's long-suffering, endless patience with Israel and that He answers their prayers once they repent, despite their habitual disobedience, idolatry, and rebellion. Likewise, Christ, even on behalf of all sinners and the very people who rejected Him, will always honor His promise and forgive all who come to Him in faith and repentance, and grant them eternal life. In Jesus, we see the perfect judge, for He brings not merely temporary deliverance from present struggles, but eternal salvation from spiritual enemies and obstacles.[14] Indeed, some scholars argue that Judges demonstrates Israel's need for a Messiah.[15] I believe the fourfold cycle not only prefigures Christ as Savior and King, but also the individual Christian's internal struggle with his sin nature, which he overcomes on a daily basis by turning to Christ through the power of the Holy Spirit. Just as spiritual warfare is real, so is the believer's ongoing struggle with his own sin nature, which he must never ignore.

The prophet Isaiah speaks to Christ's perfect judgment: "There shall come forth a shoot from the stump of Jesse, and a branch from his roots shall bear fruit. And the Spirit of the Lord shall rest upon him, the Spirit of wisdom and understanding, the Spirit of counsel and might, the Spirit of knowledge and the fear of the Lord.... He shall not judge by what his eyes see, or decide disputes by what his ears hear, but with righteousness he shall judge the poor, and decide with equity for the meek of the earth.... Righteousness shall be the belt of his waist" (Isaiah 11:1–5). The Book of Proverbs also dovetails the message of Judges and its relationship to Jesus Christ, instructing us to "trust in the Lord with all your heart and do not lean on your own understanding. In all your ways acknowledge him, and he will make straight your paths. Be not wise in your own eyes; fear the Lord, and turn away from evil" (3:5–6). We must not emulate the people during the time of the judges who did what was right in their own eyes, but fear God and place our trust in Christ, Who embodies wisdom and righteousness, and Who will deliver us unto salvation.

RUTH

◇◇◇◇◇◇◇◇◇◇

There are frequent references to the "kinsman-redeemer" in the Old Testament. He is a male who has the legal privilege or responsibility to act for a relative who is in trouble, danger, or in need of vindication.[16] He would buy back the relative's mortgaged property (Lev. 25:25–34; Jer. 32:7–8) or buy him out of slavery (Lev. 25:48–52), and preserve or restore the unity of the family.[17] The familial relationship is essential here: to redeem a person or inheritance, one has to be related to the person or estate he seeks to redeem (Lev. 25:47–49; Ruth 3:12–13; Heb. 2:14–15). To achieve the redemption, the redeemer has to pay a price (Lev. 25:27; Romans 3:24–26; 1 Peter 1:18–19; Gal. 3:13).[18]

The Book of Ruth presents a kinsman-redeemer in Boaz, a prosperous farmer who redeems land that had been owned by Ruth's deceased husband Elimelech. Boaz also takes Ruth as his wife and ensures her safety from other men who work in the field. The kinsman-redeemer is an unmistakable type of Christ.[19] Christ was our Redeemer by becoming man and taking on the sins of the world, and Isaiah specifically points to Him as a Redeemer: "And a Redeemer will come to Zion, to those in Jacob who turn from transgression" (Isaiah 59:20).

This book also supplies an essential link in the providentially arranged messianic line: Boaz and Ruth conceive and continue the family line that will include King David and eventually Jesus. The unexpected way God arranges for this line of descent assures us that He will provide for us and will honor His sovereign promises and fulfill His redemptive plans.

1 AND 2 SAMUEL

Since many of the following references span across both these books, and since the books were originally considered one book in the earliest Hebrew manuscript,[20] we'll discuss them together.

Samuel can be considered a type or at least a picture of Christ because he is a prophet, priest, and judge, though not a king.[21] As a priest, Samuel cries out to the Lord for Israel (1 Sam. 7:9), just as Christ cries out to the Father for us, as we have seen repeatedly, notably in Christ's High Priestly Prayer in John 17. "In Samuel's intercession on Israel's behalf...we see a picture of the office of Christ as our high priest," Dale Ralph Davis states. "Here is the true secret of our steadfastness: we rely on the prayers of Another whose prayers are always effectual. Nothing is quite so moving as knowing that I am a subject of Jesus' intercessory prayer."[22]

In 1 Samuel 7:9, Samuel also points to Christ by sacrificing a lamb to atone for the people's sins. This is another reminder that without the shedding of blood there is no forgiveness of sins (Heb. 9:22).[23]

These books contain several references to Samuel's mother Hannah that point to Christ: the High Priest Eli blesses Hannah before Samuel is born (1 Samuel 1:17), as the angel Gabriel blesses Mary before Jesus is born (Luke 1:26–38); Hannah brings Samuel to the Tabernacle with a sacrifice to dedicate him to God (1 Samuel 1:24–28) and Eli receives Samuel (1 Samuel 1:23), just as Mary and Joseph take Jesus to the Temple with an offering (Luke 2:22–24) and Simeon receives Him (Luke 2:25–28); Samuel's parents make an annual trip to the Tabernacle (1 Samuel 2:19), as Jesus' parents make an annual trip to the Temple (Luke 2:41); Hannah praises God in prayer in Eli's presence (1 Samuel 2:1–11),

and Mary prays a strikingly similar prayer in the priestly home of Zechariah and Elizabeth (Luke 1:46–56); and in her prayer, Hannah makes
several prophetic references to Christ and praises God as her rock—a
title, as we've seen, that is identified with Christ. Hannah also says the
Lord will judge the ends of the earth (1 Samuel 2:10; Matt. 25:31–32).[24]
Hannah's prayer, then, anticipates a future king anointed by God—and
the anointed One, the Messiah, would fulfill God's promise to establish
David's throne forever.[25]

Other references to Samuel draw parallels to Christ: Samuel (1
Samuel 2:18, 3:21) and Jesus (Luke 2:46–50) sit and serve in the Tabernacle and Temple, respectively; both Samuel (1 Samuel 2:26) and Jesus
(Luke 2:52) grow in wisdom and stature and gain favor with God and
among men; both are given to Israel after a long silence from God (1
Samuel 3:1); Samuel is a partial fulfillment of God's promise to raise a
prophet like Moses (Deut. 18:15; 1 Samuel 3:19–21), and Christ is the
perfect fulfillment of that promise (Heb. 3:1–6); and Samuel, as God's
instrument, establishes Israel's kingship (1 Samuel 10:24–25), while Jesus
establishes the true and perfect kingship of Israel and the world (Luke
1:32–33), fulfilling the Davidic Covenant.[26]

In the books of Samuel we see that David is also a type of Christ: he
is born in Bethlehem;[27] he is first a shepherd and then king; he is called
by God, an act clearly showing God's sovereign will, as even Samuel
initially resists anointing David (1 Samuel 16); he is rejected by his brothers, is in constant danger from Saul and others (inspiring many of the
Psalms he wrote, such as Psalm 22), and he takes a Gentile wife, just as
the Church is Christ's bride; he prefigures Christ as a man "after His
own heart" (1 Samuel 13:14) and who ruled sovereignly over Israel, as
will Christ;[28] and he is the standard by which all subsequent kings would
be measured, until Christ. As Kenneth Boa remarks concerning David's
reign, "Although David barely compares to the One who holds a scepter
seated at the right hand of God's throne, he comes closer than anyone
else in Scripture."[29]

Indeed, David specifically foreshadows Christ as the coming king in
the context of the Davidic Covenant, whereby God promises David an
eternal kingdom (1 Samuel 16), throne (2 Samuel 7:16), and seed, all to
be finally fulfilled in Christ (Matt. 21:9, 22:42), the "Son of David"

(Luke 1:32, 33).[30] Paul refers to Christ as being "descended from David according to the flesh" (Romans 1:3), and Jesus identifies Himself as "the root and the descendant of David" (Rev. 22:16). Interestingly, David slays Goliath in an unorthodox manner—with a sling—and Jesus defeats Satan and death with His cross.[31]

Further, David is constantly pursued by Saul, the king of Israel (1 Samuel 19), as Jesus is pursued by Herod, the king of Judah (Matt. 2:13–18); the Holy Spirit intervenes to protect both David (1 Samuel 19:18–24) and Jesus (John 18:1–11) from their enemies; both have friends and advocates who risk their lives to defend them—Jonathan for David (1 Samuel 20) and John the Baptist for Jesus (John 3:22–30); David's men eat the bread of the Presence (1 Samuel 21:1–6), and Jesus' disciples eat grain on the Sabbath (Matt. 12:1–8); and both of their experiences are reflected throughout the Psalms, often with double meanings, one applying to David in the present and the other applying to Jesus in prophecy (see Psalms 22, 31, 32, 35, 40, 41, 45, 68, 69, 109, 110).[32]

Jonathan, Saul's son and David's best friend, also prefigures Christ in that he makes a covenant and pledges love to David for the salvation of his house, just as God makes a covenant of love with Christ for the salvation of His house.[33] Charles Spurgeon, however, analogizes Jonathan's love toward David with Christ's infinite love toward men.[34]

In addition, after God delivers David from the hands of his enemies and from Saul, David talks to Him in a passage now known as the Song of David (2 Samuel 22:2–51). In that discourse, David speaks of "my rock," "my fortress," "my deliverer," and the one who brings salvation to His king. As we've seen, the New Testament identifies Jesus as our rock (1 Cor. 10:4; 1 Peter 2:7–9), the Deliverer of Israel (Romans 11:25–27), the fortress to Whom we "have fled for refuge" (Hebrews 6:18), and as our only Savior (Luke 2:11; 2 Tim. 1:10).[35]

I want to conclude this discussion by sharing an insightful recapitulation by Pastor Donald Fortner of the biblical books up to this point. He first summarizes the books preceding 1 and 2 Samuel, recalling God's covenant with Abraham in Genesis, when He promises the patriarch blessings, descendants, and a land inheritance, then Exodus through Deuteronomy, when God gives the Law to show that the people must be holy to enjoy the land promise. Fortner then observes that the people prove, time after time, that they are incapable of honoring the Law on their own, and therefore need God's grace in Jesus Christ. As Paul writes, "For by works of the law no human being will be justified in his sight, since through the law comes knowledge of sin. But now the righteousness of God has been manifested apart from the law, although the Law and the Prophets bear witness to it—the righteousness of God through faith in Jesus Christ for all who believe" (Romans 3:20–21).

In Joshua, God, through His grace, gives Israel the land, and the Book of Judges typifies the Christian's experience of ceaseless war with enemies trying to rob him of blessings (Romans 7:14–23; Gal. 5:17–23). The Book of Ruth shows how God will provide a kinsman-redeemer who will restore our relationship with Him. Finally, says Fortner, "in 1 and 2 Samuel, the Lord shows us that our Redeemer, our Savior, that One into whose hands the Lord God has entrusted the everlasting deliverance of his people is the King of Glory, into whose hands the Lord our God has put all dominion over all flesh, that he might give eternal life to all his people. Here David typifies our Savior as God's great King established upon his throne."[36]

1 AND 2 KINGS

These two books were also considered one book in the Hebrew Scriptures.[37] The Temple, which is featured in both, has replaced the Tabernacle as the place where God resides with His people. This foreshadows the dwelling of the Holy Spirit in believers in Jesus Christ. As Paul declares, "For we are the temple of the living God; as God said, 'I will make my dwelling among them and walk among them, and I will be their God, and they shall be my people'" (2 Cor. 6:16).

First Kings begins with King David's death and the reign of his son Solomon, "who excelled all the kings of the earth in riches and in wisdom" (10:23). Solomon is considered a type of Christ in numerous ways, many of which are demonstrated in Psalm 72, which speaks both of Solomon's reign and of Christ's future kingdom. Verses one and two of the psalm are a prayer for the messianic kingship of David's dynasty, and the psalm ends with praise for the Lord's glorious reign over the entire earth. "Therefore," writes Willem VanGemeren, "the prayer for the Davidic king is at the same time an expression of hope in the glorious and just rule of Jesus over the earth." The great hymnist Isaac Watts expresses this hope elegantly: "Jesus shall reign where' er the sun Does his successive journeys run; His kingdom stretch from shore to shore, Till moons shall wax and wane no more."[38]

King Solomon is also seen as a type or prefiguring of Christ in respect to his unparalleled, God-given wisdom. Paul identifies Jesus as the "wisdom from God" (1 Cor. 1:30; Col 2:3), and Jesus describes Himself as One greater than Solomon (Matt. 12:42). Philip Ryken offers fascinating insights on Solomon's coronation. Solomon, he notes, is anointed king over Israel with oil by Zadok the priest and Nathan the prophet (1 Kings 1:34–39). "King Jesus," writes Ryken, "was also anointed. Indeed, this is the very definition of the word 'Christ,' which literally means 'the Anointed one.'" Ryken points out, however, that no mere prophet or priest anointed Jesus; it was the Holy Spirit, at His baptism in the Jordan River, "when the Holy Spirit descended from heaven like a dove and rested on the Son of God" (Matt. 3:16; Luke 3:21–22). This, says Ryken, illustrates the superiority of Christ's kingship. The oil is a sign of the Spirit, but Jesus is anointed with the actual Spirit, not a symbol of it. God Himself, the third Person of the Triune Godhead, anoints the Second Person. "His kingship," writes Ryken, "was not simply a sign of God's kingly rule, therefore, but the living reality of God's dominion. The divine king was divinely anointed for divine rule."[39]

Moreover, most kingdoms go to any length to protect their king, but King Jesus surrenders Himself for crucifixion. Jesus, as our king, dies for all of our sins. According to Ryken, "The crown of thorns that was meant to make a mockery of his royal claims actually proclaimed his kingly dignity, even in death."[40] Christ's kingship, however, is permanent and spans throughout the earth. The way we serve Christ and His kingdom is to enthrone Him in our hearts.[41]

The prophet Elijah, whose ministry is largely reported in these two books, has also been depicted as a type of Christ because God empowers him to perform many miracles to prove he is a prophet. Some believe, however, that he more closely foreshadows John the Baptist.[42] Like Jesus,

Elijah raises a widow's son from the dead, upon which she proclaims, "Now I know that you are a man of God, and that the word of the Lord in your mouth is truth" (1 Kings 17:24). Similarly, in addition to raising Lazarus, Jesus raises a widow's son, causing the people to exclaim, "God has visited his people!" (Luke 7:14–15).

The prophet Elisha is also identified as prefiguring Christ,[43] evidenced by his doubling of Elijah's miracles and his feeding people on two occasions by multiplying their food (2 Kings 4:1–7, 42–44). Additionally, like Jesus, Elisha lives among the people and stresses the ideas of grace, life, and hope (2 Kings 4:8–37, 6:14–23, 8:7–15, 19:16–21).[44] Arthur Pink, however, opines that Elijah is a figure of Christ whereas Elisha, having been called, tested, and equipped for service, is a type of those servants especially called to represent Christ on earth.[45] Arguing that both conclusions are true, Donald Fortner notes that Elisha is typical of Christ in that his ministry is a source of healing and blessing, but that he is also representative of all who are called to serve Christ and to preach His Gospel.[46]

1 AND 2 CHRONICLES

We've already discussed most of the material pointing to Christ in these two books, since that material also appears in earlier biblical books. But 1 and 2 Chronicles still offer some unique indications of Jesus. For example, the tribe of Judah is placed first in the national genealogy in 1 Chronicles because God sovereignly arranged, and His prophets foretold, that the monarchy, the Temple, and the Messiah would come from the tribe of Judah (Gen. 49:10). Some scholars note that the books of Chronicles are the last books of the Hebrew Bible, so the genealogies in chapters 1–9 of 1 Chronicles form a preamble to the genealogy of Christ presented in Matthew, the first New Testament book.[47] Another notable passage in 1 Chronicles is David's thanksgiving song to God (16:33). This passage relates to God coming to judge the earth, which prefigures Matthew 25, in which Jesus says He will come to judge the earth.[48]

Second Chronicles highlights Solomon's Temple and suggests Christ's incarnation: "But will God indeed dwell with men on earth? Behold, heaven and the highest heaven cannot contain you, how much less this house that I have built!" (6:18–19).[49] Jesus invokes a similar sentiment: "I tell you, something greater than the temple is here. And if you had known what this means, 'I desire mercy, and not sacrifice,' you would not have condemned the guiltless. For the Son of Man is lord of the Sabbath'" (Matt. 12:6–8). Here, Christ is telling the Pharisees that while the Temple is holy, there is something infinitely greater and more precious. As William Hendriksen writes, "A gift from heaven immeasurably more valuable, an authority endowed with rights far more magisterial, was speaking to them."[50]

While Solomon's Temple is more permanent than the Tabernacle, like any manmade structure, it's not built to last forever—and in fact, it needs major repairs within 150 years due to decay and destruction by idolaters (2 Kings 12). We may contrast this with the temple of the Holy Spirit—believers in Jesus Christ *are* that "temple" because they are indwelled by the Holy Spirit. They will live forever because they are made not by human hands, but by God (John 1:12–13). The Holy Spirit will never leave us and has sealed us for God and His day of redemption (Eph. 1:13, 4:30). No manmade temple could ever uphold such a promise.[51] On another level, Christ identifies Himself as a temple (John 2:19), and He promises that in the New Jerusalem there will be no temple because "its temple is the Lord God the Almighty and the Lamb" (Rev. 21:22).

EZRA

Many messianic threads coalesce in Ezra. This important book relates how Zerubbabel, who is part of the messianic line as the grandson of Jeconiah (Chron. 3:17–19; Matt. 1:12–13), leads the first group of Israelites out of Babylonian captivity in 538 BC to begin rebuilding the Temple (Ezra 2:64). This is an essential link in reestablishing Israel in the Promised Land in fulfillment of the Abrahamic and later covenants, and an even more crucial link in keeping David's descendants alive in furtherance of the Davidic Covenant. God ordained, and preannounced through His prophets, that His people would have this land as an everlasting possession and that the coming Messiah would be born there, in Bethlehem (Micah 5:2). Ezra also points to Christ's work in forgiving and restoring us, as it demonstrates that God, despite Israel's perpetual disobedience and even its exile, will not give up on His people. This book illustrates, therefore, both the sovereignty and faithfulness of God.

Ezra is adamant that God's covenants with Israel remain in full force and effect, including Israel's duty to be a nation of priests and a holy people who will perform messianic functions to help usher in, from within their nation, the Messiah, for Israel and all other peoples.[52] By underscoring the importance of completing the Temple (6:15), this book signifies a deep awareness of the Temple's role in God's covenant with the people, since God will not dwell with His people unless the Temple is restored. Ezra is also messianic in expressing concern for the sacrificial system and the atonement it brings—which, of course, point to the ultimate sacrifice of the Messiah.[53] The book is filled with the theme of repentance, as poignantly demonstrated by Ezra's penitent prayer in chapter 9, whereby he acknowledges his people's repeated disobedience and expresses his heartfelt sorrow and remorse, and his profound thanksgiving for God's forgiveness.

Further, the book advances the recurring biblical theme of God's preserving a remnant for Himself. This message runs from Noah, to Lot's family in Sodom and Gomorrah, to the Israelites released from captivity in Egypt and in Babylon. In the New Testament Paul connects this theme to Christ by referring to believers as "a remnant, chosen by grace" (Romans 11:5). Not everyone accepts Christ's offer of grace, but those who do are His people and He preserves them through the power of the Holy Spirit, Who will deliver them to Him at the last day (2 Cor. 1:22; Eph. 4:30).[54] No matter how many avail themselves of God's free offer of grace, He will work His sovereign will through the remnant that He preserves. In Ezra, He works His will through Persian King Cyrus, a seemingly unlikely figure whom He guaranteed, through the prophet Isaiah more than 150 years in advance, would authorize the people's return and their rebuilding of the Temple. The book is one of hope for all Christians, showing once again that God will not abandon His people if they turn to Him in repentance.

Ezra is dedicated to the observance of God's Law, as exhibited in his public reading of it in the Book of Nehemiah and in his emphasis on laws against intermarriage (Ezra 9:2, 12). He is resolute that the people repent of their sins, live in accordance with God's will, and fulfill their covenantal duties to Him.

NEHEMIAH

This book opens with Nehemiah, a Jewish cupbearer to the Persian king Artaxerxes, sharing his concern about the Jews in Jerusalem. These people, having returned from exile, are troubled to find the city walls and gates in disrepair. Nehemiah immediately turns to prayer, reverentially thanking God for His faithfulness and confessing the sins of the people of Israel. He reminds God of His vow to scatter the people for their disobedience but regather them to the land if they return to Him in faith and keep His commandments.

Later, when Artaxerxes asks Nehemiah what is bothering him, Nehemiah relates his sorrow over the land and his people, hoping to persuade the king to reverse his earlier order to stop the rebuilding of Jerusalem. A sympathetic Artaxerxes issues a decree on March 5, 444 BC, authorizing the city's reconstruction, in fulfillment of Daniel's prophecy some ninety-five years earlier.[55] Returning to Jerusalem, Nehemiah supervises the rebuilding of the city walls, which is completed in fifty-two days despite substantial opposition (Neh. 6:15).

Upon completion of the wall, Ezra displays his dedication to God's Law by reading from the Book of the Law of Moses for six hours to the people gathered in the square before the Water Gate (Neh. 8:1–8). Ezra's deep devotion to the Law foreshadows Christ's reaffirmations of the Law, including His proclamation that He came not to abolish it, but to fulfill it (Matt. 5:17–18).

Nehemiah shares Ezra's fervent desire that Israel should uphold its covenantal duties with God (Neh. 1:5, 9:8, 32).[56] That means being able to worship God securely and freely, which is one reason he is so passionate about rebuilding the city walls (Neh. 2:1–3:32). By playing an instrumental

that Satan, despite inflicting damage, would have no chance of derailing God's ultimate purposes.

Van Groningen notes the unlikely rise to prominence of Mordecai and Esther in the Persian Empire as instrumental agents for the Jews' ultimate delivery. This, he argues, further highlights God's sovereignty over the nations of the world. Though Van Groningen doesn't mention it, we see similar events occurring throughout the Bible, such as God elevating Joseph to an instrumental role in the Egyptian empire, from whence he can direct the safe delivery of the Jewish people. I never cease to marvel at the parallel threads coursing through Scripture, all heading inexorably to fulfill God's unfolding purposes.

There are other noteworthy parallels to Christ below the surface narrative of this book. For example, Pastor Timothy Keller observes that just as Nehemiah left his high position in the Persian royal court to serve his people, Esther "risked losing the palace to identify with her people, but Jesus Christ, the ultimate Esther, lost his place, the ultimate palace, heaven, in order to come to earth and identify with his people. That's faithfulness. If you rest in him and you know because he did that for you that you now are safe, you are loved no matter what, and your sins are paid for, now and only now will you be as dedicated as Esther. Until you see the one to whom Esther points, you'll never be like Esther."[67]

Esther is indeed like Christ, putting herself in harm's way to save her people.[68] British pastor Rev. W. Burrows shows how the concept of kinsman-redeemer is also at work here: "Esther was boldly self-sacrificing. Unbidden she came to the king, bearing her life in her hands. A noble type of the sacrifice and intercession of Christ is presented by this scene in the life of Esther. In entire self-forgetfulness and self-surrender she ventured her life in order to plead for her kindred; and Christ gave his life that, now within the veil, he might make intercession for his kinsman after the flesh."[69] The ESV Study Bible puts it succinctly: "God providentially brings deliverance to his people through Esther, prefiguring final deliverance through Christ."[70] Esther's intercession, like Christ's, is not based on the merits of the people for whom she advocates, but on her love for her people. Her success in delivering her people, like Christ's, is not based on *their* worthiness, but upon the king's love for the intercessor[71]—in our case, the Father's love for His Son.

This completes our review of the historical books, where we have seen Christ at every turn. We will now examine the Bible's five poetical books and their abundant prefigurings of Jesus Christ.

CHAPTER 13

CHRIST IN EVERY BOOK
THE POETICAL BOOKS

The poetic books show the aspiration of the nation for
Christ in spiritual and moral matters. In Job the aspiration
is for mediation *(see 9:33), of which Christ is the ultimate*
fulfillment (1 Tim. 2:5). In Psalms the aspiration is for communion *with God, which is also fulfilled in Christ who*
taught us to pray (Matt. 6:5–15). Proverbs manifests the
aspiration for wisdom, *which Christ personified for "in*
[Him] are hidden all the treasures of wisdom and knowl-
edge" (Col. 2:3). In Ecclesiastes the aspiration is for ulti-
mate satisfaction *(1:8) found only in the "one Shepherd"*
(see 12:11–13). And in the Song of Solomon the aspiration
is for intimate union *with the Lover of our souls. Hence,*
all the poetic books find their ultimate focus in Christ.

—NORMAN L. GEISLER[1]

N ext we turn to the five poetical books of Job, Psalms, Proverbs, Ecclesiastes, and Song of Solomon. Poetry appears elsewhere throughout the Bible, but these five books are
particularly noted for their unique blend of poetic language and form.
Consequently, these books address the most meaningful problems that
human beings face with a mixture of deep insight and elegant expression.[2] If you've never studied Hebrew poetry you might discover it, as I
did, to be delightful. The Hebrew variant is significantly different from
what we ordinarily consider to be poetry, which tends to feature meter
and rhyme. Hebrew poetry relies more on meter than rhyme, but the

meter depends more on stress or accent for its rhythmic quality.[3] Whatever rhyme might be present in the original language doesn't usually translate into English as such.

A more distinguishing feature of Hebrew poetry is parallelism, which involves repetition of thought or similar language over two or more lines or verses, or even within two parts of the same line. Stated simply, it is the repetition of the same general idea in the second line or verse but with different wording. When reading scriptural passages, I've sometimes wondered why thoughts are often repeated back to back. The most likely reason is that repetition facilitates learning and retention, and helps to clarify and expand upon ideas. But with Hebrew poetry this repetition isn't static—it amplifies, as the repeated thought is usually stated more strongly or colorfully. This has the effect, I think, not just of planting it in our minds but of making a deeper impression, so long as we pay attention to the words and their progression. Professor Thomas Howe notes that in parallel structure the second colon or line is usually more important and almost climactic.[4] "The predominant pattern of biblical poetry," Robert Alter writes, "is to move from a standard term in the first verset to a more literary or highfalutin term in the second verset."[5]

Alter uses examples to illustrate how this progression is both clarifying and intensifying. "Your granaries will be filled with abundance / with new wine your vats will burst" (Prov. 3:10). The verbs, says Alter, reflect a movement toward intensification, "from being filled to bursting."

Consider the more complex example in Psalms 88:11–12: "Will your kindness be told in the grave, your faithfulness in perdition? // Will your wonder be known in the darkness, your bounty in the land of oblivion?"[6] Alter says one set of matched terms in these two lines remains stable: "kindness" is linked conceptually to "faithfulness," and "wonder" is linked to "bounty." But there is a second set of matched terms that "carries forward a progressive imaginative realization of death: from the familiar and localized 'grave' to 'perdition,' a poetic synonym that is quasi-mythic and grimly explicit about the fate of extinction the grave holds; then, to another everyday word, 'darkness,' which is…a sensory realization of the experience of death, and then to a second poetic term for the underworld, 'the land of oblivion,' which summarizes and generalizes the series, giving emphatic closure to the idea that death is a realm where human beings are utterly forgotten and extinct, and where there can be no question of God's greatness being recalled."[7] This may seem a bit esoteric, but it really is a fascinating concept. Alter's point is that the psalmist is using a sophisticated form of parallelism to intensify the meaning with descriptive word pictures that move the reader.

With these examples, I wanted to introduce you to Hebrew poetry and give you a glimpse of its beauty. Though much is lost in translation, a great deal of literary richness remains that will enhance your appreciation for the poetic books, if you read them with this perspective.

Hebrew poetry is a complex subject, and scholars don't always agree how to classify the types of parallelism, such as synonymous parallelism, antithetical parallelism, synthetic parallelism or semantic parallelism. It is far beyond my purpose to explore this more deeply, but I wanted to present some of the ideas and terms because I believe your understanding and enjoyment will be enriched if you read Hebrew poetry with an eye toward the poetic devices the authors use. If you want to dig deeper, there are abundant resources.

The Hebrews produced very little writings apart from the Scriptures, yet what they did compose—the Old Testament writings, especially the poetical books—are widely considered to be among the greatest works of literature ever produced.[8] Even renowned skeptic H. L. Mencken called the Bible "unquestionably the most beautiful book in the world."[9]

These books are sometimes called "wisdom literature" because their style is similar to the extra-biblical literature that goes by that name, and also because the subject of wisdom is thematic to these books, especially Job, Proverbs, and Ecclesiastes. This type of literature examines the moral substance of true wisdom (as in Proverbs) and the contemplations of wise men exploring the fundamental problems of human existence (such as in Job and Ecclesiastes).[10] The wisdom books examine how the world works, humanity's role in it, and how all of this fits together under God's superintending sovereignty.[11] The Books of Job and Ecclesiastes explore the universal human problem of evil and the purpose of life, respectively; the Song of Solomon is a mini-theology of intimacy; Proverbs probes the various aspects of practical and godly wisdom; and

Psalms is a treasure trove of human beings sharing the range of their experiences, thoughts, and emotions with their creator.

Enraptured with the literary beauty of the Bible, biblical scholar Leland Ryken maintains that just because the Bible is a book of religious authority doesn't mean it's some dry, boring "theological outline with proof texts attached." To the contrary, says Ryken, "If we look at how the Bible presents its material, it resembles a literary work more than anything else. It is filled with stories, poems, visions, and letters."[12]

As such, Ryken employs a literary approach in studying the Bible that recognizes the interrelationship between the form of the text and its meaning. Nevertheless, he acknowledges that the "literature of the Bible is intermingled with theology and history."[13] Ryken elaborates on this point in his fascinating book, *Words of Delight, A Literary Introduction to the Bible*: "The Bible is a continuously religious book. It is always ready to sacrifice literary concerns for didactic ones, and even when it does not do so, its literary dimension is permeated with religious and moral preoccupations."[14] He quotes the writer of Ecclesiastes (most likely Solomon), telling us how he approaches his task as a writer: "Besides being wise, the Preacher also taught the people knowledge, weighing and studying and arranging proverbs with great care. The preacher sought to find pleasing words, and uprightly he wrote words of truth" (12:9–10).

I refer to Ryken's book because it helps us grasp the character of the poetical books and why this biblical genre is a sort of hybrid between poetry and wisdom literature. The quote from Ecclesiastes is particularly clarifying because it underscores the writer's determination to impart wisdom—not just by sharing the content of the proverbs, but by carefully arranging it to maximize the readers' understanding. His method, as he says, includes the use of "pleasing words," and above all, "words of truth." This statement captures the approach employed by all the biblical writers. They write intending to teach, but they also often craft their words to stimulate our appreciation for the art, which in turn facilitates our understanding of the message.

Reading and contemplating the poetical books, then, helps us to understand the nagging philosophical issues we confront in life, to gain a deeper appreciation for the literary splendor of the Bible, and to understand the essence of godly wisdom and apply it to our lives. Providing a blueprint for communicating with God, these books give us deeper insight into the entire Bible. Now I turn to the individual books of poetry to introduce their basic contents and message, and more important, to illustrate their role in foreshadowing Christ.

JOB

The Book of Job deals with the timeless and universal question of why God allows righteous people to suffer. If He is all-powerful and all-loving, why doesn't He spare us this agony? While God doesn't give us a simple, neat, and direct answer, He *shows* us the reasons—for no biblical book, in my view, better demonstrates God's awesome power and His inscrutable ways, thereby teaching the indispensability of having a relationship with Him. It's not enough that we *know about* God, we must seek to *know Him*, which is the ultimate message God imparts to Job. In getting to know God, one must learn to trust Him, and believe that He knows and will do what is best for us and for all of His creation.

Those frustrated with God's failure to provide a direct answer to Job should note that Job himself doesn't end up frustrated—and he is the one who lost everything in various calamitous events. Additionally, God ultimately rewards Job for his faith, giving him even more prosperity and blessings than he initially had. In responding to his questions, God takes Job on a tour of His wondrous creation and shows that contrary to doubts some may have about His love and concern for His creation, or suspicions that He acts arbitrarily with us, He in fact cares for every hair on our heads and superintends every aspect of His creation.

This exchange constitutes the final answer to the Deist who cynically contends that his god is on permanent sabbatical following his acts of creation. Not the true God. Not the God of the Bible, who is here with us now and forever. Whereas Job begins the book as a righteous man who generally obeys God, in the end Job comes to truly know Him. He acquires this knowledge through his unimaginable suffering. He could never have learned these lessons from a tightly crafted but detached essay. Job is transformed into a thoroughly godly person whose ultimate response to God is a model for Christians. If only we could have a fraction of his faith.

The Book of Job points to Christ in numerous ways. It's noteworthy that when Job initially asks God for an answer to the problem of suffering, God is silent. Some see an analogy here to God's apparent silence when Christ cries out to Him on the cross, "My God, my God, why have you forsaken me?" (Matt. 27:46).[15] We are perplexed that God doesn't respond immediately and directly to Job's questions, yet we tend to overlook that He also didn't, then and there, answer Jesus, His One and only Son.

Of course, the book's predominant theme is human suffering and the seeming unfairness, heartlessness, and injustice of it. While Job provides no pat answers immediately satisfying to the logical human mind, it teaches the foundational lesson that we must come to know God, trust Him, and abide in Him. Christ, of course, is the final and perfect answer to our suffering because it is He with Whom we develop a personal relationship, and He is the exact image of God the Father (Heb. 1:3; John 14:9). He identifies with our suffering: "For we do not have a high priest who is unable to sympathize with our weaknesses, but one who in every respect has been tempted as we are, yet without sin" (Heb. 4:15). As He has given everything for us, we can "with confidence draw near to the throne of grace, that we may receive mercy and find grace to help in time of need" (Heb. 4:16).

Job asks God for a mediator—an advocate who will plead his case before God (Job 9:33). At first blush this appears absurd. Why would an all-powerful, all-knowing, perfectly just God be moved by any mediator on Job's behalf? Why go through such futile motions when the outcome is surely already determined, as God will make the perfect decision irrespective of any eloquent arguments a mediator could muster? Additionally, why would God allow someone to advocate against His own position? I addressed this in *Jesus On Trial*, noting that on closer examination it's not that far-fetched, because when God sent His Son, that was precisely what He was doing—providing an advocate for us. Jesus is, in fact, the Consummate Mediator who bridges the gap between our wretched sinfulness and God's perfect justice. He is the One Who, having lived a sinless life as a human being and as God, reconciles God's perfect love with His perfect mercy by taking our sins upon Himself on the cross.

God isn't acting against His own interests or principles in providing this Mediator; He is serving His interests in reuniting us with Himself without compromising His principles or His perfect nature. No other book of the Bible, in my opinion, better anticipates our need for the perfect Mediator than Job. While we've seen that Job teaches that man must come not just to know about God, but to *know* God, the best—and only—avenue to arrive at that destination is faith in Jesus Christ. As the writer of Hebrews says of Christ, "He is able to save to the uttermost those who draw near to God through him, since he always lives to make intercession for them" (7:25). Similarly, John writes, "My little children, I am writing these things to you so that you may not sin. But if anyone does sin, we have an advocate with the Father, Jesus Christ the righteous. He is the propitiation for our sins, and not for ours only but also for the sins of the whole world" (1 John 2:1). Jesus Himself is the final and perfect answer to the question of human suffering and evil in the world. God's Son suffered death on our behalf in order to conquer death for us and grant us eternal life in Him.

The Book of Job further demonstrates, perhaps ironically, that suffering need not separate humans from God. In fact, it is through the very process of suffering that Job draws closer to God and comes to know Him. Indeed, those like Job who remain steadfast are blessed by God (James 5:11). There is an obvious parallel to Christ, Who in His suffering, though temporarily separated from the Father on our behalf, ultimately draws closer to Him.[16]

It's also significant that Job, in his conversation with his friends, expresses confidence in his Redeemer: "For I know that my Redeemer lives, and at the last he will stand upon the earth. And after my skin has been thus destroyed, yet in my flesh I shall see God, whom I shall see for myself, and my eyes shall behold, and not another. My heart faints within me!" (Job 19:25). This is widely considered to be a messianic prophecy. Indeed, Professor Walter Elwell suggests that in this passage Job, though having no specific knowledge of Christ, is longing for a champion in his "lawsuit" against God. The "paramount fulfillment of Job's need for a mediator and legal advocate," writes Elwell, "has now been found in the person of Jesus Christ."[17] Note that a little later in the book the terms "mediator" and "angel" are used in association with the phrase, "I have found a ransom" (Job 33:23, 24). That caught my eye because Christ gave "his life as a ransom for many" (Mark 10:45). As Robert Alden observes, "Many of the words in these two verses become theologically freighted in the New Testament: angel, mediator, grace, ransom. For the Christian, Christ is the gracious mediator who ransoms the believer's soul from everlasting death."[18]

In contemplating the reasons for his suffering, Job poses several significant questions, all of which are answered in the Person and Work of Christ. Job asks, "Who can bring a clean thing out of an unclean?" (Job 14:4). The Bible teaches that we are powerless to purify ourselves apart from Christ. Because God is holy and we are sinful, a great chasm separates us from Him. But Christ, having paid the penalty for our sins, makes it possible for His righteousness to be imputed to us, making us acceptable in God's sight and eliminating the chasm (Heb. 10:14; Col. 1:21–23; 2 Cor. 5:17). Job also asks, "If a man dies, shall he live again?" (Job 14:14). Without Christ, the answer is yes, though in an eternity in the "outer darkness" apart from God (Matt. 25:30). But with Christ, it is eternal life in heaven with Him.[19]

PSALMS

The Book of Psalms is a collection of poems that was used as a hymnbook for the Hebrew people. It constitutes a conversation between the people and God on diverse issues spanning the gamut of human experience and emotions. In a sense it can be considered a prayer manual, for it illustrates how God's people bare their souls to their Maker. Sometimes readers are shocked at how frank the psalmists are with God, especially as they register their complaints against Him. "Rarely has human history enjoyed the luxury of a literature so cathartic," remarks C. Hassell Bullock.[20]

The Hebrews, however, aren't simply revealing their innermost thoughts, fears, and passions to God. By preserving this record for us, they (and God, of course) unveil their naked souls freely to all mankind.

There is no better way to understand the spirit of Hebrew history and the faith of the Hebrew people, says Bullock, than through this book.[21] It shows us how to communicate intimately with God and how to worship Him. The psalms give us the courage to fully open up to God honestly and completely. "The Psalms lift our hearts and minds to God and bring God down to us so that we can experience true fellowship," Ray Stedman explains. "Whether your heart is singing or sighing right now, you can turn to the Psalms to find those feelings translated into moving, inspired poetry."[22] He adds, "No matter what mood you may be in, you'll find a psalm to give expression to that mood."[23]

The psalms impart another transcendent message that we can't afford to overlook. The entire Bible reveals man's fallen nature and his emptiness without God. The psalms, in particular, "stand as a monumental witness to the timeless and universal nature of man."[24] But they also reaffirm that despite our depraved nature, God remains faithful to us. They show our utter inadequacy apart from God—but in direct proportion, they also demonstrate God's all-sufficiency and His willingness to lift us up and restore us, in preparation for an eternal relationship with Him.

Christ is everywhere in the Book of Psalms, which includes more than twenty-two messianic prophecies. Jesus expressly confirms that the psalms speak about Him (Luke 24:44). "It is the profound Christian persuasion that Christ walks within the Psalms," explains Patrick Henry Reardon, "and this is the reason that the Book of Psalms is the Old Testament book most often quoted in the New Testament."[25] Its importance is borne out at the very formation of the Church: right after Jesus' ascension, as 120 Christian brothers await Pentecost in the upper room, Peter goes directly to the Book of Psalms for authority to replace Judas. "In those days Peter stood up among the brothers...and said, 'Brothers, the Scripture had to be fulfilled, which the Holy Spirit spoke beforehand by the mouth of David concerning Judas, who became a guide to those who arrested Jesus. For he was numbered among us and was allotted his share in the ministry.... For it is written in the Book of Psalms, 'May his camp become desolate, and let there be no one to dwell in it' and 'Let another take his office'" (Acts 1:15–20).

Furthermore, their first sermon on Pentecost is an exposition of two psalms (Acts 2:25–35).[26] In Jerusalem, shortly before Paul is converted, a psalm is used in a Christian worship service, and they pray from the psalms (Acts 4:24–30). "Christ," writes Reardon, "is the referential center of the Book of Psalms."[27] The psalms cover Christ's incarnation, His deity, His eternal Sonship, His offices of prophet, priest, and king, His agony, His rejection and betrayal by men, His crucifixion, His resurrection, His ascension and exaltation, and His second coming—in judgment.[28] Indeed, Christ's presence is so pervasive throughout Psalms that it will be difficult to do more than scratch the surface in this short section. Nevertheless, I hope I can offer sufficient evidence to put some doubting minds to rest.

DOES GOD SPEAK THROUGH THE PSALMISTS?

Before examining the messianic nature of Psalms, I want to briefly address an interesting question: If the psalmists are expressing their innermost, subjective feelings and thoughts to God, how can we know they are inspired by God? After all, these communications are going from human writers to God, which is the opposite direction from which revelation flows. In his perceptive argument that the psalms can indeed be considered revelation, Gerard Van Groningen acknowledges that neither Psalms, Proverbs, Ecclesiastes, nor the Song of Solomon contain the familiar phrases indicating that God is speaking, such as, "Thus saith the Lord," "the Lord spoke," or "God came in a vision (or dream) or an oracle." These writings also lack any indication that God is speaking through the poets. But these writers did have the previous scriptural writings, knowledge of the historical circumstances then unfolding, and their own experiences and those of their people. Therefore, says Van Groningen, the poet would "give expression to his experiences and to his reactions to the historical circumstances and to his awareness of [God's] revelation in the past and in the present."

Still, Van Groningen is left wondering, "How are these 'personal' expressions to be considered revelation from [God] when they give such eloquent expression of the believing poets' heart, mind, and experiences? The answer," he says, "is that God, by his Holy Spirit, employed the poets as his spokesmen.... When they...expressed themselves, the Spirit of God carried them, guided them, and 'moved' them to speak God's words (cf. 2 Pet. 1:21)." To remove any doubt, Van Groningen quotes David, who writes, "The Spirit of the Lord speaks by me; his word is on my tongue. The God of Israel has spoken; the Rock of Israel has said to me:…" (2 Samuel 23:2–3).[29]

Of course, this does not mean every word spoken by the poets is a statement of God per se. In the context of these divinely inspired revelations, the poet or prophet sometimes interrupts what God is proclaiming through them and says or sings their inspired response, which is also true of some of Paul's New Testament writings.[30] So in Psalms, for example, we see the psalmists praying to God, and these communications, while inspired by Him, are nevertheless the heartfelt expressions of the poets. Again, this is why many people consider Psalms a prayer manual. The psalmists are showing us, under the inspiration of the Holy Spirit, how to open up and express ourselves to God in prayer.

MESSIANIC PROPHECIES IN PSALMS

Let's now look at the abundance of messianic prophecies in this book, which should be sufficient to impress all but the most unyielding materialist: He would be the Son of God (Psalms 2:7, fulfilled in Matt. 3:17); all things would be put under His feet (Psalms 8:6, fulfilled in Heb. 2:8); He would be resurrected (Psalms 16:8–10, fulfilled in Acts 2:27 and Mark 16:6, 7); God would forsake Him (Psalms 22:1, fulfilled in Matt. 27:46 and Mark 15:34); He would be mocked (Psalms 22:7–8, fulfilled in Luke 23:35–39); His hands and feet would be pierced (Psalms 22:16, fulfilled in John 20:25, 27 and Matt. 27:31, 35–36); they would cast lots for His clothes (Psalms 22:18, fulfilled in Matt. 27:35, 36); none of His bones would be broken (Psalms 34:20, fulfilled in John 19:32, 33); He would be falsely accused (Psalms 35:11, fulfilled in Mark 14:57); He would be hated without cause (Psalms 35:19, fulfilled in John 15:25); He would come to do God's will (Psalms 40:7, 8, fulfilled in Heb. 10:7); He would be betrayed by a friend (Psalms 41:9, fulfilled in Luke 22:47); His throne would be forever (Psalms 45:6, fulfilled in Heb. 1:8); He would ascend to God's right hand (Psalms 68:18, fulfilled in Mark 16:19); He would be consumed by zeal for God's house (Psalms 69:9, fulfilled in John 2:17); He would be given sour wine to drink (Psalms 69:21, fulfilled in Matt. 27:34); He would pray for His enemies (Psalms 109:4, fulfilled in Luke 23:34); His betrayer would be replaced (Psalms 109:8, fulfilled in Acts 1:20); His enemies would be placed under His feet (Psalms 110:1, fulfilled in Matt. 22:44); He would be a priest after the order of Melchizedek (Psalms 110:4, fulfilled in Heb. 5:6); He would become the stone that the builders rejected (Psalms 118:22, fulfilled in Matt. 21:42); and He would come in the name of the Lord (Psalms 118:26, fulfilled in Matt. 21:9).

CHRIST IN THE PSALMS

The psalms often have double meanings—they describe the psalmist's own experience while also putting forward a messianic or other prophetic message of which the writer may be unaware. Disbelieving any supernatural events, some critical scholars ignore the prophecies in these writings, but I personally find the dual meanings to be a compelling testimony to the psalmists' divine inspiration. How amazing that our sovereign God could arrange the outworking of history to allow the writers, in the course of describing their own circumstances, to foretell future events! Let's take a closer look at some remarkable examples.

PSALM 2

In this psalm Christ is depicted as the Son Whom God has begotten (2:7) and for Whom God will "make the nations your heritage, and the ends of the earth your possession" (2:8). The psalmist further declares, "Blessed are all who take refuge in him" (2:12). The king envisioned here, the Anointed Ruler, will rule over God's people and execute judgment against other kings who rebel against Him, but all nations can enjoy peace, blessings, and security if they serve and submit to Him.[31]

In its historical context, this psalm could apply to David or a king in the Davidic line, but it also points to the enthronement of the future Messiah in fulfillment of the Davidic Covenant.[32]

The reference to "his Anointed" in verse 2 of this psalm has a double meaning. The psalm begins, "Why do the nations rage and the peoples plot in vain? The kings of the earth set themselves, and the rulers take counsel together, against the Lord and against his Anointed, saying, 'Let us burst their bonds apart and cast away their cords from us.'" The term "anointed," which in Scripture refers to people God appoints to various offices, is undoubtedly used in that sense here. In fact, this psalm was probably a royal coronation hymn honoring the enthronement of David or Solomon, and was possibly recited again when succeeding kings were crowned. Additionally, in the progress of revelation, the future Messiah came to be known as "the Anointed One," and this verse has that second meaning as well.[33] Note that in chapter 4 of the Book of Acts, the early Christians apply this verse to Jesus, referring to Him as the coming Messiah against Whom Herod and Pilate were "raging" (4:25–26).[34]

PSALM 8

Marveling at God's created universe, the psalmist here wonders why God even bothers to think about something as seemingly insignificant as man (8:4). Yet God has made man "a little lower than the heavenly beings (angels) and crowned him with glory and honor" and has "given him dominion over the works of your hands…(and) put all things under his feet" (8:5–6). The writer of Hebrews expressly applies this language to Jesus Christ, Who "for a little while was made lower than the angels, namely Jesus, crowned with glory and honor because of the suffering of death, so that by the grace of God he might taste death for everyone" (2:5–9). While the verses speak as if God had already subjected all things to Christ, this had not yet occurred at the time Hebrews was written (and indeed still has not happened today), so the passage definitely speaks of future occurrences.[35] Donald Fortner aptly summarizes this psalm as "the Son of God becoming the Son of man in order that we might be made the sons of God."[36]

PSALM 16

Acts records that on the day of Pentecost, Peter quotes verses 8–11 of this psalm as a prophecy of Christ's resurrection. He says, in part, "For you will not abandon my soul to Hades, or let your Holy One see corruption" (2:27). Affirming God's promises both of an eternal Davidic King and of Christ's resurrection, Peter then exclaims, "Brothers, I may say to you with confidence about the patriarch David that he both died and was buried, and his tomb is with us to this day. Being therefore a prophet, and knowing that God had sworn with an oath to him that he would set one of his descendants on his throne, he foresaw and spoke about the resurrection of the Christ, that he was not abandoned to Hades, nor did his flesh see corruption. This Jesus God raised up, and of that we are all witnesses" (Acts 2: 29–32). While debating the Jews of Antioch in Pisidia, Paul also cites this psalm as predictive of Christ's resurrection (Acts 13:35).[37]

PSALM 22

This is one of my favorite passages in the Bible. It can be deeply disturbing, but viewed in the proper spirit it is wonderfully uplifting. It is undeniably a graphic picture of Christ on the cross. Many believe this psalm is purely messianic, meaning that it has no historical basis in the life of the psalmist, David.[38] In fact, the ancient Church believed that Christ, not David, was the speaker in this psalm.[39]

Taken together with Isaiah 53, we see an astonishingly accurate record of the crucifixion of Christ as recorded in the New Testament, with Psalm 22 focusing on His sufferings and Isaiah 53 directed to the sin-atoning aspects of His death.[40] Psalm 22 says the Messiah would be taunted and mocked (22:6–8), suffer terrible agony (22:14–16), have His bones wrenched out of joint (22:14), suffer incredible thirst (22:15), have His hands and feet pierced (22:16), have His garments divided and they would cast lots for His clothes (22:18), and be brought to death (22:15). Psalm 22 is powerful—so powerful in fact that Christ, in His agony on the cross, quotes from it, asking the Father why He had forsaken Him (Mark 15:34).

Other Scriptures predict additional details of Christ's fate: Psalms 41:9 says He would be betrayed by a friend; Psalms 35:11 foretells that He would be falsely accused; Isaiah 50:6 says He would be spat upon: and Psalms 34:20 relates that His bones would not be broken. Before His death, Christ Himself, through His own prophecies, completes the picture of His death and crucifixion (Matt. 12:38–42, 16:21, 17:22–23, 20:18–19, 26:31; Mark 8:31, 9:31, 10:32–34; Luke 9:22, 44, 18:31–33; John 12:32–33).[41]

PSALMS 22, 23, AND 24:
THE SHEPHERD PSALMS

These psalms together are referred to as the shepherd psalms because Psalm 22, read in conjunction with John 10:11, pictures Christ as the Good Shepherd Who lays down His life for the sheep. Psalm 23, viewed in light of Hebrews 13:20–21, depicts Christ as the Great Shepherd, and Psalm 24, read together with 1 Peter 5:4, sees Christ as the Chief Shepherd.[42] As J. Vernon McGee observes, "In Psalm 22 we see the *cross*, in Psalm 23 the *crook* (the Shepherd's crook), and in Psalm 24 the *crown* (the King's crown). In Psalm 22 Christ is the *Savior*, in Psalm 23 He is the *Satisfier*; in Psalm 24 He is the *Sovereign*."[43]

PSALM 40

Verses 7–9 of this psalm, according to the writer of Hebrews, depict Christ's obedient and willing sacrifice on the cross, which replaces the Old Testament sacrifices (10:5–10).

PSALM 41

In the Gospel of John, Jesus applies Psalm 41:9 to Judas' betrayal, saying "I am not speaking of all of you; I know whom I have chosen. But the Scripture will be fulfilled, 'He who ate my bread has lifted his heel against me.' I am telling you this now, before it takes place, that when it does take place you may believe that I am he" (13:18–19).

PSALM 45

Beginning at verse 6, this psalm reads, "Your throne, O God, is forever and ever. The scepter of your kingdom is a scepter of uprightness; you have loved righteousness and hated wickedness. Therefore God, your God, has anointed you with the oil of gladness beyond your companions." I don't see how a believing heart can reasonably doubt that these are references to Christ as God's Anointed, Who will be on the throne forever and rule in righteousness. Hebrews 1:7–12 specifically applies this psalm to Christ. I'm particularly moved by the phrase "God, your God," which suggests two of the three Persons of the Trinity. Bible scholar John MacArthur affirms this is "an indication that God is communing with the Son."[44] Henry Halley summarizes these passages: "Here is depicted the glorious reign of a king, bearing the name of God, seated on an eternal throne. It can refer to no other than the eternal King who would come from David's family. It is a wedding song of Christ and His bride, the church."[45]

PSALM 68

In his letter to the Ephesians, Paul quotes Psalms 68:18 to describe Christ's ascension to heaven and His distribution of gifts to the Church: "You ascended on high, leading a host of captives in your train and receiving gifts among men, even among the rebellious, that the Lord God may dwell there" (Eph. 4:8).[46]

PSALM 69

Jesus quotes Psalms 69:4—"those who hate me without a cause"—in John 15:25. Referring to Christ earlier in his Gospel, John quotes Psalms 69:9: "zeal for your house has consumed me" (John 2:17). Additionally, in John 19:28, Christ is described as quoting Psalms 69:21—"I thirst"—in order "to fulfill the Scripture." It is interesting to note, however, that while those passages are affirmed in the New Testament as references to Jesus, the entire psalm cannot be read as a predictive vision of Christ, as the psalmist admits his own sinfulness in verse 5 and his vindictiveness in verses 22–29.[47] Sometimes, in His mysterious ways,

God combines the simple with the complex, which adds to, rather than detracts from, the Bible's credibility. Note that Psalms 69:9 is quoted in Romans 15:3; Psalms 69:21 in Matthew 27:34; and Psalms 69:25 in Acts 1:20.[48]

PSALM 72

This psalm, writes Gerard Van Groningen, "has been considered the outstanding messianic royal psalm."[49] It describes a kingdom with a "dominion from sea to sea, and from the River to the ends of the earth!" (Psalms 72:8). More important, it depicts the kingdom as endless (Psalms 72:5), which is humanly unattainable. Most important of all, the king described in this psalm is vividly portrayed as both human and divine.[50] Further, Psalm 72 exalts the qualities of the ideal king and the virtues of a perfect government.[51] In a broader sense, five stanzas of this psalm describe five qualities that characterize the kingdom of Christ: its character (72:1–4), duration (72:5–7), expanse (72:8–11), nature (72:12–14), and blessing (72:15–17).[52]

PSALM 78

Verse 2 of this psalm foreshadows Christ's practice of preaching in parables: "I will open my mouth in a parable; I will utter dark sayings from of old." Matthew 13:34–35 quotes the verse as applying to Christ.

PSALM 89

This psalm projects the Davidic kingdom through eternity (89:3, 4), describing the throne as being grounded in the godly attributes of righteousness and justice (89:14). It says God will make the king the firstborn, the highest of the kings of the earth (89:27) and "my covenant will stand firm for him" (89:28). Again, David's throne shall last forever (89:35–37), which is only conceivable in view of Christ's permanent kingdom. The psalmist, however, then expresses dismay at being abandoned for a time, as if the Davidic promises are about to fail. Some commentators believe this prefigures Christ's suffering and rejection (Matt. 27:44; Luke 18:32; Acts 2:30, 13:22; Rev. 1:5, 19:16).[53] I see an analogy here with Christ's expressing His feeling of rejection in the Garden of Gethsemane and on the cross while simultaneously praising God. This psalm includes both sentiments.

PSALM 93

This psalm describes a theocracy, but not in the sense that it existed in ancient Israel with God's direct rule over the Hebrews. Instead, it depicts God's kingship of the entire earth and universe. "Yes, the world is established; it shall never be moved. Your throne is established from of old; you are from everlasting" (93:1–2). The psalm further describes the godly nature of His rule: "Your decrees are very trustworthy; holiness befits your house" (93:5).[54] Indeed, commentators say that Psalms 93 and 95–99 comprise a series of psalms that exalt the Lord as king. These psalms were recited before and after the United Kingdom but became particularly important in worship afterward, when they began to be interpreted messianically.[55]

PSALM 102

Hebrews quotes this psalm: "You, Lord, laid the foundation of the earth in the beginning, and the heavens are the work of your hands" (1:10, quoting Psalms 102:25). It describes Christ's eternality (Heb. 1:11–12, quoting Psalms 102:25–27).

PSALM 109

The psalmist here foresees the One who is despised and rejected without cause (109:1–5). It describes those rejecting Him and their fate (109:6–20), and anticipates Christ in His sorrow (109:21–25).[56] In Acts 1:20, Peter paraphrases Psalms 109:8, predicting Christ's betrayer: "For it is written in the Book of Psalms, 'May his camp become desolate, and let there be no one to dwell in it'; and 'Let another take his office.'"

PSALM 110

The New Testament quotes this psalm fourteen times—more than any other text in the Old Testament. In every instance, the quotes apply the psalm to Christ.[57] Jesus, in the familiar passage in which He addresses the question of whose son Christ is, quotes this psalm: "Now while the Pharisees were gathered together, Jesus asked them a question, saying 'What do you think about the Christ? Whose son is he?' They said to him, 'The son of David.' He said to them, 'How is it then that David, in the Spirit, calls him Lord, saying, "The Lord said to my Lord, 'Sit at my right hand, until I put your enemies under your feet'"? If then David calls him Lord, how is he his son?'" (Matt. 22:41–45. See also Acts 2:32–36; 1 Cor. 15:23–24; Heb. 1:13, 10:11–13). The psalm also describes Christ as an eternal priest after the order of Melchizedek (Psalms 110:4), while Hebrews, as noted, applies this quote to Christ (7:11–25). The psalm contains a series of truths concerning the Person and work of Christ, including His kingship, priesthood, and role as judge.

PSALM 118

Here Christ is foreseen as "the stone the builders rejected" Who "has become the cornerstone. This is the Lord's doing; it is marvelous in our eyes" (118:22–23). Christ applies this to Himself in Matthew 21:42: "Have you never read in the Scriptures: 'the stone that the builders rejected has become the cornerstone; this was the Lord's doing, and it is marvelous in our eyes'?" In his letter to the Ephesians, Paul affirms this as well: "Christ Jesus himself being the cornerstone" (Eph. 2:20). Other New Testament passages in some way refer to this psalm, such as Matthew 21:9, 15, 23:39; Mark 12:10; Luke 20:17; John 12:13; Acts 4:11; Romans 9:33; 1 Corinthians 3:11; Hebrews 13:6; and 1 Peter 2:7. Most of these passages reference the Messiah.[58]

PROVERBS

If the Book of Psalms is an instruction manual on prayer and developing a relationship with God, the Book of Proverbs is a handbook on acquiring wisdom, which is a precondition for developing a right relationship with Him. As Psalms relates, "The fear of the Lord is the beginning of knowledge (wisdom)" (1:7). We can't become wise without fearing God—that is, having profound respect and reverence for Him—and putting Him first in our lives, which will also help us to live more meaningfully and morally.

The proverbs teach us precepts for right and godly living. These revealed principles, as context shows, apply to all people, not just the Hebrews. They teach us, consistent with the admonition to fear God, that to become wise we must humbly accept our limitations. The acquisition of biblical wisdom involves our plumbing of Scripture to gain the insight and knowledge to live godly lives and then applying that knowledge to our daily experiences. We don't gain wisdom through book learning alone, but we learn from our experiences and through our mistakes, and we further refine what we've learned by revisiting Scripture.

Acquiring wisdom, then, involves a pattern of behavior: steeping ourselves in God's Word, applying the principles from it to our experiences, then incorporating those lessons to gain greater insight that will in turn enhance our next readings of Scripture. We should repeat this process endlessly while asking God's strength and guidance to help us act wisely. There is no shortcut—no machine that can instantly inject us with wisdom, especially not godly wisdom. It is a long, continuous, sometimes laborious, but always profitable process. We are and will always be, this side of heaven at least, works in progress, and will never be perfectly wise or have a perfect relationship with God—but we must never stop pursuing these goals. God created us with an innate desire to learn and grow, and ultimately for a relationship with Him. We must obediently make the most of this opportunity.

These themes flow directly into the Christ-centered aspects of the Book of Proverbs, as our "fear" of God and our pursuit of godly wisdom lead us to Christ, Who is Wisdom Personified and "in whom are hidden all the treasures of wisdom and knowledge" (Col. 2:3). Don't assume that Christ "became" wisdom in the sense that He is a created being or that He somehow grew in divine wisdom. He is eternal—and as we've mentioned, He was with the Father and the Holy Spirit since before time, having been instrumental in creating all things. Christ always was, is, and forever shall be, the embodiment of wisdom.

Indeed, Proverbs assures us that when God "established the heavens I was there; when he drew a circle on the face of the deep, when he made firm the skies above, when he established the fountains of the deep, when he assigned to the sea its limit, so that the waters might not transgress his command, when he marked out the foundations of the earth, then I was beside him, like a master workman" (8:27–30). If you doubt this refers to Christ, the Second Person of the Triune Godhead, read a few verses down: "For whoever finds me finds life and obtains favor from the Lord, but he who fails to find me injures himself; all who hate me love death" (8:35–36). Read in the context of the New Testament, it's clear that this proverb points to Christ, for it is through faith in Him that we find life (John 3:16). Proverbs 3 also emphasizes that wisdom is the pathway to blessing and life: "Blessed is the one who finds wisdom.... Long life is in her right hand.... She is a tree of life to those who lay hold of her; those who hold her fast are called blessed" (3:13, 16, 18).

By applying the principles of Wisdom set out in Proverbs, we will grow wiser. But if we order our priorities in a worldly direction we will fall short, because the foolishness of the world will seduce us into being wise in our own eyes. Proverbs instructs us, however, to "be not wise in your own eyes; fear the Lord, and turn away from evil. It will be healing to your flesh and refreshment to your bones" (3:7). Nevertheless, "there is a way that seems right to a man, but its end is the way to death" (14:12). We will acquire godly wisdom if, through faith, we pursue Christ and Christ-likeness. "The book of Proverbs points us to Christ," argues Gary Everett. "It leads us down the path that leads to Christlikeness."[59] According to James, "If any of you lacks wisdom, let him ask God, who gives generously to all without reproach, and it will be given him. But let him ask in faith, with no doubting" (James 1:5–6). Similarly, Paul tells us that Christ "became to us wisdom from God, righteousness and sanctification and redemption, so that, as it is written, 'Let the one who boasts, boast in the Lord'" (1 Cor. 1:30–31).[60] And Proverbs affirms that faith is the avenue to wisdom: "Trust in the Lord with all your heart, and do not lean on your own understanding. In all your ways acknowledge him, and he will make straight your paths" (3:5–6).

The principles taught in Proverbs lead us to Christ because no mere man can always measure up to the standards they prescribe, any more than mortals can live up to the standards Jesus taught in His Sermon on the Mount. It is through knowing Christ that you gain true wisdom (1 Cor. 1:24, 30), and through His Word, that you receive wisdom for right living.[61]

There is at least one messianic prophecy in Proverbs—also seen in other books—which points to the Son of God: "Who has ascended to heaven and come down? Who has gathered the wind in his fists? Who has wrapped up the waters in a garment? Who has established all the ends of the earth? What is his name, and what is his son's name? Surely you know!" (30:4).

My friend Pastor Dan Phillips suggests that Proverbs points to Christ in numerous ways, including some we haven't yet mentioned here. "Christ," writes Phillips, "is the way (John 14:6) and the life lived in believing union with Him is the way (Acts 9:2; 19:9, 23; 22:4; 24:14, 22)." Proverbs, he says, confronts us with two different paths we could pursue—that of wisdom and that of folly, of death and life, of cursing and blessing, of joy and sorrow. But this is not a works-based set of instructions—for Phillips reminds us that the very beginning of the book establishes the foundational principle of fearing God as the beginning of wisdom. We want to become wise and we want to behave wisely. Jesus Christ, notes Phillips, "embodies both the way and those values which characterize it, such as truth and life (John 14:6). In this way, Proverbs points us to Christ, the very embodiment of the way of God, of wisdom, of life, of truth, of blessing and joy."[62]

Phillips highlights another important way that Proverbs points to Christ. Jesus and His apostles admonish converted believers to be "wise as serpents and innocent as doves" (Matt. 10:16), and to walk in a wise manner (Eph. 5:15; Col. 4:5). But where, asks Phillips, "can a Christian find details, principles, directions, instruction?" His answer: "We find this instruction in the Bible of Christ and the apostles: in the book of Proverbs."[63]

ECCLESIASTES

The Book of Ecclesiastes, it occurs to me, is strikingly complementary to Proverbs in that it illustrates, rather painfully, that human existence is meaningless apart from God. The book contains a sermon of sorts from the "preacher," who I believe is Solomon, recounting his own experiences with the futility of life. Looking back on his life, the preacher bemoans that even after pursuing all the good and wonderful things that the material life can offer, from pleasure to wealth, he finds that none of them have any enduring worth or provides long-term happiness and fulfillment. "Vanity of vanities, says the Preacher, vanity of vanities! All is vanity" (1:2). Even acquiring humanly and earthly wisdom, he concedes, is "but a striving after wind" (1:16).

Readers shouldn't be discouraged by this book's pessimism, for in the final analysis, its message is actually inspiring. Only by seeing the abject futility of chasing after temporal happiness apart from God will we understand the imperative of seeking God, which is the only path to fulfillment, meaning, significance, and lasting joy in our lives.

Most of the book until the last few verses, with a few scattered exceptions, is discouraging beyond comprehension. But in these last few verses, which would be much less impactful without their predicate, the preacher gives us the primary and overriding exception that obliterates the foregoing rule: "The end of the matter; all has been heard. Fear God and keep his commandments, for this is the whole duty of man. For God will bring every deed into judgment, with every secret thing, whether good or evil." Not only is life meaningless without God, but we are all, every single one of us, whether or not we choose to accept it, accountable to Him. What could be a better foundation to the New Testament than these truths? What could better demonstrate our need for a Savior than these sobering lessons?

In *Jesus on Trial* I explained that the one thing that best revitalizes my faith during intermittent moments of doubt is, paradoxically, the pervasiveness of evil, suffering, and despair that we see all around us, and the inexplicably twisted values that increasingly define our culture. This unfathomability of the human condition, this perverse moral inversion we witness, this willing abandonment of logic and distortion of the language, cannot possibly be understood, in my view, apart from the Bible. Without the Bible, none of this makes any sense to me, but with it, I see how sin entered the world in the fall and how it has corrupted God's perfect creation. Yet the Bible also shows that despite all that, there is hope to be found in Jesus Christ—for in Christ we find our meaning, our fulfillment, our joy, and eternal life.

So Ecclesiastes contains harsh realism—a bitter jolt, warning us not to become complacent and accept our fate as if there were no light at the end of the tunnel. Its authenticity inheres in its refusal to candy-coat our fallen state and sanitize life just to superficially placate us while ultimately leaving us in despair, with no answers. To be sure, it convinces us of our emptiness, but it also reveals that each person has eternity in his heart (3:11), and that only Christ can fill that void and provide us with sustaining satisfaction, joy, and wisdom.

Yes, this book forces us to take a hard, close, uncomfortable look at the human condition and at ourselves, but it also reminds us that even after the fall, we remain beings created by God, and we retain a glimmer of His divine image. We are "fixable" thanks to that glimmer and the eternity He placed in our hearts. But we cannot fix ourselves, and this book confirms that as well as anything could. There is, however, a way. Man's path to wisdom and the highest good is to be found through faith in "one Shepherd" (Eccl. 12:11), who will give him life and give it abundantly (John 10:9, 10).[64] Every disappointment, heartache, and personal failing has its solution in Jesus Christ, Who alone can give life real meaning. No matter how despairing life may be, in heaven there will be no more tears, no more death, no more mourning, and no more pain, for those things will have passed away (Rev. 7:17, 21:4).

SONG OF SOLOMON

The Song of Solomon is a lyric poem or song in the form of a dialogue that describes Solomon's love for a woman. The book, writes Paul Benware, "elevates human, sexual love to the place that God intended. Although the Bible often warns of the negative consequences of immorality, it also extols the blessings that come from moral behavior...and shows the joys of physical love within the boundaries of marital commitment."[65]

Many question how such a book could merit inclusion in the biblical canon. But the institution of marriage is central to God's organization of human society. And why shouldn't a book that describes that institution in its godly sense be useful as part of God's revealed message to man? It is perfectly fitting because God created man and woman (Gen. 1:27, 2:20–23) and established the sacred institution of marriage (Gen. 2:24).[66] "Solomon's ancient love song exalts the purity of marital affection and romance," says John MacArthur. "It parallels and enhances other portions of Scripture which portray God's plan for marriage, including the beauty and sanctity of sexual intimacy between husband and wife."[67] Perhaps if we had a higher view of God's institution, we'd have a less cynical view of this biblical book.

Though there are no direct messianic references in Song of Solomon, it nevertheless points us to Christ through strong analogy. Like some of the psalms (and other parts of Scripture), there is a double meaning in the story—it's a contemporary account of a man and a woman in human history as well as a future-oriented look to Christ. Many commentators see this love story as a prefiguring of Christ's relationship with the Church, His bride.[68] This is hardly a case of Bible scholars trying to find Christ under every rock, seeing as Paul penned an entire section in his letter to the Ephesians analogizing husbands' love for their wives to Christ's love for and relationship with the Church (Eph. 5:25–32).

The first few verses in that passage deserve our special attention. Paul reminds us that Christ loved the Church and gave Himself up to sanctify it, "having cleansed her by the washing of water with the word, so that he might present the church to himself in splendor, without spot or wrinkle or any such thing, that she might be holy and without blemish" (Eph. 5:25–27). This is intriguing when read alongside verse 4:7 of Song of Solomon: "You are altogether beautiful, my love; there is no flaw in you." Because of Christ, we—the Church body—are no longer marred by sin. When God looks upon us on the day of judgment, He doesn't see our sin-stained bodies because our "spots" have been removed and there "is no flaw" in us. I believe it's worth repeating

Charles Spurgeon's eloquent observation on this: "If God shall look upon us as we are He must be displeased; but when He sees Christ Jesus He is well pleased for His righteousness sake. When the Lord looks this way we hide behind the veil, and the eyes of the Lord behold the exceeding glories of the veil, to wit the person of His own dear Son, and He is so pleased with the cover that he forbears to remember the defilement and deformity of those whom it covers."[69]

The last three verses of this section of Ephesians are particularly interesting. Paul writes, "For no one ever hated his own flesh, but nourishes and cherishes it, just as Christ does the church, because we are members of his body. 'Therefore a man shall leave his father and mother and hold fast to his wife, and the two shall become one flesh.' This mystery is profound, and I am saying that it refers to Christ and the church" (5:31–32). What is this mystery to which Paul refers? Archibald Robertson maintains that "the comparison of marriage to the union of Christ and the Church is the mystery."[70] William Hendriksen believes Paul refers to this as a mystery because Christ, living in bliss with the Father and the Holy Spirit in eternity past, nevertheless "plunged himself into the *dreadful darkness and awful anguish of Calvary* in order to save his *rebellious people*, gathered from among all the nations, and even to dwell in their hearts through his Spirit and at last to present *them*—even these utterly undeserving ones—to himself as his own bride, with whom he becomes united in such intimate fellowship that no early metaphor can ever do justice to it, *this* even in and by itself is a mystery."[71]

Paul is not the only New Testament writer who uses the analogy of Christ and His bride. In the Book of Revelation, John does so in two separate passages: 19:7–9 and 21:9. Other passages of the Old Testament apply the metaphor of God as the Husband of those He loves. For example, Isaiah writes, "Fear not...for...the reproach of your widowhood you will remember no more. For your Maker is your husband, the Lord of hosts is his name" (Isaiah 54:4–5; see also Jer. 2:2; Ezek. 16:8–14; Hosea 2:16).

I like Donald Fortner's assessment of the Christ-centeredness of this book and his description of how Song of Solomon and Ecclesiastes complement one another. "The Song of Solomon," writes Fortner, "is set in the Scriptures in direct contrast to Ecclesiastes. Ecclesiastes shows us the emptiness of life without Christ. The Song of Solomon shows us the fullness of life in Christ. Ecclesiastes expounds the first part of our Lord's statement to the Samaritan woman—'Whosoever drinketh of this water shall thirst again.' The Song of Solomon expounds the second part of his statement to her—'Whosoever drinketh of the water that I shall give him shall never thirst.'"[72]

Similarly, Robert Lee writes that Ecclesiastes teaches that we cannot be satisfied, even if we possess the entire world, because "the heart is too large for the object." But a beautiful discovery awaits readers of the Song of Solomon—that if we shift our focus away from the world and turn toward Christ, "we cannot fathom the infinite preciousness of His love—the Object is too large for the heart."[73]

This completes our review of the poetical books. We turn next to the prophetic books, which teem with messianic prophecies and other foreshadowings of our Savior.

CHAPTER 14

CHRIST IN EVERY BOOK
PROPHETS OBADIAH THROUGH ISAIAH

Augustine, in his interpretation of the Cana miracle where Jesus turned water into wine, wrote of the difference that Christ makes in understanding the OT: "Read all the prophetic books; and if Christ be not understood therein, what canst thou find so insipid and silly? Understand Christ in them [however], and what thou readest not only has a taste but even inebriates thee."

—FREDERICK BRUNER[1]

THE OLD TESTAMENT PROPHETS

S ome think of prophets as those who foretell the future, but that's only part of what the biblical prophets do. They are primarily "forthtellers." Think of them as preachers who have a direct line to God on certain matters, who communicate to the people on behalf of God, and who, in some cases, also engage in "foretelling." The prophets' primary task is to correct moral and religious abuses and to proclaim the great moral and religious truths flowing from God's character that inhere in the foundation of His government.[2]

God called more people to serve as prophets than those who wrote books that made it into the Old Testament canon. Those who minister only through the spoken word are called oral prophets, and those who communicate both through preaching and as authors of Old Testament books are considered writing prophets.[3] Elijah, Elisha, and the female prophetess Huldah are examples of oral prophets, while Isaiah and Malachi are writing prophets.

The prophets, as God's mouthpieces, communicate messages to a disobedient Israel. Their messages include God's holiness, the sin and disobedience of God's people, calls to repentance, warnings of God's impending judgment on the Israelites, warnings of His judgment on surrounding nations, the return of the people from captivity, the coming of the Messiah, the second coming of the Messiah, and others.[4]

We'll mainly deal here with the sixteen writing prophets, how their ministries fit into Old Testament history, and how their writings point to Christ. There are sixteen writing prophets who authored the seventeen Old Testament prophetic books—Jeremiah is believed to have written both Jeremiah and Lamentations. (Some call Moses a writing prophet as well,[5] but he wrote the first five books of the Bible, not any of the books classified as prophetic books.) These sixteen are categorized into the Major Prophets (Isaiah, Jeremiah, Ezekiel, and Daniel) and the Minor Prophets (Obadiah, Joel, Jonah, Amos, Hosea, Micah, Nahum, Zephaniah, Habakkuk, Haggai, Zechariah, and Malachi). The Major Prophets aren't designated as such because their ministries were more important, but because their books are longer than those of the Minor Prophets.[6] The books of the Major Prophets each took an entire parchment roll, whereas the Minor ones fit together into only one—the Roll of the Twelve Prophets.[7]

Bible scholars classify the writing prophets, Major and Minor, according to two main criteria. The first is the biblical period during which they ministered. These divide into three periods:

1. *The pre-exilic*—this includes both those who ministered before the Assyrian captivity of the Northern Kingdom in 722 BC and those who ministered before the Babylonian captivity in 586 BC.

2. *The exilic*—those who ministered during the Babylonian exile.

3. *The post-exilic*—those who ministered during the people's return to the land following the Babylonian exile.[8]

The pre-exilic prophets are Isaiah, Jeremiah, Hosea, Joel, Amos, Obadiah, Jonah, Micah, Nahum, Habakkuk, and Zephaniah; the exilic prophets are Ezekiel and Daniel; and the post-exilic prophets are Haggai, Zechariah, and Malachi.[9]

The second criteria for classifying the writing prophets is based on whom the prophets primarily ministered to (mostly Israel or Judah, but some largely ministered to foreign nations, such as Obadiah's ministry to Edom, and Jonah's and Nahum's ministries to the Assyrian capital of Nineveh).[10]

The dominant subject addressed by the Major and Minor Prophets is God's dealings with the Northern and Southern Kingdoms of the Israelites—though the ministries to foreign nations are also important, for they show that God works among the Gentiles as well.[11] The prophets frequently preach about the coming Messiah, both about His suffering (in His first coming) and His triumphant kingship in His second coming.[12] "The preaching of the great prophets," observes British Old Testament scholar R. E. Clements, "supplied a kind of God-given commentary on the events that took place: forewarning that they would happen, offering reasons why they must happen, and seeing in them the judgment of God upon a sinful people." Along with these warnings, Clements writes, the prophets also "provided Israel and Judah with a message of hope, looking beyond the defeat and national humiliation to eventual renewal and restoration."[13]

Grouped together, the seventeen prophetic books do not appear in strict chronological order in the Bible. For example, the Major Prophets appear first beginning with Isaiah, who wrote in the mid-eighth century BC, even though Obadiah, whose ministry was the first of the writing prophets, worked in the mid-ninth century BC. The following chart shows when and to whom the prophets ministered,[14] though some dates are debated. After the chart, we'll look at the prophetic books in their chronological order.

OLD TESTAMENT PROPHETS		
PROPHET	MINISTERED TO	IN THE YEARS
Obadiah	Edom	850–840 BC
Joel	Judah	835–796 BC
Jonah	Nineveh	784–774 BC
Amos	Israel	763–755 BC
Hosea	Israel	755–710 BC
Isaiah	Judah	739–680 BC
Micah	Judah	735–710 BC
Nahum	Nineveh	650–630 BC
Zephaniah	Judah	635–625 BC
Jeremiah	Judah	627–570 BC
Habakkuk	Judah	620–605 BC
Daniel	Jews in Babylon	605–536 BC
Ezekiel	Jews in Babylon	593–570 BC
Haggai	Judah	520–505 BC
Zechariah	Judah	520–470 BC
Malachi	Judah	433–424 BC

OBADIAH

Obadiah was probably written around 850–840 BC, but some scholars date it much later—in 586 BC—because it describes Edom's attack on Jerusalem. Though it's debated whether that attack occurred during the assault by the Philistines and Arabians on Jerusalem in 848–841 BC or during the attack by Babylonian King Nebuchadnezzar in 586 BC, most scholars prefer the former date.[15] This is one of the three prophetic books directed mostly to a foreign nation: Edom, a country south of Israel whose people descended from Jacob's brother Esau and were a constant thorn in Israel's side. Having denied Moses passage through their land (Num. 20:14–21), the Edomites opposed two of the three kings of the United Kingdom—Saul (1 Sam. 14:47) and Solomon (1 Kings 11:14–25)—as well as Judean kings Jehoshaphat (2 Chron. 20:22) and Jehoram (2 Chron. 21:8).[16] Obadiah prophesies Edom's destruction (Obad. 1:18) due to the violence it inflicted on Jerusalem and its arrogant gloating over the attack. This prophecy is dramatically fulfilled when the Edomites are removed from their land and subsequently disappear from history, with their land eventually becoming "a place of foreigners."[17]

There are no direct, obvious messianic references in this book, but there are important prefigurings and connections. As a further outworking of the prophesied enmity between Edom and God's people, Herod the Great, who rules Judea when Jesus is born and attempts to kill Him in His infancy, descends from the Edomites (Matt. 2:13).[18]

Obadiah also emphasizes the Lord's judgment against Israel's enemies (Obad. 15, 16), thereby anticipating the judgment that is to be administered by Christ, Who is the Savior of Israel (Obad. 17–20)[19] and the One Who Possesses the kingdom (Obad. 21).[20] Israel will eventually triumph through Christ.[21]

Furthermore, David Field points out that the first half of Obadiah prefigures Christ in that God's nation is betrayed, mocked, and stripped of its possessions and dignity, then exiled and humiliated. Obadiah's outrage at this injustice foreshadows our outrage as we see God's Son on the cross. As the story unfolds, Field explains, "God's own is delivered, restored, vindicated, set apart, given possession, triumph and rule, taking over the world under the kingship of God, surrounded by the mocking of those who should have known better, restored to enter the inheritance promised by God." This pattern, he contends, points to "God's own"—Jesus Christ.[22] Similarly, Gary Staats observes that Edom represents all those who will fall under God's judgment when Christ returns. He points to Jesus' words, "I say to you, as you did it to one of the least of these my brothers, you did it to me" (Matt. 25:40).[23] Like Christ, the prophet Obadiah doesn't avoid the world and its challenges. He is willing to get his hands dirty, plunging into the world to denounce the wickedness he witnesses.[24]

JOEL

Joel writes during the period of the Divided Kingdom to warn Judah of the "Day of the Lord" (1:15, 2:1, 11, 31, 3:14). Like the psalms discussed in the previous chapter, this prophecy has dual meanings that apply to the time of the writing and also to a future day of judgment.[25] Though Joel initially invokes the "day of the Lord" to describe God's judgment on Israel by a plague of locusts (1:15–2:11), he also refers to a final day of the Lord far into the future (2:31, 3:14–17).[26] While there will be a future day of judgment for Israel's enemies, the future day of the Lord will be a time of glorious blessing and prosperity for Israel (3:18–21). The phrase is also used by Amos and Zephaniah (Amos 5:18; Zeph. 1:7) and by New Testament writers, who speak of "the day of our Lord Jesus Christ" (1 Cor. 1:8; 2 Cor. 1:14) and "the day of God" (2 Peter 3:12; Rev. 16:14).

Furthermore, just before He ascends into heaven, Jesus assures His disciples He will send the Holy Spirit upon them (John 16:7–15; Acts 1:8). Joel had prophesied that Christ would return and pour out His Spirit on all flesh (Joel 2:28), gather and judge the nations (Joel 3:2, 12), and be a refuge to His people (Joel 3:16).[27] While these events did occur at Pentecost during the early days of the Church as recorded in the Book of Acts, John Walvoord argues that the prophecy awaits complete fulfillment at Christ's second coming.[28]

Joel also anticipates a gathering of all nations in the Valley of Jehoshaphat, where the Anointed One of God would judge them (Joel 3:2, 12). When the Old Testament addresses the subject of God's judgment against sin, whether it's speaking of individual or national sin, it's usually foreshadowing the coming judgment of Christ. Christ's judgment on that day will be unbearable except for those who have placed their faith in Him[29]—for with that promise of judgment is an assurance of grace. Peter, in his sermon at Pentecost, quotes the Book of Joel, concluding with, "And it shall come to pass that everyone who calls upon the name of the Lord shall be saved" (Acts 2:17–21).

JONAH

Jonah also writes during the Divided Kingdom period, having been ordered by God to direct his message toward Israel's enemy Assyria—though it's also a message for Israel. G. Campbell Morgan notes that God's commission to a foreign nation must have seemed odd to Jonah.[30] He initially flees to the far-away city of Tarshish to avoid God's command, but after God disciplines him, Jonah obediently travels to Nineveh and tells the Assyrians to repent or face God's imminent judgment. When they believe the message and repent (Jonah 3:5), God spares them from disaster.

Curiously, this angers Jonah, who admits that he initially disobeyed God's order to minister at Nineveh because he opposed God's sparing of the Assyrians. God teaches Jonah a lesson by scorching a plant that is protecting him from the sun. When Jonah grieves for the plant, God rebukes him, saying, "You pity the plant, for which you did not labor, nor did you make it grow, which came into being in a night and perished in a night. And should not I pity Nineveh, that great city, in which there are more than 120,000 persons who do not know their right hand from their left, and also much cattle?" (Jonah 4:10–11). God is denouncing Jonah's callousness about the damnation of hundreds of thousands of human beings God created while becoming heartbroken over the death of a plant that Jonah had not created.

Perhaps Jonah's lack of compassion for his enemies is shown to highlight the stark contrast between his attitude and God's love toward all His creatures. Though human beings are often slow to absolve their enemies, God is forgiving, and His forgiveness extends to the Gentiles. According to Scottish theologian George Adam Smith, "That God has granted to the Gentiles also repentance unto life is nowhere else in the Old Testament so vividly illustrated."[31] J. Sidlow Baxter suggests that the revelation of God in the closing three verses of Jonah "is perhaps the tenderest anticipation of John 3:16, and the parable of the prodigal son, and the world-embracing message of the Gospel, to be found anywhere in the Old Testament."[32] Scottish Presbyterian minister James Hastings adds, "Nowhere in pre-Christian literature can be found a broader, purer, loftier, tenderer conception of God than in this little anonymous Hebrew tract. [German theologian Carl Heinrich] Cornill describes it as 'one of the deepest and grandest things ever written.'"[33]

Baxter notes that Jonah has to learn that God's election of Israel doesn't mean the rejection of other peoples—a point we've made repeatedly.

"Israel," writes Baxter, "had not been chosen simply for Israel's own sake, but to fulfill a Divine purpose, the end of which was the blessing of *all* peoples."[34] Indeed, the Book of Jonah provides the first blueprint for foreign missions—some eight hundred years before the birth of Christ.[35]

This book includes the classic story of Jonah being swallowed by a fish and spending three days in its belly. Some treat the story as allegorical, but Jesus affirms it as historical (Matt. 12:40), even implying it is a prefiguring sign of His resurrection: "For just as Jonah was three days and three nights in the belly of the great fish, so will the Son of Man be three days and three nights in the heart of the earth" (Matt. 12:40).

Perhaps it's fitting that Jesus would give a sign to a hard-hearted audience not by unlocking the mystery for them then and there, but by hinting at something that most of them would understand only after He had arisen on the third day. That sign would wholly vindicate Him and His authority while repudiating theirs. We noted that sometimes the Old Testament prophets may not have fully understood the future implications of their prophecies, as part of the process of progressive revelation. But in this case, the One delivering the message is no ordinary prophet—it is the Son of God Himself. As such, He is undoubtedly aware of its full ramifications but, it seems, He doesn't want to translate this sign right away.

Jesus also contrasts the Ninevites' repentance in response to the preaching of a mere mortal, with the Pharisees and teachers of the Law who are rejecting One "greater than Jonah" (Matt. 12:41). Consider the gravity of this lesson. The Pharisees are of God's chosen people yet they turn blind eyes and deaf ears to God in the flesh, while the Gentiles had embraced the message of a human messenger. "The Pharisees were Israelites, participants in the covenant God had made with that nation," states Charles Price. "They had failed to recognize Christ, yet both Nineveh, the capital city of Assyria, and the Queen of Sheba who were outside of the covenant Israel enjoyed with God had recognized and responded to the truth."[36]

The message of repentance and salvation through faith is universal: it applies to the Ninevites, to the Pharisees and Law teachers, and to the Gentiles and all nations (Jonah 2:9; John 14:6; Luke 2:32; Acts 9:15, 11:18; Gal. 2:2). In Romans, Paul asks, "Or is God the God of Jews only?

Is he not the God of Gentiles also? Yes, of Gentiles also, since God is one—who will justify the circumcised by faith and the uncircumcised through faith" (3:29–30).

This book is extraordinarily Christ-centered and forward looking, as Christ likens Jonah to Himself, cites Jonah's experience as foreshadowing His culminating act of salvation in death and resurrection, and uses the story to point to the Gospel's universal applicability to all who will place their faith in Him. It gives us a foretaste of the Great Commission wherein Jesus Christ commands His disciples, "All authority in heaven and on earth has been given to me. Go therefore and make disciples of all nations, baptizing them in the name of the Father and of the Son and of the Holy Spirit, teaching them to observe all that I have commanded you" (Matt. 28:18–20).

AMOS

Amos ministers around 760 BC, during the period of the Divided Kingdom when King Jeroboam II rules Israel. This is a time of prosperity and relative peace and political stability for both kingdoms. Trade routes traversing the area enrich many people,[37] some of whom own winter and summer homes (Amos 3:15), expensive furniture, ivory beds, and luxurious couches (6:4). They drink wine by the bowlful and anoint themselves with the finest oils (6:6).

Instead of accepting their good fortune with humility and thanksgiving to God, the people congratulate themselves, exclaiming, "Have we not by our own strength captured Karnaim for ourselves?" (6:13). Soon the sins of idolatry, corruption, and greed proliferate, and the rich and powerful oppress the poor. The privileged people sell "the righteous for silver, and the needy for a pair of sandals," trampling "the head of the poor into the dust of the earth" and turning "aside the way of the afflicted" (2:6–7). They lose their souls in the process. Amos issues a stern warning first to other nations and then to the Northern Kingdom of Israel, predicting that God will use Assyria to punish the Hebrews for their sinfulness, pride, and complacency. "Woe to those who are at ease in Zion, and to those who feel secure on the mountain of Samaria," he declares (Amos 6:1).

The people dismiss Amos' warnings, wrongly assuming their prosperity signifies God's blessings—a mistake some Christians make to this day. Amos continues to warn of Israel's imminent demise (5:2), invoking images of flight, ruin, death (2:13–16),[38] and "wailing all around" (5:16–17) that stand in blunt contrast to their current condition. Christians should not assume the seeming harshness and finality of this message was rendered moot by the New Covenant, for the New Covenant avails us of nothing if we don't appropriate its promised blessings. Indeed, the certainty of judgment is the very reason we need the Gospel. As Old Testament professor Robert Martin-Achard reminds us, "The Gospel does not in fact make us take his indictment and his verdict, pronounced twenty-eight centuries ago, any less seriously; on the contrary, it should show us its truth and its relevance for today."[39]

Amos' message is not entirely negative, however. He prophesies that the Messiah will come and that the true Israel of God will be restored and revived. "In that day I will raise up the booth of David that is fallen and repair its breaches, and raise up its ruins and rebuild it as in the days of old, that they may possess the remnant of Edom.... I will restore the fortunes of my people Israel.... I will plant them on their land, and they shall never again be uprooted" (Amos 9:11–15).[40]

The Book of Acts records that James quotes these verses in affirming that Amos rightly foretold that God would raise up and deliver His people in accordance with His covenant promises, including the land promise:[41] "And with this the words of the prophets agree, just as it is written, 'After this I will return, and I will rebuild the tent of David that has fallen; I will rebuild its ruins, and I will restore it, that the remnant of mankind may seek the Lord, and all the Gentiles who are called by my name, says the Lord, who makes these things known from of old'" (15:15–17). Clearly, the promise to "plant them on their land" reiterates the land promise first made to Abraham as part of the Abrahamic Covenant and later reaffirmed in the Palestinian Covenant.

The theme of the redemption of God's remnant, as we've seen, is carried forward into the New Testament, where Paul writes, "And Isaiah cries out concerning Israel: 'Though the number of the sons of Israel be as the sand of the sea, only a remnant of them will be saved" (Romans 9:27). He adds, "So too at the present time there is a remnant chosen by grace.... And in this way all Israel will be saved, as it is written, 'The Deliverer will come from Zion, he will banish ungodliness from Jacob'; and this will be my covenant with them when I take away their sins'" (Romans 11:5, 26–27).

In the prophecies, Amos refers not only to the coming blessing of the remnant of God's people, but of all the nations, which are to be beneficiaries of God's covenant promises with Israel—for it is in the Promised Land, and through the Davidic line, that the Messiah will reign and bestow His blessings to all. "Though most of Amos's prophecy is about God's authority to judge an apathetic and ungrateful nation," notes Kenneth Boa, "he ends his book with the promise that God will restore His people and raise up the 'Tabernacle of David' (Amos 9:11). This obviously refers to more than just the kingdom of David and the Temple his son Solomon built. It speaks of the fulfillment of the Davidic dynasty, which finds its focus in the Son of David—Jesus."[42] So despite God's judgment on His people being forecast by Amos, an heir of David—Jesus Christ—would arrive someday to bless them and all the world and give them peace.[43]

Many believe that Amos 8:9—"I will make the sun go down at noon and darken the earth in broad daylight"—is a messianic prophecy about the crucifixion that is fulfilled in Matthew 27:45,[44] and that it also prophesies Christ's second coming (fulfilled in Matt. 24:29; Acts 2:20; Rev. 6:12). Shadows of Christ (Luke 4:18, 6:20, 7:22, 11:41, 14:13, 21, 18:22, 19:8, 21:2–3) can also be seen in Amos' call on his people to be righteous and to care for the poor, themes likewise emphasized by Paul (1 Cor. 11:22) and James (James 1:27, 2:1–10, 5:1–6).

HOSEA

Hosea prophesies during the period of the Divided Kingdom in the latter years of Jeroboam II's reign and, like Amos, he ministers primarily to Israel. This book focuses on one event: Hosea's tragic marriage.[45] When Hosea's wife Gomer is unfaithful, he separates from her but later accepts her back. Many interpret the book as wholly allegorical because they doubt God would instruct Hosea to marry a woman who is or would become a prostitute (Hosea 1:2). But most conservative scholars believe in the book's historicity, arguing that God uses Hosea's painful experience to equip him for this particular ministry to the adulterous nation of Israel. Hosea can better understand Israel's betrayal of God because of what he suffered with Gomer. When God tells Hosea to love Gomer despite her sin, he is made to understand, firsthand, God's deep and abiding love for His people.[46] Though Hosea is anguished by his wife's betrayal, his love for her remains unshakable. Thus, the book's overriding theme is God's inexhaustible love for His people, even when they turn away from Him.[47]

The book vividly reminds us why God insisted His people remove the Canaanites completely from the land, lest they lure the Israelites into idolatry and debauchery. Israel disobeyed that command, and in the time of Hosea the Canaanites and their religion remain in the area. According to H. D. Beeby, this false religion insidiously intermixes with the Israelites' true religion, yielding a "disastrous syncretistic mixture which threatened to distort and possibly engulf the faith once delivered to Moses."[48] The Hebrew faith having become so debased that it bears little resemblance to the true religion,[49] God commissions Hosea to demand repentance.

Chapter 11 sets forth the book's main theme: God has elected Israel and bestowed countless blessings on her, but "the more they were called, the more they went away: they kept sacrificing to the Baals and burning offerings to idols" (11:1–2). Despite God's loving-kindness, Israel turns further astray, leading to God's just punishment. But God's love endures and He would eventually save them—for it is precisely God's unbounded love for His people that leads to His judgment, as He disciplines those He loves (Heb. 12:6; Prov. 3:12).

But it's more than that. God doesn't become angry with Israel's apostasy because He is a jealous God Who demands full devotion for His own sake; it's for their sake—and our sake—that He commands that they—and we—love Him and worship Him, the only true God, because we were created in His image for an intimate relationship with Him, which is impossible if we are "whoring" with false gods. John Peter Lange observes: "Love is indeed angry and most deeply so, but it is and remains nothing but love, for it is pained that it must be angry, and with all its wrath it can only aim to remove that which interrupts and prevents the display of itself to the object beloved, and must ever aim to secure salvation, reconciliation, and restoration, else it would itself stand in the way of realizing its object, and would thus contribute most surely to its own failure."[50]

Duane A. Garrett, professor of Old Testament Interpretation, agrees that the Book of Hosea uses the metaphor of the unfaithful wife to depict the apostasy of Israel, but says that is only half the story. To be sure, Hosea has a wife, but he also has three children. Gomer, he says, represents the "leadership, institutions, and culture of Israel," while the children represent "the ordinary men and women who are trained and nurtured in that culture." The mother not only breaks her wedding vows with Hosea, but also leads her children away from God to serve Baal. Their only chance for salvation is to abandon their Mother Israel and turn back to their Father, Yahweh (God). Yet not only do they fail to repent, but they don't "even understand the need for it, nor recognize that Baal is a lie." God, then, has no choice but to "strip Mother Israel of all she has.... The institutions of Israel must die" and the mother and her children must "again wander in the wilderness."[51] Only then will they distinguish between truth and lies and return to God.

Hosea, like all Old Testament books, has a profound message for Christians. The book, writes Lloyd J. Ogilvie, "is disturbing before it is comforting. We are drawn irresistibly into the book and find ourselves inside the skin of Hosea as he endures the pain of his marriage and realizes the anguish of God. But we will also be forced to identify with Israel and be led into a deeper realization of our own need to return to the Lord."[52] Thus, the book's entire message is ultimately centered on Christ.

In addition, a central theme of Hosea that extends through other Old Testament prophets such as Jeremiah and Ezekiel and into the New Testament (Eph. 5:22–33), is that God's covenantal relationship with mankind, his love relationship with us, is mirrored by the institution of marriage.[53] An even more compelling prefiguring of Jesus is seen not simply in marriage generally, but specifically in Hosea's marriage to Gomer and Gomer's unfaithfulness to him. "The picture is of our God who loves us even as we stray away from Him and into sin," Earl Radmacher remarks. "As Hosea brought back his wife despite her adultery, so God, through His Son Jesus, identified with our plight and lovingly paid the cost of our freedom with His blood."[54] Indeed, we can view Hosea's redemption of Gomer from slavery—after she had betrayed him—as a shadow of Christ's redemptive work on our behalf.

There are a few messianic prophecies in Hosea, such as Israel being restored: "the Children of Israel shall return and seek the Lord their God, and David their king, and they shall come in fear to the Lord and to his goodness in the latter days" (Hosea 3:5, fulfilled in Romans 11:25–27). Additionally, in his Gospel Matthew quotes Hosea 11:1: "This was to fulfill what the Lord had spoken by the prophet, 'Out of Egypt I called my son'" (2:15). Matthew here is casting Israel's exodus as a prefiguring of the calling of Jesus out of Egypt during His childhood. And just as God used Jonah to preach to the Gentiles as a foreshadowing of Christ's blessings of salvation to all nations, God delivers His promise of blessing through Hosea to those who are not originally God's people: "And I will have mercy on No Mercy, and I will say to Not My People, 'You are my people'; and he shall say, 'You are my God'" (Hosea 2:23). Paul quotes this passage in his letter to the Romans (9:25–26).

ISAIAH

Many consider Isaiah to be the greatest of the writing prophets. His book, the first of the Major Prophets, is one of the longest and contains more messianic prophecies than any other prophetic book. "Isaiah ('Jehovah is salvation') is the great messianic prophet and prince of OT prophets," writes Old Testament scholar Merrill Unger. "For splendor of diction, brilliance of imagery, versatility and beauty of style, profundity and breadth of prophetic vision, he is without peer."[55] New Testament writers highly esteem the Book of Isaiah, which was cited repeatedly by Christ Himself[56] and is the second most quoted Old Testament book in the New Testament. (Psalms is first.)[57] As we'll see, it preannounces Christ's incarnation, His earthly ministry and atoning death, His second coming, and His global kingship.

Isaiah ministers from 739 to 680 BC, mostly to Judah but also to Israel. He lives when Israel is declining and Assyria is on the ascent.

While it's difficult to summarize Isaiah's voluminous and multifaceted message, it seems to convey three central points to Judah:

1. You've broken God's covenant through disobedience, idolatry, social injustice, and improper religious practices.
2. You've been called to repent but have refused, so judgment will come upon you as well as upon the nations.
3. There is hope beyond the judgment for a glorious future restoration for God's chosen people and the nations.[58]

This sequence demonstrates that sin must be rectified before a proper relationship with God can be restored. Judgment, then, as emphasized in chapters 1–39, is the purifying force that leads to the forgiveness of sins, which is the focus of chapters 40–66. This final redemption must come from the Messiah.[59] Aiming to comfort those taken captive and those threatened with captivity,[60] Isaiah affirms that there would be reconciliation and redemption through three different people: Isaiah himself, King Cyrus, and the Messiah. Isaiah would pray for his people, Cyrus would be their political deliverer (from the future Babylonian captivity), and the Messiah, of course, would be the centerpiece of redemption, the Suffering Servant who would commit no sin and would deliver Israel and the world from their sins.[61]

Emphasizing present suffering but also future glory, Isaiah applies these themes both to the coming Messiah, Who will suffer in His first coming and reign gloriously in His second, and to the nation of Israel, which experiences great hardship and suffering but will be glorified in the end.[62] James Smith views Isaiah's ultimate message as coinciding with the meaning of his name, "Yahweh (God) is salvation."[63] Some compare Isaiah to Paul's New Testament Book of Romans in that it first makes a strong case against sinning and the depravity of the human heart, but then reveals the path to salvation for Israel. Like Paul, Isaiah, as God's spokesman, preaches repentance and promises forgiveness. It's thus unsurprising that Paul quotes Isaiah seventeen times in Romans.[64]

Most scholars agree that Isaiah falls into two main sections—chapters 1–39 and 40–66. Chapters 36–39 serve as a kind of historical bridge or "hinge" that connects the two sections together. Chapters 1–35 deal with the threat from the Assyrian Empire—the world's leading power at the time—and chapters 36–37 bring this subject to a climax with Assyrian King Sennacherib's unsuccessful attack on Jerusalem. Then chapters 38–39 serve as an introduction to material concerning the Babylonian problem, which follows in chapters 40–66.[65]

Having witnessed Assyria's conquest of the Northern Kingdom of Israel, Isaiah is intimately familiar with God's judgment on His people for sustained disobedience. As such, from his ministry in Jerusalem, he tries to warn Judah—the Southern Kingdom—to avoid the same fate. God does intervene to spare Jerusalem from the Assyrians just in the nick of time, prompting Isaiah's exclamatory message, "God has saved." But Isaiah warns Judean King Hezekiah that his nation will fall to the Babylonians, not the Assyrians. Nevertheless Isaiah also delivers a promise of restoration: God would not abandon His covenant and would restore the people to the land.

Judah's predicted return from captivity foreshadows a far more significant future event prophesied by Isaiah. In the words of Derek Thomas, this occurrence would be "the recovery of the heavens and the earth to the glory that was originally intended, but which had been ruined by the Fall and the introduction of sin into the beauty that God had created—a transformation so spectacular and magnificent that it makes Isaiah's prophecy a thrilling and captivating read. Truly, the Lord delivers!"[66]

The Book of Isaiah, located in the center of the Bible, can be seen as a microcosm of the Bible in that it contains sixty-six chapters (the Bible has sixty-six books), and the first thirty-nine chapters (the same number of books of the Old Testament) focus on judgment and condemnation. The last twenty-seven chapters, like the New Testament's twenty-seven books, deal mostly with redemption.[67] Additionally, the first thirty-nine chapters of Isaiah correspond with the Old Testament in pointing to the coming Messiah. The last twenty-seven chapters parallel the New Testament in dealing with the Messiah and His messianic kingdom.

Finally, the New Testament begins with the history of John the Baptist and ends with the Book of Revelation, with the new heaven and the new earth. Chapter 40 of Isaiah is the beginning of the second part of the book, and it contains the prophetic passage predicting the coming of John the Baptist: "A voice cries: 'In the wilderness prepare the way of the Lord; make straight in the desert a highway for our God'" (Isaiah 40:3). John the Baptist, in fact, says he fulfills this passage (John 1:23), and the other Gospel writers confirm it (Matt. 3:1–4; Mark 1:1–4; Luke 1:76–78). Acting as a perfectly matched bookend, the last chapter of Isaiah—chapter 66—discusses the new heavens and the new earth (66:22).[68]

A BRIEF REPLY TO CRITICAL SCHOLARS

Before moving on to the messianic threads of Isaiah, I want to say a word about critical scholars who question the authorship of Isaiah and other biblical books. Some critics argue that two or even three authors wrote the Book of Isaiah. As evidence, they cite stylistic, theological, and thematic differences between two sections (chapters 1–39 and 40–66) or three sections (chapters 1–39, 40–54, and 55–66) of the book. Conservative scholars, with whom I agree, believe the entire book was written by one author—the prophet Isaiah—because, among other reasons, there is structural unity between the two sections, and the similarities in style between those sections are more significant than the differences. What differences there are likely stem from Isaiah writing in different settings and about different subject matter in the different sections. Critics deny there is structural unity, but the inclusion of the historical hinge suggests that a single author intended to present a cohesive message. Interestingly, the hinge chapters are written mostly in prose while the two major sections are mostly poetry.[69]

Professor Herbert Wolf outlines the verbal and stylistic relationships pointing to unity between Isaiah 1–39 and 40–66. The most impressive example, he says, is the continuity in Isaiah's distinctive title for God, "the Holy One of Israel," which occurs twelve times in the first section and fourteen times in the second. This title appears only four other times in the entire Old Testament. Wolf concludes, "Since the doctrine of God's holiness was so important to Isaiah, he used this title repeatedly, and it became an unmistakable sign of his authorship."[70] Dr. Charles Ryrie further notes there are forty to fifty instances of the same sentence or phrase appearing in both sections. (For example, compare 1:20 with 40:5 and 58:14; 11:6–9 with 65:25; and 35:6 with 41:18.)[71] It's also significant that Isaiah writes from a distinctly Palestinian perspective in both sections, which would likely not be the case if a second author had written the second section in the 500s BC, as some critics suggest.[72] Dr. Ryrie argues that if a second Isaiah lived in Babylon, it's odd that he demonstrates little knowledge of Babylonian geography but great familiarity with Palestine (41:19, 43:14, 44:14).[73]

In fact, no one seriously questioned the single authorship before 1789, when J. C. Doederlein proposed that a "Second Isaiah" or "Deutero-Isaiah" wrote chapters 40–66.[74] Then in 1892, B. Duhm theorized that chapters 40–66 were actually written by two different authors, with a "Third Isaiah" or "Trito-Isaiah" having penned chapters 55–66.[75] Yet when the Great Isaiah Scroll was later found with other Dead Sea Scrolls, it wasn't divided in three—it was one long scroll (about twenty-four feet) of all sixty-six chapters.

Overall, I believe one of the main reasons certain scholars question single authorship is that many of Isaiah's prophecies were so intricately fulfilled. For example, in the latter chapters of the book Isaiah predicts events related to the Babylonian captivity and the people's later return, so the critics conclude the material must have been added by a post-exilic "Deutero-Isaiah." Another example is Isaiah's prophecy, mentioned earlier, in which he names King Cyrus of Persia more than 150 years before his birth. But this is not a unique occurrence in biblical prophecy, as we've already seen—King Josiah was prophesied by name some three hundred years before his time (1 Kings 13:1–3, fulfilled in 2 Kings 23:15–20), and the prophet Micah identified the town of Jesus' birth (Micah 5:2) seven centuries prior to the event.

The critics' skepticism is rooted in their disbelief in supernatural occurrences or divinely revealed prophecy, which has always struck me as incredibly bizarre coming from any Bible scholar, who one would assume believes in the supernatural; otherwise how could he believe in the God of the Bible? Edward Young answers these critics plainly: "If it be asked how Isaiah in the eighth century BC could predict Christ, the answer is that God revealed His words to the prophet and the prophet spoke them forth. Prophecy can really be understood only upon the presuppositions of true Christian theism."[76]

Don't take Young's word for it. The Apostle Peter affirms that the prophecies of Christ and our salvation were written by the prophets under the guidance of the Holy Spirit (1 Peter 10–12).[77] Those who deny Isaiah's authorship due to the stunning accuracy of his predictions must realize they are denying the authenticity, inspiration, and reliability of the Bible. Of course we must doubt that a mere human being acting on his own power and limited knowledge could pen such prophecies unaided by God. But if you believe in the Triune God of the Bible, it's not difficult to believe that these prophets, under the inspiration of the Holy Spirit, accurately predicted the future.

Critics have devised various theories to undermine the authenticity and authorship not just of Isaiah, but of other biblical books as well. These include the entire Pentateuch (the first five books of the Bible), which they claim Moses didn't write, and Daniel, which they argue must have been written after the time that some of Daniel's mind-blowing prophecies were fulfilled. I mention all this only because students of the Bible should be aware of these disagreements and understand that while these critical scholars seem to get the most attention, there are plenty of brilliant scholars with impeccable credentials who defend the Bible's integrity and its divine inspiration and inerrancy.

Finally, I must add that Jesus Christ Himself essentially affirms that the entire Book of Isaiah was written by Isaiah. When Jesus is in Nazareth, He customarily goes to the synagogue on the Sabbath day. Luke records that on one such occasion He stands up to read and "the scroll of the prophet Isaiah was given to him. He unrolled the scroll and found the place where it was written, 'The Spirit of the Lord is upon me, because he has anointed me to proclaim good news to the poor. He has sent me to proclaim liberty to the captives and recovering of sight to the blind, to set at liberty those who are oppressed, to proclaim the year of the Lord's favor'" (Luke 4:17–19). After rolling up the scroll and giving it back to the attendant, Jesus sits down and when all eyes are fixed on him He says, "Today this Scripture has been fulfilled in your hearing" (Luke 4:21).[78] Jesus not only professes the inspiration of all Scripture on several other occasions, as we've said, but through this reading He confirms that Isaiah had written that passage, which was in the very last section of the book (Isaiah 61:1–2).[79] He knows, and wants us to know, that the prophet Isaiah was speaking of Him, our Savior!

CHRIST IN THE BOOK OF ISAIAH

Christ permeates the Book of Isaiah. The book's voluminous messianic prophecies are more explicit than those of any other Old Testament book.[80] These include: repentance for the nations (Isaiah 2:2–4, fulfilled in Luke 24:27); hearts are hardened (Isaiah 6:9–10, fulfilled in Matt. 13:14, 15; John 12:39, 40; Acts 28:25–27); born of a virgin (Isaiah 7:14, fulfilled in Matt. 1:22, 23); a rock of offense (Isaiah 8:14, 15, fulfilled in Romans 9:33; 1 Peter 2:8); a light out of darkness (Isaiah 9:1, 2, fulfilled in Matt. 4:14–16; Luke 2:32); God would literally be born in human flesh and live with us (Isaiah 9:6, 7, fulfilled in Matt. 1:21, 23; Luke 1:32, 33; John 8:58, 10:30, 14:19; 2 Cor. 5:19; Col. 2:9); from the seed of Jesse (Isaiah 11:1, fulfilled in Romans 1:3); full of wisdom and power (Isaiah 11:1–10, fulfilled in Matt. 3:16; John 3:34; Romans 15:12; Heb. 1:9); reigning in mercy (Isaiah 16:45, fulfilled in Luke 1:31–33); peg in a sure place (Isaiah 22:21–25, fulfilled in Rev. 3:7); death swallowed up in victory (Isaiah 25:6–12, fulfilled in 1 Cor. 15:54); a stone in Zion (Isaiah 28:16, fulfilled in Romans 9:33; 1 Peter 2:6); the deaf hear, the blind see (Isaiah 29:18–19, fulfilled in Matt. 5:3, 11:5; John 9:39); King of kings, Lord of lords (Isaiah 32:1–4, fulfilled in Rev. 19:16, 20:6); Son of the Highest (Isaiah 33:22, fulfilled in Luke 1:32; 1 Tim. 1:17, 6:15); a highway to Zion for the redeemed (Isaiah 35:8–9, fulfilled in John 14:1–6); healing for the needy (Isaiah 35:4–10, fulfilled in Matt. 9:30, 11:5, 12:22, 20:34, 21:14; Mark 7:30; John 5:9); make ready the way of the Lord (Isaiah 40:3–5, fulfilled in Matt. 3:1–12; Mark 1:3; Luke 3:4–5; John 1:23); the Shepherd dies for his sheep (Isaiah 40:10–11, fulfilled in John 10:11; Heb. 13:20; 1 Peter 2:24–25); the meek Servant (Isaiah 42:1–16, fulfilled in Matt. 12:17–21; Luke 2:32); a light to the Gentiles (Isaiah 49:6–12, fulfilled in Acts 13:47; 2 Cor. 6:2); scourged and spat upon (Isaiah 50:6, fulfilled in Matt. 26:67, 27:26, 30; Mark

14:65, 15:15, 19; Luke 22:63–65; John 19:1); rejected by his people (Isaiah 52:13–53:12, fulfilled in Matt. 8:17, 27:1–2, 12–14, 38); suffered vicariously (Isaiah 53:4–5, fulfilled in Mark 15:3–4, 27–28; Luke 23:1–25, 32–34); the Suffering Servant, silent when accused, like a lamb led to the slaughter (Isaiah 53:7, fulfilled in John 1:29, 11:49–52); crucified with transgressors (Isaiah 53:12, fulfilled in John 12:37–38; Acts 8:28–35); buried with the rich (Isaiah 53:9, fulfilled in Acts 10:43, 13:38–39; 1 Cor. 15:3; Eph. 1:7; 1 Peter 2:21–25; 1 John 1:7, 9); all thirsty to come and drink (Isaiah 55:1, fulfilled in Rev. 22:17); calling of those not a people (Isaiah 55:4, 5, fulfilled in John 18:37; Romans 9:25–26; Rev. 1:5); deliverer out of Zion (Isaiah 59:16–20, fulfilled in Romans 11:26–27); nations walk in the light (Isaiah 60:1–3, fulfilled in Luke 2:32); anointed to preach liberty (Isaiah 60:1–2, fulfilled in Luke 4:17–19; Acts 10:38); gives liberty to the spiritual captives and brings the redemption of salvation (Isaiah 61:1–4, fulfilled in Luke 4:16–21); called by a new name (Isaiah 62:2, fulfilled in Luke 2:32; Rev. 3:12); the King cometh (Isaiah 62:11, fulfilled in Matt. 21:5); a vesture dipped in blood (Isaiah 63:1–3, fulfilled in Rev. 19:13); afflicted with the afflicted (Isaiah 63:8–9, fulfilled in Matt. 25:34–40); the elect shall inherit (Isaiah 65:9, fulfilled in Romans 11:5, 7; Heb. 7:14; Rev. 5:5); and new heavens and a new earth (Isaiah 65:17–25, fulfilled in 2 Peter 3:13; Rev. 21:1–22).

As others have aptly noted, in some places Isaiah sounds more like a New Testament writer than an Old Testament prophet.[81] The book prefigures Jesus' earthly ministry, His passion, His return to earth as a reigning king, and much more, as you see from the prophecies above. Though scholars sometimes view the main message of this complex book differently, many believe Christ is the dominant theme. For example, we previously noted that James Smith sees the main theme in the meaning of Isaiah's name, "God is salvation," which points to Christ. The ESV Study Bible offers another view that also points to Christ. It emphasizes verses 1:2–2:5, wherein God accuses the people of having received so much privilege from Him that they ought to be grateful children, but instead they are rebellious and "they have despised the Holy One of Israel" (1:2–4).[82] Doesn't this perfectly and succinctly relate the fate of Christ? He does everything for His people, yet He is despised and put to death.

One long passage in the book (52:13–53:12) is so amazingly detailed and is fulfilled so completely that the only way to deny it points specifically to Jesus Christ is to disbelieve that it was written before Christ's incarnation—an absurd proposition on its face because, among other reasons, the Great Isaiah Scroll predates Christ by more than one hundred years. People have been moved to convert to Christianity from reading this passage alone, as I described in *Jesus on Trial*.[83] The five stanzas of this passage, according to Ken Boa and Bruce Wilkinson,[84] also represent the five different sacrificial offerings we discussed in Chapter 11: Isaiah 52:13–15 represents Christ's wholehearted sacrifice (the burnt offering); Isaiah 53:1–3 represents His perfect character (the grain or meal offering); Isaiah 53:4–6 represents that Christ brought atonement that results in peace with God (the peace offering); Isaiah 53:7–9 shows that He paid for the transgression of the people (the sin offering); and Isaiah 53:10–12 depicts Him as dying for the effects of our sins (the trespass offering).[85]

This section, because of its remarkably minute prophecies that were so perfectly fulfilled in history, has incalculable worth as proof that Scripture is divinely inspired and that Jesus Christ is the Son of God. R. W. L. Moberly points to its opening lines: "Behold, my servant shall act wisely; he shall be high and lifted up, and shall be exalted" (52:13). He says that in this passage Isaiah uses the same terms he applied to Yahweh (God) in an earlier passage: "In the year that King Uzziah died I saw the Lord sitting upon a throne, high and lifted up; and the train of his robe filled the temple" (6:1). He uses the same language again in 57:15: "For thus says the One who is high and lifted up, who inhabits eternity, whose name is Holy." Why would Isaiah use such lofty language to describe a mere human being, albeit a noble, sacrificial one? Would that not be a clear case of blasphemy, unthinkable by a holy prophet? Moberly notes, "No matter how much one tries with historical imagination to think of a figure in the world of captive Judah as the primary referent for the prophetic vision (where I am inclined to envisage the prophet himself as taking on Isaiah's role as servant, and suffering on Israel's behalf), the resonance of the language with the New Testament's portrayal of the suffering, death, and resurrection of Jesus is inescapable for the Christian imagination."[86]

Finally, why would Isaiah, writing hundreds of years before Jesus the human being was born, tell us that a man of sorrows, who is despised and rejected by men and punished for *our* iniquities, can bring us peace and heal our wounds? Indeed, why would a Jewish sage writing in 700 BC say that God puts that burden on another mere mortal so that everyone else's sins can be propitiated? It's not hard to believe that men could be falsely accused and punished for the wrongs of others—that has surely occurred throughout human history. And it's not inconceivable that such men, through their sacrifices, have brought a measure of peace to others, for a time. But the language of Isaiah—and, of course, the New Testament—tells us that this Man brings peace to an unlimited number of people and actually heals their wounds.

There's another relevant twist. This particular Man not only volunteers to take on the punishment rightly due others; the very God of the universe "laid on him the iniquity of us all" (Isaiah 53:6). Jesus volunteered to die for us; of that, there can be no question. But He was joined in that decision by the Father, Who was the active agent in carrying out the judgment against Him, directing His full wrath at Him for all of our past, present, and future sins. "It was the will of the Lord to crush him" (Isaiah 53:10). As the great British pastor Charles Spurgeon explains, "The text does not say that our sins were laid on Christ Jesus by accident, but 'the Lord hath laid on him the iniquity of us all.' We sing sometimes, 'I lay my sins on Jesus'; that is a very sweet act of faith, but at the bottom of it there is another laying, namely, that act in which it pleased the Lord to lay our sins on Jesus, for apart from the Lord's doing it our sins could never have been transferred to the Redeemer."[87]

Furthermore, this passage doesn't just say that this Man brings peace alone to other human beings through His sacrifice, but that through His substitutionary death, this Suffering Servant shall "make many to be accounted righteous" (Isaiah 53:11). I'm sorry, but no matter how selflessly a human being may sacrifice himself for the benefit of another, he cannot impute to that other person his own righteousness. And besides, no mere human being has righteousness sufficient to save himself spiritually, much less others. He can spare him pain, he can even save his physical life, but he cannot make him righteous.

Jesus Christ, however, is no mere man; He is God incarnate, and by His stripes we *are* healed. By His death on our behalf, we are made righteous and as spotless as Christ Himself in God's eyes on the Day of Judgment, if we place our faith in Him. This prophecy is utterly nonsensical unless inspired by God Himself, and it points to Christ's substitutionary work on behalf of believers. But the prophecy *was* made under His inspiration and demonstrates that the Bible is, was from the beginning, and forever will be a record of God's gracious plan from before the beginning of the world, to redeem those who by faith appropriate the finished work of Jesus Christ on the cross.

CHAPTER 15

CHRIST IN EVERY BOOK
PROPHETS
MICAH THROUGH
HABAKKUK

The Old Testament prophetic books are filled with descriptions of (what we now know to be) two comings of the One called the Anointed, or the Messiah. His lineage, place of birth, nature of His birth (by a virgin), and the fact that He will die for the sins of His people (Isa. 53) are all predicted, and were fulfilled in His first coming. His second coming as the King over Israel and the world is also clearly foretold. In fact, hundreds of verses describe this coming and its impact on the Jews, the Middle East, and all humanity. Whole chapters describe how the land will be changed, nature harnessed, evil punished, health increased, and that the nations will truly know God and His Messiah. These themes occupy much of the content of the major and minor prophets.

—MAL COUCH[1]

MICAH

Micah is a contemporary of Isaiah but preaches mostly in the country, whereas Isaiah speaks in the city.[2] Micah ministers to the Southern Kingdom of Judah during a period of religious revival, but his visions warn of a time of judgment that will precede the people's deliverance. Like Amos, he preaches against social sins, and he denounces the rich for defrauding the poor of their lands and for evicting widows from their property. Like Isaiah, however, he also infuses his message of impending judgment with one of hope, grounded in the coming Messiah.[3] Micah's main purpose is to call Judah to righteousness by turning back to the Lord, because God would bring judgment on sinners and bestow blessings on those who repent.[4]

Micah's prediction of Jesus' city of birth, by name, seven hundred years before the event, is one of the Bible's most extraordinary messianic prophecies: "But you, O Bethlehem Ephrathah, who are too little to be among the clans of Judah, from you shall come forth for me one who is to be ruler in Israel, whose coming forth is from of old, from ancient days" (Micah 5:2). There is no ambiguity here—He is to be from "ancient days," which would make no sense apart from Jesus' eternal existence, and He is to be ruler in Israel, in fulfillment of the Davidic and other covenants. The clear intent of this passage is confirmed in the Gospel of Matthew, which records that when Herod asks the chief priests and scribes where the Christ will be born, they cite Micah's prediction (2:1–6). In addition, Micah 2:12, 13; 4:1–8; and 5:4, 5 provide a clear description of the righteous reign of Christ throughout the world.[5]

Micah further prophesies that Christ, as the Shepherd, will regather the remnant of Israel to the land and lead His people as their king (Micah 2:12–13).[6] He foretells that Christ's kingdom will be established; the Temple will be restored; people from all over will be attracted to Jerusalem; the Lord will be the judge at Jerusalem; Israel will dwell in peace, security, and strength; peace will be universal; and Jerusalem will have dominion (Micah 4:1–8).[7]

It's fascinating that Micah 5:1 not only prophesies Christ's suffering—"with a rod they strike the judge of Israel on the cheek"—but it reminds us of the original Gospel announcement of Genesis 3:15: "he shall bruise your head, and you shall bruise his heel." The language in both these passages indicates that the blows against Christ will not be enough to keep Him from perfecting His saving work. This is another gripping example of the unity of Scripture and its all-embracing message of redemption.

Finally we see redemptive and messianic themes in the last three verses of the book, which describe God's pardoning of iniquities, His casting "all our sins into the depths of the sea," and His showing "faithfulness to Jacob and steadfast love to Abraham, as [He has] sworn to our fathers from the days of old." This is elegantly efficient language affirming God's covenants with His people, which will all culminate in Jesus Christ, Who will pardon our iniquities and cast all our sins (not just some of them) into the depths (not merely the shallow part) of the sea, never to surface again. In this little Book of Micah, we have resounding reassurance of God's promises of redemption and salvation.

NAHUM

Like Jonah, Nahum preaches to the Assyrians, but more than a century later. Some consider the book as a sort of sequel to Jonah. After repenting before Jonah, the Assyrians have now resumed and escalated their sins. Nahum warns them of God's coming judgment, offering a lesson that transcends time and the particular plight of the Assyrians: the long-suffering of God has limits.[8] Despite God's revealing Himself to them, the Assyrians have turned away and failed to pass on to their children the good news of His gracious redemption. Judgment of the unrepentant, of course, even of those whose fathers had repented, is perfectly consistent with the holiness of God. As the saying goes, "God has no grandchildren," i.e., we are all individually accountable to God.

The book is also a powerful statement of God's sovereignty—no matter how mighty Assyria is in its heyday, it's like a twig in God's hands: "Thus says the Lord, 'Though they are at full strength and many, they will be cut down and pass away.... No more shall your name be perpetuated; from the house of your gods I will cut off the carved image and the metal image. I will make your grave, for you are vile" (Nahum 1:12, 14). Nearly every verse from 1:15 through 3:19 speaks of Nineveh's coming destruction, which finally occurs at the hands of a Babylonian-led army in 612 BC.

There are no messianic prophecies in this book, but Nahum's name is a prefiguring of Christ—it means "comfort," and Christ is the "Comforter."

Nahum speaks eloquently of God's divine attributes in verses 1:2–8, which parallel Christ's prophesied role as the judge of all nations at His return. Verse 1:15 describes the "feet" of the messenger who preaches the good news of the demise of Assyria, which will bring peace. "The New Testament," notes Kendell Easley, "sees Jesus Christ as God's ultimate messenger, preaching God's peace for the world (Acts 10:36)." Paul quotes this verse (and Isaiah 52:7) in his letter to the Romans, praising those who preach the Gospel of Jesus Christ: "How beautiful are the feet of those who preach the good news!" (Romans 10:15). This metaphor illustrates that in order to spread the Gospel, one must go to others, using his feet, and preach the Word. "So faith comes from hearing," Paul declares, "and hearing through the Word of Christ" (Romans 10:17).

Additionally, we see a prefiguring of Christ in Nahum's depiction of God as "the One Who rebukes seas and dries up rivers" (Nahum 1:4), just as "Jesus rebukes the sea and calms the storm (Matt. 8:26)."[9]

With our immense gratitude for the Good News Christ brings, we sometimes forget that His grace and redemptive work are necessary because of God's perfect justice and His abhorrence of sin. This means that along with His provision of salvation He will also judge the nations—both actions are part of God's salvation history. In describing God's firm judgment on Assyria, Nahum reminds us of this. But he also demonstrates that while judgment is necessary and inescapable, God provides for us a Substitute in Jesus Christ. As Julie Woods affirms, "The Suffering Servant took the wrath so that those who repent may escape [future] judgment."[10]

ZEPHANIAH

Though Zephaniah preaches to Judah during the days of King Josiah, who had instituted spiritual reforms in the kingdom, the prophet warns of impending, severe judgment. Right off the bat, in the book's second verse, Zephaniah begins, "'I will utterly sweep away everything from the face of the earth,' declares the Lord. 'I will sweep away man and beast; I will sweep away the birds of the heavens and the fish of the sea, and the rubble with the wicked. I will cut off mankind from the face of the earth,' declares the Lord" (Zeph. 1:2–3). Like many prophets, especially Joel, he warns of the coming "day of the Lord," when sin will be punished, justice will prevail, and the faithful remnant will be saved.[11] The immediate judgment will be Babylonia's conquest of Judah and the people's captivity, but the ultimate judgment for both God's people (3:1–7) and the nations (3:8) will be in the future, after which there will be blessings both for the Gentiles (3:9–10) and the Jews (3:11–20).

When reading Zephaniah from the perspective of the New Testament and the words of Jesus, we see that the prophet is talking about Christ's second coming and His judgment of all nations on the day of the Lord (Romans 2:16; 1 Cor. 1:8; Phil. 1:6, 10, 2:16; 2 Tim. 4:8). In fact, Jesus alludes to two separate passages from this book (Zeph. 1:3 in Matt. 13:41, and Zeph. 1:15 in Matt. 24:29), both relating to Christ's return, His judgment, and His victorious reign. On the first occasion Jesus describes His gathering "out of his kingdom all causes of sin and all law-breakers" (Matt. 13:41). On the second, He refers to Zephaniah's account of a day of darkness, gloom, and devastation (Matt. 24:29–31). Zephaniah doesn't expressly identify the Messiah as the deliverer of this judgment, but as other commentators have noted, who else could gather His people together and secure a complete and final victory over all the nations as Zephaniah prophesies?[12]

Though the judgment will be harsh and complete, the victorious reign will be wonderful. Zephaniah 3:9–20 details the conversion of the nations, when Christ will "change the speech of the peoples to a pure speech, that all of them may call upon the name of the Lord and serve him with one accord" (Zeph. 3:9). Who besides Christ could bring about such a sweeping victory and transform all the people? Who else could fulfill a promise to restore Jerusalem, clear away all its enemies, and reign in the midst of its people (Zeph. 3:14–17)?

Zephaniah depicts Christ as the righteous Lord within Israel (Zeph. 3:5), the judge of all the nations (Zeph. 3:8), and the King of Israel, the Lord who is in their midst (Zeph. 3:15). Jesus, of course, is designated King of the Jews at His crucifixion (Mark 15:26). According to Old Testament Professor Mark Mangano, "The 'day of the Lord' of Zephaniah with its multifaceted focus in the New Testament centers on the coming of Jesus Christ to inaugurate the kingdom of God."[13] As Anglican priest Robert Hawker aptly puts it, "This chapter opens in sharp reproofs to Jerusalem, but ends in blessed promises. It contains much of Gospel mercies, and sweetly points to the Lord Jesus Christ."[14]

JEREMIAH

Jeremiah's prophetic ministry spans some fifty years, from King Josiah's reign until after Nebuchadnezzar's conquest of Jerusalem and destruction of the Temple. He is called the "weeping prophet" for good reason—constantly warning of the coming judgment against Judah's apostasy, he provokes fierce opposition from the spiritually decadent people. Yet he isn't an incorrigible pessimist, for he also delivers God's message of ultimate restoration. These themes appear in the book's opening declaration, in which the prophet relates what God told him: "See, I have set you this day over nations and over kingdoms, to pluck up and to break down, to destroy and to over-throw, to build and to plant" (Jer. 1:10). Essentially, God has instructed him to preach against sin and to warn of the coming destruction of Jerusalem. But the book's predominant message is one of renewal amid the background of deep and immeasurable suffering, causing some commentators to refer to Jeremiah as the "prophet of hope."[15] These themes of sin, destruction, hope, and renewal appear throughout the book (Jer. 18:7–11, 31:28, and 45:4).[16]

Jeremiah's long ministry continues into the last days of Judah in the exile period, when he warns King Jehoiakim to submit to the Babylonian king, since God is directing these events in judgment of Israel. He warns his people remaining in Jerusalem not to be fooled by the false prophets who are filling them "with vain hopes" and who speak "visions of their own minds, not from the mouth of the Lord.... They say continu-ally ... 'No disaster shall come upon you'" (Jer. 23:16–17). He also warns the exiles not to believe false prophets who predict they will soon return to their land (Jer. 29:8–9). Jeremiah insists God will bring them back only after seventy years in Babylonian captivity (Jer. 29:10).

Due to his unwelcome warnings, Jeremiah is persecuted, abandoned by his people, and imprisoned: "Now Pashhur the priest, the son of

Immer, who was chief officer in the house of the Lord, heard Jeremiah prophesying these things. Then Pashhur beat Jeremiah the prophet, and put him in the stocks that were in the upper Benjamin Gate of the house of the Lord" (Jer. 20:1–2). At the end of his ministry, Jeremiah witnesses the wholesale destruction of Judah and the obliteration of the Temple. The Book of Lamentations, commonly believed to have been written by Jeremiah, expresses the author's agony over these events.

Many Old Testament scholars emphasize the extent to which Jeremiah lives his message—he wholly identifies with his mission as the anguish of his warnings plays out in his own life, even before the predicted calamities come to pass. J. Sidlow Baxter describes this beautifully: "It is this man who, of all the prophets, gives us the fullest revelation of his own character. This is because the man and his message are in such passionate oneness under such tragic circumstances. Jeremiah's nature was such that he simply could not be merely a *transmitter*, able to detach his own feelings from that which he was commissioned to declare. With an intensity of love and sympathy, he himself lived and felt and suffered in his message. His own heartstrings vibrated to every major and every minor chord. The man and his message were one."[17]

Old Testament professor F. B. Huey Jr. observes that Jeremiah would probably be considered an abysmal failure by modern standards, as he preaches for forty years without even convincing some people he is a prophet of God, much less persuading them to heed his warnings. Huey insists, however, that we should not judge him by human standards but by God's, Who values obedience. Jeremiah obeys God's call to present a clear message to the people, and he's not responsible for their failure to respond. He is remembered now and forever because of his selfless servanthood, while all the powerful kings of his time have fallen into disrepute.[18]

Jeremiah's message couldn't have been more relevant at a time when the people have forgotten God, abandoned Him, and replaced Him with pagan idols. Speaking against the grain of the culture, Jeremiah is ridiculed and persecuted. But he persists in faithful obedience to God, knowing that the people will find hope and life if they return to Him.

Jeremiah's timeless message is just as relevant for us today, as our dominant culture upholds false gods. We Christians find our values rejected and scorned in society, but that doesn't relieve us of the responsibility to promote those values to unreceptive ears and to preach the Gospel at home and to the ends of the earth. To the contrary, writes E. Martens, we must "confront evils in a world where evil is normalized;...protest against preachers of an 'easy grace' which promises endless benefits without responsibility; (and)...present a God who demands righteous living and sends his wrath against all evil." F. B. Huey adds, "Just as 'Jeremiah...challenged their falsely based security, their doublethink, their manipulative ways, their god-substitutes,' we too must challenge people today in all their sin by proclaiming God's Word, which brings life to those who repent."[19] Rather than look at Jeremiah as some freakish counter-cultural eccentric of a bygone era, Huey argues, we should regard him as "a model whom we should imitate in proclaiming God's word."[20]

Foreshadowings of Christ appear throughout the Book of Jeremiah in numerous messianic prophecies: Christ will be the Lord of our righteousness (23:5–6, 33:16, fulfilled in Romans 3:22; 1 Cor. 1:30; 2 Cor. 5:21; Phil. 3:9); He will be born a King (30:9, fulfilled in Luke 1:69; John 18:37; Acts 13:23; Rev. 1:5); the infants will be killed (31:15, fulfilled in Matt. 2:17–18); and there is the announcement of the New Covenant (31:31–34, fulfilled in Matt. 26:27–29; Mark 14:22–24; Luke 22:15–20; 1 Cor. 11:25; Heb. 8:8–12, 10:15–17, 12:24, 13–20).

Furthermore, Christ is seen in chapter 23 as the righteous Branch Whom God will raise up from the line of David, Who shall reign as king, and Who will execute justice and righteousness in the land. Jeremiah foretells of the time when God will no longer be known only for bringing His people out of Egypt, but for regathering Israel back to the Promised Land. Christ's people will finally recognize Him as their Messiah as He provides salvation for Judah (Jer. 23:6; Romans 11:26). And as we've seen, Jeremiah announces God's coming New Covenant with the house of Israel, promising He would fulfill His previous covenants with Abraham, Moses, David, and the people of Israel, and put His Law within them and write it on their hearts. He "will forgive their iniquity, and...remember their sin no more" (Jer. 31:34).

Jeremiah portrays Christ as the Fountain of Living Waters (Jer. 2:13); the Great Physician (Jer. 8:22); the Good Shepherd (Jer. 31:10, 23:4);

David the King (Jer. 30:9); our Redeemer (Jer. 50:34); a righteous Branch (Jer. 23:5), and the Lord our Righteousness (Jer. 23:6).[21] Moreover, through his personal sufferings, Jeremiah prefigures the sufferings of Jesus. "Jesus Christ suffered in precisely the ways Jeremiah suffered," Philip Ryken writes. "He suffered physically…domestically…(and) socially."[22] Like Christ and Nehemiah, Jeremiah weeps over Jerusalem (Jer. 9:1; Neh. 1:4; Luke 19:41), and like Christ, he predicts the destruction of the Temple (Jer. 7:11–15; Matt. 24:1, 2).[23]

Moreover, Jeremiah points to the Gospel in his admonition that we must not trust in ourselves or become boastful, but boast only about our knowledge of the Lord: "Thus says the Lord: 'Let not the wise man boast in his wisdom, let not the mighty man boast in his might, let not the rich man boast in his riches, but let him who boasts boast in this, that he understands and knows me, that I am the Lord who practices steadfast love, justice and righteousness in the earth. For in these things I delight, declares the Lord'" (Jer. 9:23–24). This reminds us that man cannot save himself, that he is dependent on God, and that all blessings and gifts come from God. This calls to mind Paul's statement to the Ephesians: "For by grace you have been saved through faith. And this is not your own doing; it is the gift of God, not a result of works, so that no one may boast" (Eph. 2:8–9). Paul paraphrases Jeremiah's admonition twice: "Let him who boasts, boast in the Lord" (1 Cor. 1:31; 2 Cor. 10:17). This Jeremiah passage, read in conjunction with verse 17:7—"Blessed is the man who trusts in the Lord, whose trust is the Lord"—presents a crystal clear picture of the Gospel message.

Jeremiah points to man's helplessness apart from Christ in another respect, writes Philip Ryken. Jeremiah asks the people, "How long will it be before you are made clean?" (Jer. 13:27). "The answer," writes Ryken, "is that you will remain unclean for as long as you insist on cleaning yourself. As long as you try to reform your own life you will remain unclean. There is nothing a sinner can do to change his or her sinful nature. The point of Jeremiah's famous proverb is that you are a dyed-in-the-wool sinner: 'Can the Ethiopian change his skin or the leopard its spots?'" (Jer. 13:23).[24]

Finally, it's instructive that the people surrounding Jesus speak of an association between Him and Jeremiah. For example, Jesus asks His disciples, "'Who do people say that the Son of Man is?' And they said, 'Some say John the Baptist, others say Elijah, and others say Jeremiah or one of the prophets'" (Matt. 16:13–14). This is unsurprising because, as we've noted, Jeremiah weeps over Jerusalem, suffers, and is rejected due to his unequivocal denunciation of evil, and feels the people's suffering to the core of his spirit. Furthermore, he is driven from his native Ananoth much as Christ is driven from Nazareth (Jer. 12:6),[25] and he even compares himself to a lamb led to the slaughter (Jer. 11:19).[26]

LAMENTATIONS

Jewish tradition holds that Jeremiah also wrote Lamentations,[27] which serves as a sequel to the Book of Jeremiah.[28] Whereas the Book of Jeremiah prophesies the fall of Jerusalem to the Babylonians, Lamentations chronicles Jeremiah's lament after the city is conquered.[29] Tremper Longman suggests that Jeremiah's deep anguish follows his "discovery that the power behind the carnage that had just befallen Jerusalem was ultimately not the Babylonian war machine, but God Himself."[30] While other Old Testament books, such as Job and Psalms, give us a glimpse into the personal suffering of the writer, in Lamentations Jeremiah laments the conditions of the entire nation.[31] In that sense, it seems that Jeremiah exhibits a Christ-like quality of selfless concern for others.

As I discussed in *Jesus on Trial*, the structure of Lamentations corresponds to its message. It's an alphabetic acrostic poem in which each successive line or stanza begins with sequential letters of the Hebrew alphabet.[32] Though this doesn't come through in the English translations, the original composition is a thing of beauty. The book contains five chapters, each forming a distinct poem with twenty-two stanzas of three lines each. The structure becomes more complex from chapter to chapter until the third chapter, which is the apex of the book's complexity, where each line of every stanza, not just the first line, begins with the same letter of the Hebrew alphabet. In the book's last two chapters the complexity of the structure diminishes. Correspondingly, the subject matter of the book builds in intensity from the beginning and hits its climax in the middle of the third chapter, after which the intensity begins to diminish. Just when Jeremiah is filled to his limit with anguish and despair in verse 3:18—"My endurance has perished; so has my hope from the Lord"—He remembers that God is a God of unfailing faithfulness. He then exclaims, "The steadfast love of the Lord never ceases" (3:22), and "The Lord is my portion...therefore I will hope in him" (3:23–24).

The book illustrates one of my main points—that throughout Old Testament history, God calls His people to remember what He has done for them, and that the Bible's account of these acts of remembrance exemplify the unity of Scripture. In this case, Jeremiah recalls God's loving-kindness without any recorded prompting from God, and at the very point of his remembrance, he turns on a dime from the deepest despair to the grandest hope. Jeremiah's ultimate hope is grounded in his faith in God's salvation (3:26).

The book's main theme is God's judgment of the sins of the people of Judah—though a corollary theme is that the people are still justified in hoping for God's compassion. Underlying these themes is the constant refrain that God and His judgment are sovereign. His perfect holiness demands that Judah's sin finally be punished in their prophesied destruction. Just as God used the evil Assyrian Empire to bring judgment against the Northern Kingdom of Israel, He uses Babylon to punish the Southern Kingdom of Judah.[33]

Note that God does not relent in His promised punishment. But Jeremiah is uplifted by his remembrance of God's faithfulness and his conviction that God will not forsake His people in the end. Imagine the depth of faith required for you to accept the destruction of your beloved city and your nation, and having enough honesty of mind, emotion, and spirit to recognize that your people deserve this fate. God's fairness cannot be questioned here, especially since the Judeans already knew that the Northern Kingdom's sinfulness had brought about its demise. Jeremiah, a man of unique faith, understands that despite the calamitous judgment on Judah, God's promises are still in full force and effect. He would deliver His people in the future. As William LaSor notes, Jeremiah's faith was doubtlessly inspirational to his people. "The poet's strong faith must have heartened generations of fellow Jews," says LaSor. "To find hope in the midst of disaster and lead others to do the same takes the deepest knowledge of God."[34]

Not only is Jeremiah a type of Christ as a man of sorrows (Lam. 1:12, 3:19), and one who is despised and mocked by his enemies (Lam. 2:15, 16, 3:14, 30),[35] but his message of hope points to Christ and all His redemptive work—for Christ will redeem those who place their saving faith in Him and will one day wipe away all tears (Rev. 7:17, 21:4). In fact, many commentators cite verse 1:12 as prefiguring Christ's suffering on the cross: "Is it nothing to you, all who pass by? Look and see if there is any sorrow like my sorrow, which was brought upon me, which the Lord inflicted on the day of his fierce anger." And in whom else but Jesus could Jeremiah have been placing his hope when he exclaimed, "The Lord is my portion...therefore I will hope in him" (Lam. 3:24).

HABAKKUK

Like Job, Habakkuk writes a partially philosophical book that directly questions some of God's actions. He is particularly troubled by the notion that God would use a wicked empire like Babylon to accomplish His divine will to punish Judah. He expresses a dilemma that many still contemplate today: Why do evil people seem to prosper and go unpunished while the righteous suffer at their hands? Why does God sometimes seem to ignore our pleas for justice? He writes, "How long shall I cry for help, and you will not hear? ...Why do you make me see iniquity, and why do you idly look at wrong? Destruction and violence are before me; strife and contention arise. So the law is paralyzed, and justice never goes forth. For the wicked surround the righteous; so justice goes forth perverted" (Hab. 1:2–4).

God replies that He is raising up the "dreaded and fearsome" Babylonians—"guilty men, whose might is their god!" (1:6, 7, 11)—for a particular purpose. Habakkuk persists in asking why God would use the evil Babylonians to do His work: "O Lord, you have ordained them as a judgment, and you, O Rock, have established them for reproof. You who are of purer eyes than to see evil and cannot look at wrong, why do you idly look at traitors and remain silent when the wicked swallows up the man more righteous than he?" (1:12–13).

Just as with Job, God doesn't provide a direct answer, though one is implicit in His response. He informs Habakkuk that people must trust Him to administer judgment and justice in their appointed times. He will eventually punish the wicked nations, and in the meantime the righteous must have faith in Him and be patient, knowing He is a God of perfect justice: "For still the vision awaits its appointed time.... If it seems slow, wait for it; it will surely come.... but the righteous shall live by his faith.... Woe to him who gets evil gain for his house...who builds a town with blood and founds a city on iniquity! ...For the earth will be filled with the knowledge of the glory of the Lord as the waters cover the sea.... The cup in the Lord's right hand will come around to you, and utter shame will come upon your glory!" (2:3, 4, 9, 12, 14).

Habakkuk's response shows that he fully understands God's message, and that he indeed fears God and thoroughly trusts He will deliver justice: "I hear, and my body trembles; my lips quiver at the sound;...my legs tremble beneath me. Yet I will quietly wait for the day of trouble to come upon people who invade us" (3:16). Habakkuk closes by affirming his renewed faith in God. Even if he sees no immediate evidence of God's justice and present circumstances seem terrible, even if "the free tree should not blossom, nor fruit be on the vines, the produce of the olive fail and the fields yield no food, the flock be cut off from the fold and there be no herd in the stalls" (3:17), he will nevertheless "rejoice in the Lord; I will take joy in the God of my salvation" (3:18).

It's important to distinguish between God not answering our questions and His giving answers we don't expect or don't want to hear. In this case, He does respond to Habakkuk's question. His response reveals, like His response to Job, that in our finitude we can't possibly understand all of His ways. Habakkuk, in conversing with God, comes to understand that in the end it's not important for us to comprehend every one of God's actions. What's paramount is that we come to know Him, which seems to be precisely what happens with Habakkuk in this exchange, just as it did with Job.

God's answer to Habakkuk conveys the essence of the book's Christ-centered message. He is acknowledging that things sometimes appear unjust to us, but that He is all powerful and all knowing and perfectly just, and that in His time He will make all things right. To get ourselves aligned with Him, we must trust Him to be fair. But our faith cannot be confined to His administration of justice; we must have faith in Him because that is the path to eternal life, which is perhaps *the* central theme of the Bible. Faith is not just a salve to keep our patience in check as we await the future judgment; it is the key to life in Him—a revelation that will become clearer and more specific in the New Testament, which teaches faith in Jesus Christ. "That [the righteous shall live by faith] is the central revelation of the prophecy," G. Campbell Morgan avers. "It is a contrast between the 'puffed up' and the 'just.' The former is not upright, and therefore is condemned; the latter acts on faith, and therefore lives." Morgan continues, "The first is self-centered, and therefore doomed; the second is God-centered, and therefore permanent."[36]

Affirming the centrality of this verse—"that the righteous shall live by his faith" (Hab. 2:4)—Scottish theologian Alexander Whyte writes,

> What Habakkuk wrote six hundred years before Christ on the gates, and walls, and pillars of Jerusalem—that very same word of God the Holy Spirit of God is writing on the tables that are in the believing hearts of all God's people still: "Being justified by faith we have peace with God": "By grace ye are saved through faith": "The just shall live by his faith": He shall live—not so much by the fulfillment of all God's promises; nor by God's full answers to his prayers and expectations; nor by the full deliverance of his soul from his bitter enemies; nor by the final expulsion of the Chaldeans: but he shall live, amid all these troubles, and till they come to an end forever—he shall live by his firm faith in God, and in the future which is all in God's hand. And thus it is that, whatever our oppression and persecution may be, whatever our prayer and wherever and whatever our waiting tower, still this old and ever new vision and answer comes: Faith: Faith: and Faith only. Rest and trust in God.[37]

Permit me one more quote from an old master, Scottish theologian Thomas Boston, who writes, "Nothing but an infinite good can satisfy the desires of the human soul, and here it is. Here in Christ, like Habakkuk, you may find a source of joy and strength, when all other comforts fail. As nothing but the mother's breast can satisfy the hungry infant, so nothing but Christ can satisfy your souls aright: 'Whosoever drinketh of the water (saith Jesus) that I shall give him, shall never thirst; but the water that I shall give him shall be in him a well of living water, springing up into everlasting life'" (John 4:14).[38]

As for messianic prophecies in Habakkuk, scholars cite 2:14 as one example: "For the earth will be filled with the knowledge of the glory of the Lord as the waters cover the sea." This partially mirrors the language of Isaiah 11:9—"For the earth shall be full of the knowledge of the Lord as the waters cover the sea"—and of Psalms 72:19—"Blessed be his glorious name forever; may the whole earth be filled with his glory!" Similar language is found in Numbers 14:21 and Isaiah 6:3. Some of these verses celebrate the day the earth will be filled with the knowledge of the Lord, while other verses, like that of Habakkuk, anticipate the day it will be filled with the knowledge of His glory. These are obviously interrelated—if people have knowledge of God, inevitably they will have knowledge of His glory because to truly know Him is to know His glory. This prophecy (and promise) means that when Christ rules in His kingdom upon His return, there will be worldwide knowledge of the Lord.[39]

Jeremiah describes the expansiveness of this knowledge when he unveils the New Covenant: "'And I will be their God, and they shall be my people. And no longer shall each one teach his neighbor and each his brother, saying, "Know the Lord," for they shall all know me, from the least of them to the greatest, declares the Lord. For I will forgive their iniquity, and I will remember their sin no more'" (Jer. 31:33–34). So widespread, so universal will be the knowledge of God that people will not need to be told about Him. That work will apparently already be complete, along with the forgiveness of the sins of all who "know" (place their faith in) Him.

Mark Dever observes that Habakkuk expresses his great contentment in God at the end of chapter 3, after he has been praying and meditating on Him.[40] The lesson is that the more we abide in God, the more content we will be. Like Job, what Habakkuk really wants, whether he fully realizes it or not, is not so much God's answers to troubling questions but God Himself. As St. Augustine writes in his *Confessions*, "Thou awakes us to delight in Thy praise; for Thou madest us for Thyself, and our heart is restless, until it repose in Thee."[41] R. C. Sproul reinforces this message: "With Habakkuk we are called to live life in the presence of God, under his authority, and to his glory."[42] For the Christian, to know Christ is to know God, because Christ, as we've noted, "is the radiance of the glory of God and the exact imprint of his nature" (Heb. 1:3). He "is the image of God" (2 Cor. 4:4).

Another Christ-pointing verse in Habakkuk is 2:4, quoted above: "The righteous shall live by his faith." New Testament writers cite this verse several times (Romans 1:17; Gal. 3:11; Heb. 10:38) to reaffirm the doctrine of justification by faith.[43] We not only attain our eternal life through faith, but faith sustains our Christian walk. It is part of our sanctification process, our path to holiness.

Habakkuk, then, gives us a foretaste of the New Testament message that life in God's presence will be eternal, but it's also available to the faithful in this life. Elizabeth Achtemeier notes that this life-sustaining knowledge of God, given to Habakkuk by God Himself, provides him joy and certainty amid his turbulent and evil circumstances. Our faith in the afterlife, our trust in God, gives us contentment unavailable otherwise. As Paul writes, "Rejoice in the Lord always; again I will say, rejoice.... The Lord is at hand, do not be anxious about anything.... I have learned in whatever situation I am to be content" (Philip. 4:4, 6, 11). Achtemeier observes, "By such faithfulness, God tells Habakkuk, the prophet can live an abundant life in his time and place. That is the message Habakkuk passes on to his contemporaries, to us, and to all the faithful who find that they must live 'in the meantime,' between the revealing of God's purposes for his world and the final realization of those purposes. Countless faithful in Israel and in the church for over twenty-five hundred years have found God true to his word."[44]

Habakkuk emphasizes the importance of placing our faith in God. In our final chapter, we will turn to the prophet Daniel, who demonstrates the awesome power of such faith against overwhelming odds. We will also examine how the remaining prophetic books are centered in the divine object of that faith: Jesus Christ.

CHAPTER 16

CHRIST IN EVERY BOOK
PROPHETS
DANIEL THROUGH
MALACHI

*In one of his conversations with a mixed group of neighbors
and priests, William Tyndale (1494–1536) said: "Now the
Scriptures are a clue which we must follow, without turning aside, until we arrive at Christ; for Christ is the end."
"And I tell you," shouted out a priest, "that the Scriptures
are a Daedalian labyrinth, rather than Ariadne's clue—a
conjuring book wherein everybody finds what he wants."
"Alas!" replied Tyndale; "you read them without Jesus
Christ; that's why they are an obscure book to you."*

—GARY H. EVERETT[1]

DANIEL

D aniel is among the first group of exiles taken to Babylon
around 605 BC. Despite being selected to serve Babylonian
King Nebuchadnezzar, he inspires his fellow exiles by remaining unflinchingly loyal to God. Critical scholars argue that the book was
authored in the second century BC by some unknown person or persons
who wrote "prophecies after the fact" and put them in the mouth of

Daniel circa 600 BC.[2] Without this sort of makeshift explanation, it's hard for these critics to deny that Daniel's amazingly accurate prophecies were inspired by God. Conservative scholars make a stronger case, in accordance with both Jewish and Christian tradition, that the book was written during Daniel's captivity in Babylon.

A storehouse of phenomenal prophecy, the Book of Daniel lays the groundwork upon which many other prophecies are built. For example, in the Book of Revelation, John writes as if the reader is familiar with Daniel's predictions, which serve as a backdrop for some of John's own prophecies. "Daniel is to the Old Testament what the Book of Revelation is to the New Testament," writes Warren Wiersbe, "in fact, we cannot fully understand one without the other. Prophetically, Daniel deals with the "times of the Gentiles (see Luke 21:24), that period of time that began in 606 B.C. with the captivity of Jerusalem and will end when Christ returns to earth to judge the Gentile nations and establish His kingdom."[3]

The book serves as an object lesson in faith under trial and adversity. Daniel unfailingly trusts God to deliver him from dangerous predicaments. In turn, God richly rewards Daniel and his friends for their faithfulness by protecting them against hostile forces determined to kill them because of their refusal to bow to the worldly powers. Daniel's faith serves as a timeless example that Christians should emulate. "Daniel's righteousness," argues Larry Richards, "stood to the exiles as a beacon, pointing them toward the way to live for God no matter where they might be."[4] Daniel remains a uniquely inspiring example for Christians today.

The book's main theme is that God alone is sovereign in history and over human affairs.[5] Daniel's ancillary themes, according to John Walvoord, are that God is "loving, omnipotent, omniscient, righteous, and merciful. He is the God of Israel, but He is also the God of the Gentiles."[6] God is the One who guides the powers and principalities of the material world: "He changes times and seasons; he removes kings and sets up kings; he gives wisdom to the wise and knowledge to those who have understanding" (Daniel 2:21).

God is eternal. By contrast, all the powerful men in history—men who built cities, or transformed societies, or created great armies that toppled other nations like toothpicks—were here and gone in the blink of an eye. In the end, as hymnist Isaac Watts reminds us, "Time, like an ever-rolling stream, bears all its sons away."[7] This message is applicable to Christians, especially those who are prosperous or influential—success is wonderful, as long as we remember Who is in control. "It is God who lifts up and who puts down," Mark Dever insists. "Do not forget that. If you are a follower of Christ in a position of power and authority, do not let yourself be fooled by that power and authority. It did not come from you, you will not keep it, and you will be held accountable for how you use it."[8]

The Jewish exiles in Babylon are reassured by the message that God is in control, for they naturally wonder whether God's everlasting promises to Israel concerning the land and the Davidic kingdom are still in force. After all, they had been whisked from their land with seemingly no possibility of return. Daniel's remarkable prophecies resoundingly answer these questions: the Jews would occupy the land again, though not completely, until the time preceding Christ's second coming.

The exiles must have felt conflicted. On the one hand, having been vanquished, taken captive, and seen their Temple destroyed, they could conclude that their God had been defeated. This could have been enough, says C. Hassell Bullock, "to turn orthodoxy to agnosticism, piety to skepticism, and faith to irresolution."[9] On the other hand, wasn't history playing out exactly as God, through His prophets, said it would? Babylonia had utterly destroyed Judah and exiled its people, then the Babylonians in turn had been defeated by the Medo-Persians as if they were pawns on a divine chessboard.

God's sovereignty is further affirmed by His numerous interventions in history, as recorded by Daniel. These include His supernatural interpretation of dreams, His protection of Daniel's friends from the fiery furnace, His deliverance of Daniel from the lions' den, and Daniel's prophetic visions. To top it off, there is the miraculous appearance of handwriting on the wall of King Belshazzar's palace. This occurs during a feast in which the king and his lords, wives, and concubines are blasphemously drinking wine from the vessels of gold and silver that his father, Nebuchadnezzar, had looted from God's Temple. This haunting event presages the death of Belshazzar and the fall of his empire at the hands of Darius the Mede, which transpires that very night (Daniel 5:1–30).[10]

Through Daniel, God furnishes overwhelming evidence of His sovereign hand of protection over His exiled people to assure them He had not abandoned them, was still protecting them, was administering justice on the world's powers, and still had a plan for them. "Daniel was written to encourage the exiled Jews by revealing God's program for them, both during and after the time of Gentile power in the world," observes John MacArthur. "Prominent above every other theme in the book is God's sovereign control over the affairs of all rulers and nations, and their final replacement with the True King."[11]

Interestingly, except for chapter 1, which is a historical introduction, the first half of the Book of Daniel (chapters 2–7) is written in Aramaic and the second half (chapters 8–12) in Hebrew. It's unlikely this was accidental, as the first section is mostly a prophetic history of the Gentile nations, and the last section relates a prophetic history of the Jews.[12] J. Sidlow Baxter persuasively argues that the use of the two languages points to the earlier date for the book's authorship. He explains that before Daniel's time Jews did not understand Aramaic (see 2 Kings 18:26), and after his time they had difficulty understanding Hebrew (see Neh. 8:8). In Daniel's time, however, the people understood both languages. So why, asks Baxter, would an imposter of Daniel writing four hundred years after the fact, who was on a mission to console his people, write half the book in a language unintelligible to them? Alternatively, if he wanted it preserved in the Hebrew language for future reference only, why would he write half of it in the common tongue of his own day?[13]

There are numerous messianic prophecies in Daniel. Christ is the Stone "cut out by no human hand" that will crush the kingdoms of this world upon His return (Daniel 2:34, 35, 44, fulfilled in Luke 1:33; 1 Cor. 15:24; 2 Peter 1:11; Rev. 11:15). He is the Son of Man who "was given dominion and glory and a kingdom, that all peoples, nations, and languages should serve him; his dominion is an everlasting dominion, which shall not pass away, and his kingdom one that shall not be destroyed" (Daniel 7:13, 14, fulfilled in Matt 26:27–29; Mark 14:22–24; Luke 22:15–20; 1 Cor. 11:25; Heb. 8:8–12, 10:15–17, 12:24, 13:20).

Furthermore, His kingdom "shall be given to the people of the saints of the Most High" (Daniel 7:27, fulfilled in Luke 1:33; 1 Cor. 15:24; Rev. 11:15, 20:4, 22:5).

In one of the most remarkable of all messianic prophecies—of all *biblical* prophecies, in fact—Daniel predicts the precise date of Christ's Triumphal Entry into Jerusalem. That prophecy is even more extraordinary than it seems. The prediction, which I believe is clearest in the NIV Bible, reads as follows:

> "Seventy 'sevens' are decreed for your people and your holy city to finish transgression, to put an end to sin, to atone for wickedness, to bring in everlasting righteousness, to seal up vision and prophecy and to anoint the Most Holy Place.
>
> "Know and understand this: From the time the word goes out to restore and rebuild Jerusalem until the Anointed One, the ruler, comes, there will be seven 'sevens,' and sixty-two 'sevens.' It will be rebuilt with streets and a trench, but in times of trouble. After the sixty-two 'sevens,' the Anointed One will be put to death and will have nothing. The people of the ruler who will come will destroy the city and the sanctuary. The end will come like a flood: War will continue until the end, and desolations have been decreed. He will confirm a covenant with many for one 'seven.' In the middle of the 'seven' he will put an end to sacrifice and offering. And at the temple he will set up an abomination that causes desolation, until the end that is decreed is poured out on him" (Daniel 9:24–27).

It was customary (and seen elsewhere in Scripture, e.g., Gen. 29:26–27)[14] to speak of seven years as a week, so "seventy weeks" in this prophecy means seventy periods of seven years, or a total of 490 years. Conservative scholars, therefore, interpret this prophecy to describe God's plans for and dealings with the nation of Israel and its land over a period of 490 years (though not wholly continuous years). After 490 years He will "bring in everlasting righteousness," meaning the establishment of the messianic kingdom at the second coming of Christ, as the ultimate fulfillment of the Davidic Covenant and other covenants by Jesus Christ.

This 490-year period breaks down into three chronological periods:

1. Seven weeks (forty-nine years).
2. Sixty-two weeks (434 years).
3. A final week (seven years).

As described in verse 9:25, the 490-year period begins "from the time the word goes out to restore and build Jerusalem." Though Persian King Cyrus issued his decree in 538 BC permitting the Israelites to return from exile and rebuild their Temple, this is not the triggering event described in this prophecy. That event is the later decree issued by King Artaxerxes (Neh. 2) that authorized the Israelites to reconstruct Jerusalem's city walls. Nehemiah 2:1–8 pinpoints the date of this decree as "in the month of Nisan, in the twentieth year of King Artaxerxes," which we know to be March 5, 444 BC.[15] The 490-year period begins on this date.

So the first of the three periods—lasting seven "weeks," or forty-nine years—begins in 444 BC, and many scholars believe this was how long it took the people to rebuild the city walls, the Temple, the streets, and a trench, and to fully remove the city's debris.[16] The second period of sixty-two "weeks" (434 years), according to the text of the prophecy, runs consecutively with the first period for a total of 483 years. Thus, from Artaxerxes' decree on March 5, 444 BC, "until the Anointed One, the ruler, comes, there will be seven 'sevens,' and sixty-two 'sevens'" (Daniel 9:25). Some have posited that this 483-year period, calculated according to the Jewish calendar (consisting of 360-day years), would end on March 30, 33 AD, or Nisan 10 in AD 33—believed to be the precise date of Jesus' Triumphal Entry into Jerusalem.[17]

It's astonishing that a prediction made hundreds of years before Jesus was born could be so accurate. Rejecting the possibility of supernatural intervention, however, some critical scholars deny that the Book of Daniel was actually written by Daniel, arguing that some of his remarkable prophecies must have been written after the fact. But the discovery of the Dead Sea Scrolls proves that the Book of Daniel must have been completed before 200 BC. Therefore this prophecy, which pertains to Christ, must have been written well before the prophesied events.

Continuing with this prophecy, verse 9:26 says that after the 483-year period, the Anointed One will be put to death and the city and the sanctuary will be destroyed. Conservative scholars believe the language suggests an interval between the second and third periods, and that Christ's crucifixion occurred in that interval, as did the sacking of Jerusalem and the destruction of the Temple by the Roman Titus in 70 AD. Many scholars also believe we are still in this interval period, which is the present Church age, and that the final "week" (seven years) will begin sometime after the Rapture, when believers will be "caught up" to meet the Lord (Thes. 4:17). Known as the Great Tribulation, this seven-year period will end with Christ's arrival and His establishing His millennial kingdom, in fulfillment of God's covenants and in culmination of God's redemptive and salvation history.

There are differing views as to when and even if the Rapture will occur. Some scholars believe it will happen in the middle of the tribulation period while others predict it will be afterward. Some claim it will occur only partially (meaning only certain believers will be raptured) and some argue it will not occur at all.[18] Indeed, there are various views on many other aspects of these future events, including Christ's millennial kingdom, all of which are beyond this book's scope.

Daniel features several other prophecies that also point to Christ's return and His future kingdom. A prophecy in chapter 2 involves a dream of Babylonian King Nebuchadnezzar that no one in the kingdom but Daniel can describe and interpret. Daniel tells the king that in his dream, the king saw a large statue with a head of pure gold, a chest and arms of silver, a lower body and thighs of bronze, legs of iron, and feet partly of iron and partly of baked clay. "A rock was cut out, but not by human hands," which "struck the statue on its feet of iron and clay and smashed them." Then the entire statue disintegrated into fine pieces, and the rock grew into a huge mountain filling the whole earth. Daniel explains to the king that the different body parts represent different earthly empires (the first three being identified in chapter 8 as Babylon, Medo-Persia, and Greece, respectively, while scholars believe the fourth to be Rome). The crushing rock represents a kingdom established by God, which scholars interpret as Christ's future kingdom.

Another prophecy in chapter 7 resembles the chapter 2 prophecy except that Daniel himself has the dream, in which he envisions four great beasts representing the same four empires. This dream is more complex, involving the Anti-Christ and other matters, but it also predicts Christ's everlasting kingdom. The interrelated prophecies of chapters 2, 7, and also 8 include predictions of the coming Messiah and His future reign.

Many see verses 12:1–2—describing the final resurrection of the just and unjust—as a prophecy of Christ judging people for eternal life and eternal punishment, as described in John 5:28–29.[19] Additionally, some regard God's protection of Daniel's friends Shadrach, Meshach, and Abednego from the fiery furnace and His defense of Daniel in the lions' den as foreshadowings of the salvation Christ offers us.[20]

EZEKIEL

Poor Ezekiel—God calls on him to communicate a message containing exotic, surreal visions that he is commanded to act out in a way seemingly akin to the game of charades. He's told to construct a miniature model of Jerusalem under siege, with camps arranged outside it and battering rams planted against it all around. He is then to place an iron griddle "as an iron wall" between himself and the city, "and set your face toward it and let it be in a state of siege, and press the siege against it." This, God tells Ezekiel, is a sign for Israel (4:3)—a warning of the coming Babylonian siege of Jerusalem.

Then God tells him to lie on his left side for 390 days, signifying that "the house of Israel" would be punished for 390 years. Next, he should lie down on his right side for forty days, representing forty years that "the house of Judah" would be punished (Ezek. 4:3–6). He's also instructed to bind himself up in ropes inside his house (3:25). God makes Ezekiel's tongue cling to the roof of his mouth to prevent him from reproving the rebellious people (3:26–27). God tells him He's going to take his wife from him but he would not be allowed to mourn the loss

(24:15–16). Ezekiel is carried off in visions (8:7) to witness what God has in store. In another such "living parable," he's told to simulate an escape by preparing "an exile's baggage" and digging through the wall at night with his baggage as a sign of Judah's coming captivity (12:1–6).

Ezekiel obeys God's commands. As a result, the people think he's deranged—and some still do. According to one scholarly paper ostensibly employing a Freudian analysis of Ezekiel's behavior, Ezekiel is "a true psychotic characterized by a narcissistic-masochistic conflict, with attendant fantasies of castration and unconscious sexual regression…schizophrenic withdrawal…and delusions of persecution and grandeur."[21] Others speculate that he's catatonic, a paranoid schizophrenic, given to fits of ecstasy, or has a tendency toward psychic abnormality.[22] All of this illustrates the lengths some scholars will go to avoid any hint of the supernatural, as if it's difficult to believe that a God who created the universe could instruct one of His prophets to engage in apparently bizarre behavior to deliver His messages to the people—or even transport him to another place and time, which happens repeatedly in the book (8:3, 37:1–14, 40:1).

Ezekiel ministers mostly in captivity in Babylonia, directing his messages both to his fellow exiles and to the Jews remaining in Judah. He warns his people that Judah will fall due to the people's sins, though many believe that the worst has passed and that Judah will survive. After Judah does fall, Ezekiel shifts his message to one of hope for its future restoration.[23]

Establishing its principal theme, the book begins by relating the prophet's vision of God's glory (chapters 1–3). Then chapters 4–39, in essence, describe God's glory departing from Israel and God's rationale for removing it—though chapters 25–32 switch themes to describe God's judgment on the nations. Subsequently, chapters 33–39 offer a message of hope for the coming glory that is prophesied in chapters 40–48, which close out the book by portraying God's glory returning to Israel in future days.

Though God will restore Israel in the future, He always acts in furtherance of His own glory. God illustrates this principle when He states, "It is not for your sake, O house of Israel, that I am about to act, but for the sake of my holy name, which you have profaned among the nations to which you came. And I will vindicate the holiness of my great name, which has been profaned among the nations, and which you have profaned among them. And the nations will know that I am the Lord, declares the Lord God, when through you I vindicate my holiness before their eyes. I will take you from the nations and gather you from all countries and bring you into your own land" (Ezek. 36:22–24). According to the ESV Study Bible, "The primary purpose of Ezekiel's message was to restore God's glory before the people who had spurned it in view of the watching nations."[24]

Put simply, God is demonstrating His sovereignty. He will accomplish His salvation purposes for mankind through His chosen nation of Israel, and He will restore Israel itself despite its recurring disobedience. Israel may forfeit its blessings in the short run, even for prolonged periods, but in the end, God's redemptive plan will not be thwarted. C. Hassell Bullock explains this vividly in his description of God's reaction throughout history to the Hebrews' disobedience. Even after Jerusalem falls, the people remain morally inflexible, unchanged, and unrepentant. "Ezekiel," writes Bullock, "as clearly as any of the prophets, set up the opposite poles and then showed how Yahweh (God) resolved the polarization."[25] God says He will turn His face from Israel (7:22), yet He will not hide His face from them anymore (39:29); Israel drives God from the sanctuary (8:6), but He nevertheless gives them instructions for a new Temple where He will reside everlastingly (37:26–28, 40–48). God's glory moves from the Temple (11:23) and returns (43:1–5). He gives up the land for the people throughout biblical history (14:12–20), but then returns them to it (47:13–48:35). Israel breaks the Mosaic covenant (16:59), but God establishes an everlasting covenant with them. The shepherds neglect His flock (34:10), and He responds by becoming the good Shepherd (34:11).

Throughout, says Bullock, Israel's apostasy stands in stark contrast to God's holiness. But to remedy this deplorable state of affairs, God doesn't emphasize Israel's repentance. Rather, He proactively moves to bring about major changes to save and restore Israel. Ezekiel (and the other prophets) had tirelessly warned Israel to no avail, and disaster came upon it. "And now in the face of appalling destruction and despair," writes Bullock, "hope could be found only in the Person and actions of Yahweh Himself."[26] It seems that, in the end, the more Israel sins, the more God's grace abounds. In fact, that's what Paul says in his explanation of Christianity to the Romans. Due to Christ's sacrifice, Paul writes, "where sin abounded, grace abounded much more" (Romans 5:20).

Messianic prophecies fill the Book of Ezekiel, including the following: the Lord, the sanctuary (Ezek. 11:16–20, fulfilled in Rev. 21:22); a tree planted by God, a tender twig that becomes a stately cedar on a lofty mountain (Ezek. 17:22–24, fulfilled in Matt. 13:31–32); the humble are exalted; the rightful king (Ezek. 21:26–27, fulfilled in Luke 1:52); the good and faithful shepherd (Ezek. 34:23–24, fulfilled in John 10:11); the great purification (Ezek. 36:25–36, fulfilled in John 1:25–28); and the great resurrection and gift of the Spirit (Ezek. 37:1–14, fulfilled in John chapter 20 and Acts 2:33).[27] Many also see the prophecies of Ezekiel 44–48 as pertaining to the second coming of Christ.[28] Gary Staats sees chapter 48 as depicting a type of the heavenly Jerusalem that is described in Revelation 21–22, where Christ is with His Father.[29]

The Book of Ezekiel is Christ-directed in many other respects. Ezekiel addresses the Davidic kingship, with his oracles of doom against those currently occupying David's throne (Ezek. 17:1–21, 19:1–9, 10–14, 21:25–27, 30–32); his oracles of hope for a future Davidic dynasty that would rule over God's people regathered from exile (Ezek. 17:22–24; 29:21); and his visions of a prince and his future successors, who would be stewards of the new Temple, administer social justice, and correct the Davidic dynasty's past abuses of the people (Ezek. 44:1–3, 45:7–9, 16–25, 46:1–24, 48:21–22).[30]

In addition, the term "Son of man"—the phrase Jesus invokes most often to refer to Himself in the New Testament—is used more than ninety times in this book to address Ezekiel. The term has two separate meanings, connoting either a human being or a divine one. Jesus applies it to Himself in both ways,[31] as He is fully God and fully man.

Finally, like Jeremiah, Ezekiel announces the New Covenant, predicting that one day God will inaugurate a new covenant with the House of Israel and the House of Judah, and that God will give His people a new heart and a new birth (Ezek. 34:25–31, 36:24–27, 37:26–28, fulfilled in John 3:1–16).

HAGGAI

One of the main reasons the returning Jewish exiles manage to rebuild the Temple despite persistent opposition is that the prophets Haggai and Zechariah shame them and exhort them to finish the task. Ministering in Judah in 520 BC, Haggai is the first prophet in Jerusalem after the return. He scathingly rebukes the people for living in their paneled houses while allowing the house of God to lie in rubble. But Haggai isn't speaking on his own behalf; no prophet does. He relates that God is commanding the people to "go up to the hills and bring wood and build the house, that I may take pleasure in it and that I may be glorified" (Haggai 1:8). God also reminds His people again of the covenant He'd made with them when He brought them out of Egypt. Rebuild His Temple, He tells them, and He "will fill this house with glory . . . and the latter glory of this house shall be greater than the former. . . . And in this place I will give peace. . . . From this day on I will bless you" (Haggai 2:7–9, 19).

What a perfect illustration of God's patience and grace! Israel has constantly disobeyed and disappointed Him, even after He returned them to their land, and has forgotten and neglected His faithfulness and blessings. Nevertheless, He is anxious to forgive them and to dwell with them and bestow His peace and glory upon them.

Haggai attaches profound importance to rebuilding the Temple. It's no mere symbolic exercise, but an integral part of the messianic program God had promised through His prophets and His covenants. Gerard Van Groningen explains that if "the messianic promises concerning the royal Person of the Davidic house and the kingdom were to be realized, it was necessary that the remnant of the covenant people do their part. They were to build the temple, the symbol of Yahweh's presence with them and the type of him who was to come and dwell among them (John 1:14–18)."[32]

The Temple is a symbol of God's presence, to be sure, but it's much more. It's an important and ongoing reminder of God's special relationship with His people. When God freed them from captivity in Egypt He commanded them to build a dwelling place for Him—the Tabernacle (Exodus 26:1, 35:4–29). Once it had been built, God entered into it and filled it with His glory (Exodus 40:33, 34–37). Dwelling among His people, God would lead and sustain them.[33] The same was true for Solomon's Temple that replaced the Tabernacle. Once it was completed, not only was the Ark of the Covenant placed inside it, but it was filled with God's glory cloud (1 Kings 8:10; 2 Chron. 5:13). Haggai's announcements make clear that God is not only still present among His people, but also that His covenants remain in full force and effect.

Haggai's essential declaration is in verse 1:13: "I am with you." This, says Van Groningen, is at the core of the covenant promises God had made to Abraham, Moses, Joshua, David, and Solomon. Note that this is simply a shortened form of the statement we identified earlier as the promise underlying all God's covenants: "I will be their God and they shall be my people." God's promises are unchanging and completely reliable; the people's disobedience does not nullify the covenant promises.

As the first post-exilic prophet, Haggai's message is crucial because the people have to understand that no matter what hardships they've endured or whatever doubts they might have about God's faithfulness, all his promises are still valid. Therefore, it is vital that the Temple be rebuilt and that the three Old Testament offices—prophet, priest, and king—resume functioning to help carry out God's covenant plans. Another key "building" project must be resumed as well: "the building of the Davidic house that represented God's kingdom"[34]—meaning the Davidic dynasty that God promised to establish forever.

Ultimately, this book teaches that we must keep our hearts and minds set on God and not allow our earthly priorities to lead us away from Him. It's a comforting reminder to us that even in seemingly dark times God is faithful. We can rely on Him to honor His promises.

We Christian readers of the Old Testament must be forever mindful, as we've stressed repeatedly, that in the Bible God not only unfolds the progressive revelation of His salvation history, but that He is always superintending history and directing it toward its final conclusion in Jesus Christ. Many Israelites, especially during their exile, and continuing into their return and restoration, seem to have lost faith in God's sweeping control of history and His blessed promises, not all of which are fully realized in their days. We Christians have an advantage over our Old Testament brothers in that we have read the rest of the story, and we also have the entire Old Testament laid out before us in a way that demonstrates the continuity and integrity of God's plan—both in revelation and in actual history. Haggai's admonitions to the Jewish remnant concerning God's covenant promises are important for us to remember, constituting another example of the Old Testament's relevance today.

The Book of Haggai also demonstrates that we must put God first in our lives. It may seem like a costly sacrifice to turn ourselves toward God when we're caught up in our daily struggles, but in the end we'll be richly rewarded through our renewed connection with Him. Moreover, while we acknowledge that God is sovereign and carries the laboring oar, we are not relieved of our duty to do our part. God was fully capable of building the Temple by Himself and is fully capable of building our "temple," but He wants us to participate. He wants us to be engaged.

Haggai, though not among the Major Prophets or even among the most profound of the Minor Prophets, is an undeniably courageous and godly man who steps out in faith against formidable opposition. He is also an effective messenger, successfully coaxing the people into completing the Temple project.

Haggai stresses that this second Temple will have even greater glory than the original and that God will give peace there (Haggai 2:9). This points to the essential role of the second Temple in God's redemptive plan.[35] There is also a foreshadowing of the Messiah in Zerubbabel, the governor of Judah and descendant of David who led the first band of Israelites back to the land and helped erect the Temple's altar and its foundation.[36] In Haggai 2:23, Zerubbabel is referred to with the messianic title, "My Servant" (cf. 2 Samuel 3:18; 1 Kings 11:34; Isaiah 42:1–9; Ezek. 37:24, 25). That verse has further messianic significance because God tells Zerubbabel He will make him like a signet ring, "for I have chosen you." A signet ring is a symbol of honor, authority, and power, like a king's scepter, used to seal letters and decrees.[37] What makes Zerubbabel unique in the Davidic line is that he resumes and reestablishes the line after its interruption by the exile. He thereby becomes like a signet ring in the center of the messianic line that seals both branches together.[38] Significantly, Zerubbabel is in the line of Christ on both Joseph's side (Matt. 1:12) and Mary's side (Luke 3:27).[39]

Finally, Haggai writes, "For thus says the Lord of hosts: 'Yet once more, in a little while, I will shake the heavens and the earth and the sea and the dry land. And I will shake the nations, so that the treasures of all nations shall come in, and I will fill this house with glory, says the Lord of hosts'" (Haggai 2:6). The writer of Hebrews quotes this passage and applies it to Christ as the final king in His unshakable kingdom (12:25–29).

ZECHARIAH

Zechariah is a contemporary of Haggai's who also encourages the people to complete the Temple. But he focuses more on the people's need to repent and renew their covenant with God, a theme also found in the Book of Haggai but is more prominent here. Zechariah has the long view in mind. He does not, Warren Wiersbe reminds us, "see a weak nation in a ruined city; he looked down the centuries and saw the future of the city and the coming of Jerusalem's King, the Messiah."[40] Zechariah not only insists that the people rebuild the Temple, but that they grasp the moral and spiritual truths concerning their faith and their God. Without this, writes James Hastings, "the Temple and its worship would be hollow mockery."[41] As Dr. Thomas Howe observes, "God was not concerned with the glory of the temple except in the sense that the neglect of the temple was a sign of their lack of commitment to Him.... The dilapidated condition of the temple reflected on the nature of God.... The glory of Israel is not her physical temple, but the spiritual temple, and ultimately her Messiah. All those who oppose her will be crushed. All those who trust will be rescued. Ultimately, the nations will be subjugated and come to serve and worship the Lord at Zion."[42]

The messages of Haggai and Zechariah are so consistent that some scholars suggest we should view the short Book of Haggai as an introduction to the longer Zechariah, which amplifies Haggai's key message—"From this day on I will bless you" (Haggai 2:19).[43] Haggai tells the people that God wants them to remember the exodus from Egypt and His covenant with them, and Zechariah stresses this theme of remembrance even more. In fact the name "Zechariah" means "The Lord remembers," signifying that God has not forgotten His people despite their conquest by a foreign empire. God is always present with His people even if their difficult circumstances make it seem otherwise.[44] Zechariah encourages the people spiritually as they re-engage in the Temple project (see Ezra 5:2), promising them future blessings on the nation including the coming Messiah. As John MacArthur puts it, Haggai "was used to start the revival, while Zechariah was used to keep it going strong with a more positive emphasis, calling the people to repentance and reassuring them regarding future blessings."[45]

Indeed, MacArthur deems Zechariah the most messianic book of the Old Testament. There's a reason for that even aside from the book's abundant messianic prophecies: the gospels quote or allude to as many or more passages from Zechariah as from any other prophet.[46] Because the prophets would soon be silent for some four hundred years, argues MacArthur, God is using Zechariah "to bring a rich, abundant outburst of promise for the future to sustain the faithful remnant through those silent years."[47]

The book's messianic prophecies include: God living among His people and dwelling in their midst (Zech. 2:10–13, fulfilled in Rev. 21:3, 24); a new priesthood (Zech. 3:8, fulfilled in Eph. 20–21; 1 Peter 2:5); Christ as the Enthroned High Priest (Zech. 6:12–13, fulfilled in Heb. 5:5–10, 7:11–28, 8:1, 2); Christ riding on a donkey during the Triumphal Entry (Zech. 9:9–12, fulfilled in Matt. 21:4–6; Mark 11:1–10; Luke 19:28–38; John 12:13–15); He is the Lord who shall save His flock (Zech. 9:16, fulfilled in John 3:16); betrayed by a friend and sold for thirty pieces of silver (Zech. 11:12–13, fulfilled in Matt. 26:14–15, 27:9); the money was used to buy the potter's field (Zech. 11:12–13, fulfilled in Matt. 27:9–10); His body was pierced (Zech. 12:10, fulfilled in John 19:34, 37); and He is the Shepherd Who was smitten and the sheep were scattered (Zech. 13:1, 6–7, fulfilled in Matt. 26:31; John 16:32).

In this book Christ is portrayed in His first and second comings as Servant and King, Man and God. Zechariah further anticipates Christ in the following passages: He is seen as the Angel of the Lord Who commands the salvation of His people (Zech. 3:1–5; Rev. 10); the Righteous

Branch (Zech. 3:8, 6:12, 13); the Servant of God Whom He shall bring forth (Zech. 3:8; Mark 10:45); the Foundation Stone with seven eyes upon which God's Church and kingdom is built and Who will remove the iniquity of the land (Zech. 3:9; 1 Cor. 3:10–11; 1 Peter 2:6–8); the king-priest (Zech. 6:13); the humble king (Zech. 9:9, 10); the cornerstone, tent peg, and battle bow (Zech. 10:4); the Good Shepherd (Zech. 11:4–13); the cleansing fountain and Savior of Israel, whose blood covers the sins and uncleanliness of the people (Zech. 13:1); and the coming Judge and righteous king (Zech. 14)[48] Who shall stand on Mount Olive when He returns (Zech. 14:4; Acts 1:6–11).

Finally, some commentators suggest Zechariah presents Christ's dual nature: as man (6:12) and as God: "Awake, O sword, against my shepherd, against the man who stands next to me" (13:7).[49] F. W. Lindsey writes, "In Zechariah 13:7 the Lord is claiming identity of nature or unity of essence with His Shepherd, thus strongly affirming the Messiah's deity."[50]

MALACHI

Most scholars believe this book was written late in the fifth century BC, probably during Nehemiah's return to Persia around 433–424 BC. At the time, the people are back in the land, the Temple is standing, and sacrifices are being made there. Yet the people are discouraged because they have not experienced the glories prophesied by Isaiah.[51] Malachi rails against the spiritual decadence shown by their corrupted worship practices, resumption of intermarriage with pagans, dishonoring of God's name in worship, withholding of tithes, and their criticism of God Himself.

Malachi is more concerned, though, with the cynical attitude these sins reflect than the sins themselves.[52] Spiritual practices are not supposed to be by rote; their acceptance to God depends on the sincerity and purity of those making the offerings.[53] One is not righteous because he goes through the motions of external obedience to the Law. God looks at the heart. The people have apparently come to take God's promises of future blessing for granted, but Malachi sets them straight, telling them that the Messiah would also come in judgment. "Behold, he is coming...but who can endure the day of his coming, and who can stand when he appears? For He is like a refiner's fire and like fullers' soap. He will sit as a refiner and purifier of silver, and he will purify the sons of Levi and refine them like gold and silver" (Mal. 3:1–3).

So Malachi is, in essence, appealing to the people to repent of their sins and return to God, and promising that if they respond they will be blessed, but if not they will be judged. J. Sidlow Baxter confirms that "the coming One who was the nation's hope of future blessing was coming to *judge* (not merely, as was being presumed, to bless the nation indiscriminately!)."[54] Indeed, "Malachi now shows them that the Divine promise is a two-edged sword. Not only will the coming 'Day' slay the enemies *outside* the nation, but also the wicked *inside* the nation."[55]

The book is structured as a formal dispute or debate between God and His people. God, through Malachi, asks the people questions and they often respond disrespectfully, even questioning His authority. We should read carefully the six oracles (direct communications from God) and the people's responses. Take, for example, the fourth (2:17–3:6) and sixth oracles (3:13–4:3), in which God accuses the people of using hard words against Him. In each case the people question the charge, presumptuously demanding proof. Addressing their response to the fourth oracle, God says that they have wearied Him by complaining that "everyone who does evil is good in the sight of the Lord, and he delights in them," or by asking "Where is the God of justice?" (2:17). Speaking to their response to the sixth oracle, God explains again how they have used hard words against him: "You have said, 'It is vain to serve God. What is the profit of our keeping his charge or of walking as in mourning before the Lord of hosts? And now we call the arrogant blessed. Evildoers not only prosper but they put God to the test and they escape'" (3:14–15).

In both cases the people accuse God of allowing the righteous to suffer and the evil to prosper. Intending to indict God's fairness and justice, they indict themselves instead, for the responses reveal their impure hearts and their abject superficiality. Are they only serving God for what they can get out of the bargain? Do none of their actions flow from love and obedience? Is it all a matter of a cynical negotiation to them by which they will obey God only as long as there's something to be gained?

Christians today should take Malachi's message to heart—we must not be selfish, calculating, and shortsighted. Our faith must be properly motivated. Malachi speaks to us as Christians concerning our own spiritual apathy. It's easy to become complacent and to fall away if times get tough or if we lose sight of God's overall plan. But in the end, God sees our hearts, so there's no point in fooling ourselves. We don't get right with God by merely going through the motions. Yes, we should do good works, but those works must flow from a heart that is in a proper relationship with God.

The Book of Malachi has several key messianic prophecies, including verse 3:1: the Messiah would be preceded by a forerunner, a messenger who will prepare the way before Him. This is fulfilled by John the Baptist (Matt. 11:10; Mark 1:2; Luke 7:27) and by Jesus, Who physically came to the Temple. To fulfull this prediction, the Messiah had to come before the Temple was destroyed in 70 AD. Additionally, verses 4:5–6 promise that Elijah will return before the day of the Lord comes. This too is believed to predict the coming of John the Baptist, who will precede Christ (Matt. 11:14, 17:10–12; Mark 9:11–13; Luke 1:17). It's noteworthy that Malachi makes two references to John the Baptist because John is the prophet who will break the four-hundred-year silence following Malachi's ministry. Scholars believe that Malachi is prophesying both Christ's first and second comings.[56]

Finally, the reference in verse 4:2 to "the sun of righteousness" is taken by some to be a messianic prophecy, but others say it refers to the day of the Lord in general.[57] David Clark and Howard Hatton write that Christian tradition, going back to early times, interprets the phrase as relating to the coming of the Messiah. They say that may be true, but they believe the prophet's main intention was to describe the day of the Lord.[58]

Malachi's prophecy closes out the Old Testament. After him, God remained silent for four centuries. But through the warnings and exhortations of His many Old Testament prophets—both Major and Minor—He left behind clear guidance on living an obedient life. Though they did not always obey, His people now understood what God expected from them as His chosen people. An epoch of history had closed, one filled with disobedience and violence, exile and destruction—yet always infused with hope, grounded in God's promises.

Though the trying days of the Old Testament were followed by a difficult period of silence from God's prophets, God had not abandoned His people. But after this period, writes James Lee Beall, "The people were so unaccustomed to hearing God speak that they needed a messenger before the messenger.... Before people could be alerted to hear Him, they needed to be awakened through the prophetic preaching and baptism of John, the...herald."[59]

When John the Baptist arrived on the scene and broke this period of prophetic silence, many mistook him for the ultimate Prophet, but he quickly denied it, saying, "I baptize you with water, but he who is mightier than I is coming, the strap of whose sandals I am not worthy to untie. He will baptize you with the Holy Spirit and fire" (Luke 3:16).

It wasn't long before God validated John's prophecy—and indeed the entirety of Old Testament prophecy and His covenantal promises. As shepherds were keeping watch over their flock one night, "an angel of the Lord appeared to them, and the glory of the Lord shone around them, and they were filled with great fear. And the angel said to them 'Fear not, for behold, I bring you good news of great joy that will be for all the people. For unto you is born this day in the city of David a Savior, who is Christ the Lord'" (Luke 2:9–11).

God's dealings with Israel in Old Testament times and His record of those dealings in the Old Testament were the indispensable precursor for the arrival on earth of God Himself—our Savior, Jesus Christ. When Jesus arrived, His path had been laid by His many forerunners who, in ways sometimes clear and other times vaguely implied, had foretold of His coming, and the glories He would bestow on all the nations of the world.

CONCLUSION

W hen I began studying the Bible years ago, eager to get a sense of its recorded history and unifying themes, I tried various approaches to hasten the process and mostly came up short. It wasn't that the Bible was incomprehensible, it's that I was impatient—too anxious to master it like other books I'd set out to study. But the Bible isn't like any other book. What eventually unlocked the mystery of Scripture for me was learning that the Old Testament, too, is centered on Jesus Christ. Once that became clear, I truly began to understand the Bible.

I invite you to open your Bible to Luke 24:27 and reread the passage that inspired the title for this book. Then go back to the beginning of the story at Luke 24:13. Two men walking toward Emmaus, a village close to Jerusalem, are puzzling over recent events when Jesus, uninvited, begins walking with them. Now notice verse 24:16: "But their eyes were kept from recognizing him." I believe this is meant literally, but there's also another meaning—it suggests that most people at the time, including the apostles, fail to fully grasp Who Jesus is. They are deeply perplexed by His death on the cross and the sudden end of a promising ministry. The presumptive Messiah left this earth without making so much as a fizzle in redeeming Israel from its worldly tormentors.

In short order, Jesus sets them straight, telling them Who He is, disabusing them of their errors, and showing them how every page of their Bible—the Old Testament—points to Himself. We can only imagine their range of emotions as waves of understanding pour over them and they come to realize Who Christ is, the significance of His ministry, and how Scripture has pointed to Him all along. Like most people at the time, they hadn't truly seen Jesus because "their eyes were kept from recognizing him."

But in His time, Christ showed them Who He is—and since we today are no less important to Him than they were, He also wants *us* to recognize Him on every page of the Old Testament. Jesus wasted no time in His earthly ministry, especially during His resurrection appearances. Every minute counted, yet He chose to reveal Himself to those two men—and to record the encounter in Scripture for our benefit. He wants us to see exactly what they saw. And with the New Testament, He shows us.

The sovereignly orchestrated encounter on the Emmaus road has special significance for me, for it parallels my own experience in finally beginning to understand the Bible. I'm not surprised that some people are intimidated by parts of the Old Testament, but to think it can be ignored or downplayed is inconceivable. If God intended the Christian Bible to consist of the New Testament alone, He wouldn't have arranged for it to include the Old Testament. But He did, which is all the proof we need of its relevance and indispensability.

Yet knowing it is relevant and understanding how and why are different things. Until I tapped into the answers to those questions, I remained in a theological fog, unable to fully understand the Bible's message. Thankfully, I came across several books that emphasized Christ's centrality to the Old Testament. It was as if I'd put on my first pair of glasses. Discovering Christ in the Old Testament gave me a better understanding of the flow of Old Testament history. Scripture—both

Old and New Testaments—came into focus like never before. Thereafter, Bible study became richer and more fulfilling.

With my own Emmaus road epiphany, I was itching to share my discoveries with others. As noted in the Introduction, after a false start a few decades ago, this book is the culmination of my Christ-centered Old Testament studies. Its organization reflects my own avenue of study, which is why I devoted considerable space outlining Old Testament history.

I pray that this book has helped you to get a better handle on that history, gain an appreciation for the foundational importance of the Old Testament to the New Testament, and most important, develop a heightened awareness of Christ's dominating presence in every Old Testament book. The New Testament, as we've shown, does not supersede the Old, though the New Covenant supersedes the Old Covenant. With humility, I hope that if the Old Testament was intimidating or seemed irrelevant to you before, it will be less so after reading this book, and that the Old Testament will come alive for you as it has for me.

I've tried to demonstrate Christ's dominating presence in the entirety of Scripture and also in history, from the creation of the universe. God foreknew that man would sin, and although His perfect justice required Him to judge us, He designed from the very beginning a plan for our redemption. He first revealed His salvation plan in shadowy form and with few details, but with a firm, unconditional covenant to bless mankind. As history unfolded, God, through His dealings with Israel and in turn through progressive revelation in Scripture, amplified and clarified His promise-plan with increasing specificity. What began as a vague but certain divine promise of blessing grew into a guarantee of the Messiah, and ultimately ripened into the appearance of Jesus Christ—God in the flesh—born for the purpose of dying a substitutionary death for our sins.

Some critical scholars maintain that the idea of a coming Messiah originated in the mind of ancient man and evolved, over time, into the form that is recorded in Scripture. To the contrary, writes Gerard Van Groningen, "It had its origin in divine revelation. It did not rise in pagan political and religious settings; it did not come from reflection on past, present, and future political, economic, military, or religious events, prospects or hopes. The messianic concept was given its first expression in the creation of man and woman as God's royal agents. After mankind's fall into sin, when the royal status could have been lost forever, God intervened to maintain and restore it. He did so by promising and providing a royal mediator who would fully and perfectly restore what had been so severely distorted."[1]

Indeed, as we study the Old Testament through our New Testament lenses and with our eyes focused on Christ, we see His image in the portraits, the types, the Christophanies, the Old Testament offices, His work in creating and sustaining the universe, His redemptive activities on behalf of the Israelites, His names and titles, and in the stunning messianic prophecies. We see that all God's promises and covenants are fulfilled in Him. With the benefit of New Testament revelation we now see Him clearly in every Old Testament book, which enlivens us, renews our faith, and magnifies our gratitude for our Savior, Who created us for an eternal, personal, loving relationship with Himself.

God knew us before He formed us in the womb. Before the beginning of time He had a redemptive plan for us. This plan, grounded in God's irrevocable promises and culminating in Jesus Christ, His Son, is plainly revealed for all students of Scripture. We must cherish the entire Bible, as it is our roadmap to eternal salvation.

Jesus Christ lives and He saves, and because He saves we may live.

ACKNOWLEDGMENTS

It's hard for me to believe, but this is my seventh book, and every one has been with Regnery Publishing, with whom I have a wonderful relationship. I have nothing but sincere praise for everyone there. The entire staff demonstrates professionalism, integrity, and excellence in every department and all aspects of the publishing business: acquisition, editing, layout, marketing, accounting, and management. My sincere thanks to Marji Ross for her support and personal encouragement for my books, and her openness to new ideas and directions. I will always be especially grateful to Harry Crocker, whose friendship and loyalty have highlighted my sustained relationship with the company. He is solid in every respect and I highly value his professional judgment and advice, which I seek liberally. As with *Jesus on Trial*, Maria Ruhl was a pleasure to work with in copy editing and proofing the manuscript, and always willing to make every effort to accommodate my requested changes.

This is the fourth book in a row in which I have worked with the editor par excellence, Jack Langer, a gifted writer and editor, who never met a sentence he couldn't tighten and a paragraph he couldn't improve, all without altering the voice, or the substance—except when necessary. He has a keen eye for weak, inconsistent, or questionable arguments, and always calls them to my attention, which forces me to rethink and clarify, resulting, obviously, in a much better end product. He is incredibly conscientious, industrious, and cooperative—amazingly easy to work with. On numerous occasions we were trading emails and phone calls as late as 1:00 a.m., and he sounded like he was just getting warmed up.

Many thanks to my longtime friend Greg Mueller and his team at Creative Response Concepts for quarterbacking the promotion and marketing of this book, along with the excellent marketing staff at Regnery. I must renew my gratitude to Greg for bringing me to the bookwriting dance in the first place, which has changed my life. Thank you, Greg, for also expressing such confidence in *Jesus on Trial*.

As this is my second book on Christianity, I must reiterate my thanks to certain mentors along the way. My friend Dr. Steve Johnson helped to guide me through the beginning phases of my journey, tirelessly answered my endless questions on theology, and helped keep me on the right theological path early on and away from error. I am very grateful.

Ron Watts, my extraordinary pastor and friend, has been an enormous blessing to me and to every other member of his congregation. His Christian example and leadership have helped La Croix become an amazingly successful, seeker-friendly, biblically solid church with a balanced approach to theology, discipleship, and service. His consistently outstanding sermons have educated, inspired, and uplifted thousands. The entire staff of La Croix is Christ-centered and focused on spreading the Gospel to the "unchurched." They impart to the congregation the essential messages of service and discipleship, and help to train all members with the skills necessary for both.

No one has been more important to my spiritual walk than my wife Lisa, my best friend and mother of our five children, who was patient and understanding through my doubting years, always confident I would come to Christ. As with *Jesus on Trial*, she was the first to read my completed manuscript. She jumped to the task on a moment's notice, read it thoroughly, and provided invaluable suggestions, which have helped to make the book better and, in places, easier to understand.

My friend Frank Turek read this book as he did *Jesus on Trial*, vetting it for theological accuracy and making numerous helpful suggestions. Frank is a rock; I can always count on him to sacrifice the time to help and to offer solid, reliable ideas. His organization, CrossExamined. org, is doing amazing apologetics work on our college campuses, combating the secular message that dominates America's universities. I am proud to be a CrossExamined board member.

My friend Sean Hannity has always been supportive of all my books and other professional endeavors. Sean is a humble, kind, and generous man despite his celebrity and phenomenal success. I am proud to call him my very close friend.

Mark Levin is a very close friend whose loyalty exceeds anything any friend would ever deserve. As usual, he has been extremely supportive of this project, for which I am grateful.

Finally, I again want to thank my brother Rush for inspiring me, for opening up doors for me directly and indirectly, and for doing wonderful work for this nation we both love from the bottom of our hearts. He has always supported me and my career pursuits, unfailingly encouraging and cheering me on. I am blessed and grateful to have such a generous, caring, and thoughtful brother, who makes a difference every day in working to keep this nation true to its founding principles. He doesn't get nearly the credit he deserves.

APPENDIX

MESSIANIC PROPHECIES OF THE OLD TESTAMENT		
PROPHECY	OLD TESTAMENT REFERENCES	NEW TESTAMENT FULFILLMENT
Seed of the woman	Gen. 3:15	Gal. 4:4; Heb. 2:14
Through Noah's sons	Gen. 9:27	Luke 6:36
Seed of Abraham	Gen. 12:3	Matt. 1:1; Gal. 3:8,16
Seed of Isaac	Gen. 17:19	Rom. 9:7; Heb. 11:18
Blessing to nations	Gen. 18:18	Gal. 3:8
Seed of Isaac	Gen. 21:12	Rom. 9:7; Heb. 11:18
Blessing to Gentiles	Gen. 22:18	Gal. 3:8,16; Heb. 6:14
Blessing to Gentiles	Gen. 26:4	Gal. 3:8,16; Heb. 6:14
Blessing through Abraham	Gen. 28:14	Gal. 3:8,16; Heb. 6:14
Of the tribe of Judah	Gen. 49:10	Rev. 5:5
No bone broken	Exod. 12:46	John 19:36
Blessing to firstborn son	Exod. 13:2	Luke 2:23
No bone broken	Num. 9:12	John 19:36
Serpent in wilderness	Num. 21:8-9	John 3:14-15
A star out of Jacob	Num. 24:17-19	Matt. 2:2; Luke 1:33,78; Rev. 22:16

MESSIANIC PROPHECIES OF THE OLD TESTAMENT

PROPHECY	OLD TESTAMENT REFERENCES	NEW TESTAMENT FULFILLMENT
As a prophet	Deut. 18:15,18-19	John 6:14; 7:40; Acts 3:22-23
Cursed on the tree	Deut. 21:23	Gal. 3:13
The throne of David established forever	2 Sam. 7:12-13,16,25-26; 1 Chron. 17:11-14, 23-27; 2 Chron. 21:7	Matt. 19:28; 21:4; 25:31; Mark 12:37; Luke 1:32; John 7:4; Acts 2:30; 13:23; Rom. 1:3; 2 Tim. 2:8; Heb. 1:5,8; 8:1; 12:2; Rev. 22:1
A promised Redeemer	Job 19:25-27	John 5:28-29; Gal. 4:4; Eph. 1:7,11,14
Declared to be the Son of God	Ps. 2:1-12	Matt. 3:17; Mark 1:11; Acts 4:25-26; 13:33; Heb. 1:5; 5:5; Rev. 2:26-27; 19:15-16
His resurrection	Ps. 16:8-10	Acts 2:27; 13:35; 26:23
Hands and feet pierced	Ps. 22:1-31	Matt. 27:31,35-36
Mocked and insulted	Ps. 22:7-8	Matt. 27:39-43,45-49
Soldiers cast lots for coat	Ps. 22:18	Mark 15:20,24-25,34; Luke 19:24; 23:35; John 19:15-18,23-24,34; Acts 2:23-24
Accused by false witnesses	Ps. 27:12	Matt. 26:60-61
He commits His spirit	Ps. 31:5	Luke 23:46
No bone broken	Ps. 34:20	John 19:36
Accused by false witnesses	Ps. 35:11	Matt. 26:59-61; Mark 14:57-58
Hated without reason	Ps. 35:19	John 15:24-25
Friends stand far off	Ps. 38:11	Matt. 27:55; Mark 15:40; Luke 23:49
"I come to do Thy will"	Ps. 40:6-8	Heb. 10:5-9

MESSIANIC PROPHECIES OF THE OLD TESTAMENT

PROPHECY	OLD TESTAMENT REFERENCES	NEW TESTAMENT FULFILLMENT
Betrayed by a friend	Ps. 41:9	Matt. 26:14-16,47,50; Mark 14:17-21; Luke 22:19-23; John 13:18-19
Known for righteousness	Ps. 45:2,6-7	Heb. 1:8-9
His resurrection	Ps. 49:15	Mark 16:6
Betrayed by a friend	Ps. 55:12-14	John 13:18
His ascension	Ps. 68:18	Eph. 4:8
Hated without reason	Ps. 69:4	John 15:25
Stung by reproaches	Ps. 69:9	John 2:17; Rom. 15:3
Given gall and vinegar	Ps. 69:21	Matt. 27:34,48; Mark 15:23; Luke 23:36; John 19:29
Exalted by God	Ps. 72:1-19	Matt. 2:2; Phil. 2:9-11; Heb. 1-8
He speaks in parables	Ps. 78:2	Matt. 13:34–35:34
Seed of David exalted	Ps. 89:3-4,19,27-29,35-37	Luke 1:32; Acts 2:30; 13:23; Rom. 1:3; 2 Tim. 2:8
Son of Man comes in glory	Ps. 102:16	Luke 21:24,27; Rev. 12:5-10
"Thou remainest"	Ps. 102:24-27	Heb. 1:10-12
Prays for His enemies	Ps. 109:4	Luke 23:34
Another to succeed Judas	Ps. 109:7-8	Acts 1:16-20
A priest like Melchizedek	Ps. 110:1-7	Matt. 22:41-45; 26:64; Mark 12:35-37; 16:19; Acts 7:56; Eph. 1:20; Col. 1:20; Heb. 1:13; 2:8; 5:6; 6:20; 7:21; 8:1; 10:11-13; 12:2

MESSIANIC PROPHECIES OF THE OLD TESTAMENT

PROPHECY	OLD TESTAMENT REFERENCES	NEW TESTAMENT FULFILLMENT
The chief corner stone	Ps. 118:22-23	Matt. 21:42; Mark 12:10-11; Luke 20:17; John 1:11; Acts 4:11; Eph. 2:20; 1 Pet. 2:4
The King comes in the name of the Lord	Ps. 118:26	Matt. 21:9; 23:39; Mark 11:9; Luke 13:35; 19:38; John 12:13
David's seed to reign	Ps. 132:11 cf. 2 Sam.7:12-13 , 16 , 25-26, 29	Matt. 1:1
Declared to be the Son of God	Prov. 30:4	Matt. 3:17; Mark 14:61-62; Luke 1:35; John 3:13; 9:35-38; 11:21; Rom. 1:2-4; 10:6-9; 2 Pet. 1:17
Repentance for the nations	Isa. 2:2-4	Luke 24:47
Hearts are hardened	Isa. 6:9-10	Matt. 13:14-15 ; John 12:39-40 ; Acts 28:25-27
Born of a virgin	Isa. 7:14	Matt. 1:22-23
A rock of offense	Isa. 8:14,15	Rom. 9:33; 1 Pet. 2:8
Light out of darkness	Isa. 9:1,2	Matt. 4:14-16; Luke 2:32
God with us	Isa. 9:6,7	Matt. 1:21,23; Luke 1:32-33; John 8:58; 10:30; 14:19; 2 Cor. 5:19; Col. 2:9
Full of wisdom and power	Isa. 11:1-10	Matt. 3:16; John 3:34; Rom. 15:12; Heb. 1:9
Reigning in mercy	Isa. 16:4-5	Luke 1:31-33
Peg in a sure place	Isa. 22:21-25	Rev. 3:7
Death swallowed up in victory	Isa. 25:6-12	1 Cor. 15:54
A stone in Zion	Isa. 28:16	Rom. 9:33; 1 Pet. 2:6
The deaf hear, the blind see	Isa. 29:18-19	Matt. 5:3; 11:5; John 9:39

MESSIANIC PROPHECIES OF THE OLD TESTAMENT

PROPHECY	OLD TESTAMENT REFERENCES	NEW TESTAMENT FULFILLMENT
King of kings, Lord of lords	Isa. 32:1-4	Rev. 19:16; 20:6
Son of the Highest	Isa. 33:22	Luke 1:32; 1 Tim. 1:17; 6:15
Healing for the needy	Isa. 35:4-10	Matt. 9:30; 11:5; 12:22; 20:34; 21:14; Mark 7:30; John 5:9
Make ready the way of the Lord	Isa. 40:3-5	Matt. 3:3; Mark 1:3; Luke 3:4-5; John 1:23
The Shepherd dies for His sheep	Isa. 40:10-11	John 10:11; Heb. 13:20; 1 Pet. 2:24-25
The meek Servant	Isa. 42:1-16	Matt. 12:17-21; Luke 2:32
A light to the Gentiles	Isa. 49:6-12	Acts 13:47; 2 Cor. 6:2
Scourged and spat upon	Isa. 50:6	Matt. 26:67; 27:26,30; Mark 14:65; 15:15-19; Luke 22:63-65; John 19:1
Rejected by His people	Isa. 52:13-53:12	Matt. 8:17; 27:1-2,12-14,38
Suffered vicariously	Isa. 53:4-5	Mark 15:3-4 , 27-28 ; Luke 23:1-25 , 32-34
Silent when accused	Isa. 53:7	John 1:29 ; 11:49-52
Crucified with transgressors	Isa. 53:12	John 12:37-38 ; Acts 8:28-35
Buried with the rich	Isa. 53:9	Acts 10:43; 13:38-39; 1 Cor. 15:3; Eph. 7; 1 Pet. 2:21-25; 1 John 1:7,9
Calling of those not a people	Isa. 55:4,5	John 18:37; Rom. 9:25-26; Rev. 1:5
Deliver out of Zion	Isa. 59:16-20	Rom. 11:26-29
Nations walk in the light	Isa. 60:1-3	Luke 2:32
Anointed to preach liberty	Isa. 60:1-2	Luke 4:17-19; Acts 10:38
Called by a new name	Isa. 62:11	Luke 2:32; Rev. 3:12

MESSIANIC PROPHECIES OF THE OLD TESTAMENT

PROPHECY	OLD TESTAMENT REFERENCES	NEW TESTAMENT FULFILLMENT
The King cometh	Isa. 62:11	Matt. 21:5
A vesture dipped in blood	Isa. 63:1-3	Rev. 19:13
Afflicted with the afflicted	Isa. 63:8-9	Matt. 25:34-40
The elect shall inherit	Isa. 65:9	Rom. 11:5,7; Heb. 7:14; Rev. 5:5
New heavens and a new earth	Isa. 65:17-25	2 Pet. 3:13; Rev. 21:1
The Lord our righteousness	Jer. 23:5,6	John 2:19-21; Rom. 1:3-4; Eph. 2:20-21; 1 Pet. 2:5
Born a King	Jer. 30:9	John 18:37; Rev. 1:5
Massacre of infants	Jer. 31:15	Matt. 2:17-18
Conceived by the Holy Spirit	Jer. 31:22	Matt. 1:20; Luke 1:35
A New Covenant	Jer. 31:31-34	Matt. 26:27-29; Mark 14:22-24; Luke 22:15-20; 1 Cor. 11:25; Heb. 8:8-12; 10:15-17; 12:24; 13:20
A spiritual house	Jer. 33:15-17	John 2:19-21; Eph. 2:20-21; 1 Pet. 2:5
A tree planted by God	Ezek. 17:22-24	Matt. 13:31-32
The humble exalted	Ezek. 21:26-27	Luke 1:52
The good Shepherd	Ezek. 34:23-24	John 10:11
Stone cut without hands	Dan. 2:34-35	Acts 4:10-12
His kingdom triumphant	Dan. 2:44-45	Luke 1:33; 1 Cor. 15-24; Rev. 11:15
An everlasting dominion	Dan. 7:13-14	Matt. 24:30; 25:31; 26:64; Mark 14:61-62; Acts 1:9-11; Rev. 1:7
Kingdom for the saints	Dan. 7:27	Luke 1:33; 1 Cor. 15:24; Rev. 11:15
Time of His birth	Dan. 9:24-27	Matt. 24:15-21; Luke 3:1
Israel restored	Hos. 3:5	John 18:37; Rom. 11:25-27
Flight into Egypt	Hos. 11:1	Matt. 2:15

MESSIANIC PROPHECIES OF THE OLD TESTAMENT

PROPHECY	OLD TESTAMENT REFERENCES	NEW TESTAMENT FULFILLMENT
Promise of the Spirit	Joel 2:28-32	Acts 2:17-21; Rom. 15:13
The sun darkened	Amos 8:9	Matt. 24:29; Acts 2:20; Rev. 6:12
Restoration of tabernacle	Amos 9:11-12	Acts 15:16-18
Israel regathered	Mic. 2:12-13	John 10:14 , 26
The Kingdom established	Mic. 4:1-8	Luke 1:33
Born in Bethlehem	Mic. 5:1-5	Matt. 2:1; Luke 2:4 , 10-11
Earth filled with knowledge of the glory of the Lord	Hab. 2:14	Rom. 11:26; Rev. 21:23-26
The Lamb on the throne	Zech. 2:10-13	Rev. 5:13; 6:9; 21:24; 22:1-5
A holy priesthood	Zech. 3:8	John 2:19-21; Eph. 2:20-21; 1 Pet. 2:5
A heavenly High Priest	Zech. 6:12-13	Heb. 4:4; 8:1-2
Triumphal entry	Zech. 9:9-10	Matt. 21:4-5; Mark 11:9-10; Luke 20:38; John 12:13-15
Sold for pieces of silver	Zech. 11:12-13	Matt. 26:14-15
Money buys potter's field	Zech. 11:12-13	Matt. 27:9
Piercing of His body	Zech. 12:10	John 19:34,37
Shepherd smitten—sheep scattered	Zech. 13:1,6-7	Matt. 26:31; John 16:32
Preceded by forerunner	Mal. 3:1	Matt. 11:10; Mark 1:2; Luke 7:27
Our sins purged	Mal. 3:3	Heb. 1:3
The light of the world	Mal. 4:2-3	Luke 1:78; John 1:9; 12:46; 2 Pet. 1:19; Rev. 2:28; 19:11-16; 22:16
The coming of Elijah	Mal. 4:5-6	Matt. 11:14; 17:10-12

Chart contents used by permission: Holman Bible Dictionary
(Nashville, TN: B&H Publishing Group), pages 1,089–91.

NOTES

INTRODUCTION

1. S. D. Toussaint, "Acts," in J. F. Walvoord and R. B. Zuck, eds., *The Bible Knowledge Commentary: An Exposition of the Scriptures* (Wheaton, IL: Victor Books, 1985), vol. 2, 423.

2. Udo Schnelle, *Apostle Paul: His Life and Theology*, trans. M. E. Boring (Grand Rapids, MI: Baker Academic, 2012), 384.

3. John B. Polhill, *Acts* (Nashville, TN: Broadman & Holman Publishers, 1992), vol. 26, 484.

CHAPTER 1: IN DEFENSE OF THE OLD TESTAMENT

1. Sidney Greidanus, *Preaching Christ from Ecclesiastes: Foundations for Expository Sermons* (Grand Rapids, MI; Cambridge, UK: William B. Eerdmans Publishing Company, 2010), 48.

2. John Blanchard, *The Complete Gathered Gold: A Treasury of Quotations for Christians* (Webster, NY; Darlington, England: Evangelical Press, 2006), 42.

3. Thomas S. Kepler, ed., *The Table Talk of Martin Luther* (Mineola, NY: Dover, 2005), 197.

4. Roy E. Gingrich, *Old Testament Survey* (Memphis, TN: Riverside Printing, 2001), 4.

5. Biblical theology, as distinguished from systematic theology, is the study of the Bible focusing on what the biblical writers, under divine guidance, believed, described, and taught in the context of their times. Walter A. Elwell, in *Evangelical Dictionary of Biblical Theology*, electronic ed. (Grand Rapids, MI: Baker Book House, 1996). It is "that branch of theological science which deals systematically with the historically conditioned progress of self-revelation of God as deposited in the Bible," Charles C. Ryrie, *Biblical Theology of the New Testament* (Chicago, IL: Moody, 1959), 12. See also the helpful brief discussion in Charles C. Ryrie, *Basic Theology* (Wheaton, IL: Victor Books, 1986), 14. Systematic theology can be defined as "any study that answers the question, 'What does the whole Bible teach us today?' about any given topic. This definition indicates that systematic theology involves collecting and understanding all the relevant passages in the Bible on various topics and then summarizing their teachings clearly so that we know what to believe about each topic." Wayne A. Grudem, *Systematic Theology: An Introduction to Biblical Doctrine* (Leicester, England; Grand Rapids, MI: InterVarsity Press; Zondervan Publishing House, 2004), 21.

6. L. R. Helyer, *The Witness of Jesus, Paul and John: An Exploration in Biblical Theology* (Downers Grove, IL: InterVarsity Press, 2008), 40.

7. Warren W. Wiersbe, *Wiersbe's Expository Outlines on the Old Testament* (Wheaton, IL: Victor Books, 1993), 13.

8. John F. Walvoord, *Jesus Christ Our Lord* (Chicago, IL: Moody Bible Institute of Chicago, 1975, 2008), 36.

9. Eugene H. Merrill, *Everlasting Dominion* (Nashville, TN: B&H Publishing Group, 2006).

10. R. B. Zuck, *Basic Bible Interpretation: A Practical Guide to Discovering Biblical Truth* (Colorado Springs, CO: David C. Cook, 1991), 251.

11. Carl F. H. Henry, *Revelation and the Bible* (Grand Rapids, MI: Baker, 1958), 137–51.

12. Zuck, *Basic Bible Interpretation*, 251.

13. Ray C. Stedman, "God Spoke in Time Past," RayStedman.org, December 1, 1963.

14. Stephen Charnock, *The Complete Works of Stephen Charnock* (Edinburgh; London; Dublin: James Nichol; James Nisbet and Co.; W. Robertson; G. Herbert, 1864–1866), vol. 2, 7–8.

15. Vern S. Poythress, *The Shadow of Christ in the Law of Moses* (Phillipsburg, NJ: P & R Publishing, 1991), 4–5.

16. John F. MacArthur Jr., "The Glory of the New Covenant (1994)," *John MacArthur Sermon Archive* (Panorama City, CA: Grace to You, 2014).

17. Eugene H. Merrill, *Everlasting Dominion* (Nashville, TN: B&H, 2006).

18. Robert A. Morey, *How the Old and New Testaments Relate to Each Other* (Las Vegas, NV: Christian Scholars Press, 2002), 13–14.

19. J. D. Hannah, "Exodus," in J. F. Walvoord and R. B. Zuck, eds., *The Bible Knowledge Commentary: An Exposition of the Scriptures* (Wheaton, IL: Victor Books, 1985), vol. 1, 140; Norman Geisler, *Systematic Theology, Volume Four: Church, Last Things* (Minneapolis, MN: Bethany House Publishers, 2005), 236.

20. Kenneth Boa and Robert M. Bowman Jr., *An Unchanging Faith in a Changing World: Understanding and Responding to Critical Issues that Christians Face Today* (Nashville, TN: Oliver Nelson, 1997), 261.

21. Hans K. LaRondelle and Jon Paulien, *The Bible Jesus Interpreted* (Loma Linda, CA: Jon Paulien, 2014), 39.

22. Augustine of Hippo, *The City of God*, in P. Schaff, ed., M. Dods, trans., *St. Augustin's City of God and Christian Doctrine* (Buffalo, NY: Christian Literature Company, 1887), vol. 2, 326.

23. Philip Schaff, ed., *Saint Augustin: Anti-Pelagian Writings* (New York: Christian Literature Company, 1887), vol. 5, 35.

24. LaRondelle and Paulien, *The Bible Jesus Interpreted*, 39.

25. Ibid.

26. Vern S. Poythress, *The Shadow of Christ in the Law of Moses* (Phillipsburg, NJ: P & R Publishing, 1991), 7.

27. Ibid.

28. Ray C. Stedman, *Adventuring through the Old Testament* (Grand Rapids, MI: Discovery House Publishers, 2011), Kindle locations 441–463.

29. Ibid.

30. Graeme Goldsworthy in his foreword to Mark Dever and Graeme Goldsworthy, *The Message of the Old Testament: Promises Made* (Wheaton, IL: Crossway, 2006).

31. Readers sometimes infer that this passage means God cannot be moved in prayer. The *Faithlife Study Bible* assures us, however, that this text doesn't imply that God cannot change His mind—as there are many examples in Scripture of Him doing so. Rather, it means that God will not change something He has decreed or promised. His Word, in other words, is totally reliable and dependable. John D. Barry et al., *Faithlife Study Bible* (Bellingham, WA: Logos Bible Software, 2012), notes for Num. 23:19. Other scholars, however, have a different view. See Got Questions Ministries, "Does God Change His Mind?," *Got Questions? Bible Questions Answered* (Bellingham, WA: Logos Bible Software, 2010). For another view see Walter C. Kaiser et al., *Hard Sayings of the Bible* (Downers Grove, IL: InterVarsity, 1996), 108–9. Finally, my friend Frank Turek observes that the Bible is written from an observational perspective. So when we see God relenting from judging Israel after Moses pleads with God (Exodus 32:14), it's not that God is literally changing His mind. From our perspective it appears that way. But since God is all knowing, He always knew Moses would pray and that He wouldn't judge Israel. Similarly, the Bible says that the sun rises and sets. Even though we know that's not literally true, we use the same observational language today.

32. Mark Dever and Graeme Goldsworthy, *The Message of the Old Testament: Promises Made* (Wheaton, IL: Crossway, 2006).

33. John Blanchard, *The Complete Gathered Gold: A Treasury of Quotations for Christians* (Webster, New York; Darlington, England: Evangelical Press, 2006), 43.

34. L. A. Barbieri Jr., "Matthew," in J. F. Walvoord and R. B. Zuck, eds., *The Bible Knowledge Commentary: An Exposition of the Scriptures* (Wheaton, IL: Victor Books, 1985), vol. 2, 30.

35. F. F. Bruce, *The Canon of Scripture* (Downers Grove, IL: InterVarsity Press, 1988), 28.

36. Ravi Zacharias, *Deliver Us From Evil, Restoring the Soul in a Disintegrating Culture* (Nashville, TN: W Publishing Group, A Division of Thomas Nelson Inc., 1997), 47–48.

37. Warren W. Wiersbe, *Wiersbe's Expository Outlines on the Old Testament* (Wheaton, IL: Victor Books, 1993), 11.

CHAPTER 2: OLD TESTAMENT HISTORY: OVERVIEW

1. Cited by J. Sidlow Baxter, *Explore the Book* (Grand Rapids, MI: Zondervan, 1960), vol. 2, 8.

2. D. Martyn Lloyd-Jones, *The Gospel in Genesis: From Fig Leaves to Faith* (P. Leominster) (Wheaton, IL: Day One Publications, 2010), 5.

3. Graeme Goldsworthy, *Preaching the Whole Bible as Christian Scripture: The Application of Biblical Theology to Expository Preaching* (Grand Rapids, MI; Cambridge: William B. Eerdmans Publishing Company, 2000), 27.

4. John D. Barry et al., *Faithlife Study Bible* (Bellingham, WA: Logos Bible Software, 2012).

5. Marsha A. Ellis Smith, June Swann, Trent C. Butler, Christopher L. Church, and David S. Dockery, *Holman Book of Biblical Charts, Maps, and Reconstructions* (Nashville, TN: Broadman & Holman Publishers, 1993), 31–32.

6. Goldsworthy, *Preaching the Whole Bible*, 27.

7. Bruce K. Waltke, with Charles Yu, *An Old Testament Theology: An Exegetical, Canonical, and Thematic Approach* (Grand Rapids, MI: Zondervan, 2007), 133.

8. Alfred Edersheim, *Bible History: Old Testament* (Oak Harbor, WA: Logos Bible Software, 1997; originally published 1876–1877), vol. 4, 2.

9. Ismael E. Amaya, *Journal of the Evangelical Theological Society* (1971): 14, 68.

10. George Eldon Ladd, "The Saving Acts of God," *Christianity Today*, January 30, 1961.

11. Roy R. Matheson, *Old Testament Survey* (Chicago, IL: Moody Bible Institute of Chicago, 1989), xii.

12. Crossway Bibles, *The ESV Study Bible* (Wheaton, IL: Crossway Bibles, 2008), 866.

13. Ibid.

14. P. J. Achtemeier, "Harper & Row and Society of Biblical Literature," in *Harper's Bible Dictionary*, 1st ed. (San Francisco, CA: Harper & Row, 1985), 166.

15. Richard Bauckham, "Reading Scripture as a Coherent Story," in Ellen F. Davis and Richard. B. Hays, eds., *The Art of Reading Scripture* (Grand Rapids, MI; Cambridge, UK: William B. Eerdmans Publishing Company, 2003), 41–42.

16. Ibid., 42.

17. C. I. Scofield, *The Scofield Reference Bible: The Holy Bible Containing the Old and New Testaments* (New York; London; Toronto; Melbourne; Bombay: Oxford University Press, 1917), v.

18. I prepared these summaries by reviewing these biblical books, consulting the introductions of the books in the ESV Bible, *The Holy Bible: English Standard Version* (Wheaton: Standard Bible Society, 2001), and the summaries of the books in other sources, including Mark Dever and Graeme Goldsworthy, *The Message of the Old Testament: Promises Made* (Wheaton, IL: Crossway, 2006); Tremper Longman III and Raymond B. Dillard, *An Introduction to the Old Testament*, 2nd ed. (Grand Rapids, MI: Zondervan, 2007); Kendell Easley, *Holman QuickSource Guide to*

Understanding the Bible (Nashville, TN: Holman Bible Publishers, 2002), and many others.

CHAPTER 3: OLD TESTAMENT HISTORY: CREATION THROUGH THE UNITED KINGDOM

1. Alfred Edersheim, *Bible History: Old Testament* (Oak Harbor, WA: Logos Bible Software, 1997; originally published 1876–1877), vol. 1, x.

2. Paul N. Benware, *Survey of the Old Testament (Revised)* (Chicago, IL: Moody Press, 1993), 18–20.

3. Jason D. DeRouchie, ed., *What the Old Testament Authors Really Cared about: A Survey of Jesus' Bible* (Grand Rapids, MI: Kregel Academic, 2013), 32.

4. Walter A. Elwell and B. J. Beitzel, in *Baker Encyclopedia of the Bible* (Grand Rapids, MI: Baker Book House, 1988), vol. 1, 448.

5. Samuel J. Schultz and Gary V. Smith, *Exploring the Old Testament* (Wheaton, IL: Crossway Books, 2001), 12; H. I. Hester, *The Heart of Hebrew History: A Study of the Old Testament*, rev. ed. (Nashville, TN: Broadman & Holman Publishers, 1962), 67.

6. Wilbur Fields, *Old Testament History: An Overview of Sacred History & Truth* (Joplin, MO: College Press Publishing Company, 1996), 14.

7. Gary Staats, *A Brief Survey through the Hebrew Scriptures: Viewing the Basic Overall Themes and Different High Points of the Books from an Ancient Near-Eastern and Christological Approach*, M. Johnson, ed. (Dr. Gary Staats, 2012), 5–6.

8. Lawrence O. Richards, *The Teacher's Commentary* (Wheaton, IL: Victor Books, 1987), 17. Richards' timeline dates the beginning of the Time of Judges to 1367 BC, creating a twenty-three-year gap between the Conquest of Canaan and the Time of Judges. This seems to be a mistake, since on page 176 he says the Time of Judges began in 1390 BC, which would eliminate the gap. Additionally, though he dates the end of the Babylonian Captivity at 538 BC, I have also included a possible end date of 516 BC, which is cited by many other scholars.

9. Martin Lloyd-Jones, *God the Father, God the Son* (Wheaton, IL: Crossway Books, 1996), 228; G. W. Bromiley, "Atonement," in G. W. Bromiley, ed., *The International Standard Bible Encyclopedia, Revised* (Grand Rapids, MI: Wm. B. Eerdmans, 1979–1988), vol. 1, 353.

10. Richard P. Belcher Jr., *Genesis, The Beginning of God's Plan of Salvation* (Scotland, UK: Christian Focus Publications Ltd., 2012), 51–52.

11. Ibid., 52.

12. Kenneth A. Mathews, *Genesis 1–11:26* (Nashville, TN: Broadman & Holman Publishers, 1996), vol. 1A, 160.

13. Roy E. Gingrich, *Old Testament Survey* (Memphis, TN: Riverside Printing, 2001), 4.

14. G. Campbell Morgan, *The Analyzed Bible: Genesis to Esther* (New York; Chicago; Toronto; London; Edinburgh: Fleming H. Revell Company, 1907), vol. 1, 18.

15. See the treatment of this subject in Richard P. Belcher Jr., *Genesis, The Beginning of God's Plan of Salvation* (Scotland, UK: Christian Focus Publications Ltd., 2012), 112.

16. John Peter Lange, Tayler Lewis, and A. Gosman, *A Commentary on the Holy Scriptures: Genesis* (Bellingham, WA: Logos Bible Software, 2008), 460, 472, 578.

17. Roy R. Matheson, *Old Testament Survey* (Chicago, IL: Moody Bible Institute of Chicago, 1989), 10.

18. G. Campbell Morgan, *Living Messages of the Books of the Bible: Old Testament* (New York: Fleming H. Revell Company, 1908), vol. 1, 32–33.

19. Roy B. Zuck, *A Biblical Theology of the Old Testament*, electronic ed. (Chicago, IL: Moody Press, 1991), 13.

20. R. L. Harris, S. J. Schultz, G. V. Smith, and W. M. Dunnett, *Exploring the Bible: A Guide to the Old and New Testaments* (Wheaton, IL: Crossway, 2002).

21. Ibid.

22. A. T. Shearman and J. Heading, eds., *Day by Day in the Psalms* (West Glamorgan, UK: Precious Seed, 1986), 315.

23. Bruce Wilkinson and Kenneth Boa, *Talk thru the Bible* (Nashville, TN: Thomas Nelson, 1983), 457.

24. Matheson, *Old Testament Survey*, 24.

25. James E. Smith, *The Pentateuch*, 2nd ed. (Joplin, MO: College Press Pub. Co.: 1993); Matheson, *Old Testament Survey*, 22.

26. Tremper Longman III, *Introducing the Old Testament: A Short Guide to Its History and Message* (Grand Rapids, MI: Zondervan, 2012), 32.

27. Charles Dyer, Eugene Merrill, Charles R. Swindoll, and Roy B. Zuck, *Nelson's Old Testament Survey: Discover the Background, Theology and Meaning of Every Book in the Old Testament* (Nashville, TN: Word, 2001), 161.

28. Bill T. Arnold and H. G. M. Williamson, in *Dictionary of the Old Testament: Historical Books* (Downers Grove, IL: InterVarsity Press, 2005), 132; C. G. Libolt, "Canaan," in Geoffrey W. Bromiley, ed., *The International Standard Bible Encyclopedia, Revised* (Grand Rapids, MI: Wm. B. Eerdmans, 1979–1988), vol. 1, 587.

29. John D. Barry et al., *Faithlife Study Bible* (Bellingham, WA: Logos Bible Software, 2012); David Noel et al., eds., in *The Anchor Yale Bible Dictionary* (New York: Doubleday, 1992), vol. 1, 831; Schultz and Smith, *Exploring the Old Testament*, 49. Note that a different source—Gingrich, *Old Testament Survey*, 9—says that Ashtoreth was Baal's wife.

30. William Sanford LaSor, David Allan Hubbard, and Frederic W. Bush, *Old Testament Survey: The Message, Form, and Background of the Old Testament*, 2nd ed. (Grand Rapids, MI: William B. Eerdmans Publishing Company), 152.

31. George Ernest Wright and Floyd V. Filson, eds., *Westminster Historical Atlas of the Bible* (Philadelphia, PA: Westminster Press, 1956), 34.

32. Schultz and Smith, *Exploring the Old Testament*, 49.

33. Eugene H. Merrill, *Kingdom of Priests: A History of Old Testament Israel*, 2nd ed. (Grand Rapids, MI: Baker Academic, 2008), 111.

34. Douglas Redford, *The History of Israel* (Cincinnati, OH: Standard Publishing, 2008), vol. 2, 9.

35. Longman, *Introducing the Old Testament*, 41–42.
36. Hester, *The Heart of Hebrew History*, 155.
37. James E. Smith, *The Books of History* (Joplin, MO: College Press, 1995).
38. Redford, *The History of Israel*, vol. 2, 33–34.
39. Gingrich, *Old Testament Survey*, 30.
40. Hester, *The Heart of Hebrew History*, 155.
41. Redford, *The History of Israel*, vol. 2, 35.
42. Gingrich, *Old Testament Survey*, 32.
43. J. W. Reed, "Ruth," in J. F. Walvoord and R. B. Zuck, eds., *The Bible Knowledge Commentary: An Exposition of the Scriptures* (Wheaton, IL: Victor Books, 1985), vol. 1, 415.
44. Jack W. Hayford et al., eds., *New Spirit-Filled Life Bible* (Nashville, TN: Thomas Nelson Bibles, 2002), 350.
45. LaSor, Hubbard, and Bush, *Old Testament Survey*, 165.
46. Ibid., 168.
47. Wayne A. Grudem, *Systematic Theology: An Introduction to Biblical Doctrine* (Leicester, England; Grand Rapids, MI: Inter-Varsity Press; Zondervan, 2004), 624.
48. J. Knox Chamblin, *Matthew: A Mentor Commentary* (Ross-shire, Great Britain: Mentor, 2010), 130.
49. James E. Smith, *The College Press NIV Commentary, 1 & 2 Samuel* (Joplin, MO: College Press Pub. Co, 2000), 138.
50. Gingrich, *Old Testament Survey*, 32.
51. Schultz and Smith, *Exploring the Old Testament*, 57.
52. Hester, *The Heart of Hebrew History*, 165.
53. Ibid.
54. Eugene H. Merrill, in Walvoord and Zuck, eds., *The Bible Knowledge Commentary*, vol. 1, 430.
55. Harris, Schultz, Smith, and Dunnett, *Exploring the Bible*.
56. Ibid.
57. Robert D. Bergen, *1, 2 Samuel* (Nashville, TN: Broadman & Holman Publishers, 1996), vol. 7, 172.
58. Eugene H. Merrill, "1 Samuel," in Walvoord and Zuck, eds., *The Bible Knowledge Commentary*, vol. 1, 449.
59. Fields, *Old Testament History*, 417.

60. Zuck, *A Biblical Theology of the Old Testament*, 118.

61. Craig A. Blaising and Darrell L. Bock, *Progressive Dispensationalism* (Grand Rapids, MI: Baker Books, 1993), 166.

62. Eugene H. Merrill, "2 Samuel," in Walvoord and Zuck, eds., *The Bible Knowledge Commentary*, vol. 1, 464.

63. R. E. Clements, "The Messianic Hope in the Old Testament," *Journal for the Study of the Old Testament* 43 (1989), 12.

64. Matheson, *Old Testament Survey*, 76.

65. Ibid.

66. Dyer, Merrill, Swindoll, and Zuck, *Nelson's Old Testament Survey*, 241.

67. Ibid., 253.

68. Ryken et al., in *Dictionary of Biblical Imagery*, electronic ed. (Downers Grove, IL: InterVarsity Press, 2000), 849.

69. Matheson, *Old Testament Survey*, 88.

CHAPTER 4: OLD TESTAMENT HISTORY: DIVIDED KINGDOM THROUGH RESTORATION

1. R. L. Drouhard, "Agriculture," in J. D. Barry et al., eds., *The Lexham Bible Dictionary* (Bellingham, WA: Lexham Press, 2012, 2013, 2014).

2. Roy R. Matheson, *Old Testament Survey* (Chicago, IL: Moody Bible Institute of Chicago, 1989), 89.

3. Wilbur Fields, *Old Testament History: An Overview of Sacred History & Truth* (Joplin, MO: College Press Publishing Company, 1996), 503–4.

4. Lawrence O. Richards, *The Teacher's Commentary* (Wheaton, IL: Victor Books, 1987), 278.

5. Ibid., 255.

6. Dale R. Davis, *2 Kings: The Power and the Fury* (Great Britain: Christian Focus Publications, 2005), 32.

7. John G. Butler, *Elisha: The Miracle Prophet* (Clinton, IA: LBC Publications, 1994), vol. 4, 38.

8. Fields, *Old Testament History*, 539.

9.   William Sanford LaSor, David Allan Hubbard, and Frederic W. Bush, *Old Testament Survey: The Message, Form, and Background of the Old Testament*, 2nd ed. (Grand Rapids, MI: William B. Eerdmans Publishing Company), 205.

10. Frank E. Gaebelin et al., *The Expositor's Bible Commentary: 1 & 2 Kings, 1 & 2 Chronicles, Ezra, Nehemiah, Esther, Job* (Grand Rapids, MI: Zondervan Publishing House, 1988), vol. 4, 176.

11. LaSor, Hubbard, and Bush, *Old Testament Survey*, 205.

12. R. L. Harris, S. J. Schultz, G. V. Smith, and W. M. Dunnett, *Exploring the Bible: A Guide to the Old and New Testaments* (Wheaton, IL: Crossway, 2002).

13. James E. Smith, *The Books of History* (Joplin, MO: College Press, 1995).

14. Matheson, *Old Testament Survey*, 93.

15. Fields, *Old Testament History*, 577.

16. Lord Byron, incidentally, describes Sennacherib's defeat in his poem "The Destruction of Sennacherib."

17. John Peter Lange et al., *A Commentary on the Holy Scriptures: Jeremiah* (Bellingham, WA: 2008), 1.

18. Crossway Bibles, *The ESV Study Bible* (Wheaton, IL: Crossway Bibles, 2008), 689.

19. T. L. Constable, "2 Kings," in J. F. Walvoord and R. B. Zuck, eds., *The Bible Knowledge Commentary: An Exposition of the Scriptures* (Wheaton, IL: Victor Books, 1985), vol. 1, 581; Dale R. Davis, *2 Kings: The Power and the Fury* (Great Britain: Christian Focus Publications, 2005), 316; D. Slager, Preface, in P. Clarke, S. Brown, L. Dorn, and D. Slager, eds., *A Handbook on 1 & 2 Kings* (New York: United Bible Societies, 2008), vols. 1–2, 1,264.

20. T. L. Constable, "2 Kings," in Walvoord and Zuck, *The Bible Knowledge Commentary*, vol. 1, 581, and Crossway Bibles, *The ESV Study Bible* (Wheaton, IL: Crossway Bibles, 2008), 689.

21. J. L. Nuelsen Orr, E. Y. Mullins, and M. O. Evans, eds., in *The International Standard Bible Encyclopaedia*, vols. 1–5 (Chicago, IL: The Howard-Severance Company, 1915), 571.

22. T. L. Constable, "2 Kings," in Walvoord and Zuck, *The Bible Knowledge Commentary*, vols. 1, 585.

23. J. Sidlow Baxter, *Explore the Book* (Grand Rapids, MI; Zondervan Publishing House, 1960), vol. 2, 117.

24. Roy E. Gingrich, *Old Testament Survey* (Memphis, TN: Riverside Printing, 2001), 4.

25. James E. Smith, *Bible History Made Simple* (Joplin, MO: College Press Publishing Company, 2009), 103.

26. James Luther Mays, ed., *Harper's Bible Commentary* (San Francisco, CA: Harper & Row, 1988), 607.

27. Alfred Edersheim, *Bible History: Old Testament* (Oak Harbor, WA: Logos Bible Software, 1997; originally published 1876–1877), vol. 7, 211.

28. D. F. Morgan, "Captivity," in G. W. Bromiley, ed., *The International Standard Bible Encyclopedia, Revised* (Grand Rapids, MI: Wm. B. Eerdmans, 1979–1988), vol. 1, 614.

29. Richards, *The Teacher's Commentary*, 292.

30. Ibid., 293.

31. Ibid.

32. C. H. Dyer, "Ezekiel," in Walvoord and Zuck, *The Bible Knowledge Commentary*, vol. 1, 1,224.

33. H. I. Hester, *The Heart of Hebrew History: A Study of the Old Testament*, rev. ed. (Nashville, TN: Broadman & Holman Publishers, 1962), 252.

34. Lamar Eugene Cooper Sr., *Ezekiel*, vol. 17, in *The New American Commentary* (Nashville, TN: Broadman & Holman Publishers, 1994), 75.

35. P. A. Beaulieu, "History of Israel 6: Babylonian Period," in B. T. Arnold and H. G. M. Williamson, eds., *Dictionary of the Old Testament: Historical Books* (Downers Grove, IL: InterVarsity Press, 2005).

36. Walter A. Elwell and B. J. Beitzel, in *Baker Encyclopedia of the Bible* (Grand Rapids, MI: Baker Book House, 1988), vol. 1, 734.

37. Francis Ernest Gigot, *Outlines of Jewish History* (New York; Cincinnati; Chicago: Benziger Brothers, 1918), 306.

38. Elwell and Beitzel, in *Baker Encyclopedia of the Bible*, vol. 1, 734.

39. Dr. Foakes-Jackson, *Biblical History of the Hebrews*, 316, in J. L. Nuelsen Orr, E. Y. Mullins, and M. O. Evans, eds., *The Interna-*

tional Standard Bible Encyclopedia, vols. 1–5 (Chicago, IL: The Howard-Severance Company, 1915), 574.

40. T. Nicol, in Orr, Mullins, and Evans, *The International Standard Bible Encyclopedia*, 574.

41. Gingrich, *Old Testament Survey*, 47; Gigot, *Outlines of Jewish History*, 308; Paul N. Benware, *Survey of the Old Testament (Revised)* (Chicago, IL: Moody Press, 1993), 135; *The Open Bible: New King James Version*, electronic ed. (Nashville, TN: Thomas Nelson Publishers, 1998).

42. *The Open Bible: New King James Version*, electronic ed. (Nashville, TN: Thomas Nelson Publishers, 1998).

43. Richards, *The Teacher's Commentary*, 291.

44. Paul N. Benware, *Survey of the Old Testament (Revised)* (Chicago, IL: Moody Press, 1993), 136.

45. John F. Walvoord, *The Prophecy Knowledge Handbook* (Wheaton, IL: Victor Books, 1990), 147.

46. F. B. Huey Jr., *Jeremiah, Lamentations* (Nashville, TN: Broadman & Holman Publishers, 1993), vol. 16, 370.

47. Bruce K. Waltke, *An Old Testament Theology: An Exegetical, Canonical, and Thematic Approach* (Grand Rapids, MI: Zondervan, 2007), 775.

48. Matheson, *Old Testament Survey*, 105.

49. Roy E. Gingrich, *Old Testament Survey* (Memphis, TN: Riverside Printing, 2001), 47; Francis Ernest Gigot, *Outlines of Jewish History* (New York; Cincinnati; Chicago: Benziger Brothers, 1918), 48.

50. Matheson, *Old Testament Survey*, 106.

51. G. A. Getz, "Nehemiah," in Walvoord and Zuck, *The Bible Knowledge Commentary*, vol. 1, 673.

CHAPTER 5: ALL ROADS LEAD TO CHRIST: BIBLICAL COVENANTS, PART 1

1. W. Graham Scroggie, *The Unfolding Drama of Redemption* (Grand Rapids, MI: Kregel Publications, 1976), vol. 1, 30.

2. Graham Scroggie quoted in Warren W. Wiersbe, *Wiersbe's Expository Outlines on the Old Testament* (Wheaton, IL: Victor Books, 1993), 12.

3. Roy E. Gingrich, *Old Testament Survey* (Memphis, TN: Riverside Printing, 2001), 4.

4. Norman L. Geisler, *To Understand the Bible Look for Jesus: The Bible Student's Guide to the Bible's Central Theme* (Eugene, OR: Wipf and Stock Publishers, 1979), 89.

5. Ray Comfort, *The Evidence Bible: Irrefutable Evidence for the Thinking Mind* (Gainesville, FL: Bridge-Logos, 2003), 142.

6. Geisler, *To Understand the Bible Look for Jesus*, 89.

7. James E. Smith, *Bible History Made Simple* (Joplin, MO: College Press Publishing Company, 2009), 10.

8. Ibid.

9. Crossway Bibles, *The ESV Study Bible* (Wheaton, IL: Crossway Bibles, 2008), 23.

10. Geisler, *To Understand the Bible Look for Jesus*, 7.

11. Scroggie, *The Unfolding Drama of Redemption*, 31.

12. Walter C. Kaiser, *The Promise-Plan of God: A Biblical Theology of the Old and New Testaments* (Grand Rapids, MI: Zondervan, 2008), 19.

13. Walter C. Kaiser, *The Messiah in the Old Testament* (Grand Rapids: MI: Zondervan Publishing House, 1995), 29.

14. Kaiser, *The Promise-Plan of God*, 19.

15. Kaiser, *The Messiah in the Old Testament*, 136.

16. Kaiser, *The Promise-Plan of God*, 19.

17. Ibid., 18.

18. Kaiser, *The Messiah in the Old Testament*, 137.

19. Ibid.

20. Larry Richards, *Every Promise in the Bible* (Nashville, TN: T. Nelson Publishers, 1998), 5.

21. O. Palmer Robertson, *The Christ of the Covenants* (Phillipsburg, NJ: Presbyterian and Reformed Publishing Co., 1980), 17.

22. Crossway Bibles, *The ESV Study Bible* (Wheaton, IL: Crossway Bibles, 2008), 24.

23. Wayne A. Grudem, *Systematic Theology: An Introduction to Biblical Doctrine* (Leicester, England; Grand Rapids, MI: InterVarsity Press; Zondervan, 2004), 515.

24. Ibid.

25. Simon J. Kistemaker and W. Hendriksen, *Exposition of the Second Epistle to the Corinthians*, (Grand Rapids, MI: Baker Book House, 1953–2001), vol. 19, 231.

26. Douglas Stuart, *Exodus* (Nashville, TN: Broadman & Holman Publishers, 2006), vol. 2, 171–72.

27. Paul S. Karleen, *The Handbook to Bible Study: With a Guide to the Scofield Study System* (New York: Oxford University Press, 1987), 318, 35.

28. Jason D. DeRouchie, ed., *What the Old Testament Authors Really Cared about: A Survey of Jesus' Bible* (Grand Rapids, MI: Kregel Academic, 2013), 32.

29. Crossway Bibles, *The ESV Study Bible* (Wheaton, IL: Crossway Bibles, 2008), 24.

30. Hans K. LaRondelle and Jon Paulie, *The Bible Jesus Interpreted* (Loma Linda, CA: Jon Paulien, 2014), 82.

31. Ibid., 83.

32. Arnold G. Fruchtenbaum, *Israelology: The Missing Link in Systematic Theology*, rev. ed. (Tustin, CA: Ariel Ministries, 1994), 345.

33. Grudem, *Systematic Theology*, 522.

34. Arnold G. Fruchtenbaum, *The Messianic Bible Study Collection* (Tustin, CA: Ariel Ministries, 1983), vol. 1, 5.

35. Lewis Sperry Chafer, in *Systematic Theology* (Grand Rapids, MI: Kregel Publications, 1993), vol. 7, 112; some scholars, however, argue that God was referring only to spiritual death, not physical death, as Adam's death is gradual, not immediate. See, e.g., Grudem, *Systematic Theology*, 516.

36. Got Questions Ministries, *Got Questions? Bible Questions Answered* (Bellingham, WA: Logos Bible Software, 2010).

37. Sung Wook Chung, "Toward the Reformed and Covenantal Theology of Premillennialism: A Proposal," in C. L. Blomberg, ed., *A Case for Historic Premillennialism: An Alternative to "Left*

Behind" Eschatology (Grand Rapids, MI: Baker Academic, 2009), 141–42.

38. Robertson, *The Christ of the Covenants*, 93.
39. Dwight J. Pentecost, *Thy Kingdom Come: Tracing God's Kingdom Program and Covenant Promises throughout History* (Grand Rapids, MI: Kregel Publications, 1995), 45.
40. C. I. Scofield, *What Do the Prophets Say?* (Philadelphia, PA: The Sunday School Times Company, 1918), 29.
41. C. I. Scofield, *The Scofield Reference Bible: The Holy Bible Containing the Old and New Testaments* (New York; London; Toronto; Melbourne; Bombay: Oxford University Press, 1917), 16; Scofield, *What Do the Prophets Say?*, 29.
42. J. Gordon McConville, and Stephen N. Williams, *Joshua* (Grand Rapids, MI; Cambridge, UK: William B. Eerdmans Publishing Company, 2010), 143.
43. Gerard Van Groningen, *Messianic Revelation in the Old Testament* (Grand Rapids, MI: Baker Book House, 1990), 127.
44. Ibid., 129.
45. Scofield, *The Scofield Reference Bible*, 1,298.
46. Van Groningen, *Messianic Revelation in the Old Testament*, 129.
47. Mark Dever and Graeme Goldsworthy, *The Message of the Old Testament: Promises Made* (Wheaton, IL: Crossway, 2006).
48. Van Groningen, *Messianic Revelation in the Old Testament*, 141.
49. Craig A. Blaising and Darrell L. Bock, *Progressive Dispensationalism* (Grand Rapids, MI: Baker Books, 1993), 189.
50. William MacDonald, *Believer's Bible Commentary: Old and New Testaments*, A. Farstad, ed. (Nashville, TN: Thomas Nelson, 1995), 41.
51. John F. Walvoord, "Millennial Series," *Bibliotheca Sacra* (1951–1952): 109, 38–40.
52. Fruchtenbaum, *The Messianic Bible Study Collection*, vol. 21, 16.
53. William Sanford LaSor, David Allan Hubbard, and Frederic W. Bush, *Old Testament Survey: The Message, Form, and Background of the Old Testament*, 2nd ed. (Grand Rapids, MI: William B. Eerdmans Publishing Company), 47.
54. Blaising and Bock, *Progressive Dispensationalism*, 141–43.

55. Ibid., 141–42.

56. Roy B. Zuck et al., *A Biblical Theology of the Old Testament*, electronic ed. (Chicago, IL: Moody Press, 1991), 32.

57. Michael Lawrence, *Biblical Theology in the Life of the Church: A Guide for Ministry* (Wheaton, IL: Crossway, 2010), 60.

58. Zuck et al., *A Biblical Theology of the Old Testament*, 33.

59. The text of the covenant is set out in Exodus 20:1–23:33. But the curses and blessings set forth in Leviticus 26 and later in Deuteronomy 28:1–68 are also part of the covenant. See Zuck et al., *A Biblical Theology of the Old Testament*, 35.

60. Zuck et al., *A Biblical Theology of the Old Testament*, 12–13.

61. Paul P. Enns, *The Moody Handbook of Theology* (Chicago, IL: Moody Press, 1989), 57; Charles Fred Lincoln, The Biblical Covenants, Part 2, *Bibliotheca Sacra*, 1943, 100:448.

62. J. Vernon McGee, *Through the Bible with J. Vernon McGee*, electronic ed. (Nashville, TN: Thomas Nelson, 1997), vol. 1, 406.

63. Fruchtenbaum, *The Messianic Bible Study Collection*, vol. 21, 18.

64. Vern S. Poythress, *The Shadow of Christ in the Law of Moses* (Phillipsburg, NJ: P & R Publishing, 1991), 43.

65. David M. Howard, "The Historical Books," in John D. Barry et al., *Faithlife Study Bible* (Bellingham, WA: Logos Bible Software, 2012).

66. Paul R. Williamson, *Sealed with an Oath* (Downers Grove, IL: InterVarsity Press, 2007), 94.

67. Blaising and Bock, *Progressive Dispensationalism*, 151.

68. Charles Spurgeon, "What Is the Purpose of the Law?," in Ray Comfort, *The Evidence Bible: Irrefutable Evidence for the Thinking Mind*, K. Cameron, ed. (Orlando, FL: Bridge-Logos, 2003), 1,528.

69. Charles Spurgeon, "The Function of the Law?," in Comfort, *The Evidence Bible*, 1528.

70. Ralph H. Alexander, *Ezekiel* (Chicago, IL: Moody Press, 1976), 60.

71. Jason D. DeRouchie, ed., *What the Old Testament Authors Really Cared about: A Survey of Jesus' Bible* (Grand Rapids, MI: Kregel Academic, 2013), 33; Scofield, *The Scofield Reference Bible*, 1,298.

72. Norman Geisler, *Systematic Theology, Volume Four: Church, Last Things* (Minneapolis, MN: Bethany House Publishers, 2005), 516–17.

73. Ibid., 517.

74. Walter C. Kaiser in Stanley N. Gundry, ed., *Five Views on Law and Gospel* (Grand Rapids, MI: Zondervan, 1999), 177.

CHAPTER 6: ALL ROADS LEAD TO CHRIST: BIBLICAL COVENANTS, PART 2

1. Larry D. Pettegrew, "The New Covenant," *Master's Seminary Journal* (Fall 1999): 10, no. 2, 250.

2. C. I. Scofield, *The Scofield Reference Bible: The Holy Bible Containing the Old and New Testaments* (New York; London; Toronto; Melbourne; Bombay: Oxford University Press, 1917), 1,298.

3. Ibid., 250.

4. Walter C. Kaiser, *The Promise-Plan of God: A Biblical Theology of the Old and New Testaments* (Grand Rapids, MI: Zondervan, 2008), 93.

5. Eugene H. Merrill, *Deuteronomy* (Nashville, TN: Broadman & Holman Publishers, 1994), vol. 4, 354.

6. William MacDonald, *Believer's Bible Commentary: Old and New Testaments*, A. Farstad, ed. (Nashville, TN: Thomas Nelson, 1995), 42.

7. Dwight J. Pentecost, *Things to Come: A Study in Biblical Eschatology* (Grand Rapids, MI: Dunham Publishing Company, 1958), 97.

8. Arnold G. Fruchtenbaum, *Israelology: The Missing Link in Systematic Theology*, rev. ed. (Tustin, CA: Ariel Ministries, 1994), 50.

9. Paul P. Enns, *The Moody Handbook of Theology* (Chicago, IL: Moody Press, 1989), 59.

10. Josh McDowell and Don Stewart, *Answers to Tough Questions* (Nashville, TN: Thomas Nelson Publishers, 1993).

11. Tony Evans, "Prophecy, God's Eternal Drama, 'The Key to Prophecy,'" TonyEvans.org, 8.

12. S. Hahn, "Covenant," in J. D. Barry et al., eds., *The Lexham Bible Dictionary* (Bellingham, WA: Lexham Press, 2012, 2013, 2014).

13. C. I. Scofield, *What Do the Prophets Say?* (Philadelphia, PA: The Sunday School Times Company, 1918), 59.

14. Crossway Bibles, *The ESV Study Bible* (Wheaton, IL: Crossway Bibles, 2008), 700.

15. Charles C. Ryrie, *Ryrie Study Bible: New International Version*, expanded ed. (Chicago, IL: Moody Publishers, 1994), 462.

16. MacDonald, *Believer's Bible Commentary*, 761.

17. Crossway Bibles, *The ESV Study Bible* (Wheaton, IL: Crossway Bibles, 2008), 554.

18. Gordon H. Johnston, "Messianic Trajectories in God's Covenant Promise to David," in *Jesus the Messiah: Tracing the Promises, Expectations, and Coming of Israel's King* (Grand Rapids, MI: Kregel Academic, 2012), 68.

19. David Murray, *Jesus on Every Page: 10 Simple Ways to Seek and Find Christ in the Old Testament* (Nashville, TN: Thomas Nelson, 2013).

20. John D. Barry et al., *Faithlife Study Bible* (Bellingham, WA: Logos Bible Software, 2012).

21. Hahn, "Covenant," in Barry et al., eds., *The Lexham Bible Dictionary*.

22. Craig A. Evans and Peter W. Flint, eds., *Eschatology, Messianism, and the Dead Sea Scrolls* (Grand Rapids, MI: William B. Eerdmans Publishing Company, 1997), 1–2.

23. G. Lanier, "Davidic Covenant," in John D. Barry et al., eds., *The Lexham Bible Dictionary* (Bellingham, WA: Lexham Press, 2012, 2013, 2014).

24. J. Daniel Hays et al., in *Dictionary of Biblical Prophecy and End Times* (Grand Rapids, MI: Zondervan Publishing House, 2007), 109.

25. William David Reyburn and Euan McGregor Fry, *A Handbook on Genesis* (New York: United Bible Societies, 1998), 1,083.

26. Gordon H. Johnston, "Messianic Trajectories in Genesis and Numbers," in *Jesus the Messiah: Tracing the Promises, Expectations,*

and Coming of Israel's King (Grand Rapids, MI: Kregel Academic, 2012), 40–41.

27. Allen C. Myers, in *The Eerdmans Bible Dictionary* (Grand Rapids, MI: Eerdmans, 1987), 121.

28. D. Stuart Briscoe and L. J. Ogilvie, *Genesis* (Nashville, TN: Thomas Nelson Inc., 1987), vol. 1, 385.

29. Eugene H. Merrill, "Numbers," in J. F. Walvoord and R. B. Zuck, eds., *The Bible Knowledge Commentary: An Exposition of the Scriptures* (Wheaton, IL: Victor Books, 1985), vol. 1, 244.

30. MacDonald, *Believer's Bible Commentary*, 42.

31. Carl F. H. Henry, *God, Revelation, and Authority* (Wheaton, IL: Crossway Books, 1999), vol. 3, 257–58.

32. T. H. Home, *Introduction to the Critical Study and Knowledge of the Holy Scriptures* (New York: R. Carter and Brothers, 1858), 1:37.

33. R. Schultz, "Hearing the Major Prophets: 'Your Ears Are Open, but You Hear Nothing' (Isa. 42:20)," in C. G. Bartholomew and D. J. H. Beldman, eds., *Hearing the Old Testament: Listening for God's Address* (Grand Rapids, MI; Cambridge, UK: William B. Eerdmans Publishing Company, 2012), 340; Kaiser, *The Promise-Plan of God*, 200.

34. Bruce A. Baker, "Israel and the Church: The Transcendental Distinction within the Dispensational Tradition," *Baptist Bible College Journal of Ministry and Theology* (2004): 8, no. 2, 56; *The Open Bible: New King James Version*, electronic ed. (Nashville, TN: Thomas Nelson Publishers, 1998).

35. MacDonald, *Believer's Bible Commentary: Old and New Testaments*, 43.

36. Renald E. Showers, *There Really Is a Difference!: A Comparison of Covenant and Dispensational Theology* (Bellmawr, NJ: The Friends of Israel Gospel Ministry, Inc., 1990).

37. Norman Geisler, *Systematic Theology, Volume Four: Church, Last Things* (Minneapolis, MN: Bethany House Publishers, 2005), 519.

38. Roy B. Zuck, *A Biblical Theology of the Old Testament*, electronic ed. (Chicago, IL: Moody Press, 1991), 355.

39. Wayne A. Grudem, *Systematic Theology: An Introduction to Biblical Doctrine* (Leicester, England; Grand Rapids, MI: InterVarsity Press; Zondervan, 2004), 522.

40. J. I. Packer, *Concise Theology: A Guide to Historic Christian Beliefs* (Wheaton, IL: Tyndale House, 1993).

41. Charles H. Spurgeon, *Christ in the Old Testament: Sermons on the Foreshadowing of Our Lord in Old Testament History, Ceremony, and Prophecy*, electronic ed. (Chattanooga, TN: AMG Publishers, 1997), 370.

42. Kaiser, *The Promise-Plan of God*, 201.

43. Walter C. Kaiser, in Stanley N. Gundry, ed., *Five Views on Law and Gospel* (Grand Rapids, MI: Zondervan, 1999), 178.

44. Wayne Strickland, quoted in Stanley N. Gundry, ed., *Five Views on Law and Gospel* (Grand Rapids, MI: Zondervan, 1999), 295.

45. Robert H. Mounce, *Romans* (Nashville, TN: Broadman & Holman Publishers, 1995), vol. 27, 165.

46. Kaiser, *The Promise-Plan of God*, 201.

47. Rev. H. D. Spence, ed., *Galatians* (London; New York: Funk & Wagnalls Company, 1909), 166.

48. O. Palmer Robertson, *The Christ of the Covenants* (Phillipsburg, NJ: Presbyterian and Reformed Publishing Co., 1980), 272.

49. Hahn, "Covenant," in Barry et al., eds., *The Lexham Bible Dictionary.*

50. Craig A. Blaising and Darrell L. Bock, *Progressive Dispensationalism* (Grand Rapids, MI: Baker Books, 1993), 175.

51. Hahn, "Covenant," in Barry et al., eds., *The Lexham Bible Dictionary.*

52. *The Open Bible: New King James Version*, electronic ed. (Nashville, TN: Thomas Nelson Publishers, 1998).

53. Kaiser, *The Promise-Plan of God*, 393.

54. Arnold G. Fruchtenbaum, *Israelology: The Missing Link in Systematic Theology*, rev. ed. (Tustin, CA: Ariel Ministries, 1994), 354.

55. Showers, *There Really Is a Difference!*

56. Geisler, *Systematic Theology, Volume Four*, 500.

57. Showers, *There Really Is a Difference!*

58. Ibid.
59. Ibid.
60. Blaising and Bock, *Progressive Dispensationalism*, 200.
61. Showers, *There Really Is a Difference!*
62. Ibid.
63. Blaising and Bock, *Progressive Dispensationalism*, 200; Showers, *There Really Is a Difference!*
64. Geisler, *Systematic Theology, Volume Four*, 524.
65. Showers, *There Really Is a Difference!*
66. Robertson, *The Christ of the Covenants*, 272–73.
67. Ibid., 51–52.

CHAPTER 7: ALL ROADS LEAD TO CHRIST: PORTRAITS, OFFICES, CREATION, AND SALVATION

1. Iain M. Duguid and Matthew P. Harmon, *Living in the Light of Inextinguishable Hope: The Gospel According to Joseph*, I. M. Duguid, ed. (Phillipsburg, NJ: P&R Publishing, 2013), x.
2. Michael P. Barrett, *Beginning at Moses: A Guide to Finding Christ in the Old Testament* (Greenville, SC; Belfast, Northern Ireland: Ambassador-Emerald International, 2001), 13.
3. Ibid.
4. Kurt Strassner, *Hints and Signs of the Coming King: Pictures of Jesus in the Old Testament*, 1st ed. (Leominster: Day One, 2010), 8.
5. J. Sidlow Baxter, *The Master Theme of the Bible* (Wheaton, IL: Tyndale House Publishers, 1973).
6. David Limbaugh, *Jesus on Trial: A Lawyer Affirms the Truth of the Gospel* (Washington, D.C.: Regnery, 2014), 334.
7. R. C. Sproul, *Can I Trust the Bible?* (Lake Mary, FL: Reformation Trust Publishing, 2009), vol. 2, 16.
8. Sidney Greidanus, *Preaching Christ from Ecclesiastes: Foundations for Expository Sermons* (Grand Rapids, MI; Cambridge, UK: William B. Eerdmans Publishing Company, 2010), 25.
9. Baxter, *The Master Theme of the Bible*, 20.

10. Ibid.

11. Duguid and Harmon, *Living in the Light of Inextinguishable Hope*, 8.

12. W. Standord Reid, in G. W. Bromiley, ed., *The International Standard Bible Encyclopedia, Revised* (Grand Rapids, MI: Wm. B. Eerdmans, 1979–1988), vol. 1, 653.

13. Ibid.

14. Wayne A. Grudem, *Systematic Theology: An Introduction to Biblical Doctrine* (Leicester, England; Grand Rapids, MI: Inter-Varsity Press; Zondervan, 2004), 624.

15. J. A. Groves, Foreword, in Tremper Longman III and J. A. Groves, eds., *Immanuel in Our Place: Seeing Christ in Israel's Worship* (Phillipsburg, NJ: P&R Publishing, 2001), 119.

16. W. Graham Scroggie, *The Unfolding Drama of Redemption* (Grand Rapids, MI: Kregel Publications, 1976), vol. 1, 30.

17. Walter A. Elwell, in *Evangelical Dictionary of Biblical Theology*, electronic ed. (Grand Rapids, MI: Baker Book House, 1996).

18. Richard D. Phillips, *Hebrews*, R. D. Phillips, P. G. Ryken, and D. M. Doriani, eds. (Phillipsburg, NJ: P&R Publishing, 2006), 17.

19. Charles C. Ryrie, *Basic Theology: A Popular Systematic Guide to Understanding Biblical Truth* (Chicago, IL: Moody Press, 1999), 292.

20. Eusebius of Caesaria, "The Church History of Eusebius," in P. Schaff and H. Wace, eds., A. C. McGiffert, trans., *Eusebius: Church History, Life of Constantine the Great, and Oration in Praise of Constantine* (New York: Christian Literature Company, 1890), vol. 1, 86.

21. W. Standord Reid, in G. W. Bromiley, ed., *The International Standard Bible Encyclopedia, Revised* (Grand Rapids, MI: Wm. B. Eerdmans, 1979–1988), vol. 1, 653.

22. Jack S. Deere, "Deuteronomy," in J. F. Walvoord and R. B. Zuck, eds., *The Bible Knowledge Commentary: An Exposition of the Scriptures* (Wheaton, IL: Victor Books, 1985), vol. 1, 323.

23. Bruce Demarest, *The Cross and Salvation: The Doctrine of Salvation* (Wheaton, IL: Crossway Books, 1997), 183.

24. Crossway Bibles, *The ESV Study Bible* (Wheaton, IL: Crossway Bibles, 2008), 2,522.

25. See the helpful chart on the Biblical Descriptions of Atonement in Crossway Bibles, *The ESV Study Bible* (Wheaton, IL: Crossway Bibles, 2008), 2,523.

26. Carl F. H. Henry, *God, Revelation, and Authority* (Wheaton, IL: Crossway Books, 1999), vol. 3, 59.

27. Charles W. Carter, "The Epistle to the Hebrews," in *Hebrews-Revelation* (Grand Rapids, MI: William B. Eerdmans Publishing Company, 1966), vol. 6, 16.

28. Thomas C. Oden, *The Living God: Systematic Theology, Vol. I.* (San Francisco, CA: HarperSanFrancisco, 1992), 248.

29. Ibid.

30. Thomas Aquinas, *Summa Theologica*, Fathers of the English Dominican Province, Trans. (Bellingham, WA: Logos Bible Software, 2009), STh., I q.45 a.6 ad 2.

31. Oden, *The Living God: Systematic Theology, Vol. I.*, 247.

32. David J. MacLeod, "The Creation of the Universe by the Word: John: 1:3–5," *Bibliotheca Sacra*, 2003, vol. 160, n. 638, 189.

33. John M. Dillon, "Providence," in D. N. Freedman, ed., *The Anchor Yale Bible Dictionary* (New York: Doubleday, 1992), vol. 5, 520.

34. John F. Walvoord, *Jesus Christ Our Lord* (Chicago, IL: Moody Bible Institute of Chicago, 1975, 2008), 49.

35. Ibid.

36. Donald Williams and L. J. Ogilvie, *Psalms 1–72* (Nashville, TN: Thomas Nelson Inc, 1986), vol. 13, 523.

37. "The doctrine of salvation (is) the branch of systematic theology that deals with the work of Christ the redeemer, and its application to the elect by the Holy Spirit"—also known as "soteriology." Alan Cairns, in *Dictionary of Theological Terms* (Belfast; Greenville, SC: Ambassador Emerald International, 2002), 425; see also Samuel Macauley Jackson, ed., in *The New Schaff-Herzog Encyclopedia of Religious Knowledge: Embracing Biblical, Historical, Doctrinal, and Practical Theology and Biblical, Theological, and Ecclesiastical Biography from the Earliest Times to the Present*

Day, vols. 1–12 (New York; London: Funk & Wagnalls, 1908–1914), vol. 3, 49.

38. John F. Walvoord, *Jesus Christ Our Lord* (Chicago, IL: Moody Bible Institute of Chicago, 1975, 2008), 56.
39. Ibid., 57.
40. Ibid.
41. Ibid., 59.
42. Leon Morris, "Hebrews," in F. E. Gaebelein, ed., *The Expositor's Bible Commentary: Hebrews through Revelation* (Grand Rapids, MI: Zondervan, 1981), vol. 12, 126.
43. Walvoord, *Jesus Christ Our Lord*, 61.
44. David K. Lowery, "1 Corinthians," in Walvoord and Zuck, *The Bible Knowledge Commentary*, vol. 2, 526.
45. Simon J. Kistemaker and William Hendriksen, *Exposition of the First Epistle to the Corinthians* (Grand Rapids, MI: Baker Book House, 1953–2001), vol. 18, 325.

CHAPTER 8: ALL ROADS LEAD TO CHRIST: TITLES, CHRISTOPHANIES, TYPOLOGY, PROPHECY, AND ANALOGY

1. Iain M. Duguid and Matthew P. Harmon, *Living in the Light of Inextinguishable Hope: The Gospel According to Joseph*, I. M. Duguid, ed. (Phillipsburg, NJ: P&R Publishing, 2013), x.
2. John F. Walvoord, *Jesus Christ Our Lord* (Chicago, IL: Moody Bible Institute of Chicago, 1975, 2008), 36.
3. Ibid., 37.
4. Ibid., 38.
5. Loraine Boettner, *Studies in Theology* (Grand Rapids, MI: Presbyterian and Reformed Publishing Company, 1947), 151.
6. Allen C. Myers, in *The Eerdmans Bible Dictionary* (Grand Rapids, MI: Eerdmans, 1987), 997.
7. James Oliver Buswell Jr., *A Systematic Theology of the Christian Religion*, 2 vols. (Grand Rapids, MI: Zondervan, 1962), 1:33.
8. James A. Borland, *Christ in the Old Testament* (Fearn, UK: Christian Focus Publications, 1999), 19.

9. Ibid.

10. Buswell, *A Systematic Theology of the Christian Religion*, 2 vols., 1:33.

11. F. L. Cross and E. A. Livingstone, eds., in *The Oxford Dictionary of the Christian Church*, 3rd ed. rev. (Oxford; New York: Oxford University Press, 2005), 1,617.

12. Michael P. Barrett, *Beginning at Moses: A Guide to Finding Christ in the Old Testament* (Greenville, SC; Belfast, Northern Ireland: Ambassador-Emerald International, 2001), 146.

13. Ibid., 154.

14. Walvoord, *Jesus Christ Our Lord*, 51–52.

15. Barrett, *Beginning at Moses*, 148.

16. Walvoord, *Jesus Christ Our Lord*, 54.

17. Barrett, *Beginning at Moses*, 160.

18. Mark G. Cambron, *Bible Doctrines: Beliefs That Matter* (Grand Rapids, MI: Zondervan, 1954), 25; Borland, *Christ in the Old Testament*, 58.

19. William George Heidt, *Angelology of the Old Testament; A Study in Biblical Theology* (Washington, D.C.: Catholic U., 1949), 97.

20. Borland, *Christ in the Old Testament*, 60–61.

21. Ibid., 61–62.

22. Barrett, *Beginning at Moses*, 153.

23. Borland, *Christ in the Old Testament*, 62–63; see also James R. Battenfield, "An Exegetical Study of the מלאך יהוה in the Old Testament," January 1971, 44–45.

24. Barrett, *Beginning at Moses*, 148.

25. Friedbert Ninow, "Typology," in D. N. Freedman, A. C. Myers, and A. B. Beck, eds., *Eerdmans Dictionary of the Bible* (Grand Rapids, MI: W.B. Eerdmans, 2000), 1,341.

26. Gareth Lee Cockerill, *The Epistle to the Hebrews* (Grand Rapids, MI; Cambridge, UK: William B. Eerdmans Publishing Company, 2012), 53–54.

27. Norman L. Geisler, *To Understand the Bible Look for Jesus: The Bible Student's Guide to the Bible's Central Theme* (Eugene, OR: Wipf and Stock Publishers, 1979), 58.

28. C. A. Myers, in *The Eerdmans Bible dictionary* (Grand Rapids, MI: Eerdmans, 1987), 24.

29. G. R. Osborne, "Type; Typology," in G. W. Bromiley, ed., *The International Standard Bible Encyclopedia, Revised* (Grand Rapids, MI: Wm. B. Eerdmans, 1979–1988), vol. 4, 930.

30. Chad L. Bird, in Robert D. Ibach, ed., "Typological Interpretation within the Old Testament: Melchizedekian Typology," (Dallas Theological Seminary, Bibliotheca Sacra, January 2000), vol. 157, 361.

31. Walvoord, *Jesus Christ Our Lord*, 63.

32. Walter A. Elwell and B. J. Beitzel, in *Baker Encyclopedia of the Bible* (Grand Rapids, MI: Baker Book House, 1988), vol. 2, 2,109.

33. Al Wolters, "The History of Old Testament Interpretation: An Anecdotal Survey," in C. G. Bartholomew and D. J. H. Beldman, eds., *Hearing the Old Testament: Listening for God's Address* (Grand Rapids, MI; Cambridge, UK: William B. Eerdmans Publishing Company, 2012), 24.

34. Walter A. Elwell and B. J. Beitzel, in *Baker Encyclopedia of the Bible*, vol. 2, 2,110.

35. J. D. Atkins, "Use of the Old Testament in the New Testament, Critical Issues," in J. D. Barry et al., eds., *The Lexham Bible Dictionary* (Bellingham, WA: Lexham Press, 2012, 2013, 2014).

36. Barrett, *Beginning at Moses*, 245–46.

37. Patrick Fairbairn, *The Typology of Scripture* (New York: Funk & Wagnalls Co., 1900), I, 1.

38. Barrett, *Beginning at Moses*, 246.

39. W. Randolph Tate, in *Handbook for Biblical Interpretation: An Essential Guide to Methods, Terms, and Concepts*, 2nd ed. (Grand Rapids, MI: Baker Academic, 2012), 255.

40. Fred John Meldau, *The Prophets Still Speak: Messiah in Both Testaments* (Bellmawr, NJ: Friends of Israel Gospel Ministry, 1988), 1.

41. Sidney Greidanus, *Preaching Christ from Genesis: Foundations for Expository Sermons* (Grand Rapids, MI; Cambridge, UK: William B. Eerdmans Publishing Company, 2007), 5, 6.

42. Ibid., 6.

CHAPTER 9: CHRIST IN EVERY BOOK: GENESIS

1. Iain M. Duguid, *Living in the Gap between Promise and Reality: The Gospel According to Abraham*, T. Longman III and J. A. Groves, eds. (Phillipsburg, NJ: P&R Publishing, 1999), 2.

2. M. R. DeHaan, *Portraits of Christ in Genesis* (Grand Rapids, MI: Kregel Publications, 1995), 14.

3. Norman L. Geisler, *Baker Encyclopedia of Christian Apologetics* (Grand Rapids, MI: Baker Books, 1999), 99.

4. DeHaan, *Portraits of Christ in Genesis*, 19.

5. Graeme Goldsworthy, *Christ-Centered Biblical Theology, Hermeneutical Foundations and Principles* (Downers Grove, IL: IVP Academic, An imprint of InterVarsity Press, 2012), Kindle locations 147–75.

6. Eugene E. Carpenter, *Exodus*, H. W. House and W. D. Barrick, eds. (Bellingham, WA: Lexham Press, 2012).

7. J. A. Witmer, "Romans," in J. F. Walvoord and R. B. Zuck, eds., *The Bible Knowledge Commentary: An Exposition of the Scriptures* (Wheaton, IL: Victor Books, 1985), vol. 2, 476.

8. Roy B. Zuck, *A Biblical Theology of the Old Testament*, electronic ed. (Chicago, IL: Moody Press, 1991), 12.

9. Daniel C. Juster, *The Irrevocable Calling: Israel's Role as a Light to the Nations* (Clarksville, MD: Messianic Jewish Publishers, 2007), 11.

10. Ibid., 12.

11. Iain M. Duguid and Matthew P. Harmon, *Living in the Light of Inextinguishable Hope: The Gospel According to Joseph* (Phillipsburg, NJ: P&R Publishing, 2013), 9.

12. G. Campbell Morgan, *Living Messages of the Books of the Bible: Old Testament* (New York: Fleming H. Revell Company, 1908), vol. 1, 32–33.

13. Goldsworthy, *Christ-Centered Biblical Theology, Hermeneutical Foundations and Principles*, Kindle location 565.

14. Ibid., Kindle location 574.

15. Ibid., Kindle locations 574–84.

16. Charles H. Spurgeon, *Christ in the Old Testament: Sermons on the Foreshadowing of Our Lord in Old Testament History, Ceremony, and Prophecy*, electronic ed. (Chattanooga, TN: AMG Publishers, 1998), 13.

17. Goldsworthy, *Christ-Centered Biblical Theology, Hermeneutical Foundations and Principles*, Kindle location 584.

18. M. R. DeHaan cites light as an example of a portrait of Christ in *Portraits of Christ in Genesis*, 19.

19. Ibid., 33.

20. Sidney Greidanus, *Preaching Christ from Genesis: Foundations for Expository Sermons* (Grand Rapids, MI; Cambridge, UK: William B. Eerdmans Publishing Company, 2007), 69.

21. Anthony A. Hoekema, *Created in God's Image* (Grand Rapids, MI; Cambridge, UK: William B. Eerdmans Publishing Company, 1994), 149.

22. Everett F. Harrison, "Romans," in F. E. Gaebelein, ed., *The Expositor's Bible Commentary: Romans through Galatians* (Grand Rapids, MI: Zondervan Publishing House, 1976), vol. 10, 63.

23. David Murray, *Jesus on Every Page: 10 Simple Ways to Seek and Find Christ in the Old Testament* (Nashville, TN: Thomas Nelson, 2013).

24. D. Martyn Lloyd-Jones, *The Gospel in Genesis: From Fig Leaves to Faith* (Wheaton, IL: Day One Publications, 2010), 35.

25. Nancy Guthrie, *The One Year Book of Discovering Jesus in the Old Testament* (Carol Stream, IL: Tyndale House Publishers, Inc., 2010), Kindle location 357.

26. Donald S. Fortner, *Discovering Christ in Genesis* (Darlington, England: Evangelical Press, 2002), 73.

27. DeHaan, *Portraits of Christ in Genesis*, 71.

28. Arthur Walkington Pink, *Gleanings in Genesis* (Bellingham, WA: Logos Bible Software, 2005), 68–69.

29. Dwight Lyman Moody, *Notes from My Bible: From Genesis to Revelation* (Chicago; New York; Toronto: Fleming H. Revell, 1895), 16.

30. G. K. Beale, *Handbook on the New Testament Use of the Old Testament: Exegesis and Interpretation* (Grand Rapids, MI: Baker Academic, 2012), 21.

31. John Peter Lange et al., *A Commentary on the Holy Scriptures: Genesis* (Bellingham, WA: Logos Bible Software, 2008), 302.

32. *Christ in the Old Testament* (Torrance, CA: Rose Publishing, 2009).

33. Arnold G. Fruchtenbaum*The Messianic Bible Study Collection* (Tustin, CA: Ariel Ministries, 1983), vol. 116, 9; Barton Warren Johnson, *The New Testament commentary, Vol. III: John* (St. Louis, MO: Christian Board of Publication, 1886).

34. Genesis 6:14 states that God told Noah to build the ark and gives him explicit instructions on how to build it. It doesn't say that Noah's family didn't help, but it doesn't say they did help.

35. Arthur Walkington Pink, *Gleanings in Genesis* (Bellingham, WA: Logos Bible Software, 2005), 96–102.

36. Zane. C. Hodges, "Hebrews," in Walvoord and Zuck, eds., *The Bible Knowledge Commentary*, vol. 2, 798.

37. John F. Walvoord, *Jesus Christ Our Lord* (Chicago, IL: Moody Bible Institute of Chicago, 1975, 2008), 68.

38. John F. MacArthur Jr., *John MacArthur Sermon Archive* (Panorama City, CA: Grace to You, 2014), 1972, the Crucifixion, Part 1.

39. Warren W. Wiersbe, *Wiersbe's Expository Outlines on the Old Testament* (Wheaton, IL: Victor Books, 1993).

40. Walvoord, *Jesus Christ Our Lord*, 66; K. Rudge, "January 28th: Christ at Peniel (Genesis 32:1–2, 24–32)," in I. Steeds, ed., *Day by Day: Christ Foreshadowed: Glimpses in the Old Testament* (West Glamorgan, UK: Precious Seed, 2002), 43.

41. Walvoord, *Jesus Christ Our Lord*, 66–67; Donald S. Fortner, *Discovering Christ in All the Scriptures* (Danville, KY: Don Fortner), 12.

42. D. Martyn Lloyd-Jones, *Glorious Christianity*, 1st U.S. ed. (Wheaton, IL: Crossway Books, 2004), vol. 4, 135.

43. Arthur Walkington Pink, *Gleanings in Genesis* (Bellingham, WA: Logos Bible Software, 2005), 388.

44. D. Mangum, Jacob, Son of Isaac, in J. D. Barry et al., eds., *The Lexham Bible Dictionary* (Bellingham, WA: Lexham Press, 2012, 2013, 2014).

45. Walvoord, *Jesus Christ Our Lord*, 66–67; Fortner, *Discovering Christ in All the Scriptures*, 65.

46. Wilbur Fields, *Old Testament History: An Overview of Sacred History & Truth* (Joplin, MO: College Press Publishing Company, 1996), 107.

47. Walvoord, *Jesus Christ Our Lord*, 66–67; Fortner, *Discovering Christ in All the Scriptures*, 69–70.

48. Charles H. Spurgeon, "Christ, the Tree of Life," *Spurgeon's Sermons*, electronic ed. (Albany, OR: Ages Software, 1998), vol. 57.

49. H. A. Ironside did refer to the Sabbath as a type of Christ in H. A. Ironside, *Addresses on the Gospel of Luke* (Neptune, NJ: Loizeaux Brothers, 1947), 180–81; as did John Calvin in John Calvin and John Owen, *Commentaries on the Prophet Jeremiah and the Lamentations* (Bellingham, WA: Logos Bible Software, 2010), vol. 2, 381.

CHAPTER 10: CHRIST IN EVERY BOOK: EXODUS

1. J. Sidlow Baxter, *Explore the Book* (Grand Rapids, MI; Zondervan Publishing House, 1960), vol. 1, 75.

2. Walter C. Kaiser, *The Promise-Plan of God: A Biblical Theology of the Old and New Testaments* (Grand Rapids, MI: Zondervan, 2008), 69.

3. Arthur Walkington Pink, *Gleanings in Exodus* (Chicago, IL: Moody Press, 1962), 8.

4. Ibid., 9–10.

5. Ibid., 7, 9.

6. Donald S. Fortner, *Discovering Christ in All the Scriptures* (Danville, KY: Don Fortner), 13.

7. Gerard Van Groningen, *Messianic Revelation in the Old Testament* (Grand Rapids, MI: Baker Book House, 1990), 201–2.

8. Earl D. Radmacher, *The NKJV Study Bible* (Nashville, TN: Thomas Nelson, 2007).

9. Paul J. Achtemeier and Elizabeth Achtemeier, *The Old Testament Roots of Our Faith*, revised ed. (Peabody, MA: Hendrickson Publishers, 1994), 66–67.

10. Katharine Doob Sakenfeld, *Journeying with God: A Commentary on the Book of Numbers* (Grand Rapids, MI; Edinburgh: Wm. B. Eerdmans Pub. Co.; Handsel Press Ltd, 1995), 82.

11. John F. Walvoord, *Jesus Christ Our Lord* (Chicago, IL: Moody Bible Institute of Chicago, 1975, 2008), 68.

12. *Christ in the Old Testament* (Torrance, CA: Rose Publishing, 2009).

13. Some of these examples were from Benjamin M. Holt, *Finding Christ in the Old Testament* (New York: Vantage Press, 1977), 17–18. Others came from John F. Walvoord, *Jesus Christ Our Lord*, 68.

14. D. Gilliland, "February 16th: Christ in Moses—The Meekest Man (Numbers 12:1–16)," in I. Steeds, ed., *Day by Day: Christ Foreshadowed: Glimpses in the Old Testament* (West Glamorgan, UK: Precious Seed, 2002), 61.

15. Achtemeier and Achtemeier, *The Old Testament Roots of Our Faith*, 68–69.

16. Gerard Van Groningen, *Messianic Revelation in the Old Testament* (Grand Rapids, MI: Baker Book House, 1990), 206.

17. Warren W. Wiersbe, *Wiersbe's Expository Outlines on the Old Testament* (Wheaton, IL: Victor Books, 1993), 85.

18. Timothy J. Keller, "The Lord of Salvation, The Gospel According to Moses: Discovering the Lost Language of Salvation, September 15, 2002, *The Timothy Keller Sermon Archive* (New York City: Redeemer Presbyterian Church, 2013).

19. Charles H. Spurgeon, *Christ in the Old Testament: Sermons on the Foreshadowing of Our Lord in Old Testament History, Ceremony, and Prophecy*, electronic ed. (Chattanooga, TN: AMG Publishers, 1997), 98.

20. Ibid., 99.

21. Roy R. Matheson, *Old Testament Survey* (Chicago, IL: Moody Bible Institute of Chicago, 1989), 20.

22. Ray Stedman, *Adventuring Through the Bible* (Grand Rapids, MI: Discovery House Books, 1997), 79.
23. Tremper Longman III, *How to Read Exodus* (Downers Grove, IL: IVP Academic, 2009), 145.
24. Van Groningen, *Messianic Revelation in the Old Testament*, 202.
25. John F. Walvoord, *Jesus Christ Our Lord* (Chicago, IL: Moody Bible Institute of Chicago, 1975, 2008), 70.
26. Van Groningen, *Messianic Revelation in the Old Testament*, 203.
27. Ibid.
28. Baxter, *Explore the Book*, vol. 1, 78–79.
29. Ibid., 79–80.
30. O. L. Johnson, *Bible Typology* (James L. Fleming, 2005).
31. H. D. M. Spence-Jones, ed., *Exodus*, vol. 2 (London; New York: Funk & Wagnalls Company, 1909), 41.
32. Philip Graham Ryken and R. K. Hughes, *Exodus: Saved for God's Glory* (Wheaton, IL: Crossway Books, 2005), 456.
33. Simon J. Kistemaker and William Hendriksen, *Exposition of the First Epistle to the Corinthians* (Grand Rapids, MI: Baker Book House, 1993), vol. 18, 324–25.
34. John G. Butler, *Analytical Bible Expositor: Exodus* (Clinton, IA: LBC Publications, 2008), 217.
35. J. V. Fesko, *Christ and the Desert Tabernacle* (Darlington, England: EP Books, 2012), 85.
36. Matheson, *Old Testament Survey*, 22.
37. Philip Peter Jenson, *Graded Holiness: A Key to the Priestly Conception of the World* (Sheffield, England: Sheffield Academic Press, 1992), 100, cited in Thomas R. Schreiner, *The King in His Beauty: A Biblical Theology of the Old and New Testaments* (Grand Rapids, MI: Baker Academic, 2013), 40.
38. Baxter, *Explore the Book*, vol. 1, 98.
39. Van Groningen, *Messianic Revelation in the Old Testament*, 228.
40. Ronald F. Youngblood et al., eds., in *Nelson's New Illustrated Bible Dictionary* (Nashville, TN: Thomas Nelson, Inc., 1995).
41. Allen C. Myers, in *The Eerdmans Bible Dictionary* (Grand Rapids, MI: Eerdmans, 1987), 733.
42. Youngblood et al., in *Nelson's New Illustrated Bible Dictionary*.

43. Roy E. Gingrich, *The Book of Genesis* (Memphis, TN: Riverside Printing, 1998), 15.

44. David Lyle Jeffrey, in *A Dictionary of Biblical Tradition in English Literature* (Grand Rapids, MI: W.B. Eerdmans, 1992).

45. Leonard Sweet and Frank Viola, *Jesus: A Theography* (Nashville, TN: Thomas Nelson, 2012).

46. The first illustration is from T. B. Dozeman, *Commentary on Exodus* (Grand Rapids, MI; Cambridge, UK: William B. Eerdmans Publishing Company, 2009), 608. The second drawing is from Marsha Smith et al., *Holman Book of Charts, Maps and Reconstructions* (Nashville, TN: B&H Publishing Group, 1993), 144.

47. David M. Levy, *The Tabernacle: Shadows of the Messiah: Its Sacrifices, Services, and Priesthood* (Bellmawr, NJ: Friends of Israel Gospel Ministry, 1993).

48. Michael P. V. Barrett, *Beginning at Moses: A Guide to Finding Christ in the Old Testament* (Greenville, SC; Belfast, Northern Ireland: Ambassador-Emerald International, 2001), 140.

49. Levy, *The Tabernacle*.

50. Baxter, *Explore the Book*, vol. 1, 104.

51. Fesko, *Christ and the Desert Tabernacle*, 110.

52. Lawrence O. Richards, *The Teacher's Commentary* (Wheaton, IL: Victor Books, 1987), 105.

53. Levy, *The Tabernacle*,

54. Ibid.

55. Warren W. Wiersbe, *Prayer: Basic Training* (Wheaton, IL: Tyndale, 1988), 8.

56. Fesko, *Christ and the Desert Tabernacle*, 89.

57. Wiersbe, *Prayer*, 9.

58. Ibid., 29.

59. Fesko, *Christ and the Desert Tabernacle*, 23.

60. Levy, *The Tabernacle*.

61. Ibid.

62. William Hendriksen and S. Kistemaker, *Exposition of the Gospel According to Matthew* (Grand Rapids, MI: Baker Book House, 1953–2001), vol. 9, 974.

63. John F. MacArthur, "Jesus Christ, the Perfect Priest," in *John MacArthur Sermon Archive* (Panorama City, CA: Grace to You, 2014).

64. Ray Stedman, *Adventuring Through the Bible* (Grand Rapids, MI: Discovery House Publishers, 1997), 83.

65. Ibid.

66. Timothy J. Keller, "Why Do We Need the Bible," in *The Timothy Keller Sermon Archive* (New York: Redeemer Presbyterian Church, 2013).

67. Kaiser, *The Promise-Plan of God*, 70–71.

68. Van Groningen, *Messianic Revelation in the Old Testament*, 220–21.

69. Ibid., 221.

70. Kaiser, *The Promise-Plan of God*, 71.

CHAPTER 11: CHRIST IN EVERY BOOK: LEVITICUS THROUGH DEUTERONOMY

1. Mark F. Rooker, *Leviticus* (Nashville, TN: Broadman & Holman Publishers, 2000), vol. 3A, 77.

2. Roy R. Matheson, *Old Testament Survey* (Chicago, IL: Moody Bible Institute of Chicago, 1989), 24.

3. Roy B. Zuck, *A Biblical Theology of the Old Testament*, electronic ed. (Chicago, IL: Moody Press, 1991), 57–58.

4. Ray Stedman, *Adventuring Through the Bible* (Grand Rapids, MI: Discovery House Books, 1997), 88.

5. Joseph S. Exell, "Leviticus," *The Biblical Illustrator* (Grand Rapids, MI: Baker Book House, 1952–1959), v.

6. Matheson, *Old Testament Survey*, 24.

7. H. Richard Niebuhr, *The Kingdom of God in America* (New York: Harper & Tow, 1959), 193.

8. Robert Laird Harris, "Leviticus," in F. E. Gaebelein, ed., *The Expositor's Bible Commentary: Genesis, Exodus, Leviticus, Numbers* (Grand Rapids, MI: Zondervan Publishing House, 1990), vol. 2, 520.

9. Warren W. Wiersbe, *Wiersbe's Expository Outlines on the Old Testament* (Wheaton, IL: Victor Books, 1993), 139.

10. Gary W. Demarest and L. J. Ogilvie, *Leviticus* (Nashville, TN: Thomas Nelson Inc., 1990), vol. 3, 170.

11. James E. Smith, *The Old Testament Books Made Simple* (Joplin, MO: College Press Publishing Company, 2009), 42–43.

12. Samuel J. Schultz, *Leviticus: God among His People* (Chicago, IL: Moody Press, 1983), 54.

13. Matheson, *Old Testament Survey*, 24.

14. Earl D. Radmacher, *The NKJV Study Bible* (Nashville, TN: Thomas Nelson, 2007).

15. F. D. Lindsey, "Leviticus," in J. F. Walvoord and R. B. Zuck, eds., *The Bible Knowledge Commentary: An Exposition of the Scriptures* (Wheaton, IL: Victor Books, 1985), vol. 1, 177.

16. Samuel J. Schultz and Gary V. Smith, *Exploring the Old Testament* (Wheaton, IL; Crossway Books, 2001), 37.

17. Matheson, *Old Testament Survey*, 25.

18. Robert I. Vasholz, *Leviticus: A Mentor Commentary* (Fearn, Tain, Ross-shire, Great Britain: Mentor, 2007), 53.

19. Ibid., 77.

20. Andrew Jukes, *The Law of the Offerings in Leviticus 1–7: Considered as the Appointed Figure of the Various Aspects of the Offering of the Body of Jesus Christ* (London: James Nisbet and Co, 1847), 166–67.

21. Edward E. Hindson and Woodrow M. Kroll, eds., *KJV Bible Commentary* (Nashville, TN: Thomas Nelson, 1994), 198.

22. John R. W. Stott, *The Cross of Christ* (Downers Grove, IL: IVP Books, 2006), 189.

23. Lindsey, "Leviticus," in Walvoord and Zuck, *The Bible Knowledge Commentary*, vol. 1, 183.

24. Robert I. Vasholz, *Leviticus: A Mentor Commentary* (Fearn, Tain, Ross-shire, Great Britain: Mentor, 2007), 77.

25. Vern S. Poythress, *The Shadow of Christ in the Law of Moses* (Phillipsburg, NJ: P & R Publishing, 1991), 60.

26. Daniel C, Juster, *The Irrevocable Calling: Israel's Role as a Light to the Nations* (Clarksville, MD: Messianic Jewish Publishers, 2007), 11.

27. Ibid., 11.

28. John F. MacArthur Jr., "Jesus: The Guarantee of a Better Covenant," in *John MacArthur Sermon Archive* (Panorama City, CA: Grace to You, 1972).

29. John F. Walvoord, *Jesus Christ Our Lord* (Chicago, IL: Moody Bible Institute of Chicago, 1975, 2008), 75.

30. Paul J. Achtemeier, in *Harper's Bible Dictionary*, 1st ed. (San Francisco, CA: Harper & Row, 1985), 80.

31. D. R. Wood and I. Howard Marshall, in *New Bible Dictionary*, 3rd ed. (Leicester, England; Downers Grove, IL: InterVarsity Press, 1996), 105.

32. James Hastings et al., eds., in *A Dictionary of Christ and the Gospels: Aaron–Zion* (Edinburgh; New York: T&T Clark; Charles Scribner's Sons, 1906), vol. 2, 157.

33. Samuel J. Schultz, *Leviticus: God among His people* (Chicago, IL: Moody Press, 1983), 105.

34. Mark F. Rooker, *Leviticus* (Nashville, TN: Broadman & Holman Publishers, 2000), vol. 3A, 281.

35. Ronald F. Youngblood et al., eds., in *Nelson's New Illustrated Bible Dictionary* (Nashville, TN: Thomas Nelson, Inc., 1995).

36. Walvoord, *Jesus Christ Our Lord*, 76.

37. Walter A. Elwell, in *Evangelical Dictionary of Biblical Theology*, electronic ed. (Grand Rapids: Baker Book House, 1996).

38. Matheson, *Old Testament Survey*, 27.

39. Arno Gaebelein, *Studies in Prophecy* (New York: Publication Office "Our Hope" 1918), 142.

40. L. McFall, "Sacred Meals," in T. D. Alexander and B. S. Rosner, eds., *New Dictionary of Biblical Theology*, electronic ed. (Downers Grove, IL: InterVarsity Press, 2000), 752.

41. Walter A. Elwell and B. J. Beitzel, in *Baker Encyclopedia of the Bible* (Grand Rapids, MI: Baker Book House, 1988), 785.

42. J. A. Groves, Foreword, in Tremper Longman III and J. A. Groves, eds., *Immanuel in Our Place: Seeing Christ in Israel's Worship* (Phillipsburg, NJ: P&R Publishing, 2001), 201–2.

43. Ibid., 207.

44. T. M. Constance, *Early History of Israel* (Dickson, TN: Explorer's Bible Study, 1988), vol. 1, 100.

45. Joseph S. Exell, *The Biblical illustrator (Acts)* (Oak Harbor, WA: Logos Research Systems, Inc., 1997), 112.

46. Allen P. Ross, *Holiness to the Lord: A Guide to the Exposition of the Book of Leviticus* (Grand Rapids, MI: Baker Academic, 2002), 438.

47. Charles C. Ryrie, *Ryrie Study Bible: New International Version*, expanded ed. (Chicago, IL: Moody Publishers, 1994), 197.

48. Stephen Kaung, *Seeing Christ in Numbers: The Walk of God (God Has Spoken—Seeing Christ in the Old Testament Book 5*, Kindle ed. (Christian Fellowship Publishers, 2014), Kindle locations 130–32.

49. Gary Staats, *The Person and Work of Jesus Christ in Each Book of the Old Testament Seen in Its New Testament Fulfillment—An Emmaus Walk*, T. Staats and J. Kitchen, eds. (Gary Staats, 2010), 22.

50. Earl D. Radmacher, *The NKJV Study Bible* (Nashville, TN: Thomas Nelson, 2007).

51. William Jones, *Numbers* (New York; London; Toronto: Funk & Wagnalls Company, 1892), 354.

52. Harold L. Willmington, *The Outline Bible* (Wheaton, IL: Tyndale House Publishers, 1999).

53. Francis A. Schaeffer, *The Complete Works of Francis A. Schaeffer: a Christian Worldview* (Westchester, IL: Crossway Books, 1982), vol. 2, 301–2.

54. Crossway Bibles, *The ESV Study Bible* (Wheaton, IL: Crossway Bibles, 2008), 325.

55. Albert H. Baylis, *From Creation to the Cross, Understanding the First Half of the Bible* (Grand Rapids, MI: Zondervan Publishing House, 1996), 150.

56. Walter Brueggemann, *The Land: Place as Gift, Promise, and Challenge in Biblical Faith*, 2nd ed. (Minneapolis, MN: Fortress Press, 2003), 55.

57. Elwell and Beitzel, in *Baker Encyclopedia of the Bible*, vol. 1, 619.

58. Mark Water, *The Books of the Bible Made Easy* (Alresford, Hampshire: John Hunt Publishing, 2000), 8.

59. Elwell and Beitzel, in *Baker Encyclopedia of the Bible*, vol. 1, 619.

60. Staats, *The Person and Work of Jesus Christ*, 26.

CHAPTER 12: CHRIST IN EVERY BOOK: JOSHUA THROUGH ESTHER

1. Francis A. Schaeffer, *The Complete Works of Francis A. Schaeffer: A Christian Worldview* (Westchester, IL: Crossway Books, 1982), vol. 2, 201.

2. Ibid., vol. 2, 153.

3. Mark Allan Powell, ed., "Joshaphat," in *The HarperCollins Bible Dictionary (Revised and Updated)*, 3rd ed. (New York: HarperCollins, 2011), 493.

4. Ray C. Stedman, "The Way to Victory: Joshua," Ray Stedman.org, 1997.

5. Warren W. Wiersbe, *Wiersbe's Expository Outlines on the Old Testament* (Wheaton, IL: Victor Books, 1993), 206.

6. J. Sidlow Baxter, *Explore the Book* (Grand Rapids, MI; Zondervan Publishing House, 1960), vol. 1, 238.

7. John F. Walvoord, *Jesus Christ Our Lord* (Chicago, IL: Moody Bible Institute of Chicago, 1975, 2008), 70–71.

8. Gary Staats, *The Person and Work of Jesus Christ in Each Book of the Old Testament Seen in Its New Testament Fulfillment—An Emmaus Walk*, T. Staats and J. Kitchen, eds. (Gary Staats, 2010), 29.

9. Walvoord, *Jesus Christ Our Lord*, 67.

10. Donald S. Fortner, *Discovering Christ in All the Scriptures* (Danville, KY: Don Fortner, 2007), 62–63.

11. *Christ in the Old Testament* (Torrance, CA: Rose Publishing, 2009).

12. *The Open Bible: New King James Version*, electronic ed. (Nashville, TN: Thomas Nelson Publishers, 1998).

13. Got Questions Ministries, *Got Questions? Bible Questions Answered* (Bellingham, WA: Logos Bible Software, 2010).

14. Staats, *The Person and Work of Jesus Christ*, 30.

15. Gerard Van Groningen, *Messianic Revelation in the Old Testament* (Grand Rapids, MI: Baker Book House, 1990), 268.

16. Walter A. Elwell, in *Evangelical Dictionary of Biblical Theology*, electronic ed. (Grand Rapids, MI: Baker Book House, 1996).

17. R. L. Hubbard Jr., "Redemption," in T. D. Alexander and B. S. Rosner, eds., *New Dictionary of Biblical Theology*, electronic ed. (Downers Grove, IL: InterVarsity Press, 2000), 717.

18. John F. Walvoord, "Series in Christology, Part 3: The Incarnation of the Son of God," *Bibliotheca Sacra Volume 105* (Dallas Theological Seminary, 1948), 291–92.

19. C. I. Scofield, *The Scofield Reference Bible: The Holy Bible Containing the Old and New Testaments* (New York; London; Toronto; Melbourne; Bombay: Oxford University Press, 1917), 765.

20. John MacArthur Jr., ed., *The MacArthur Study Bible*, electronic ed. (Nashville, TN: Word Pub, 1997), 374.

21. *The Open Bible: New King James Version*, electronic ed.

22. Dale Ralph Davis, *1 Samuel: Looking on the Heart* (Scotland: Christian Focus Publications, 2000), 76.

23. Richard D. Phillips, *1 Samuel*, P. G. Ryken and R. D. Phillips, Duguid Iain M., eds., 1st ed. (Phillipsburg, NJ: P&R Publishing, 2012),126.

24. Got Questions Ministries, *Got Questions? Bible Questions Answered* (Bellingham, WA: Logos Bible Software, 2010).

25. John F. MacArthur Jr., *The MacArthur Bible Handbook* (Nashville, TN: Thomas Nelson Publishers, 2003), 92.

26. *Christ in the Old Testament*, Rose Publishing.

27. *The Open Bible: New King James Version*, electronic ed.

28. Walvoord, *Jesus Christ Our Lord*, 65.

29. Kenneth Boa, *Jesus in the Bible* (Nashville, TN: Thomas Nelson, Inc., 2002), 24.

30. *The Open Bible: New King James Version*, electronic ed.

31. Fortner, *Discovering Christ in All the Scriptures*, 105.

32. *Christ in the Old Testament*, Rose Publishing.

33. Fortner, *Discovering Christ in All the Scriptures*, 105.

34. Charles H. Spurgeon, *Christ in the Old Testament: Sermons on the Foreshadowing of Our Lord in Old Testament History, Ceremony, and Prophecy*, electronic ed. (Chattanooga, TN: AMG Publishers, 1997), 154.

35. Got Questions Ministries, *Got Questions? Bible Questions Answered* (Bellingham, WA: Logos Bible Software, 2010).

36. Fortner, *Discovering Christ in All the Scriptures*, 109–10.

37. P. J. Achtemeier, "Harper & Row and Society of Biblical Literature," in *Harper's Bible Dictionary*, 1st ed. (San Francisco, CA: Harper & Row, 1985), 529.

38. Willem A. VanGemeren, "Psalms," in F. E. Gaebelein, ed., *The Expositor's Bible Commentary: Psalms, Proverbs, Ecclesiastes, Song of Songs* (Grand Rapids, MI: Zondervan Publishing House, 1991), vol. 5, 469.

39. Philip G. Ryken, *1 Kings*, R. D. Phillips, I. M. Duguid, and P. G. Ryken, eds. (Phillipsburg, NJ: P&R Publishing, 2011), 35.

40. Ibid., 36.

41. Ibid., 37.

42. *The Open Bible: New King James Version*, electronic ed.

43. Mark Water, *The Books of the Bible Made Easy* (Alresford, Hampshire: John Hunt Publishing, 2001), 13.

44. Boa, *Jesus in the Bible*, 26.

45. Arthur W. Pink, *Gleanings from Elisha: His Life and Miracles* (Bellingham, WA: Logos Bible Software, 2005), 16.

46. Fortner, *Discovering Christ in All the Scriptures*, 138.

47. *The Open Bible: New King James Version*, electronic ed.

48. Got Questions Ministries, *Got Questions? Bible Questions Answered* (Bellingham, WA: Logos Bible Software, 2010).

49. Boa, *Jesus in the Bible*, 30.

50. William Hendriksen and S. J. Kistemaker, *Exposition of the Gospel According to Matthew* (Grand Rapids, MI: Baker Book House, 1953–2001), vol. 9, 514.

51. Got Questions Ministries, *Got Questions? Bible Questions Answered* (Bellingham, WA: Logos Bible Software, 2010).

52. Van Groningen, *Messianic Revelation in the Old Testament*, 923.

53. Ibid., 923.

54. Got Questions Ministries, *Got Questions? Bible Questions Answered* (Bellingham, WA: Logos Bible Software, 2010).

55. Boa, *Jesus in the Bible*, 32.

56. Van Groningen, *Messianic Revelation in the Old Testament*, 924.

57. Bruce Wilkinson and Kenneth Boa, *Talk thru the Bible* (Nashville, TN: T. Nelson, 1983), 126.

58. Crossway Bibles, *The ESV Study Bible* (Wheaton, IL: Crossway Bibles, 2008), 825.

59. Jack Hayford et al., eds., *New Spirit-Filled Life Bible* (Nashville, TN: Thomas Nelson Bibles, 2002), 613.

60. *The Open Bible: New King James Version*, electronic ed.

61. Some have pointed out that God is mentioned by way of acrostics in the book, which is a fascinating notion, but one beyond the scope of this book. See J. Baxter, *Explore the Book*, vol. 2, 261; W. Graham Scroggie, *The Unfolding Drama of Redemption* (Grand Rapids, MI: Kregel Publications, 1976), vol. 1, 469–71.

62. Debra Reid, *Esther: An Introduction and Commentary* (Downers Grove, IL: InterVarsity Press, 2008), vol. 13, 29.

63. John Lowrie, *Esther and Her Times: In a Series of Lectures on the Book of Esther* (Philadelphia, PA: Presbyterian Board of Publication, 1859), 89.

64. Baxter, *Explore the Book*, vol. 2, 259.

65. Fortner, *Discovering Christ in All the Scriptures*, 195.

66. Van Groningen, *Messianic Revelation in the Old Testament*, 920.

67. Timothy J. Keller, "A New Church for the City," *The Timothy Keller Sermon Archive* (New York City: Redeemer Presbyterian Church, 2013).

68. Earl D. Radmacher, *The NKJV Study Bible* (Nashville, TN: Thomas Nelson, 2007).

69. W. Burrows, *Esther* (New York; London; Toronto: Funk & Wagnalls Company, 1892), 263–64.

70. *The ESV Study Bible* (Wheaton, IL: Crossway Bibles, 2008), 2,646.

71. Roy Gingrich, *The Book of Esther* (Memphis, TN: Riverside Printing, 2004), 25.

CHAPTER 13: CHRIST IN EVERY BOOK: THE POETICAL BOOKS

1. Norman L. Geisler, *A Popular Survey of the New Testament* (Grand Rapids, MI: Baker Books, 2014), 11.

2. Daniel J. Estes, *Handbook on the Wisdom Books and Psalms* (Grand Rapids, MI: Baker Academic, 2005), 9.

3. C. Hassell Bullock, *An Introduction to the Old Testament Poetic Books, Revised and Expanded* (Chicago, IL: Moody Press, 1979, 1988), 31–32.

4. Thomas A. Howe, Class Notes, "Old Testament Survey 2," Southern Evangelical Seminary, 2012, 199–200; 4.

5. Robert Alter, *The Art of Biblical Poetry* (New York: Basic Books, 1985).

6. I am not sure which translation Alter is using or modifying here, but it is not the version I have been using almost exclusively in this book: the English Standard Version (ESV).

7. Alter, *The Art of Biblical Poetry*, Kindle location 346 of 5126.

8. Estes, *Handbook on the Wisdom Books and Psalms*, 9.

9. He was particularly impressed with the grandeur of the King James Version. H. L. Mencken, *Treatise on the Gods* (New York: Knopf, 1946), 286.

10. Walter A. Elwell and Philip W. Comfort, in *Tyndale Bible Dictionary* (Wheaton, IL: Tyndale House Publishers, 2001), 1,305.

11. Crossway Bibles, *The ESV Study Bible* (Wheaton, IL: Crossway Bibles, 2008), 866.

12. Leland Ryken, *Words of Delight: A Literary Introduction to the Bible*, 2nd ed. (Grand Rapids, MI: Baker Academic, 1992), 9.

13. Ibid., 32.

14. Ibid., 508.

15. A Viberg, "Job," in T. D. Alexander and B. S. Rosner, eds., *New Dictionary of Biblical Theology*, electronic ed. (Downers Grove, IL: InterVarsity Press, 2000), 203.

16. Ibid., 203.

17. Walter A. Elwell, in *Evangelical Dictionary of Biblical Theology*, electronic ed. (Grand Rapids, MI: Baker Book House, 1996).

18. Robert L. Alden, *Job* (Nashville, TN: Broadman & Holman Publishers, 1993), vol. 11, 329.

19. Got Questions Ministries, *Got Questions? Bible Questions Answered* (Bellingham, WA: Logos Bible Software, 2010).

20. Bullock, *An Introduction to the Old Testament Poetic Books, Revised and Expanded*, 111.

21. Ibid.

22. Ray C. Stedman, *Adventuring Through the Old Testament* (Grand Rapids, MI: Discovery House Books, 2011).

23. Ray Stedman, *Adventuring Through the Bible* (Grand Rapids, MI: Discovery House Books, 1997), 257.

24. Bullock, *An Introduction to the Old Testament Poetic Books, Revised and Expanded*, 111.

25. Patrick Henry Reardon, *Christ in the Psalms* (Chesterton, IN: Ancient Faith Publishing, 2000), vii.

26. Ibid., viii.

27. Ibid.

28. Donald S. Fortner, *Discovering Christ in All the Scriptures* (Danville, KY: Don Fortner), 219.

29. Gerard Van Groningen, *Messianic Revelation in the Old Testament* (Grand Rapids, MI: Baker Book House, 1990), 329–30.

30. Ibid., 330.

31. Ibid., 338.

32. Herbert W. Bateman et al., *Jesus the Messiah: Tracing the Promises, Expectations, and Coming of Israel's King* (Grand Rapids, MI: Kregel Academic, 2012), 75–76.

33. Ibid.

34. Gary Staats, *The Person and Work of Jesus Christ in Each Book of the Old Testament Seen in Its New Testament Fulfillment—An*

Emmaus Walk, T. Staats and J. Kitchen, eds. (Gary Staats, 2010), 41.

35. Mal Couch, "Progressive Dispensationalism: Is Christ Now on the Throne of David?—Part II," *Conservative Theological Journal* (1998): 2, no. 5, 144.

36. Fortner, *Discovering Christ in All the Scriptures*, 221–22.

37. Gary H. Everett, *The Book of Psalms* (Gary Everett, 2011), 62.

38. Hans K. LaRondelle, *Deliverance in the Psalms: Messages of Hope for Today* (Bradenton, FL: First Impressions, 2006), 95.

39. James H. Waltner, *Psalms* (Scottdale, PA; Waterloo, ON: Herald Press, 2006), 125.

40. Fortner, *Discovering Christ in All the Scriptures*, 224.

41. John F. Walvoord, *Jesus Christ Our Lord* (Chicago, IL: Moody Bible Institute of Chicago, 1975, 2008), 92.

42. J. Vernon McGee, *Through the Bible with J. Vernon McGee*, electronic ed. (Nashville, TN: Thomas Nelson, 1997), vol. 2, 711.

43. Ibid.

44. John F. MacArthur Jr. "Creation Day 6, Part 1, *John MacArthur Sermon Archive* (Panorama City, CA: Grace to You, 1999).

45. Henry H. Halley, *Finding Jesus in the Old Testament: a Zondervan Digital Short* (Grand Rapids, MI: Zondervan, 2012).

46. John D. Barry et al., *Faithlife Study Bible* (Bellingham, WA: Logos Bible Software, 2012).

47. Ralph G. Turnbull, in *Baker's Dictionary of Practical Theology* (Grand Rapids, MI: Baker Book House, 1967), 137–38.

48. Ibid., 138.

49. Gerard Van Groningen, *Messianic Revelation in the Old Testament* (Grand Rapids, MI: Baker Book House, 1990), 379.

50. Ibid., 385.

51. Geoffrey W. Grogan, *Psalms* (Grand Rapids, MI; Cambridge, UK: William B. Eerdmans Publishing Company, 2008), 390.

52. James Montgomery Boice, *Psalms 42–106: An Expositional Commentary* (Grand Rapids, MI: Baker Books, 2005), 601.

53. Waltner, *Psalms*, 438–39.

54. Boice, *Psalms 42–106*, 761.

55. Waltner, *Psalms*, 455.

56. Arno Gaebelein, *The Annotated Bible: Ezra to Psalms* (Bellingham, WA: Logos Bible Software, 2009), vol. 3, 301.

57. Michael P. Barrett, *Beginning at Moses: A Guide to Finding Christ in the Old Testament* (Greenville, SC; Belfast, Northern Ireland: Ambassador-Emerald International, 2001), 315.

58. Gerard Van Groningen, *Messianic Revelation in the Old Testament* (Grand Rapids, MI: Baker Book House, 1990), 397.

59. Gary H. Everett, *The Book of Proverbs* (Gary Everett, 2011), 35.

60. Got Questions Ministries, *Got Questions? Bible Questions Answered* (Bellingham, WA: Logos Bible Software, 2010).

61. Warren W. Wiersbe, *Wiersbe's Expository Outlines on the Old Testament* (Wheaton, IL: Victor Books, 1993), 466.

62. Dan Phillips, *God's Wisdom in Proverbs: Hearing God's Voice in Scripture* (Woodlands, TX: Kress Biblical Resources, 2011), 394–95.

63. Ibid., 396.

64. *The Open Bible: New King James Version*, electronic ed. (Nashville, TN: Thomas Nelson Publishers, 1998).

65. Paul N. Benware, *Survey of the Old Testament (Revised)* (Chicago, IL: Moody Press, 1993), 180.

66. Charles Dyer, Eugene Merrill, Charles R. Swindoll, and Roy B. Zuck, *Nelson's Old Testament Survey: Discover the Background, Theology and Meaning of Every Book in the Old Testament* (Nashville, TN: Word, 2001), 512.

67. John MacArthur Jr., ed.), *The MacArthur Study Bible*, electronic ed. (Nashville, TN: Word Pub, 1997), 940–941.

68. John F. MacArthur Jr., *The MacArthur Bible Handbook* (Nashville, TN: Thomas Nelson Publishers, 2003), 175.

69. Charles H. Spurgeon, *Christ in the Old Testament: Sermons on the Foreshadowing of Our Lord in Old Testament History, Ceremony, and Prophecy*, electronic ed. (Chattanooga, TN: AMG Publishers, 1997), 370.

70. Archibald T. Robertson, *Word Pictures in the New Testament* (Nashville, TN: Broadman Press, 1933).

71. William Hendriksen and S. J. Kistemaker, *Exposition of Ephesians* (Grand Rapids, MI: Baker Book House, 1953–2001), vol. 7, 257.

72. Donald S. Fortner, *Discovering Christ in All the Scriptures* (Danville, KY: Don Fortner), 253.

73. Robert Lee in *The Outlined Bible* (Pickering & I, 1921), 21, in Irving L. Jensen, *Jensen's Survey of the Old Testament: Search and Discover* (Chicago, IL: Moody Press, 1978), 310.

CHAPTER 14: CHRIST IN EVERY BOOK: PROPHETS OBADIAH THROUGH ISAIAH

1.   Frederick Dale Bruner, "Tract. in Jn., 9:3:64," *Matthew: A Commentary: The Churchbook, Matthew 13–28*, revised and expanded ed. (Grand Rapids, MI; Cambridge, UK: William B. Eerdmans Publishing Company, 2007), vol. 2, 56.

2.   M. G. Easton, in *Easton's Bible Dictionary* (New York: Harper & Brothers, 1893).

3.   Irving L. Jensen, *Jensen's Survey of the Old Testament: Search and Discover* (Chicago, IL: Moody Press, 1978), 321.

4.   William MacDonald, *Believer's Bible Commentary: Old and New Testaments*, A. Farstad, ed. (Nashville, TN: Thomas Nelson, 1995), 931.

5.   Robert Laird Harris, *Exploring the Basics of the Bible* (Wheaton, IL: Crossway Books, 2002), 8.

6.   James E. Smith, *The Major Prophets* (Joplin, MO: College Press, 1991).

7.   J. Gavigan et al., eds., *Major Prophets* (Dublin; New York: Four Courts Press; Scepter Publishers, 2008), 11.

8.   Irving L. Jensen, *Jensen's Survey of the Old Testament: Search and Discover* (Chicago, IL: Moody Press, 1978), 323.

9.   John MacArthur Jr., ed., *The MacArthur Study Bible*, electronic ed. (Nashville, TN: Word Pub, 1997), 9. See also MacDonald, *Believer's Bible Commentary*, 933.

10. Julius J. Scott Jr., *Jewish Backgrounds of the New Testament* (Grand Rapids, MI: Baker Academic, 2000), 72.

11. MacDonald, *Believer's Bible Commentary*, 933; see also Scott Jr., *Jewish Backgrounds of the New Testament*, 72.

12. MacArthur Jr., *The MacArthur Study Bible*, 12.

13. R. E. Clements *Jeremiah* (Atlanta: J. Knox Press, 1988), 2.

14. MacArthur Jr., *The MacArthur Study Bible*, 9; see also Wilbur Fields, *Old Testament History: An Overview of Sacred History & Truth* (Joplin, MO: College Press Publishing Company, 1996), 589.

15. Charles C. Ryrie, *Ryrie Study Bible: New International Version*, expanded ed. (Chicago, IL: Moody Publishers, 1994), 1,365.

16. Ibid.

17. Paul R. Raabe, *Obadiah: a New Translation with Introduction and Commentary* (New Haven; London: Yale University Press, 2008), vol. 24D, 55; T. T. Perowne, *Obadiah and Jonah, with Notes and Introduction* (Cambridge: Cambridge University Press, 1889), 22; Got Questions Ministries, *Got Questions? Bible Questions Answered* (Bellingham, WA: Logos Bible Software, 2010).

18. Robert J. Utley, *The First Christian Primer: Matthew* (Marshall, TX: Bible Lessons International, 2000), vol. 9, 183; *Holman QuickSource Guide to Understanding the Bible* (Nashville, TN: Holman Bible Publishers, 2002), 191; Got Questions Ministries, *Got Questions? Bible Questions Answered* (Bellingham, WA: Logos Bible Software, 2010).

19. Earl D. Radmacher, *The NKJV Study Bible* (Nashville, TN: Thomas Nelson, 2007).

20. *The Open Bible: New King James Version*, electronic ed. (Nashville, TN: Thomas Nelson Publishers, 1998).

21. John F. MacArthur Jr., *The MacArthur Bible Handbook* (Nashville, TN: Thomas Nelson Publishers, 2003), 238.

22. David Field, *Obadiah: A Practical Commentary* (Leominster: Day One Publications, 2008), 70.

23. Gary Staats, *The Person and Work of Jesus Christ in Each Book of the Old Testament Seen in Its New Testament Fulfillment—An Emmaus Walk*, T. Staats and J. Kitchen, eds. (Gary Staats, 2010), 90.

24. Dan M. Doriani, *PC151 Theology of Everyday Life* (Bellingham, WA: Lexham Press, 2014).

25. Paul N. Benware, *Survey of the Old Testament (Revised)* (Chicago, IL: Moody Press, 1993), 203.

26. Walter A. Elwell and B. J. Beitzel, in *Baker Encyclopedia of the Bible* (Grand Rapids, MI: Baker Book House, 1988), vol. 1, 588.

27. Norman L. Geisler, *To Understand the Bible Look for Jesus: The Bible Student's Guide to the Bible's Central Theme* (Eugene, OR: Wipf and Stock Publishers, 1979), 99.

28. John F. Walvoord, *The Prophecy Knowledge Handbook* (Wheaton, IL: Victor Books, 1990), 289.

29. Got Questions Ministries, *Got Questions? Bible Questions Answered* (Bellingham, WA: Logos Bible Software, 2010).

30. G. Campbell Morgan, *The Analyzed Bible: Job to Malachi* (New York; Chicago; Toronto; London; Edinburgh: Fleming H. Revell Company, 1908), vol. 2, 212.

31. George A. Smith, "The Book of the Twelve Prophets," in W. Robertson Nicoll, ed., *The Expositor's Bible: Jeremiah to Mark* (Hartford, CT: S.S. Scranton Co., 1903), vol. 4, 680.

32. J. Sidlow Baxter, *Explore the Book* (Grand Rapids, MI; Zondervan Publishing House, 1960), vol. 4, 180.

33. James Hastings et al., in *Dictionary of the Bible* (New York: Charles Scribner's Sons, 1909), 492.

34. Baxter, *Explore the Book* (Grand Rapids, MI; Zondervan Publishing House, 1960), vol. 4, 180.

35. H. I. Hester, *The Heart of Hebrew History: a Study of the Old Testament*, rev. ed. (Nashville, TN: Broadman & Holman Publishers, 1962), 280–81.

36. Charles Price, *Matthew: Can Anything Good Come Out of Nazareth?* (Fearn, Great Britain: Christian Focus Publications, 1998), 163.

37. Michael Bentley, *Opening up Amos* (Leominster: Day One Publications, 2006), 8.

38. Robert Martin-Achard and S. Paul Re'emi, *God's People in Crisis* (Edinburgh; Grand Rapids: Handsel Press; Wm. B. Eerdmans Pub. Co, 1984), 8.

39. Ibid., 9.

40. Gordon J. Keddie, *The Lord Is His Name* (Hertfordshire, England: Evangelical Press, 1986), 82–83.

41. Donald S. Fortner, *Discovering Christ in All the Scriptures* (Danville, KY: Don Fortner), 340.

42. Kenneth Boa, *Jesus in the Bible* (Nashville, TN: Thomas Nelson, Inc., 2002), 56–57.

43. Crossway Bibles, *The ESV Study Bible* (Wheaton, IL: Crossway Bibles, 2008), 1,658.

44. Josh McDowell, *The New Evidence That Demands a Verdict* (Nashville, TN: Thomas Nelson Publishers, 1999), 192.

45. William LaSor et al., *Old Testament Survey: the Message, Form, and Background of the Old Testament*, 2nd ed. (Grand Rapids, MI: William B. Eerdmans Publishing Company, 1996), 254.

46. Lloyd J. Ogilvie, *Hosea, Joel, Amos, Obadiah, Jonah* (Nashville, TN: Thomas Nelson Inc, 1990), vol. 22, 18.

47. Roy R. Matheson, *Old Testament Survey* (Chicago, IL: Moody Bible Institute of Chicago, 1989), 201.

48. H. D. Beeby, *Grace Abounding: a Commentary on the Book of Hosea* (Grand Rapids; Edinburgh: Eerdmans; Handsel Press, 1989), 2.

49. Ibid.

50. John Peter Lange et al., *A Commentary on the Holy Scriptures: Hosea* (Bellingham, WA: Logos Bible Software, 2008), 7.

51. Duane A. Garrett, *Hosea, Joel* (Nashville, TN: Broadman & Holman Publishers, 1997), vol. 19A, 38–40.

52. Lloyd J. Ogilvie, *Hosea, Joel, Amos, Obadiah, Jonah* (Nashville, TN: Thomas Nelson Inc, 1990), vol. 22, 19.

53. Tremper Longman III and Raymond B. Dillard, *An Introduction to the Old Testament*, 2nd ed. (Grand Rapids, Michigan: Zondervan, 2007), 408.

54. Radmacher, *The NKJV Study Bible.*

55. Merrill F. Unger, *The New Unger's Bible Handbook*, rev. and updated ed. (Chicago, IL: Moody Publishers, 2005), 255.

56. Herbert M. Wolf, *Interpreting Isaiah, the Suffering and Glory of the Messiah* (Grand Rapids, MI: Zondervan Publishing House, 1985), 11.

57. MacDonald, *Believer's Bible Commentary*, 936.

58. Daniel J. Hays *Message of the Prophets: a Survey of the Prophetic and Apocalyptic Books of the Old Testament* (Grand Rapids, MI: Zondervan, 2010), 98–99.

59. J. A. Martin, "Isaiah," in J. F. Walvoord and R. B. Zuck, eds., *The Bible Knowledge Commentary: An Exposition of the Scriptures* (Wheaton, IL: Victor Books, 1985), vol. 1, 1,032.

60. Eugene H. Merrill, *An Historical Survey of the Old Testament*, 2nd ed. (Grand Rapids, MI: Baker Book House, 1991), 264.

61. C. Hassell Bullock, *An Introduction to the Old Testament Prophetic Books* (Chicago, IL: Moody Press, 1986), 156–57.

62. Roy R. Matheson, *Old Testament Survey* (Chicago, IL: Moody Bible Institute of Chicago, 1989), 160.

63. James E. Smith, *The Major Prophets* (Joplin, MO: College Press, 1992), unknown.

64. Herbert M. Wolf, *Interpreting Isaiah, the Suffering and Glory of the Messiah* (Grand Rapids, MI: Zondervan Publishing House, 1985), 11.

65. Walter A. Elwell and B. J. Beitzel, in *Baker Encyclopedia of the Bible* (Grand Rapids, MI: Baker Book House, 1988), 1048.

66. Derek Thomas, *God Delivers: Isaiah Simply Explained* (Darlington, England: Evangelical Press, 1991), 12.

67. James E. Smith, *The Major Prophets* (Joplin, MO: College Press, 1992).

68. Ray Stedman, *Adventuring Through the Bible* (Grand Rapids, MI: Discovery House Books, 1997), 309–10.

69. Elwell and B. J. Beitzel, in *Baker Encyclopedia of the Bible* (Grand Rapids, MI: Baker Book House, 1988), 1,048.

70. Herbert M. Wolf, *Interpreting Isaiah, the Suffering and Glory of the Messiah* (Grand Rapids, MI: Zondervan Publishing House, 1985), 34.

71. Charles C. Ryrie, *Ryrie Study Bible: New International Version*, expanded ed. (Chicago, IL: Moody Publishers, 1994), 1,013.

72. MacDonald, *Believer's Bible Commentary*, 936.

73. Ryrie, *Ryrie Study Bible: New International Version*, 1,013.

74. Merrill F. Unger, *The New Unger's Bible Handbook*, rev. and updated ed. (Chicago, IL: Moody Publishers, 2005), 255; MacDonald, *Believer's Bible Commentary*, 936

75. MacDonald, *Believer's Bible Commentary*, 936.

76. Edward J. Young, *The Book of Isaiah, Chapters 1–18* (Grand Rapids, MI: Wm. B. Eerdmans Publishing Co, 1965), vol. 1, 8.

77. Robert D. Culver, R. D. *Systematic Theology: Biblical and Historical* (Ross-shire, UK: Mentor, 2005), 107.

78. J. A. Martin, "Isaiah," in J. F. Walvoord and R. B. Zuck, eds., *The Bible Knowledge Commentary: An Exposition of the Scriptures* (Wheaton, IL: Victor Books, 1985), vol. 1, 1030.

79. In fact, Jesus stops in mid-verse because the rest of the verse talks about the Messiah's second coming.

80. *The Open Bible: New King James Version*, electronic ed. (Nashville, TN: Thomas Nelson Publishers, 1998).

81. Bruce Wilkinson and Kenneth Boa, *Talk thru the Bible* (Nashville, TN: T. Nelson, 1983), 192.

82. Crossway Bibles, *The ESV Study Bible* (Wheaton, IL: Crossway Bibles, 2008), 1,235.

83. David Limbaugh, *Jesus on Trial* (Washington, D.C.: Regnery Publishing Co, 2014), 42–46.

84. Radmacher, *The NKJV Study Bible*.

85. Wilkinson and Boa, *Talk thru the Bible*, 192.

86. R. W. L. Moberly, *Old Testament Theology: Reading the Hebrew Bible as Christian Scripture* (Grand Rapids, MI: Baker Academic, 2013), 174–75.

87. Charles H. Spurgeon, *Christ in the Old Testament: Sermons on the Foreshadowing of Our Lord in Old Testament History, Ceremony, and Prophecy*, electronic ed. (Chattanooga, TN: AMG Publishers, 1997), 605–6.

CHAPTER 15: CHRIST IN EVERY BOOK: PROPHETS MICAH THROUGH HABAKKUK

1. Mal Couch, "Inerrancy: The Book of Revelation," *Conservative Theological Journal* (2001): 5, no. 15, 210.

2. H. I. Hester, *The Heart of Hebrew History: A Study of the Old Testament*, rev. ed. (Nashville, TN: Broadman & Holman Publishers, 1962), 286.

3. Paul N. Benware, *Survey of the Old Testament (Revised)* (Chicago, IL: Moody Press, 1993), 226.

4. John MacArthur Jr., ed., *The MacArthur Study Bible*, electronic ed. (Nashville, TN: Word Pub, 1997), 1,299.

5. *The Open Bible: New King James Version*, electronic ed. (Nashville, TN: Thomas Nelson Publishers, 1998).

6. J. A. Martin, "Micah," in J. F. Walvoord and R. B. Zuck, eds., *The Bible Knowledge Commentary: An Exposition of the Scriptures* (Wheaton, IL: Victor Books, 1985), vol. 1, 1,481.

7. Ibid., 1,483–85.

8. Roy R. Matheson, *Old Testament Survey* (Chicago, IL: Moody Bible Institute of Chicago, 1989), 216.

9. Kendell H. Easley, *Holman QuickSource Guide to Understanding the Bible* (Nashville, TN: Holman Bible Publishers, 2002), 209.

10. Julie Woods, "The West as Nineveh: How Does Nahum's Message of Judgement Apply to Today?," *Themelios* (October 2005): 31, no. 1, 27.

11. Crossway Bibles, *The ESV Study Bible* (Wheaton, IL: Crossway Bibles, 2008), Introduction to Zephaniah.

12. Earl D. Radmacher, *The NKJV Study Bible* (Nashville, TN: Thomas Nelson, 2007).

13. Mark Mangano, *Old Testament Introduction* (Joplin, MO: College Press Pub, 2005), 599.

14. Robert Hawker, R. *Poor Man's Old Testament Commentary: Ezekiel–Malachi* (Bellingham, WA: Logos Bible Software, 2013), vol. 6, 472.

15. R. E. Clements *Jeremiah* (Atlanta: J. Knox Press, 1988), 3.

16. Crossway Bibles, *The ESV Study Bible* (Wheaton, IL: Crossway Bibles, 2008), 1370.

17. J. Sidlow Baxter, *Explore the Book* (Grand Rapids, MI; Zondervan Publishing House, 1960), vol. 3, 260.

18. F. B. Huey, Jr., *Jeremiah, Lamentations* (Nashville, TN: Broadman & Holman Publishers, 1993), vol. 16, 24.

19. Ibid., 36.

20. Ibid., 36.

21. Donald S. Fortner, *Discovering Christ in All the Scriptures* (Danville, KY: Don Fortner), 277.

22. Philip G. Ryken, *Jeremiah and Lamentations: from Sorrow to Hope* (Wheaton, IL: Crossway Books, 2001), 201.

23. Kendell Easley, *Holman QuickSource Guide to Understanding the Bible* (Nashville, TN: Holman Bible Publishers, 2002).

24. Philip G. Ryken, *Jeremiah and Lamentations: from Sorrow to Hope* (Wheaton, IL: Crossway Books, 2001), 241.

25. H. D. M. Spence-Jones, ed., *Jeremiah* (London; New York: Funk & Wagnalls Company, 1909), vol. 1, 9.

26. R. K. Harrison, *Jeremiah and Lamentations: an Introduction and Commentary* (Downers Grove, IL: InterVarsity Press, 1973), vol. 21, 40.

27. James E. Smith, *The Old Testament Books Made Simple* (Joplin, MO: College Press Publishing Company, 2009), 162.

28. Mark Water, *The Books of the Bible Made Easy* (Alresford, Hampshire: John Hunt Publishing, 2000), 25.

29. Irving L. Jensen, *Jensen's Survey of the Old Testament: Search and Discover* (Chicago, IL: Moody Press, 1978), 351.

30. Tremper Longman III & Raymond B. Dillard, *An Introduction to the Old Testament*, 2nd ed. (Grand Rapids, MI: Zondervan, 2007), 342.

31. C. Hassell Bullock, *An Introduction to the Old Testament Prophetic Books*, (Chicago, IL: Moody Press, 1986), 263.

32. A. C. Myers in *The Eerdmans Bible Dictionary* (Grand Rapids, MI: Eerdmans, 1987), 856.

33. John F. MacArthur Jr., *The MacArthur Bible Handbook* (Nashville, TN: Thomas Nelson Publishers, 2003), 202.

34. William LaSor et al., *Old Testament Survey: the Message, Form, and Background of the Old Testament*, 2nd ed. (Grand Rapids, MI: William B. Eerdmans Publishing Company, 1996), 531.

35. *The Open Bible: New King James Version*, electronic ed.

36. G. Campbell Morgan, *The Analyzed Bible: Job to Malachi* (New York; Chicago; Toronto; London; Edinburgh: Fleming H. Revell Company, 1908), vol. 2, 241–42.

37. Alexander Whyte, in C. E. Fant et al., *A Treasury of Great Preaching: Spurgeon to Meyer* (Dallas, TX: Word Publishing, 1995), vol. 6, 276.

38. Thomas Boston, *The Whole Works of Thomas Boston: Sixty-Six Sermons*, S. M'Millan, ed. (Aberdeen: George and Robert King, 1851), vol. 9, 135.

39. J. R. Blue, "Habakkuk," in Walvoord and Zuck, *The Bible Knowledge Commentary*, vol. 1, 1,515.

40. Mark Dever and Graeme Goldsworthy, *The Message of the Old Testament: Promises Made* (Wheaton, IL: Crossway, 2006).

41. Augustine, Bishop of Hippo, *The Confessions of St. Augustine*. E. B. Pusey, trans. (Oak Harbor, WA: Logos Research Systems, Inc., 1996), book I, chapter 1, 1.

42. R. C. Sproul, *Before the Face of God: Book 3: A Daily Guide for Living from the Old Testament*, electronic ed. (Grand Rapids: Baker Book House; Ligonier Ministries, 1994).

43. Got Questions Ministries, *Got Questions? Bible Questions Answered* (Bellingham, WA: Logos Bible Software, 2010).

44. Elizabeth R. Achtemeier, *Nahum–Malachi* (Atlanta, GA: John Knox Press, 1986), 48.

CHAPTER 16: CHRIST IN EVERY BOOK: PROPHETS DANIEL THROUGH MALACHI

1. Gary H. Everett, *The Epistle of Romans*, 2011, 91

2. Crossway Bibles, *The ESV Study Bible* (Wheaton, IL: Crossway Bibles, 2008), 1581.

3. Warren W. Wiersbe, *Wiersbe's Expository Outlines on the Old Testament* (Wheaton, IL: Victor Books, 1993), 550.

4. Lawrence O. Richards, *The Teacher's Commentary* (Wheaton, IL: Victor Books, 1987), 440.

5. James Montgomery Boice, *Daniel: an Expositional Commentary* (Grand Rapids, MI: Baker Books, 2003), 15; *The Open Bible: New*

King James Version, electronic ed. (Nashville, TN: Thomas Nelson Publishers, 1998).

6. John F. Walvoord, *Daniel: The Key To Prophetic Revelation* (Galaxie Software, 2008), 26.

7. "O God, Our Help in Ages Past," words by Isaac Watts, 1719, cited in Mark Dever and Graeme Goldsworthy, *The Message of the Old Testament: Promises Made* (Wheaton, IL: Crossway, 2006).

8. Dever and Goldsworthy, *The Message of the Old Testament.*

9. C. Hassell Bullock, *An Introduction to the Old Testament Prophetic Books* (Chicago, IL: Moody Press, 1986), 298.

10. Introduction to the book of Daniel, in *The Holy Bible: English Standard Version* (Wheaton: Standard Bible Society, 2001).

11. John MacArthur Jr., ed., *The MacArthur Study Bible*, electronic ed. (Nashville, TN: Word Pub, 1997), 1,225–26.

12. Roy R. Matheson, *Old Testament Survey* (Chicago, IL: Moody Bible Institute of Chicago, 1989), 184–85.

13. J. Sidlow Baxter, *Explore the Book* (Grand Rapids, MI; Zondervan Publishing House, 1960), vol. 4, 76.

14. M. R. De Haan, *Daniel the Prophet* (Grand Rapids, MI: Kregel Publications, 1995), 253–254.

15. Mervin Breneman, *Ezra, Nehemiah, Esther*, electronic ed. (Nashville, TN: Broadman & Holman Publishers, 1993), vol. 10, 42; J. D. Pentecost, "Daniel," in J. F. Walvoord and R. B. Zuck, eds., *The Bible Knowledge Commentary: An Exposition of the Scriptures* (Wheaton, IL: Victor Books, 1985), vol. 1, 1,362.

16. M. R. De Haan, *Daniel the Prophet* (Grand Rapids, MI: Kregel Publications, 1995), 257; Pentecost, "Daniel," in Walvoord and Zuck, *The Bible Knowledge Commentary*, vol. 1, 1,363.

17. Josh McDowell, *Evidence for Christianity* (Nashville, TN: Thomas Nelson Publishers, 2006), 240. Citing Harold Hoehner, who thoroughly researched this prophecy and the corresponding dates, Josh McDowell shows that the calculation involves using the Jewish prophetic year of 360 days. Hoehner writes, "Multiplying the sixty-nine weeks by seven years for each week by 360 days gives a total of 173,880 days. The difference between 444 B.C. and A.D. 33 then is 476 solar years. By multiplying 476 by 365.24219879 or by

365 days, 5 hours, 48 minutes, 45.975 seconds [there are 365 1/4 days in a year], one comes to 173,855 days, 6 hours, 52 minutes, 44 seconds, or 173,855 days. This leaves only 25 days to be accounted for between 444 B.C. and A.D. 33. By adding the 25 days to March 5 (of 444 B.C.), one comes to March 30 (of A.D. 33) which was Nisan 10 in A.D. 33. This is the triumphal entry of Jesus into Jerusalem." See Josh McDowell, *Evidence for Christianity* (Nashville, TN: Thomas Nelson Publishers, 2006), 235. Of course many dispute this precise dating and I am not insisting on it, although I think a strong case can be made for it. I just think it is astonishing that the prophecy comes anywhere close to being accurate. See also John F. Walvoord, *The Prophecy Knowledge Handbook* (Wheaton, IL: Victor Books, 1990).

18. Charles C. Ryrie, *Basic Theology* (Wheaton: Victor, 1986), 557.

19. Gary Staats, *A Brief Survey through the Hebrew Scriptures: Viewing the Basic Overall Themes and Different High Points of the Books from an Ancient Near-Eastern and Christological Approach*, M. Johnson, ed. (Dr. Gary Staats, 2012), 13; E. A. Blum, "John," in Walvoord and Zuck, *The Bible Knowledge Commentary*, vol. 2, 291.

20. Got Questions Ministries, *Got Questions? Bible Questions Answered* (Bellingham, WA: Logos Bible Software, 2010).

21. E. C. Broome, "Ezekiel's Abnormal Personality," in *Journal of Biblical Literature* 65 (1946): 277–292, at 291–292, cited in Mark Dever and Graeme Goldsworthy, *The Message of the Old Testament: Promises Made* (Wheaton, IL: Crossway, 2006).

22. R. K. Harrison, *Introduction to the Old Testament* (Grand Rapids, MI: William B. Eerdmans Publishing Company, 1969), 850.

23. Charles Dyer, Eugene Merrill, Charles R. Swindoll, and Roy B. Zuck, *Nelson's Old Testament Survey: Discover the Background, Theology and Meaning of Every Book in the Old Testament* (Nashville, TN: Word, 2001), 658.

24. Crossway Bibles, *The ESV Study Bible* (Wheaton, IL: Crossway Bibles, 2008), 1495.

25. C. Hassell Bullock, *An Introduction to the Old Testament Prophetic Books* (Chicago, IL: Moody Press, 1986), 250.

26. Ibid.

27. Anton T. Pearson, "Ezekiel," in *The Wycliffe Bible Commentary*, 705.

28. Herbert Bateman et al., *Jesus the Messiah: Tracing the Promises, Expectations, and Coming of Israel's King* (Grand Rapids, MI: Kregel Academic, 2012), 182.

29. Staats, *A Brief Survey through the Hebrew Scriptures*, 13.

30. Bateman et al., *Jesus the Messiah*, 177.

31. Kendell Easley, *Holman QuickSource Guide to Understanding the Bible* (Nashville, TN: Holman Bible Publishers, 2002), 161.

32. Gerard Van Groningen, *Messianic Revelation in the Old Testament* (Grand Rapids, MI: Baker Book House, 1990), 855.

33. Ibid., 858.

34. Ibid., 859.

35. Bruce Wilkinson and Kenneth Boa, *Talk thru the Bible* (Nashville, TN: T. Nelson, 1983), 284–85.

36. M. G. Easton, in *Easton's Bible Dictionary* (New York: Harper & Brothers, 1893).

37. Got Questions Ministries, *Got Questions? Bible Questions Answered* (Bellingham, WA: Logos Bible Software, 2010).

38. *The Open Bible: New King James Version*, electronic ed. (Nashville, TN: Thomas Nelson Publishers, 1998).

39. Got Questions Ministries, *Got Questions? Bible Questions Answered* (Bellingham, WA: Logos Bible Software, 2010).

40. Warren W. Wiersbe, *Wiersbe's Expository Outlines on the Old Testament* (Wheaton, IL: Victor Books, 1993), 626.

41. James Hastings et al., in *Dictionary of the Bible* (New York: Charles Scribner's Sons, 1909), 986.

42. Thomas A. Howe, Class Notes, "Old Testament Survey 2," Southern Evangelical Seminary, 2012, 199–200, 204.

43. J. Sidlow Baxter, *Explore the Book* (Grand Rapids, MI; Zondervan Publishing House, 1960), vol. 4, 237.

44. Roy R. Matheson, *Old Testament Survey* (Chicago, IL: Moody Bible Institute of Chicago, 1989), 75–76.

45. John MacArthur Jr., ed., *The MacArthur Study Bible*, electronic ed. (Nashville, TN: Word Pub, 1997), 1,337.

46. Kendell Easley, *Holman QuickSource Guide to Understanding the Bible* (Nashville, TN: Holman Bible Publishers, 2002), 233.

47. MacArthur, *The MacArthur Study Bible*, electronic ed., 1,338.

48. *The Open Bible: New King James Version*, electronic ed. (Nashville, TN: Thomas Nelson Publishers, 1998).

49. Donald S. Fortner, *Discovering Christ in All the Scriptures* (Danville, KY: Don Fortner), 416.

50. F. D. Lindsey, "Zechariah," in Walvoord and Zuck, *The Bible Knowledge Commentary*, vol. 1, 1,569.

51. W. Graham Scroggie, *The Unfolding Drama of Redemption* (Grand Rapids, MI: Kregel Publications, 1976), vol. 1, 483.

52. Matheson, *Old Testament Survey*, 223.

53. H. I. Hester, *The Heart of Hebrew History: A Study of the Old Testament*, rev. ed. (Nashville, TN: Broadman & Holman Publishers, 1962), 294.

54. J. Sidlow Baxter, *Explore the Book* (Grand Rapids, MI; Zondervan Publishing House, 1960), vol. 4, 263.

55. Ibid., 265.

56. Earl D. Radmacher, *The NKJV Study Bible* (Nashville, TN: Thomas Nelson, 2007), 67–68.

57. C. A. Blaising, "Malachi," in Walvoord and Zuck, *The Bible Knowledge Commentary*, vol. 1, 1,587.

58. David J. Clark and Howard A. Hatton, *A Handbook on Malachi* (New York: United Bible Societies, 2002), 462.

59. James Lee Beall, *Laying the Foundation* (Plainfield, NJ: Logos International, 1976), 130.

CONCLUSION

1. Gerard Van Groningen, *Messianic Revelation in the Old Testament* (Grand Rapids, MI: Baker Book House, 1990), 939.

INDEX